SLIME 13!

THAT TIME I GOT REINCARNATED AS A

Author:
FUSE

Artist:
TAIKI KAWAKAMI

Character design:
MITZ VAH

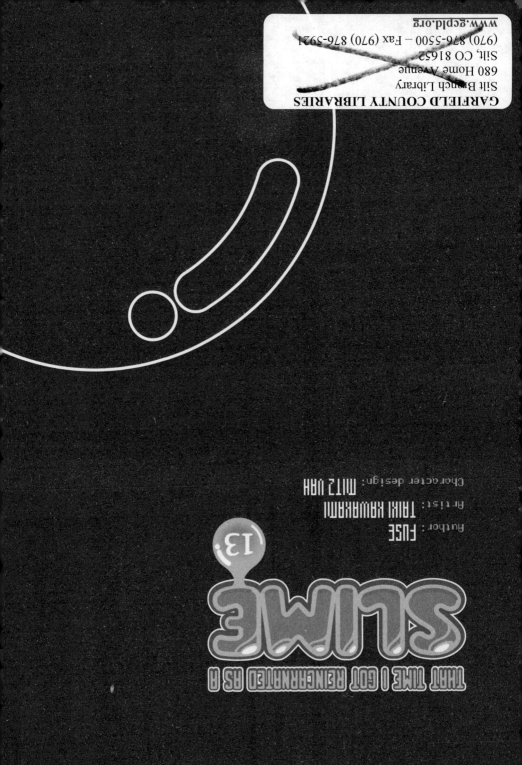

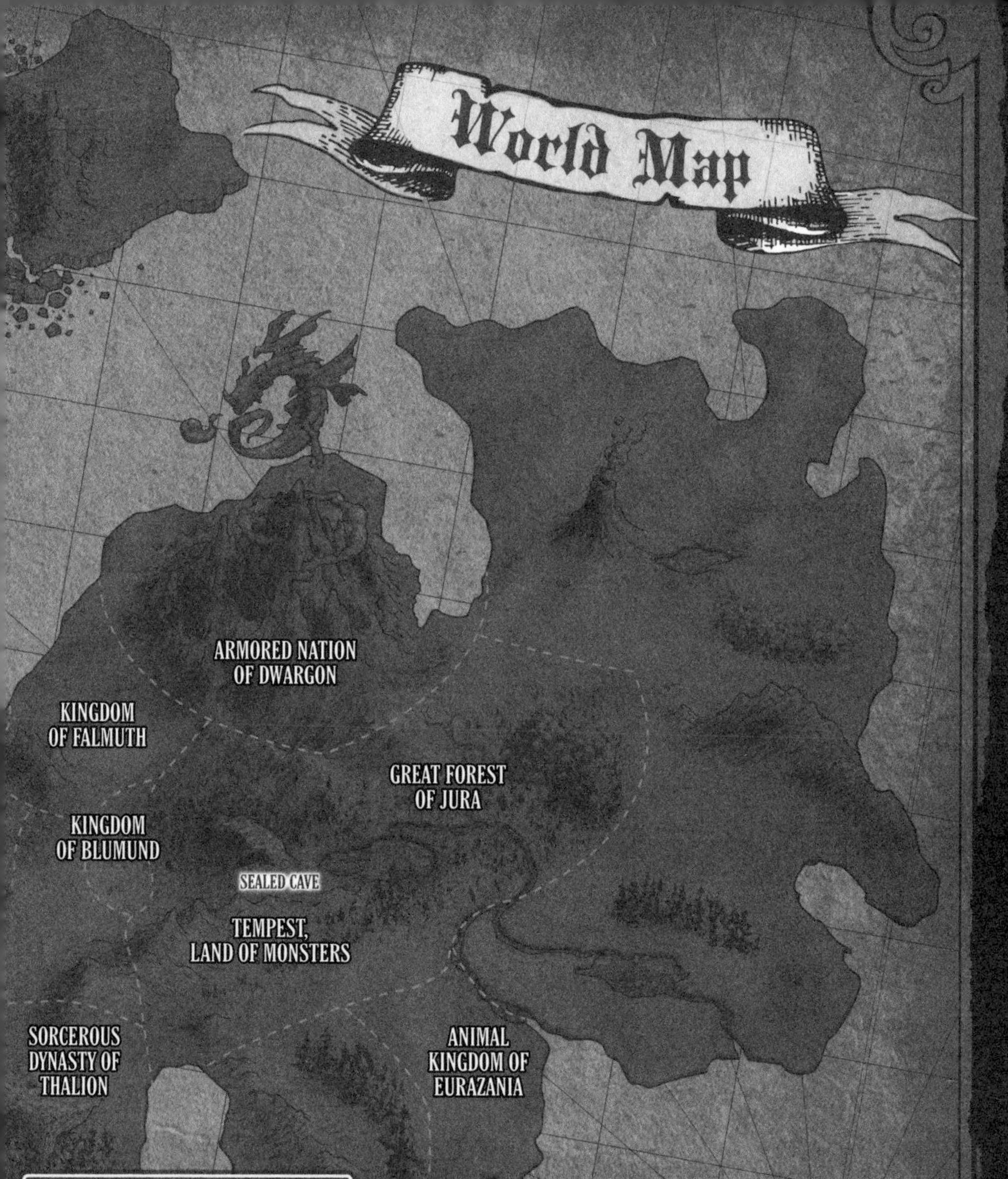
World Map
ARMORED NATION OF DWARGON
KINGDOM OF FALMUTH
GREAT FOREST OF JURA
KINGDOM OF BLUMUND
SEALED CAVE
TEMPEST, LAND OF MONSTERS
SORCEROUS DYNASTY OF THALION
ANIMAL KINGDOM OF EURAZANIA

PLOT SUMMARY

Rimuru saved the children Shizu left behind, and then put Engrassia behind him. But on the way home, he was attacked by the captain of the Western Holy Church's Crusaders, Hinata Sakaguchi. He escaped danger by using a body double as a decoy, but it delayed his return to Tempest. During that time, the city was attacked by Shogo Taguchi, Kirara Mizutani, and Kyoya Tachibana—flippant but capable otherworlders.

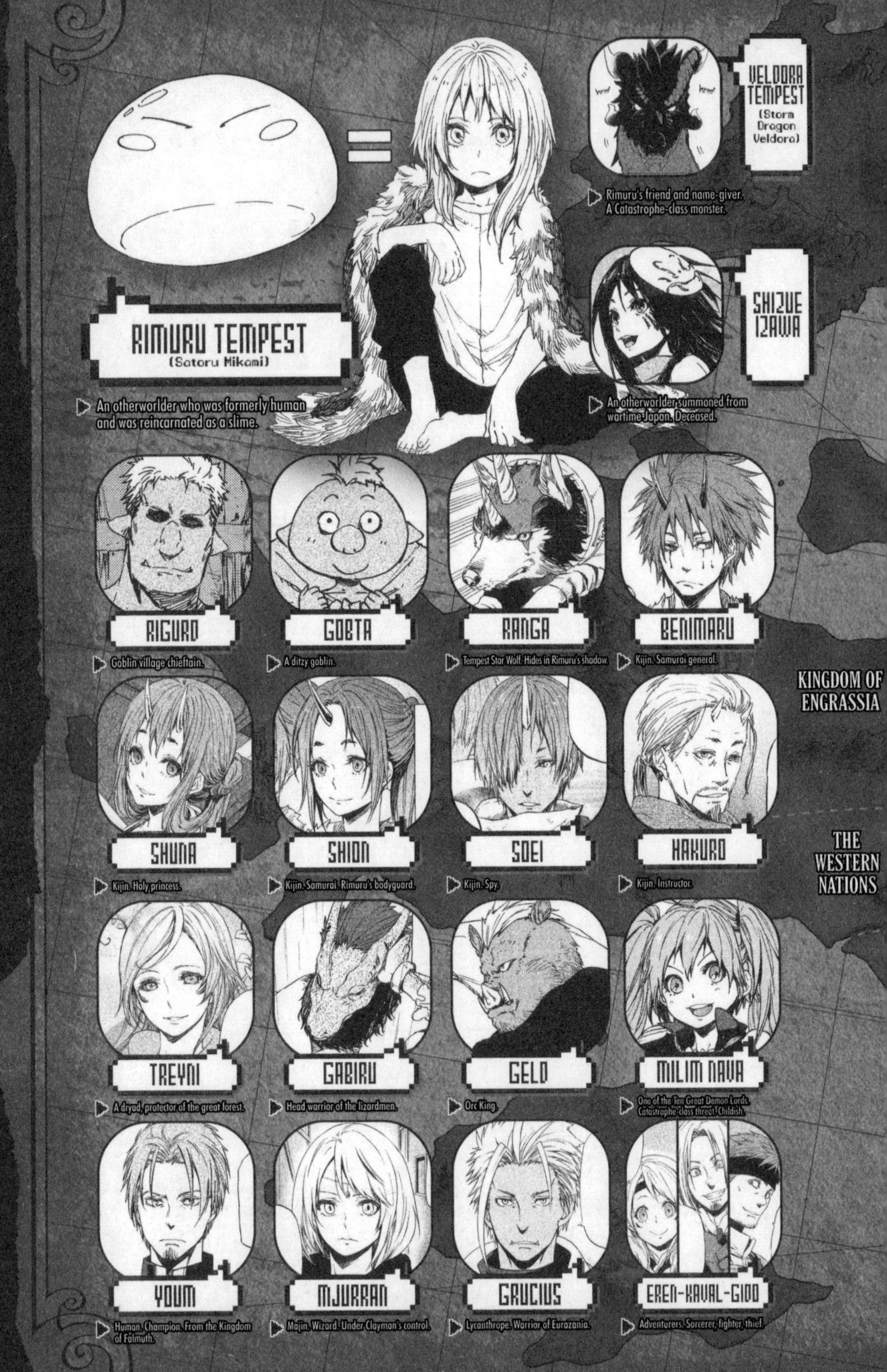
RIMURU TEMPEST
(Satoru Mikami)
An otherworlder who was formerly human and was reincarnated as a slime.
VELDORA TEMPEST
(Storm Dragon Veldora)
Rimuru's friend and name-giver. A Catastrophe-class monster.
SHIZUE IZAWA
An otherworlder summoned from wartime Japan. Deceased.
RIGURD
Goblin village chieftain.
GOBTA
A ditzy goblin.
RANGA
Tempest Star Wolf. Hides in Rimuru's shadow.
BENIMARU
Kijin. Samurai general.
KINGDOM OF ENGRASSIA
SHUNA
Kijin. Holy princess.
SHION
Kijin. Samurai. Rimuru's bodyguard.
SOEI
Kijin. Spy.
HAKURO
Kijin. Instructor.
THE WESTERN NATIONS
TREYNI
A dryad, protector of the great forest.
GABIRU
Head warrior of the lizardmen.
GELD
Orc King.
MILIM NAVA
One of the Ten Great Demon Lords. Catastrophe-class threat. Childish.
YOUM
Human. Champion. From the Kingdom of Falmuth.
MJURRAN
Majin. Wizard. Under Clayman's control.
GRUCIUS
Lycanthrope. Warrior of Eurazania.
EREN-KAVAL-GIDO
Adventurers. Sorcerer, fighter, thief.

CONTENTS

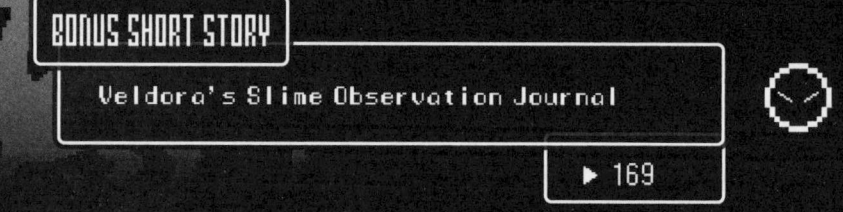

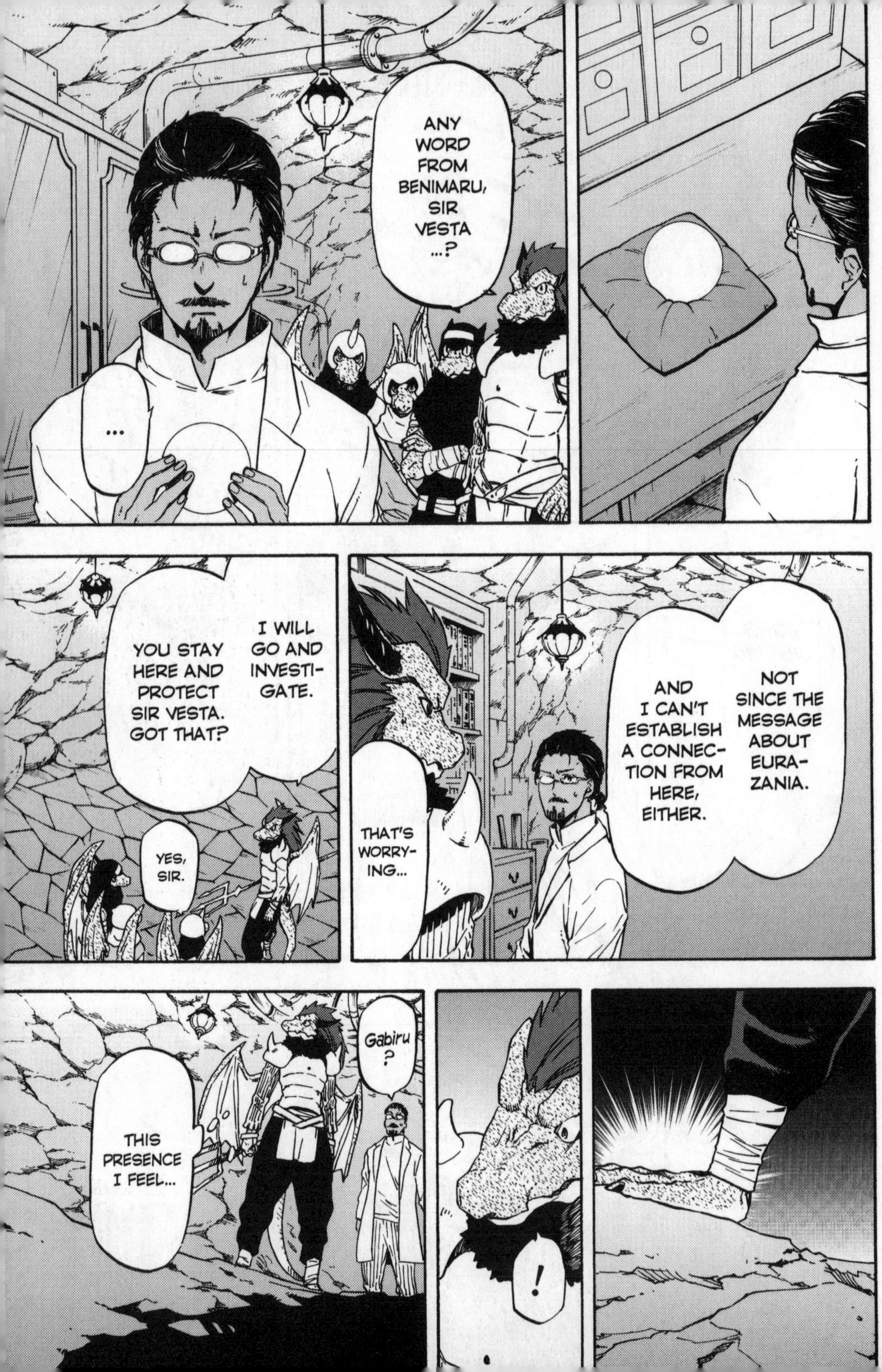
ANY WORD FROM BENIMARU, SIR VESTA ...?
...
NOT SINCE THE MESSAGE ABOUT EURA-ZANIA.
AND I CAN'T ESTABLISH A CONNEC-TION FROM HERE, EITHER.
THAT'S WORRY-ING...
I WILL GO AND INVESTI-GATE.
YOU STAY HERE AND PROTECT SIR VESTA. GOT THAT?
YES, SIR.
!
Gabiru?
THIS PRESENCE I FEEL...

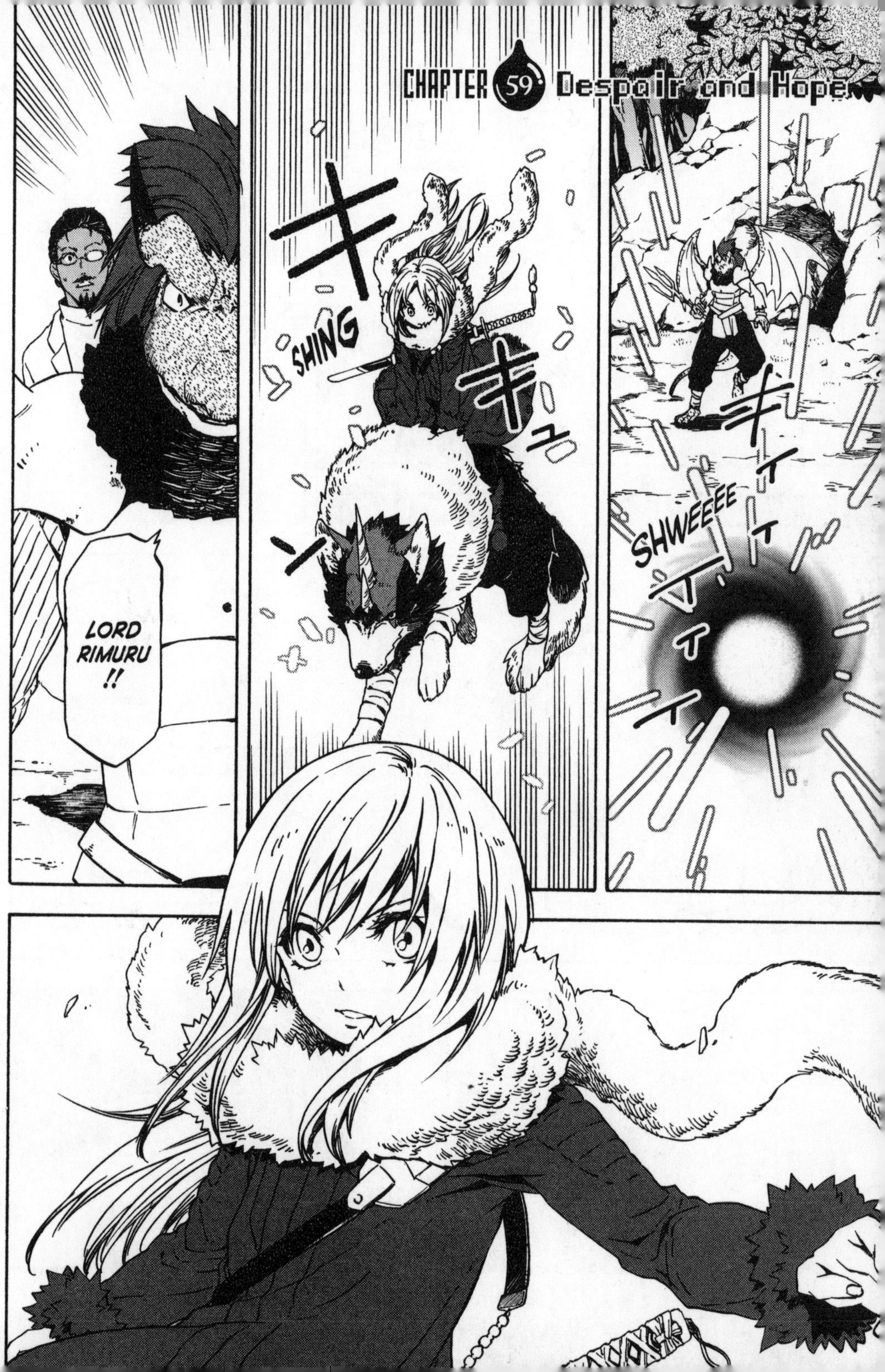
CHAPTER 59 Despair and Hope
SHWEEEE
SHING
LORD RIMURU !!

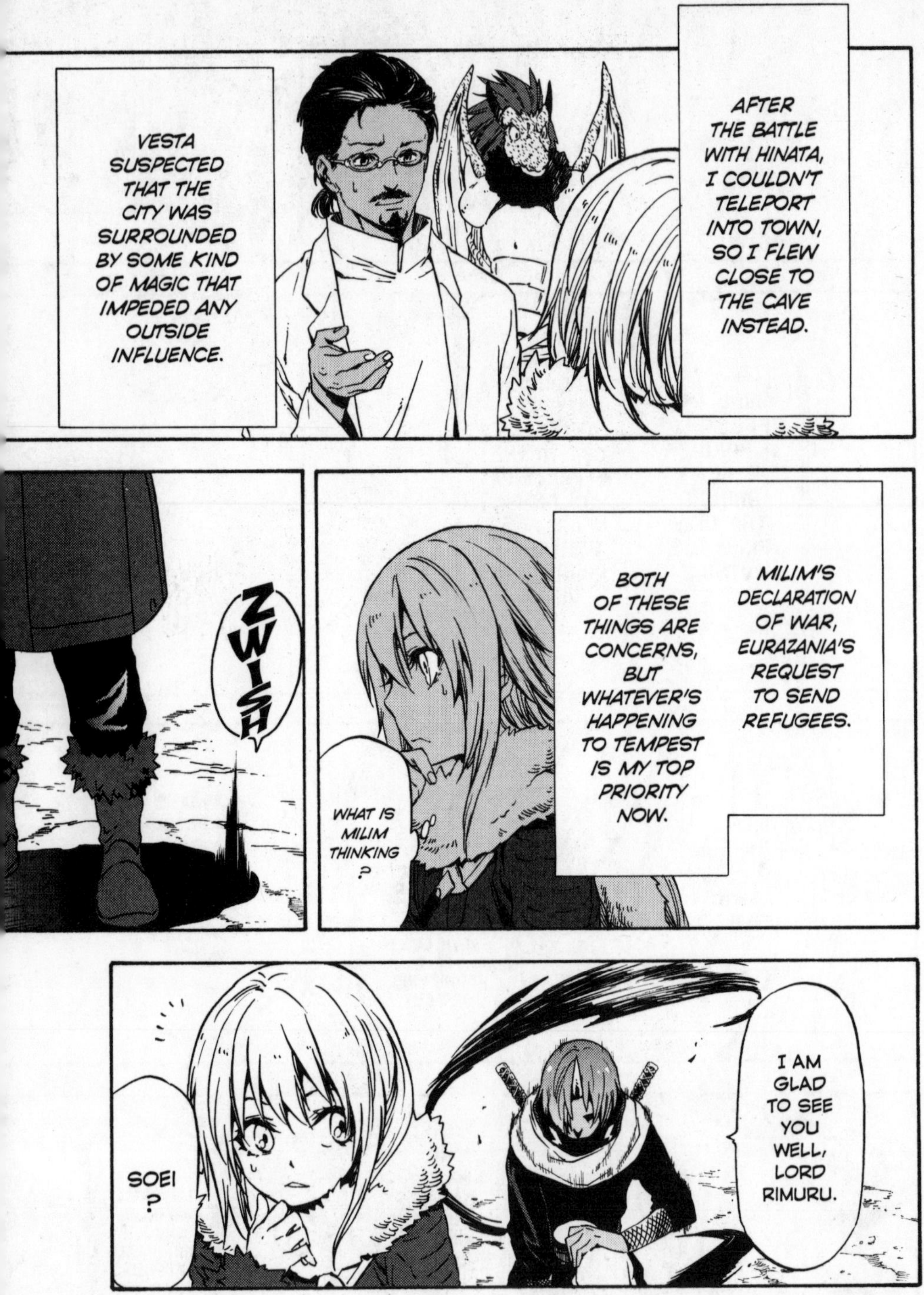
AFTER THE BATTLE WITH HINATA, I COULDN'T TELEPORT INTO TOWN, SO I FLEW CLOSE TO THE CAVE INSTEAD.
VESTA SUSPECTED THAT THE CITY WAS SURROUNDED BY SOME KIND OF MAGIC THAT IMPEDED ANY OUTSIDE INFLUENCE.
MILIM'S DECLARATION OF WAR, EURAZANIA'S REQUEST TO SEND REFUGEES.
BOTH OF THESE THINGS ARE CONCERNS, BUT WHATEVER'S HAPPENING TO TEMPEST IS MY TOP PRIORITY NOW.
WHAT IS MILIM THINKING?
ZWISH
I AM GLAD TO SEE YOU WELL, LORD RIMURU.
SOEI?

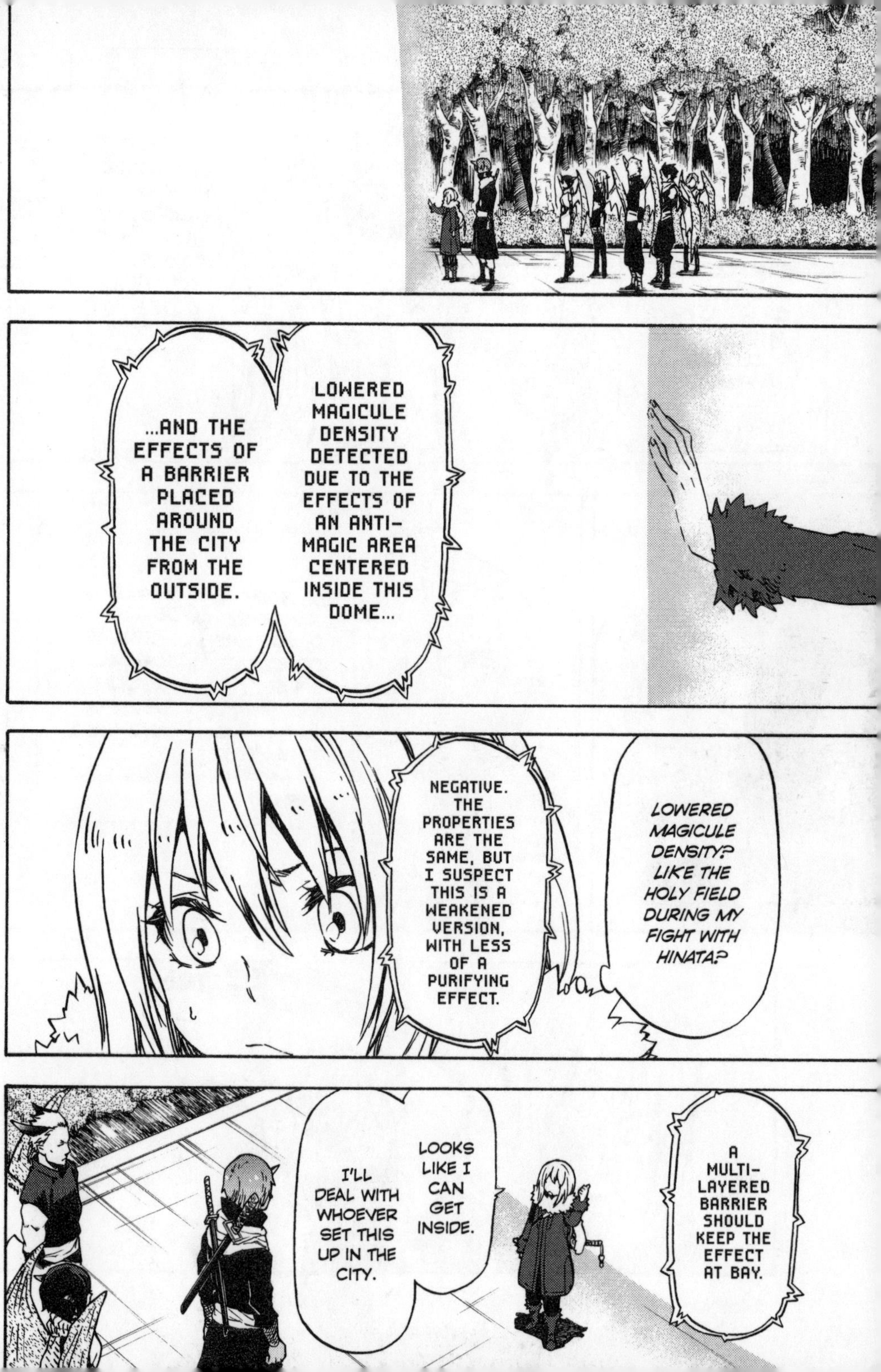
...AND THE EFFECTS OF A BARRIER PLACED AROUND THE CITY FROM THE OUTSIDE.
LOWERED MAGICULE DENSITY DETECTED DUE TO THE EFFECTS OF AN ANTI-MAGIC AREA CENTERED INSIDE THIS DOME...
LOWERED MAGICULE DENSITY? LIKE THE HOLY FIELD DURING MY FIGHT WITH HINATA?
NEGATIVE. THE PROPERTIES ARE THE SAME, BUT I SUSPECT THIS IS A WEAKENED VERSION, WITH LESS OF A PURIFYING EFFECT.
A MULTI-LAYERED BARRIER SHOULD KEEP THE EFFECT AT BAY.
LOOKS LIKE I CAN GET INSIDE.
I'LL DEAL WITH WHOEVER SET THIS UP IN THE CITY.

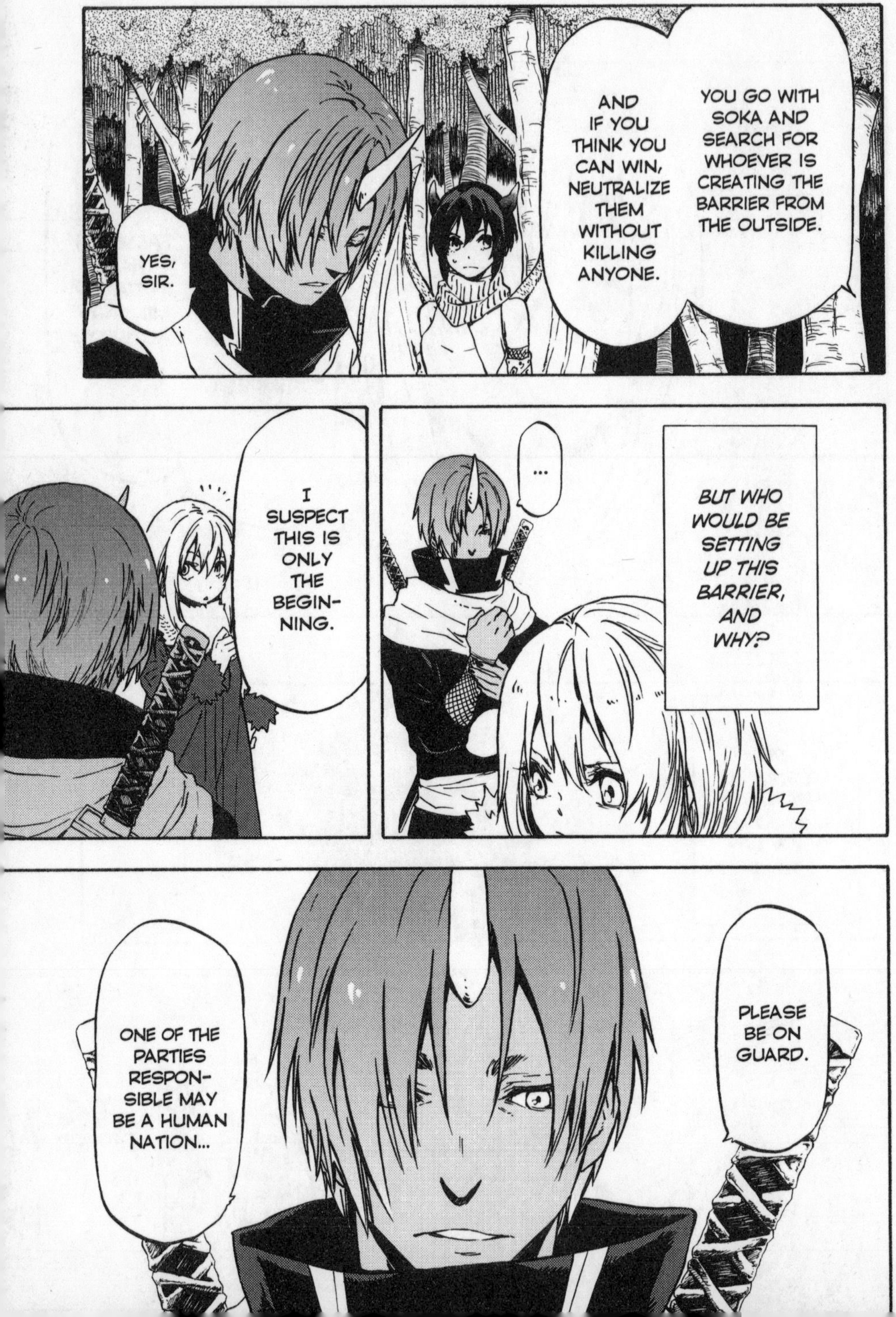
YOU GO WITH SOKA AND SEARCH FOR WHOEVER IS CREATING THE BARRIER FROM THE OUTSIDE.
AND IF YOU THINK YOU CAN WIN, NEUTRALIZE THEM WITHOUT KILLING ANYONE.
YES, SIR.
BUT WHO WOULD BE SETTING UP THIS BARRIER, AND WHY?
...
I SUSPECT THIS IS ONLY THE BEGIN-NING.
PLEASE BE ON GUARD.
ONE OF THE PARTIES RESPON-SIBLE MAY BE A HUMAN NATION...

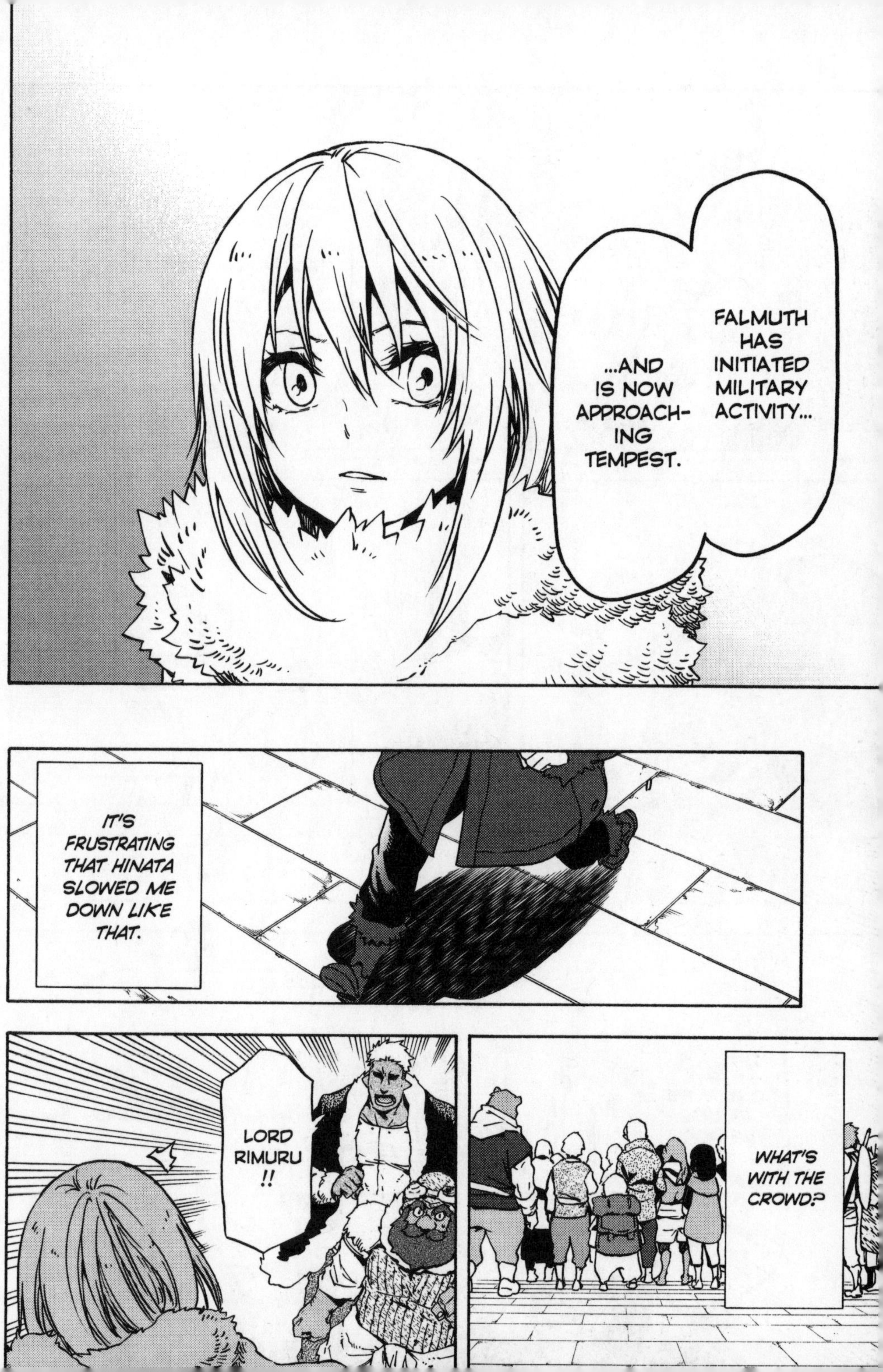
FALMUTH HAS INITIATED MILITARY ACTIVITY...
...AND IS NOW APPROACH-ING TEMPEST.
IT'S FRUSTRATING THAT HINATA SLOWED ME DOWN LIKE THAT.
WHAT'S WITH THE CROWD?
LORD RIMURU !!

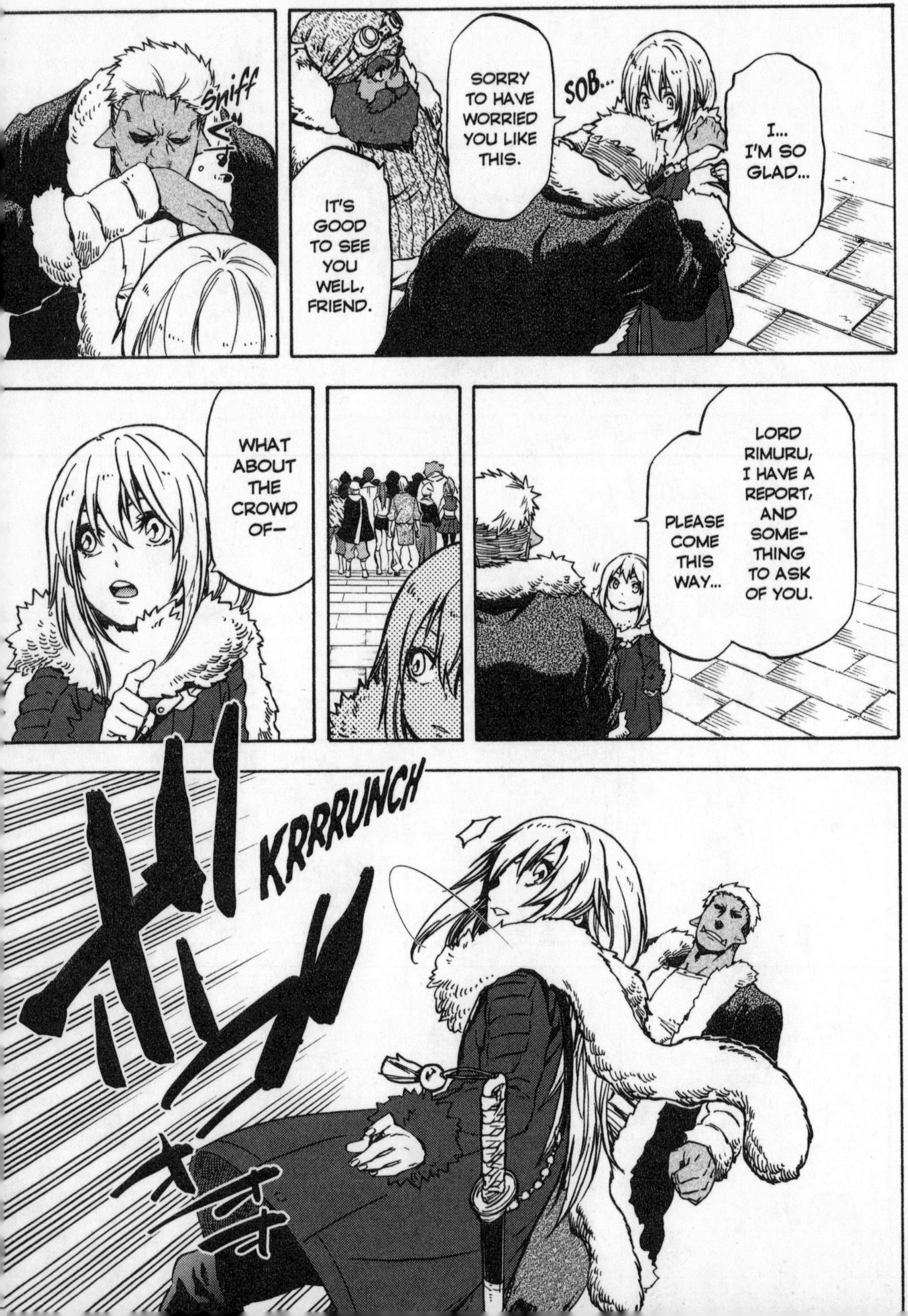
I...
I'M SO GLAD...
SOB...
SORRY TO HAVE WORRIED YOU LIKE THIS.
IT'S GOOD TO SEE YOU WELL, FRIEND.
Sniff
LORD RIMURU, I HAVE A REPORT, AND SOMETHING TO ASK OF YOU.
PLEASE COME THIS WAY...
WHAT ABOUT THE CROWD OF—
KRRRUNCH

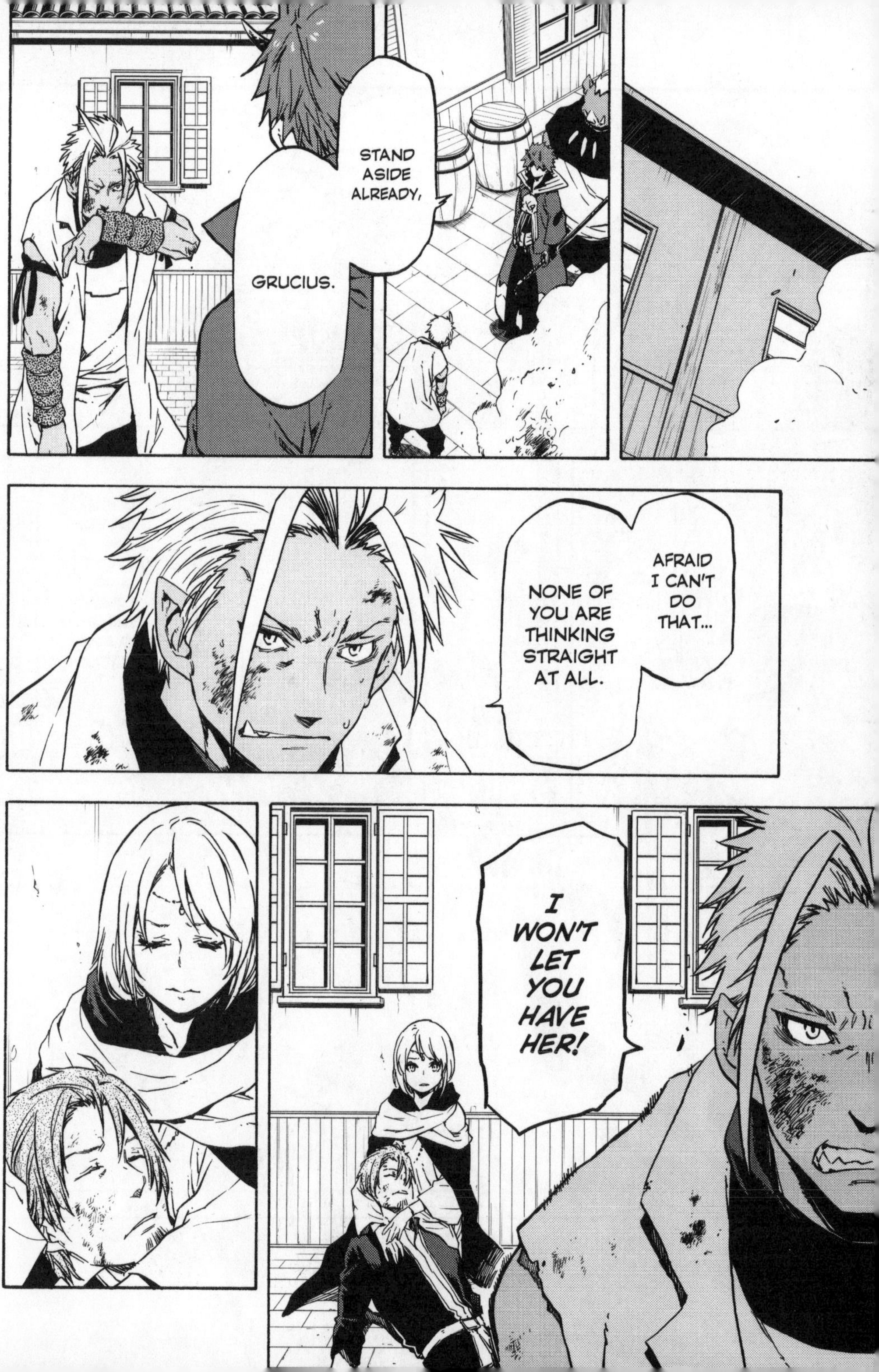
STAND ASIDE ALREADY,
GRUCIUS.
AFRAID I CAN'T DO THAT...
NONE OF YOU ARE THINKING STRAIGHT AT ALL.
I WON'T LET YOU HAVE HER!

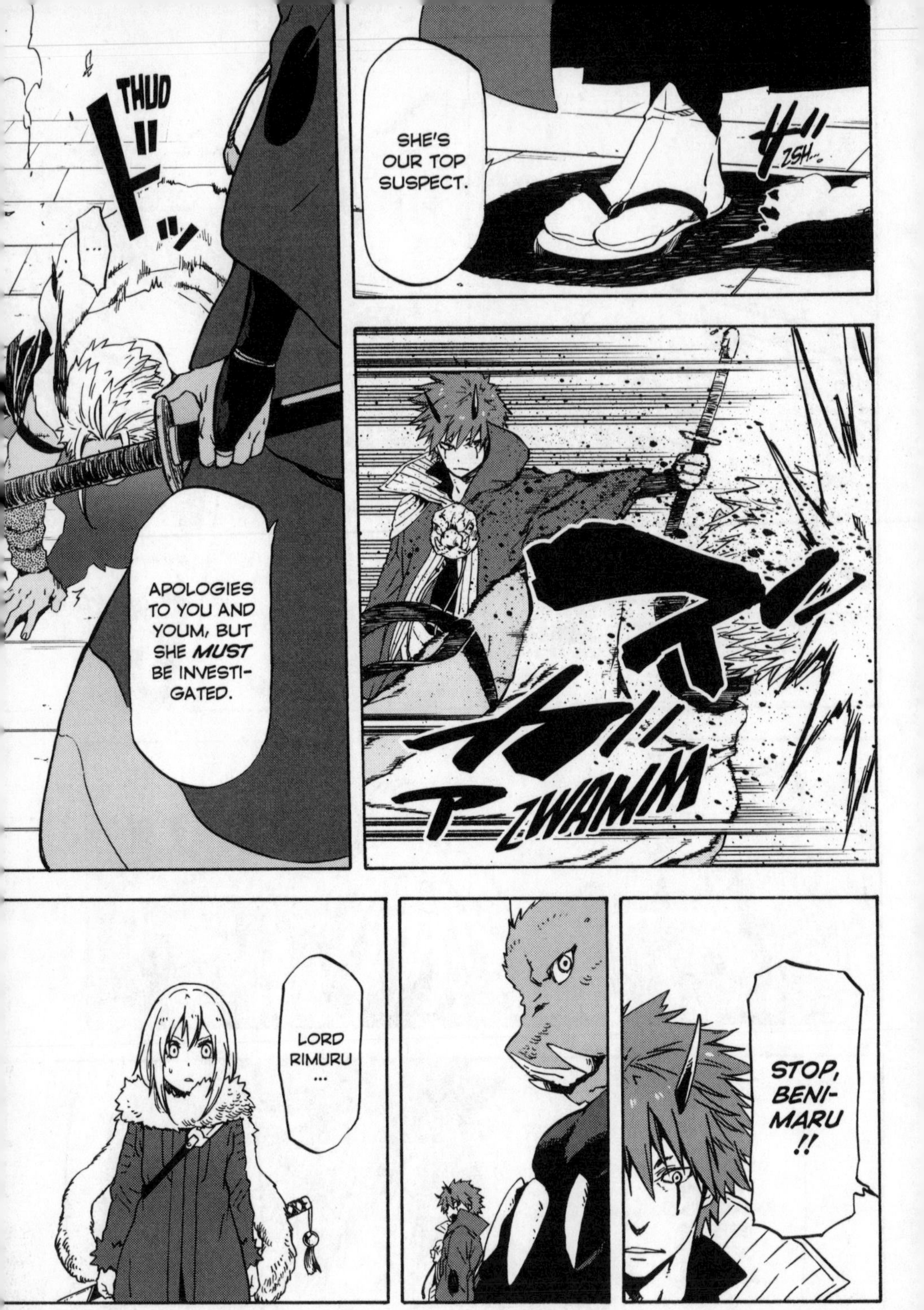
SHE'S OUR TOP SUSPECT.
ZSH...
ZWAMM
THUD
...
APOLOGIES TO YOU AND YOUM, BUT SHE *MUST* BE INVESTIGATED.
STOP, BENIMARU!!
LORD RIMURU...

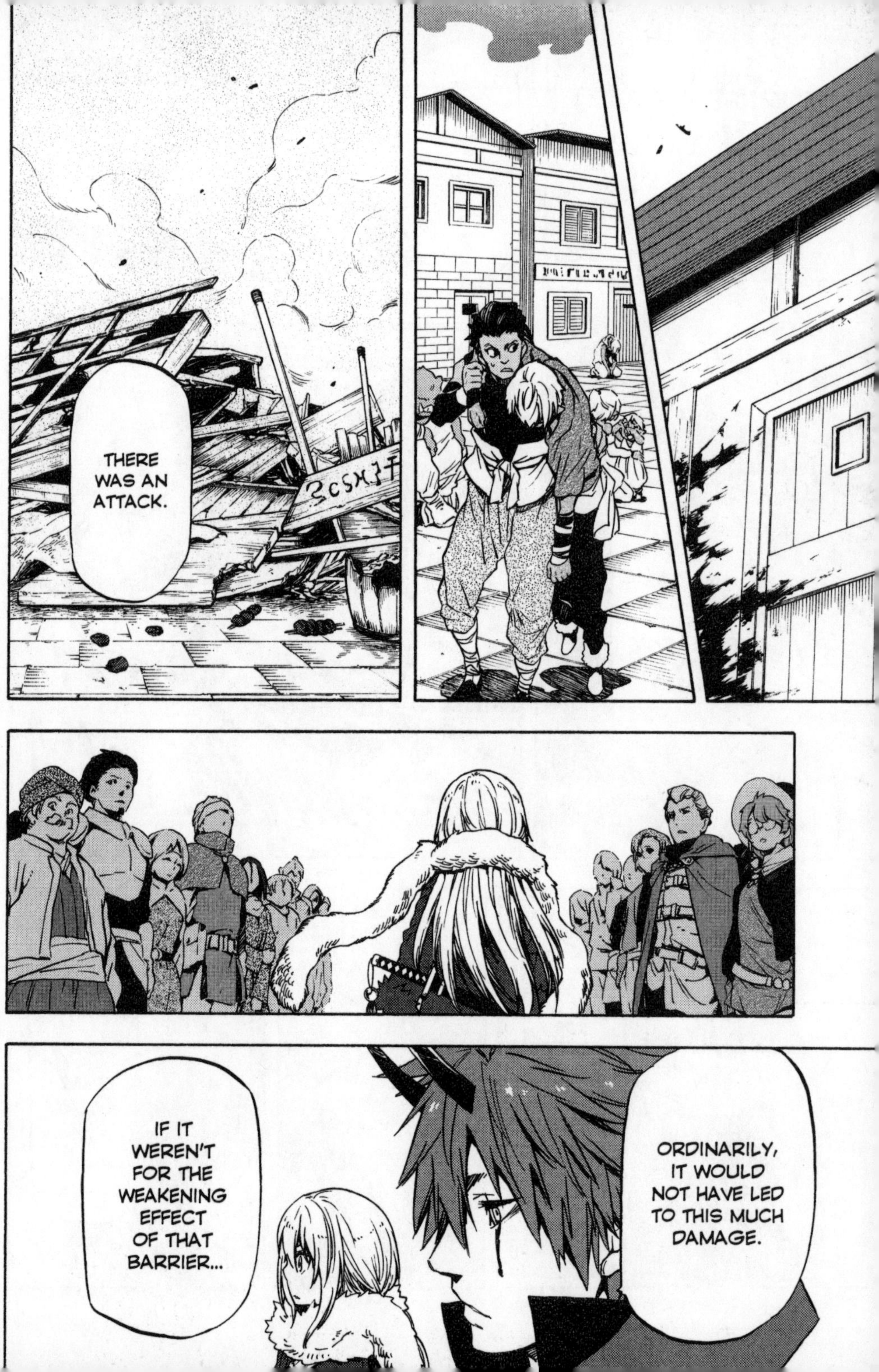
THERE WAS AN ATTACK.
ORDINARILY, IT WOULD NOT HAVE LED TO THIS MUCH DAMAGE.
IF IT WEREN'T FOR THE WEAKENING EFFECT OF THAT BARRIER...

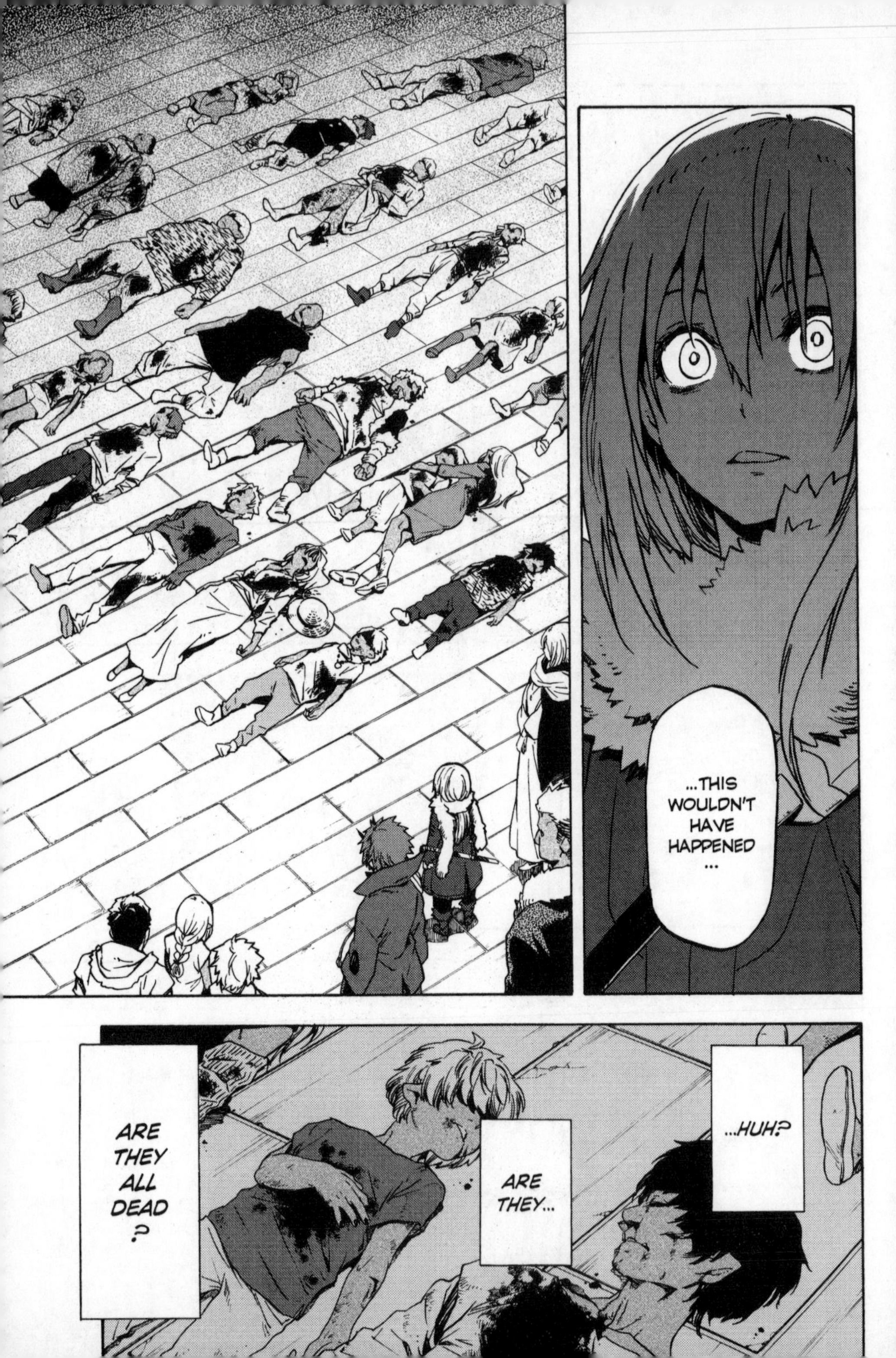
...THIS WOULDN'T HAVE HAPPENED ...
...HUH?
ARE THEY...
ARE THEY ALL DEAD ?

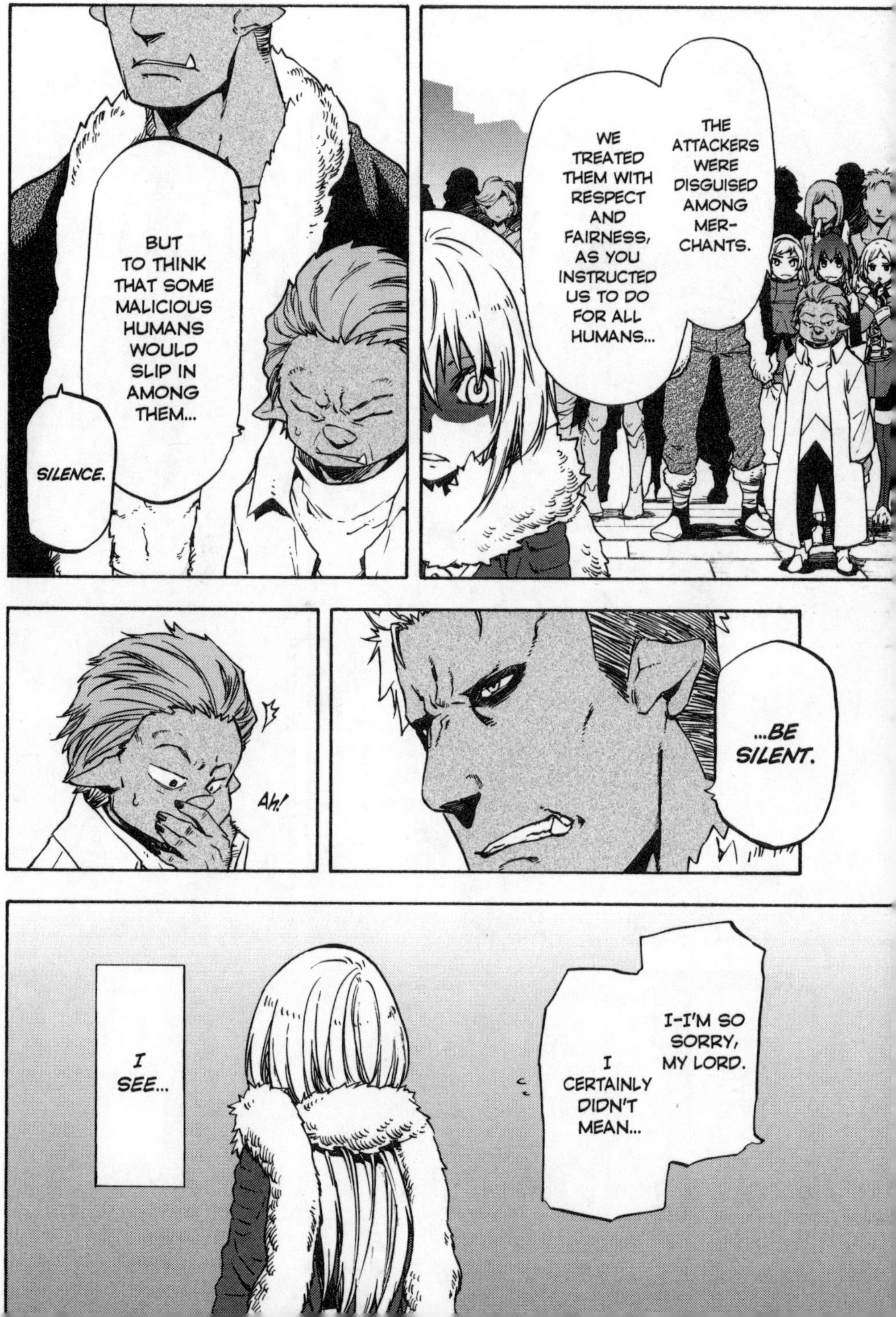
THE ATTACKERS WERE DISGUISED AMONG MER-CHANTS.
WE TREATED THEM WITH RESPECT AND FAIRNESS, AS YOU INSTRUCTED US TO DO FOR ALL HUMANS...
BUT TO THINK THAT SOME MALICIOUS HUMANS WOULD SLIP IN AMONG THEM...
SILENCE.
...BE SILENT.
Ah!
I-I'M SO SORRY, MY LORD.
I CERTAINLY DIDN'T MEAN...
I SEE...

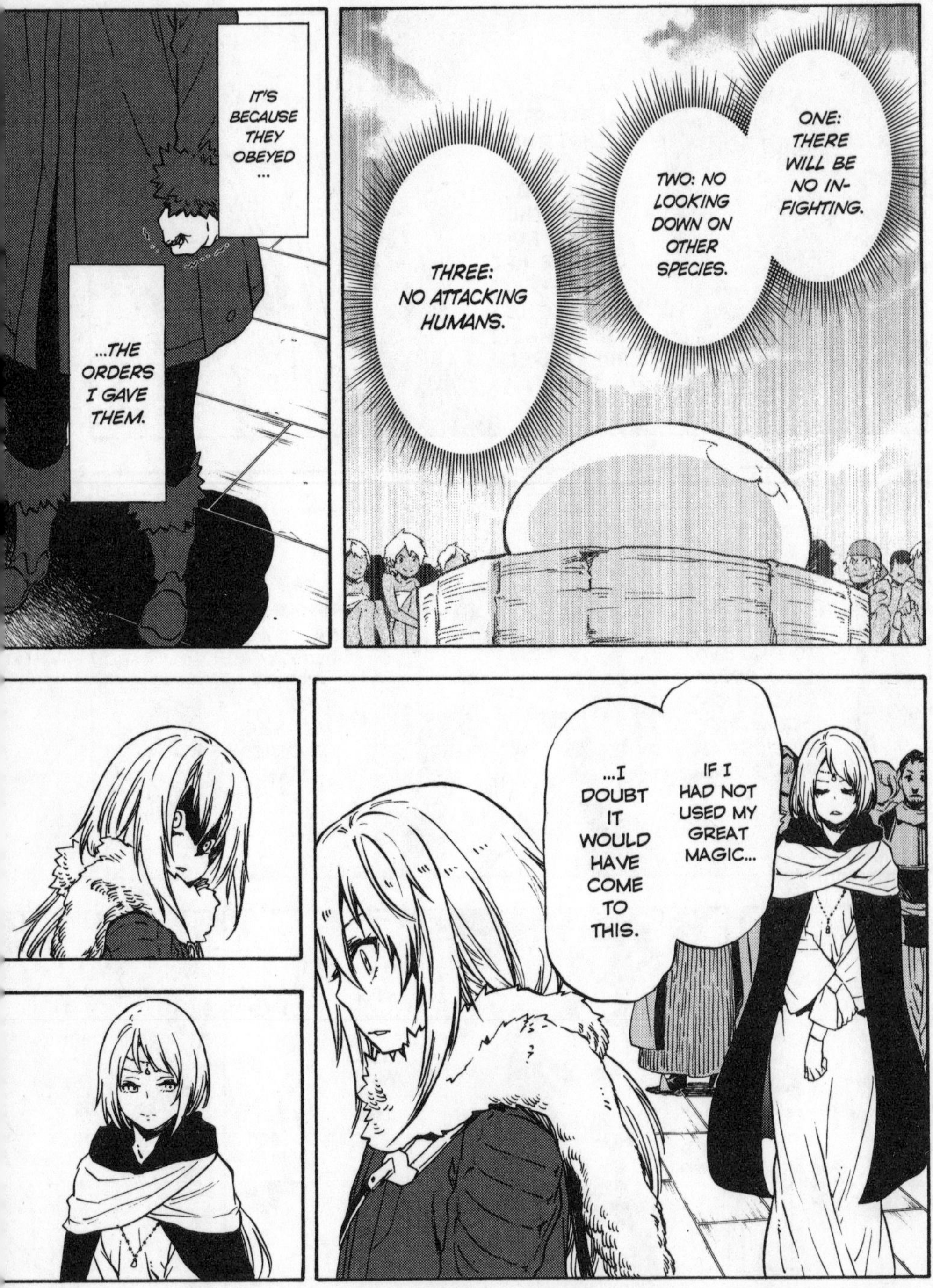
ONE: THERE WILL BE NO IN-FIGHTING.
TWO: NO LOOKING DOWN ON OTHER SPECIES.
THREE: NO ATTACKING HUMANS.
IT'S BECAUSE THEY OBEYED ...
...THE ORDERS I GAVE THEM.
IF I HAD NOT USED MY GREAT MAGIC...
...I DOUBT IT WOULD HAVE COME TO THIS.

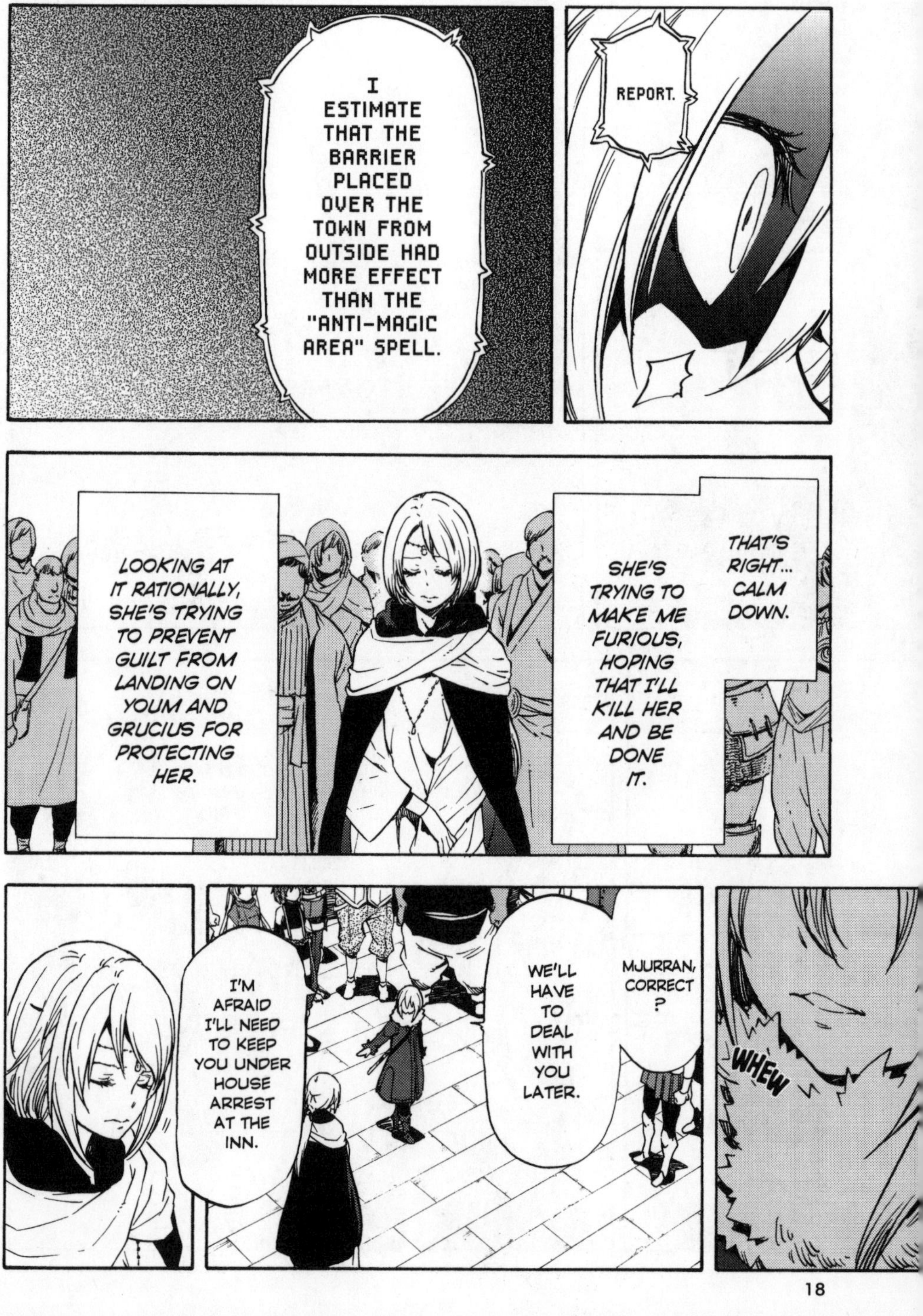
REPORT.
I ESTIMATE THAT THE BARRIER PLACED OVER THE TOWN FROM OUTSIDE HAD MORE EFFECT THAN THE "ANTI-MAGIC AREA" SPELL.
THAT'S RIGHT... CALM DOWN.
SHE'S TRYING TO MAKE ME FURIOUS, HOPING THAT I'LL KILL HER AND BE DONE IT.
LOOKING AT IT RATIONALLY, SHE'S TRYING TO PREVENT GUILT FROM LANDING ON YOUM AND GRUCIUS FOR PROTECTING HER.
WHEW
MJURRAN, CORRECT ?
WE'LL HAVE TO DEAL WITH YOU LATER.
I'M AFRAID I'LL NEED TO KEEP YOU UNDER HOUSE ARREST AT THE INN.

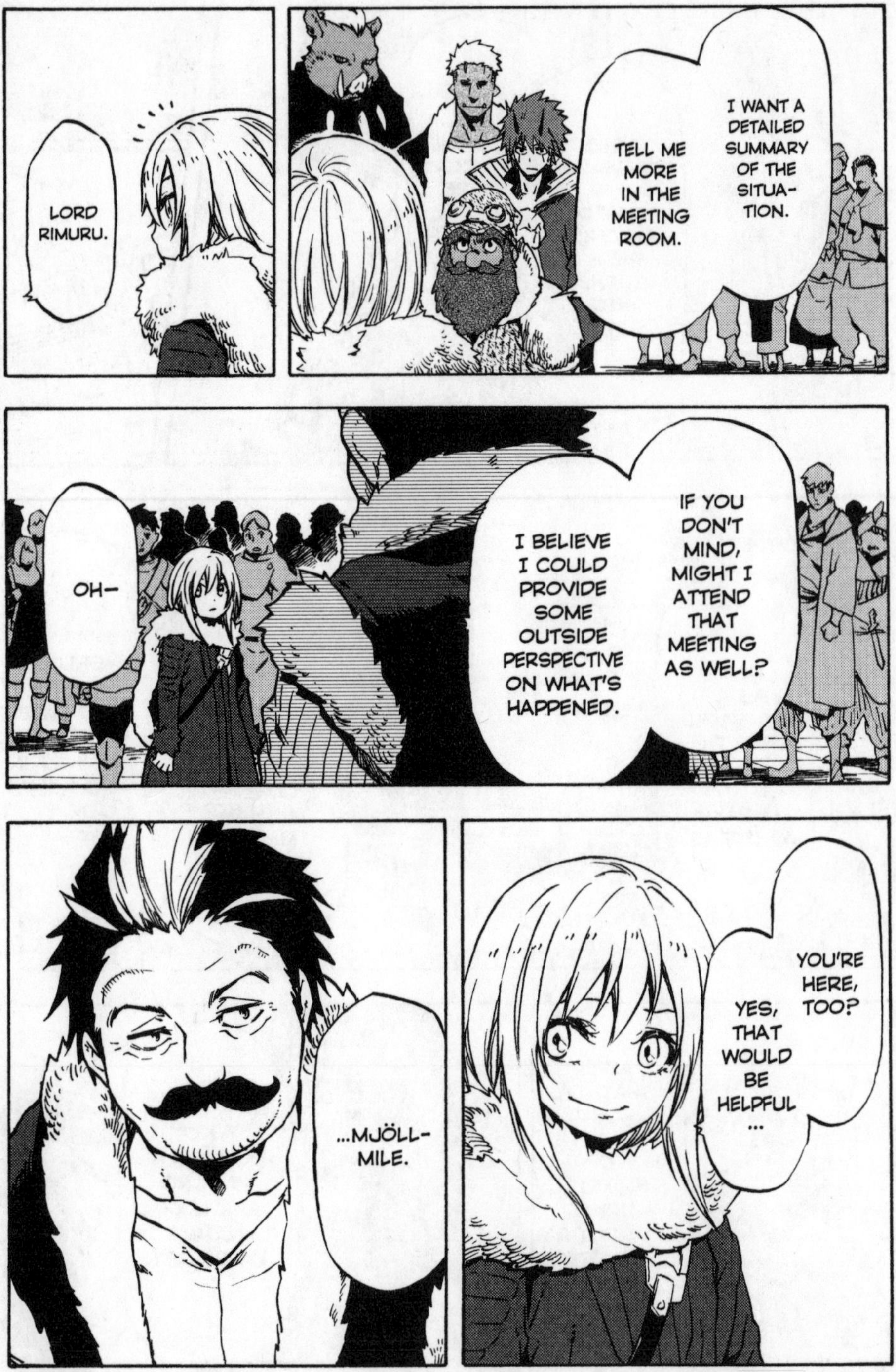
I WANT A DETAILED SUMMARY OF THE SITUA-TION.
TELL ME MORE IN THE MEETING ROOM.
LORD RIMURU.
IF YOU DON'T MIND, MIGHT I ATTEND THAT MEETING AS WELL?
I BELIEVE I COULD PROVIDE SOME OUTSIDE PERSPECTIVE ON WHAT'S HAPPENED.
OH–
YOU'RE HERE, TOO?
YES, THAT WOULD BE HELPFUL ...
...MJÖLL-MILE.

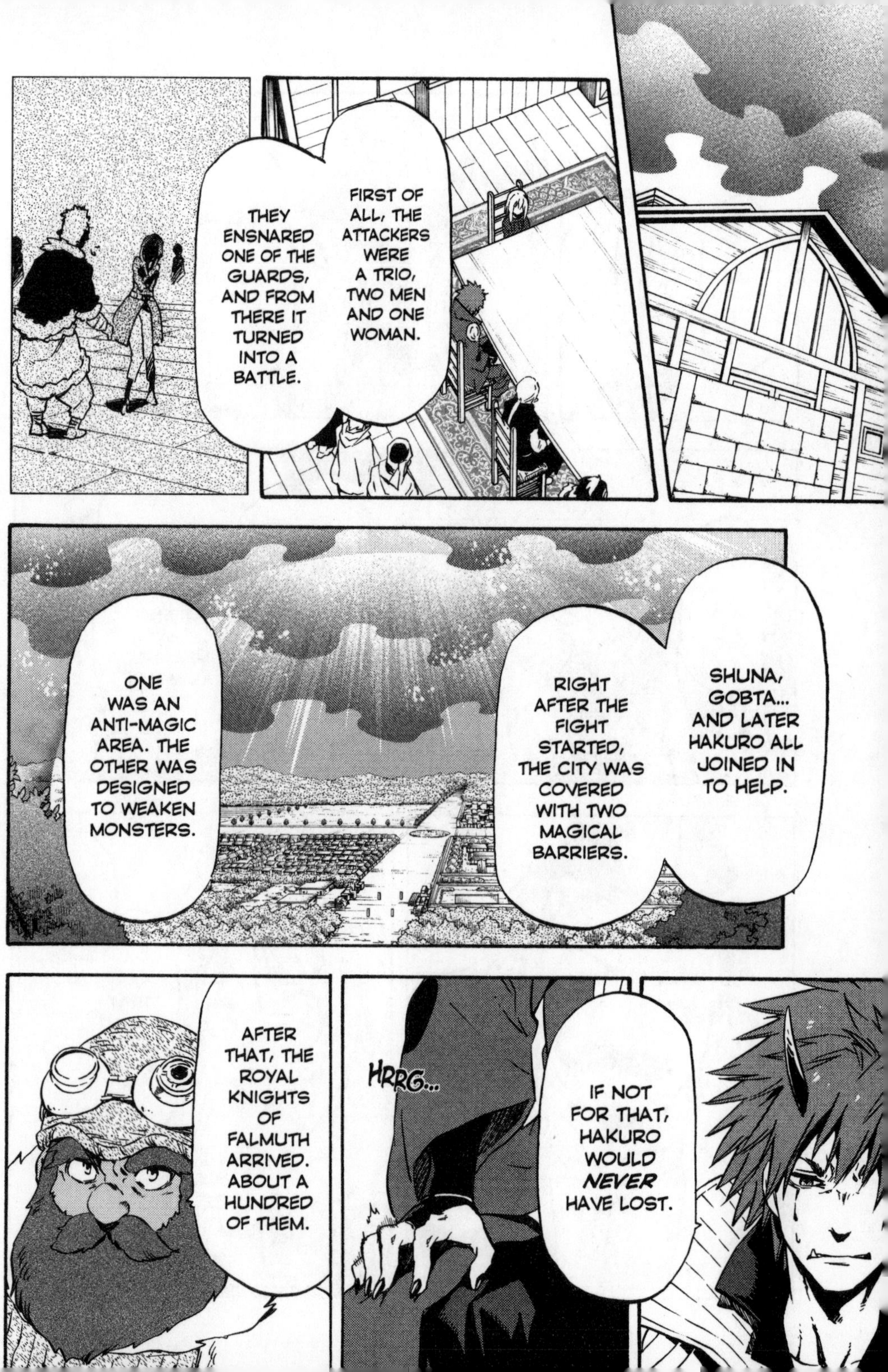
FIRST OF ALL, THE ATTACKERS WERE A TRIO, TWO MEN AND ONE WOMAN.
THEY ENSNARED ONE OF THE GUARDS, AND FROM THERE IT TURNED INTO A BATTLE.
SHUNA, GOBTA... AND LATER HAKURO ALL JOINED IN TO HELP.
RIGHT AFTER THE FIGHT STARTED, THE CITY WAS COVERED WITH TWO MAGICAL BARRIERS.
ONE WAS AN ANTI-MAGIC AREA. THE OTHER WAS DESIGNED TO WEAKEN MONSTERS.
IF NOT FOR THAT, HAKURO WOULD *NEVER* HAVE LOST.
HRRG...
AFTER THAT, THE ROYAL KNIGHTS OF FALMUTH ARRIVED. ABOUT A HUNDRED OF THEM.

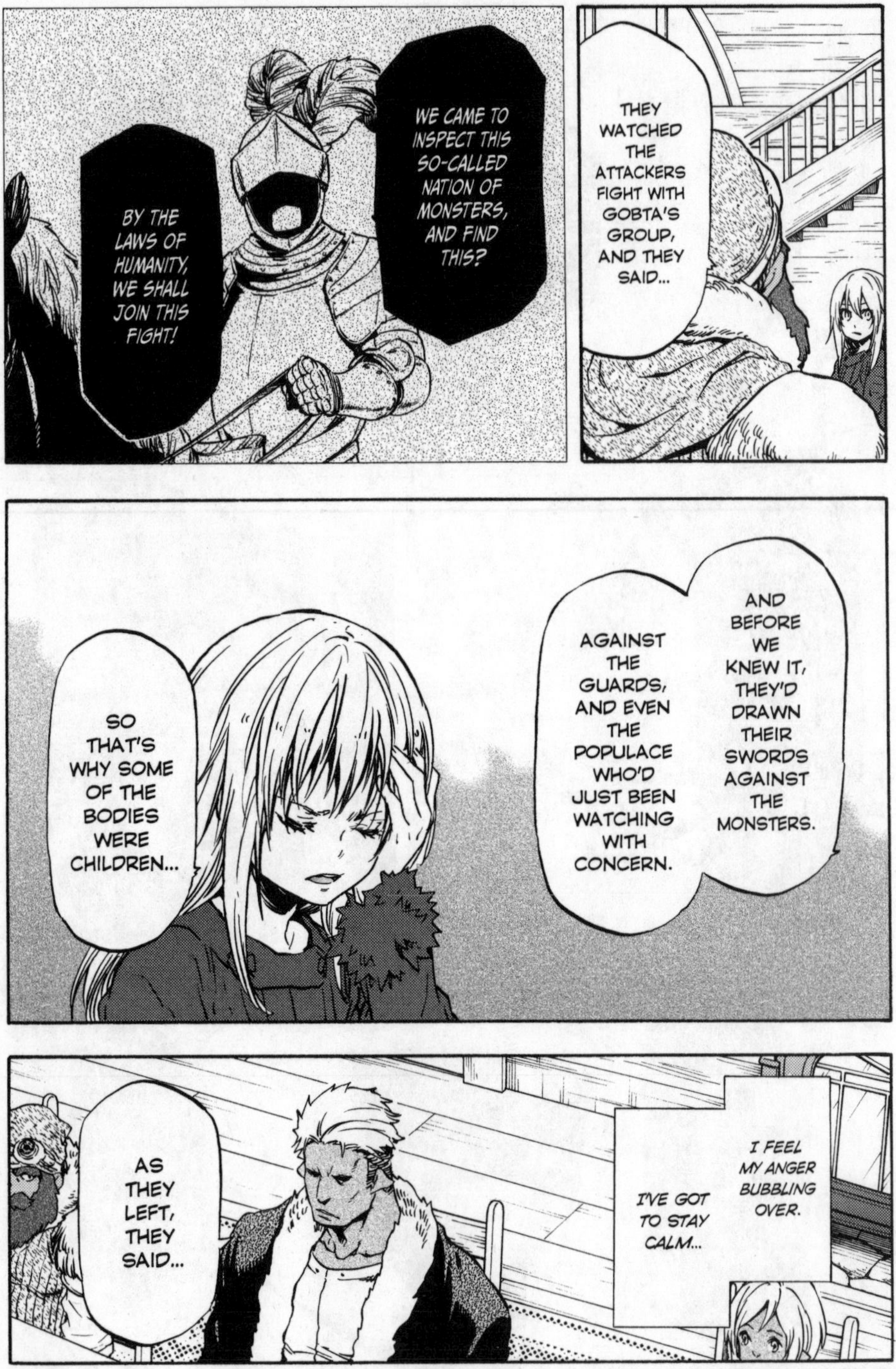
THEY WATCHED THE ATTACKERS FIGHT WITH GOBTA'S GROUP, AND THEY SAID...
WE CAME TO INSPECT THIS SO-CALLED NATION OF MONSTERS, AND FIND THIS?
BY THE LAWS OF HUMANITY, WE SHALL JOIN THIS FIGHT!
AND BEFORE WE KNEW IT, THEY'D DRAWN THEIR SWORDS AGAINST THE MONSTERS.
AGAINST THE GUARDS, AND EVEN THE POPULACE WHO'D JUST BEEN WATCHING WITH CONCERN.
SO THAT'S WHY SOME OF THE BODIES WERE CHILDREN...
I FEEL MY ANGER BUBBLING OVER.
I'VE GOT TO STAY CALM...
AS THEY LEFT, THEY SAID...

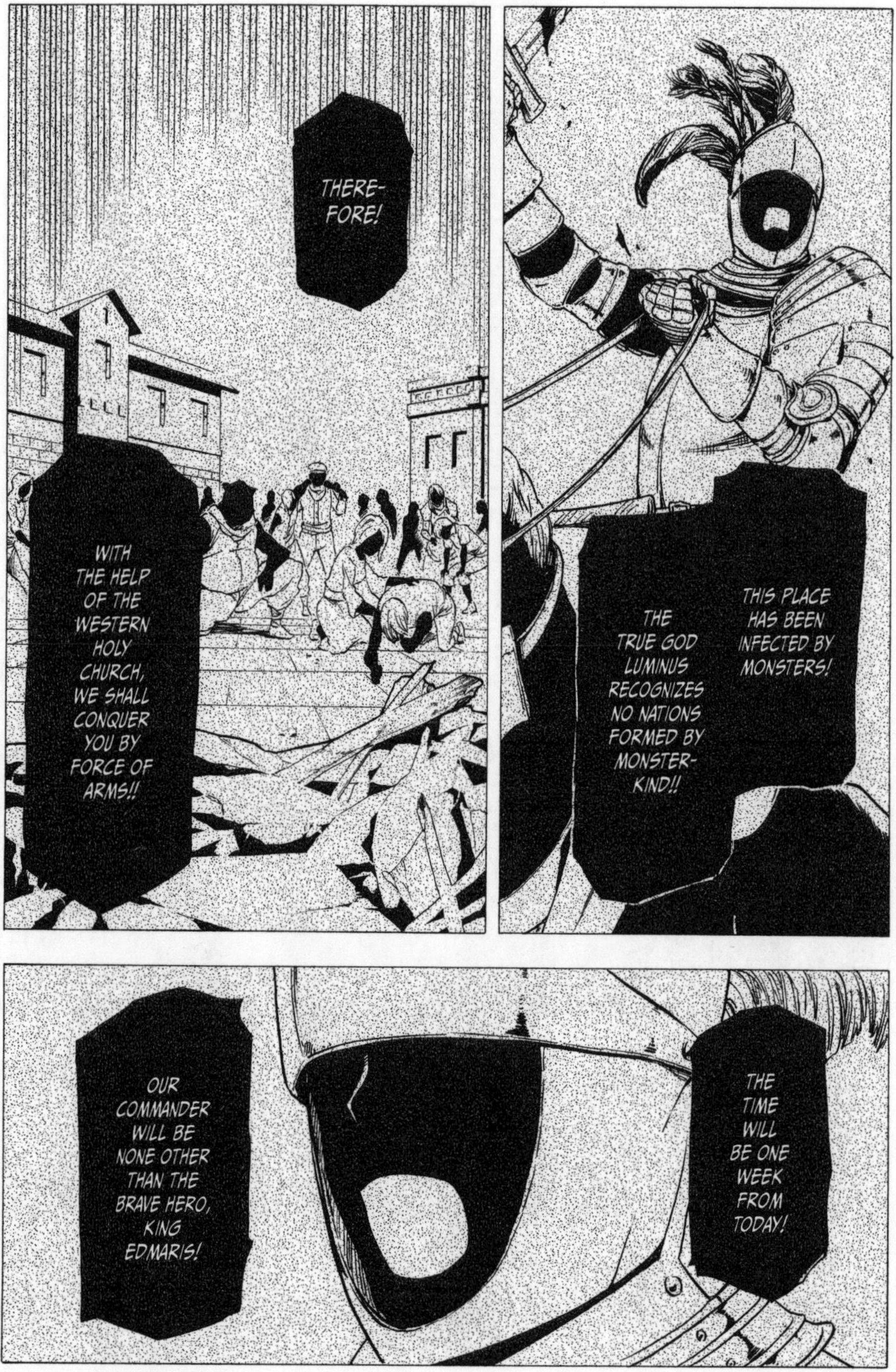
THIS PLACE HAS BEEN INFECTED BY MONSTERS!
THE TRUE GOD LUMINUS RECOGNIZES NO NATIONS FORMED BY MONSTER-KIND!!
THERE-FORE!
WITH THE HELP OF THE WESTERN HOLY CHURCH, WE SHALL CONQUER YOU BY FORCE OF ARMS!!
THE TIME WILL BE ONE WEEK FROM TODAY!
OUR COMMANDER WILL BE NONE OTHER THAN THE BRAVE HERO, KING EDMARIS!

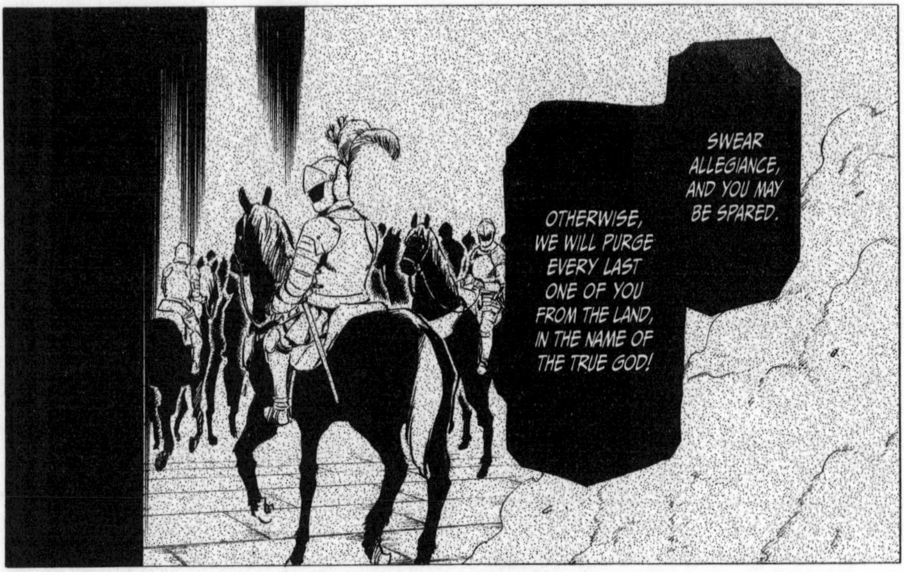
SWEAR ALLEGIANCE, AND YOU MAY BE SPARED.
OTHERWISE, WE WILL PURGE EVERY LAST ONE OF YOU FROM THE LAND, IN THE NAME OF THE TRUE GOD!

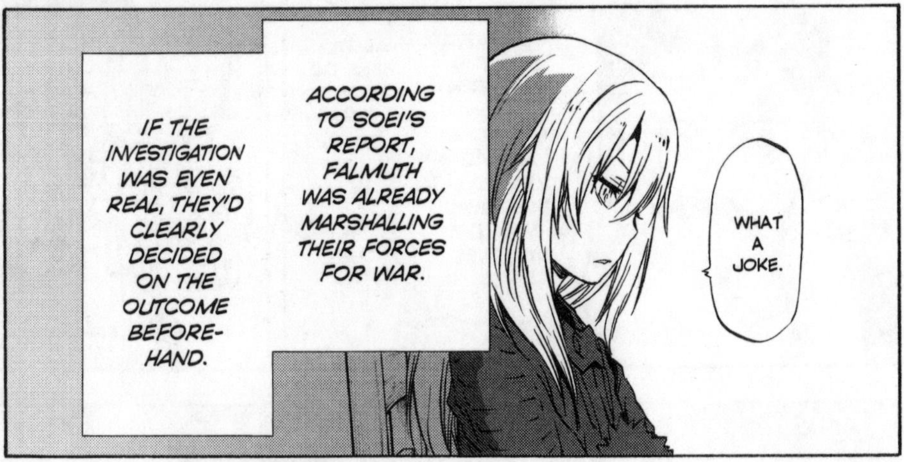
WHAT A JOKE.
ACCORDING TO SOEI'S REPORT, FALMUTH WAS ALREADY MARSHALLING THEIR FORCES FOR WAR.
IF THE INVESTIGATION WAS EVEN REAL, THEY'D CLEARLY DECIDED ON THE OUTCOME BEFORE-HAND.

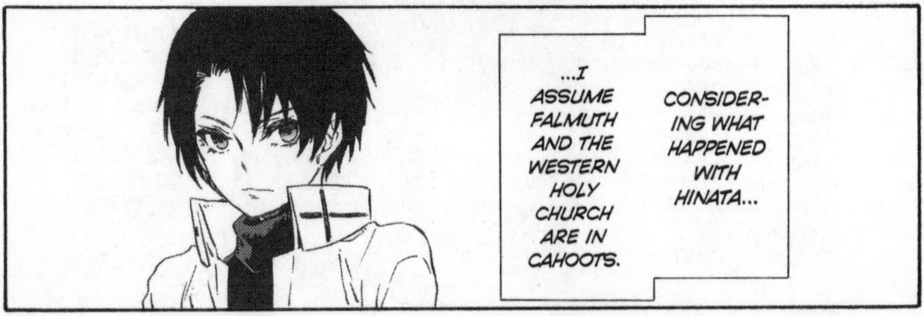
CONSIDER-ING WHAT HAPPENED WITH HINATA...
...I ASSUME FALMUTH AND THE WESTERN HOLY CHURCH ARE IN CAHOOTS.

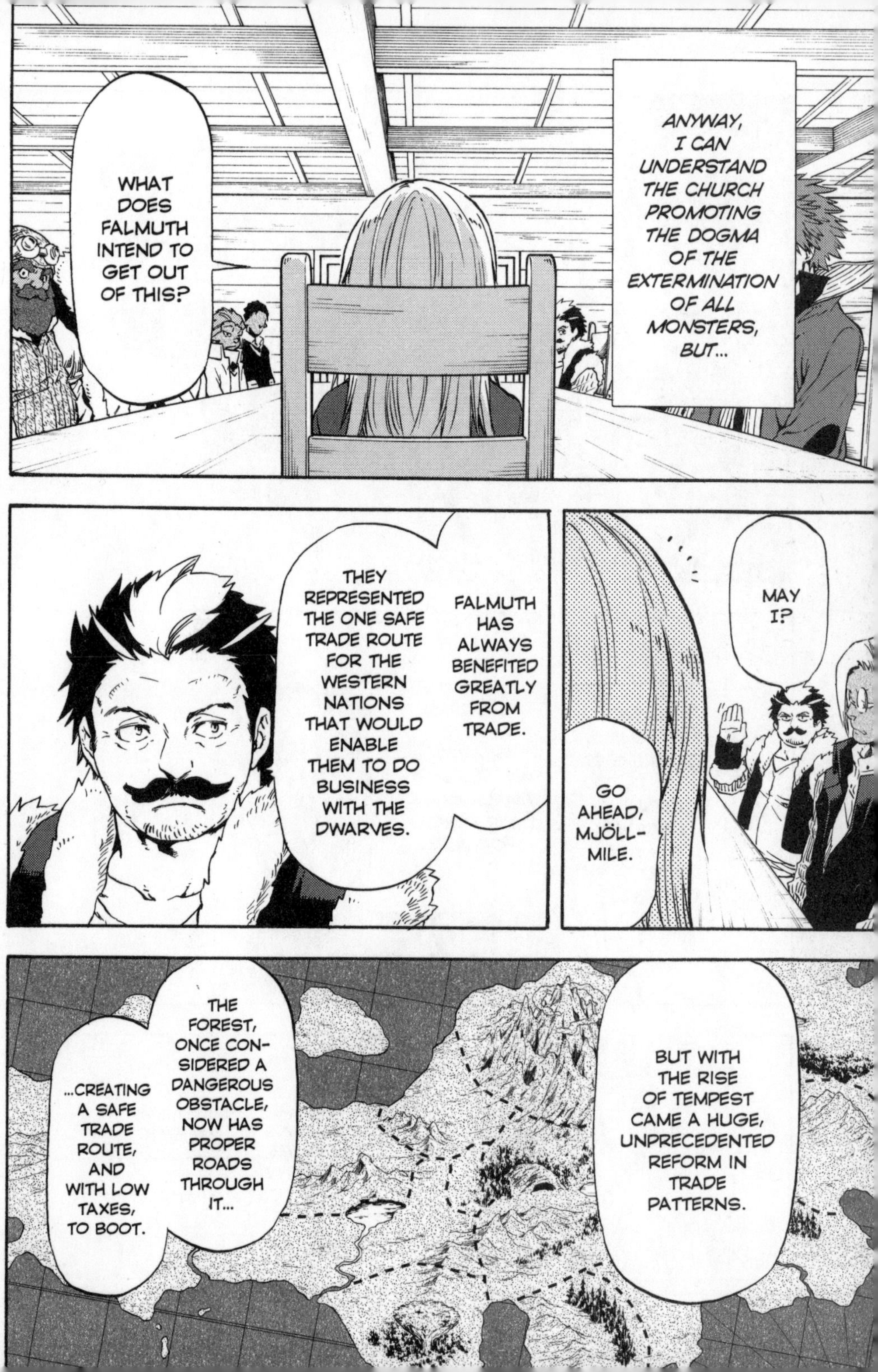
ANYWAY, I CAN UNDERSTAND THE CHURCH PROMOTING THE DOGMA OF THE EXTERMINATION OF ALL MONSTERS, BUT...
WHAT DOES FALMUTH INTEND TO GET OUT OF THIS?
MAY I?
GO AHEAD, MJÖLL-MILE.
FALMUTH HAS ALWAYS BENEFITED GREATLY FROM TRADE.
THEY REPRESENTED THE ONE SAFE TRADE ROUTE FOR THE WESTERN NATIONS THAT WOULD ENABLE THEM TO DO BUSINESS WITH THE DWARVES.
BUT WITH THE RISE OF TEMPEST CAME A HUGE, UNPRECEDENTED REFORM IN TRADE PATTERNS.
THE FOREST, ONCE CON-SIDERED A DANGEROUS OBSTACLE, NOW HAS PROPER ROADS THROUGH IT...
...CREATING A SAFE TRADE ROUTE, AND WITH LOW TAXES, TO BOOT.

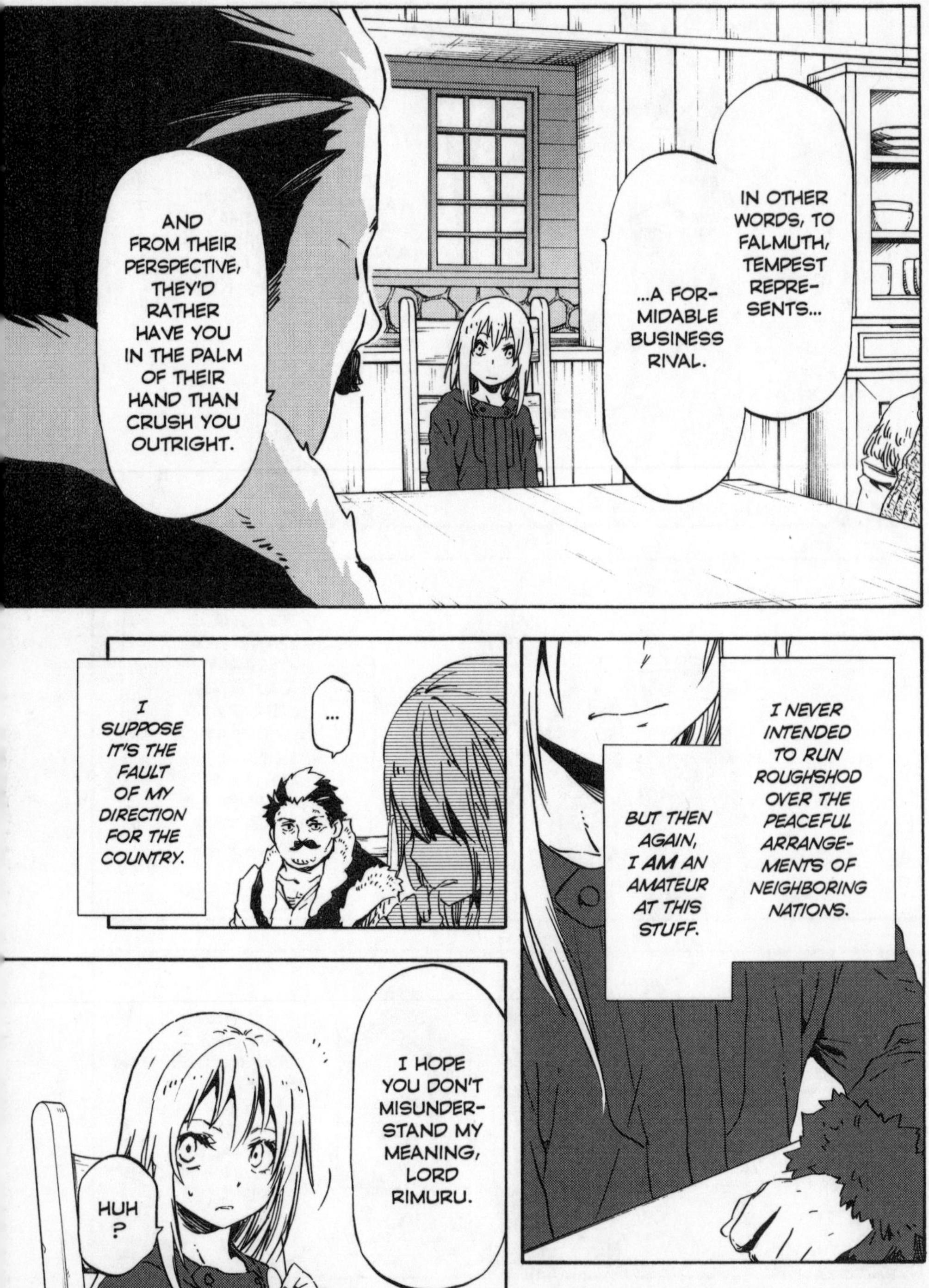
IN OTHER WORDS, TO FALMUTH, TEMPEST REPRESENTS...
...A FORMIDABLE BUSINESS RIVAL.
AND FROM THEIR PERSPECTIVE, THEY'D RATHER HAVE YOU IN THE PALM OF THEIR HAND THAN CRUSH YOU OUTRIGHT.
I NEVER INTENDED TO RUN ROUGHSHOD OVER THE PEACEFUL ARRANGEMENTS OF NEIGHBORING NATIONS.
BUT THEN AGAIN, I **AM** AN AMATEUR AT THIS STUFF.
I SUPPOSE IT'S THE FAULT OF MY DIRECTION FOR THE COUNTRY.
...
I HOPE YOU DON'T MISUNDERSTAND MY MEANING, LORD RIMURU.
HUH?

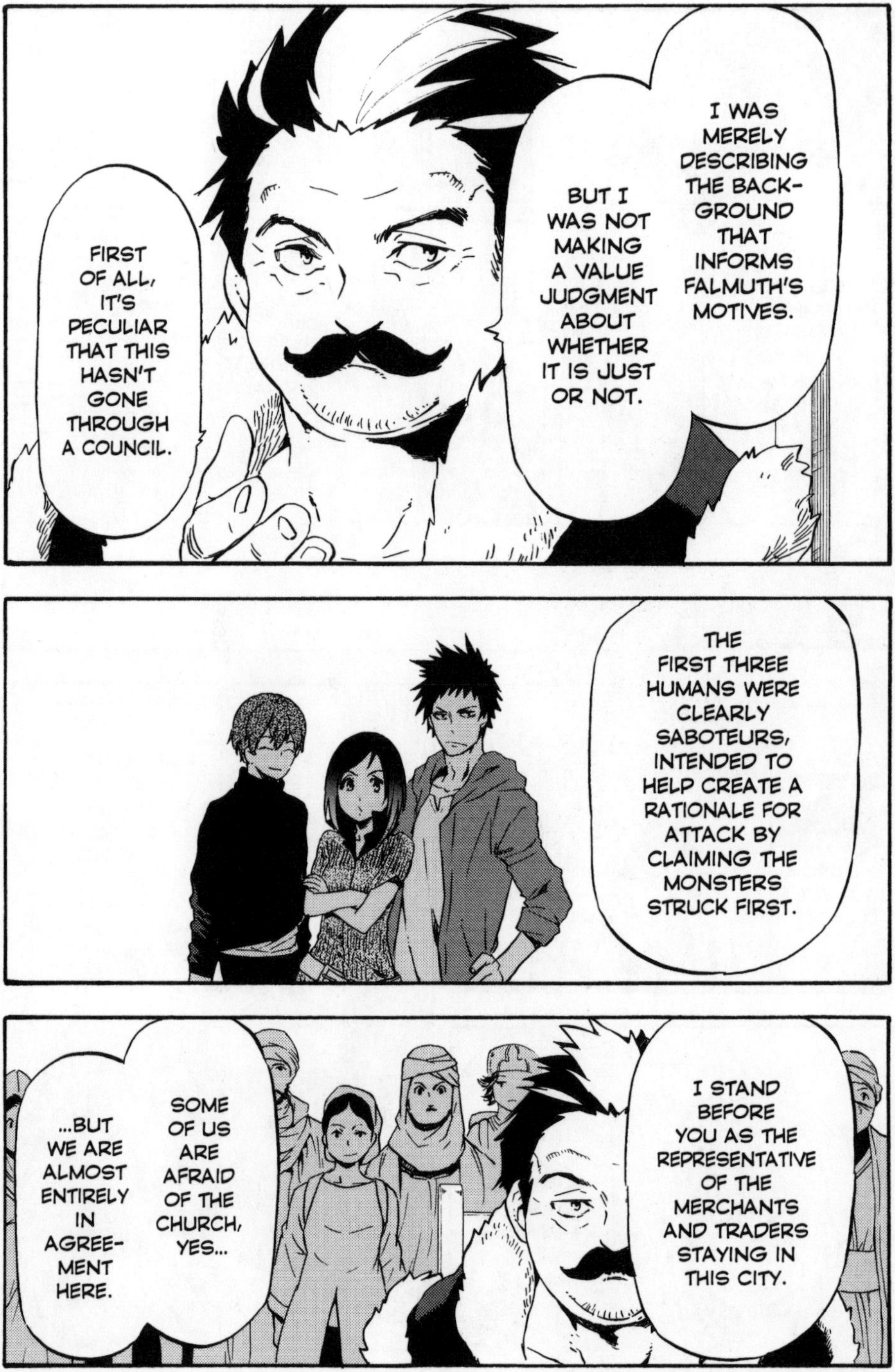
I WAS MERELY DESCRIBING THE BACK-GROUND THAT INFORMS FALMUTH'S MOTIVES.
BUT I WAS NOT MAKING A VALUE JUDGMENT ABOUT WHETHER IT IS JUST OR NOT.
FIRST OF ALL, IT'S PECULIAR THAT THIS HASN'T GONE THROUGH A COUNCIL.
THE FIRST THREE HUMANS WERE CLEARLY SABOTEURS, INTENDED TO HELP CREATE A RATIONALE FOR ATTACK BY CLAIMING THE MONSTERS STRUCK FIRST.
I STAND BEFORE YOU AS THE REPRESENTATIVE OF THE MERCHANTS AND TRADERS STAYING IN THIS CITY.
SOME OF US ARE AFRAID OF THE CHURCH, YES...
...BUT WE ARE ALMOST ENTIRELY IN AGREE-MENT HERE.

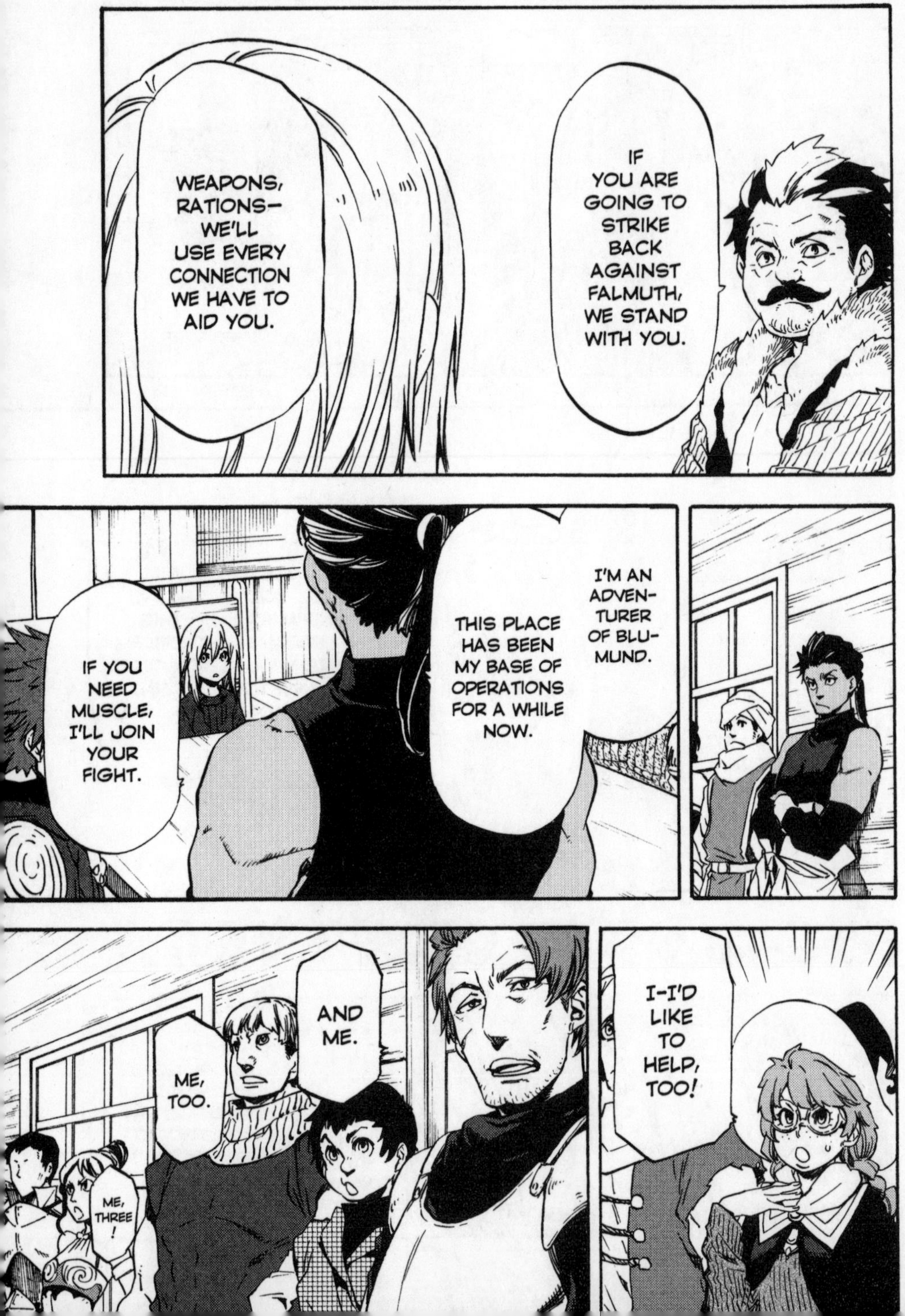
IF YOU ARE GOING TO STRIKE BACK AGAINST FALMUTH, WE STAND WITH YOU.
WEAPONS, RATIONS—WE'LL USE EVERY CONNECTION WE HAVE TO AID YOU.
I'M AN ADVEN-TURER OF BLU-MUND.
THIS PLACE HAS BEEN MY BASE OF OPERATIONS FOR A WHILE NOW.
IF YOU NEED MUSCLE, I'LL JOIN YOUR FIGHT.
I-I'D LIKE TO HELP, TOO!
AND ME.
ME, TOO.
ME, THREE!

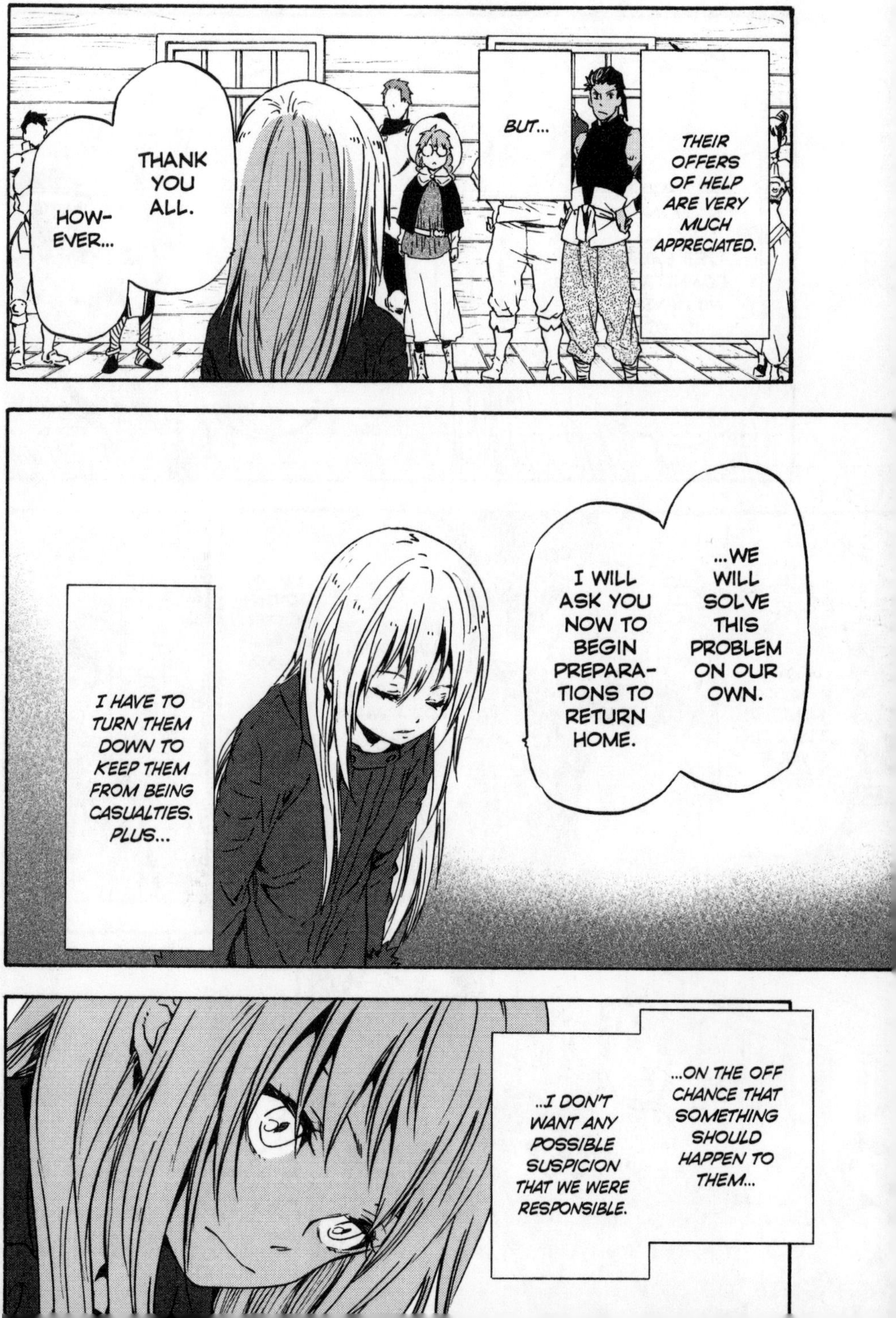
THEIR OFFERS OF HELP ARE VERY MUCH APPRECIATED.
BUT...
THANK YOU ALL.
HOW-EVER...
...WE WILL SOLVE THIS PROBLEM ON OUR OWN.
I WILL ASK YOU NOW TO BEGIN PREPARA-TIONS TO RETURN HOME.
I HAVE TO TURN THEM DOWN TO KEEP THEM FROM BEING CASUALTIES. PLUS...
...ON THE OFF CHANCE THAT SOMETHING SHOULD HAPPEN TO THEM...
...I DON'T WANT ANY POSSIBLE SUSPICION THAT WE WERE RESPONSIBLE.

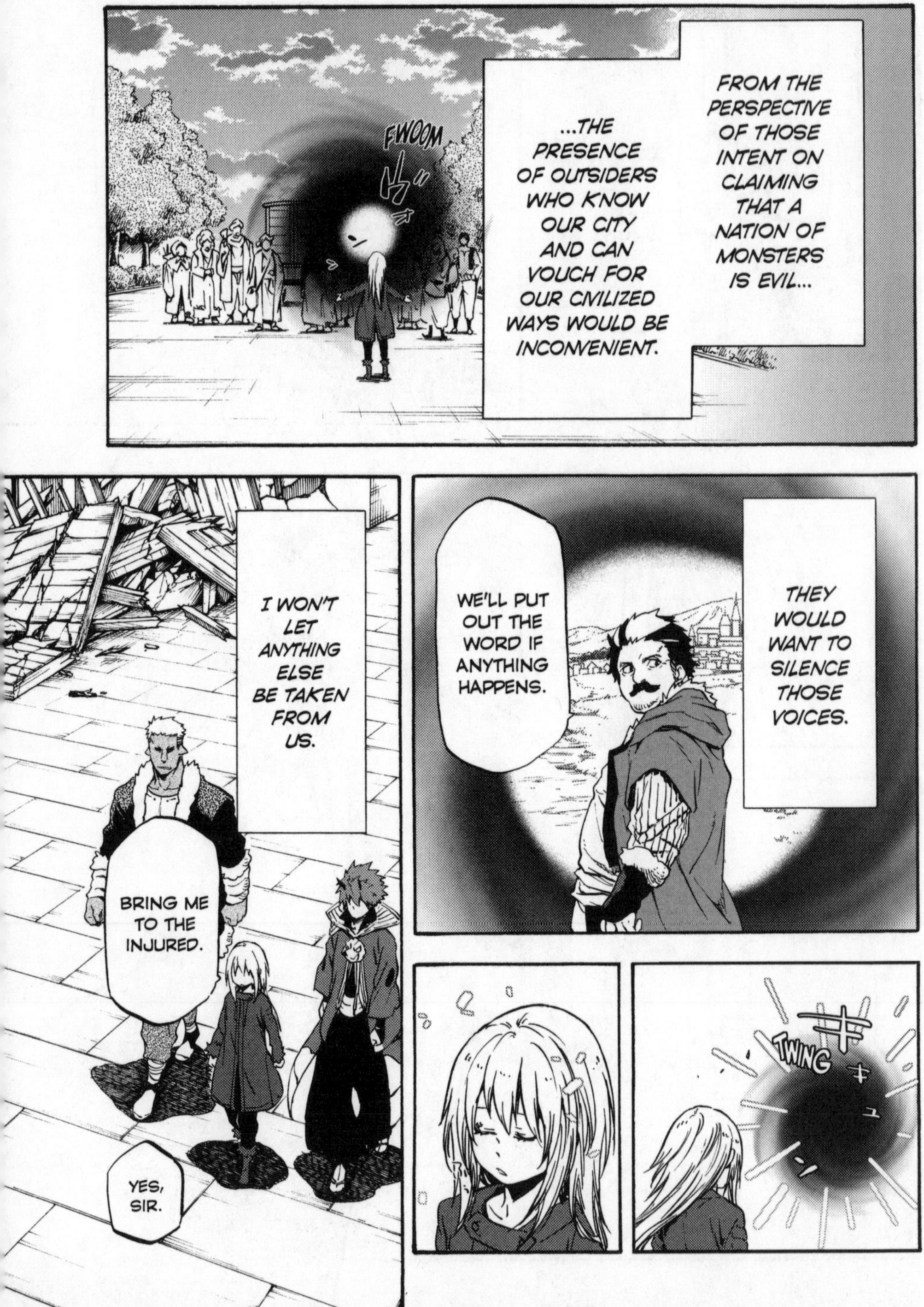
FROM THE PERSPECTIVE OF THOSE INTENT ON CLAIMING THAT A NATION OF MONSTERS IS EVIL...
...THE PRESENCE OF OUTSIDERS WHO KNOW OUR CITY AND CAN VOUCH FOR OUR CIVILIZED WAYS WOULD BE INCONVENIENT.
FWOOM
THEY WOULD WANT TO SILENCE THOSE VOICES.
WE'LL PUT OUT THE WORD IF ANYTHING HAPPENS.
TWING
I WON'T LET ANYTHING ELSE BE TAKEN FROM US.
BRING ME TO THE INJURED.
YES, SIR.

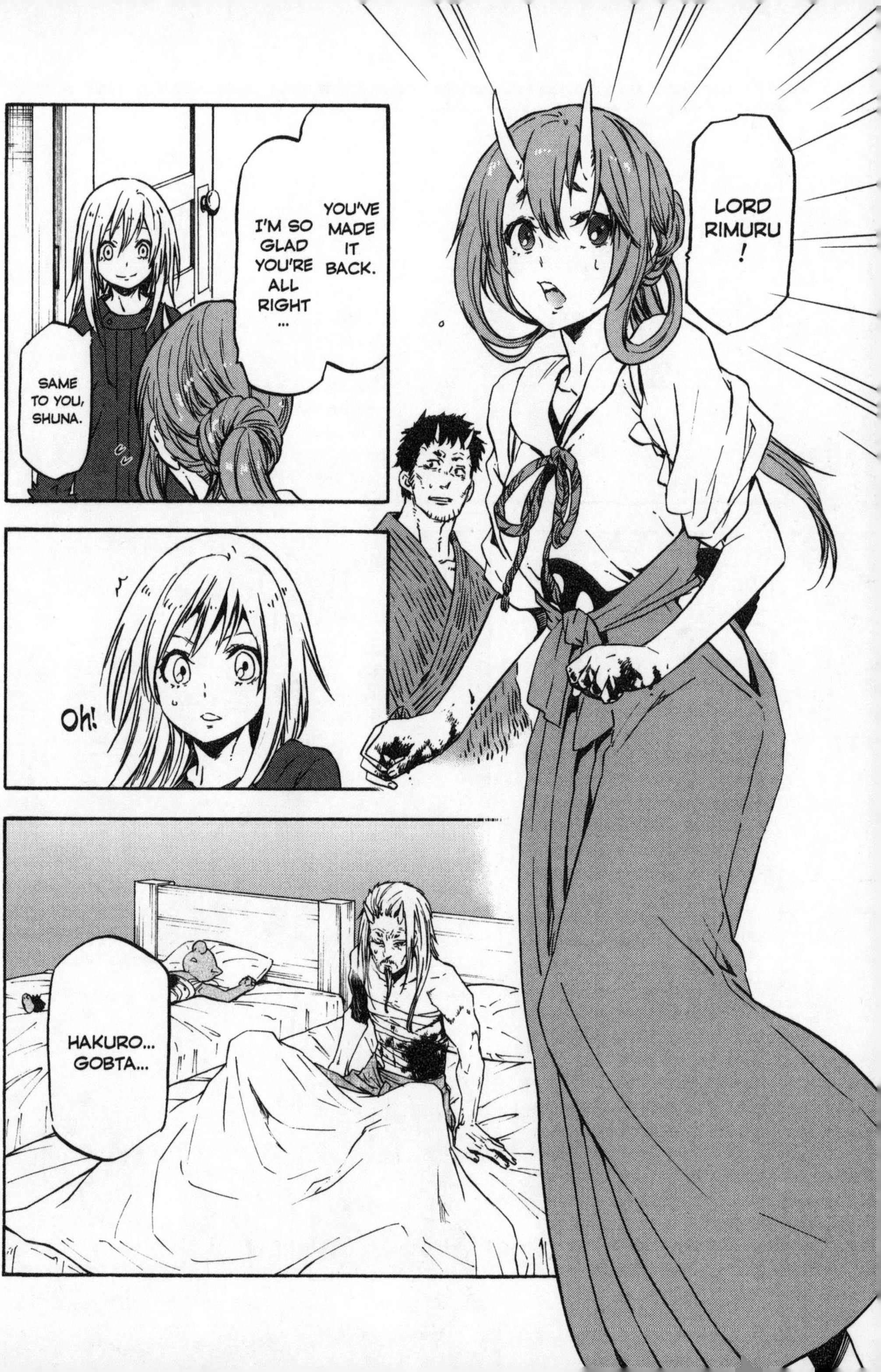
LORD RIMURU!
YOU'VE MADE IT BACK.
I'M SO GLAD YOU'RE ALL RIGHT...
SAME TO YOU, SHUNA.
Oh!
HAKURO... GOBTA...

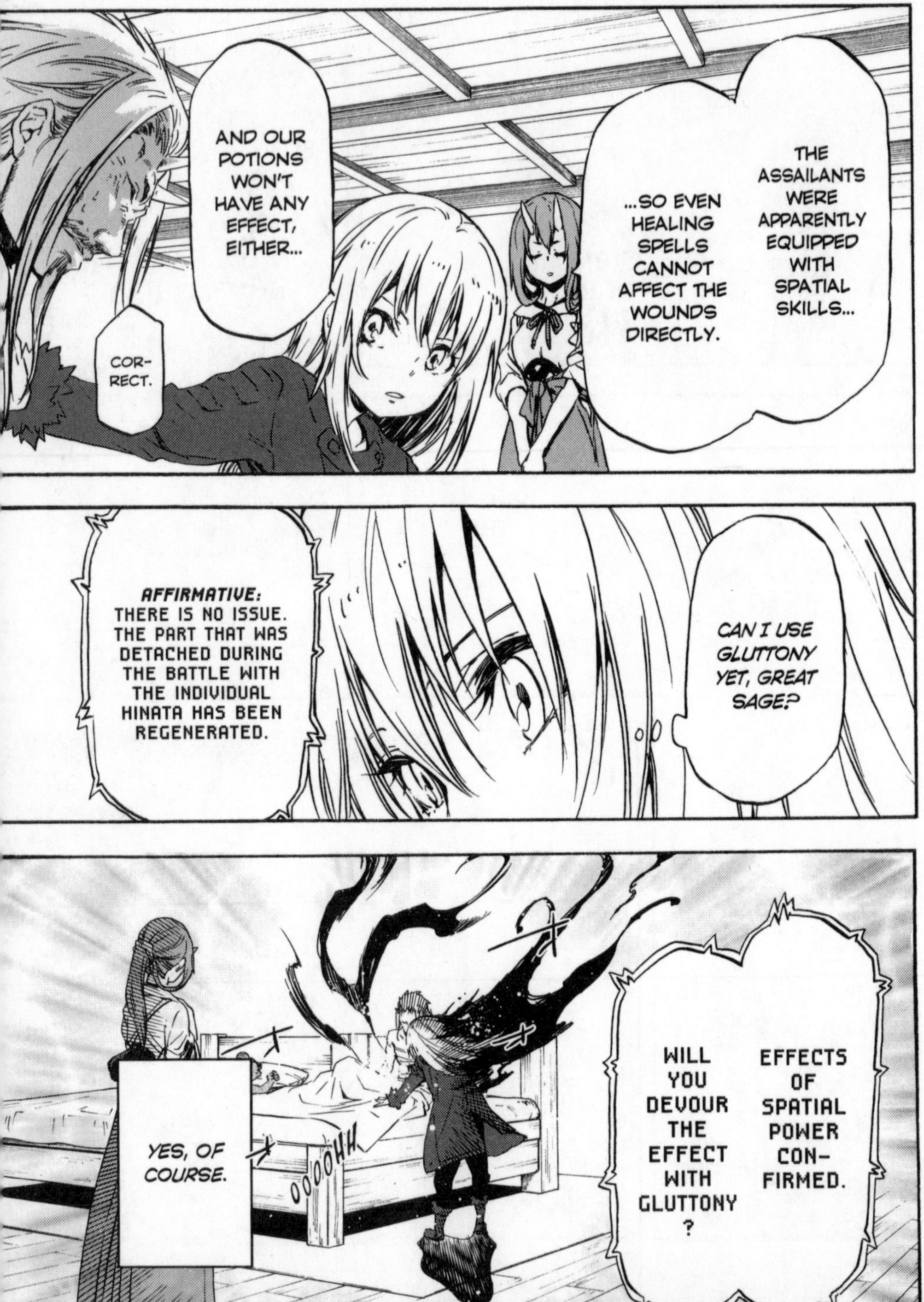
THE ASSAILANTS WERE APPARENTLY EQUIPPED WITH SPATIAL SKILLS...
...SO EVEN HEALING SPELLS CANNOT AFFECT THE WOUNDS DIRECTLY.
AND OUR POTIONS WON'T HAVE ANY EFFECT, EITHER...
COR-RECT.
CAN I USE GLUTTONY YET, GREAT SAGE?
AFFIRMATIVE: THERE IS NO ISSUE. THE PART THAT WAS DETACHED DURING THE BATTLE WITH THE INDIVIDUAL HINATA HAS BEEN REGENERATED.
EFFECTS OF SPATIAL POWER CON-FIRMED.
WILL YOU DEVOUR THE EFFECT WITH GLUTTONY?
YES, OF COURSE.
OOOOHH

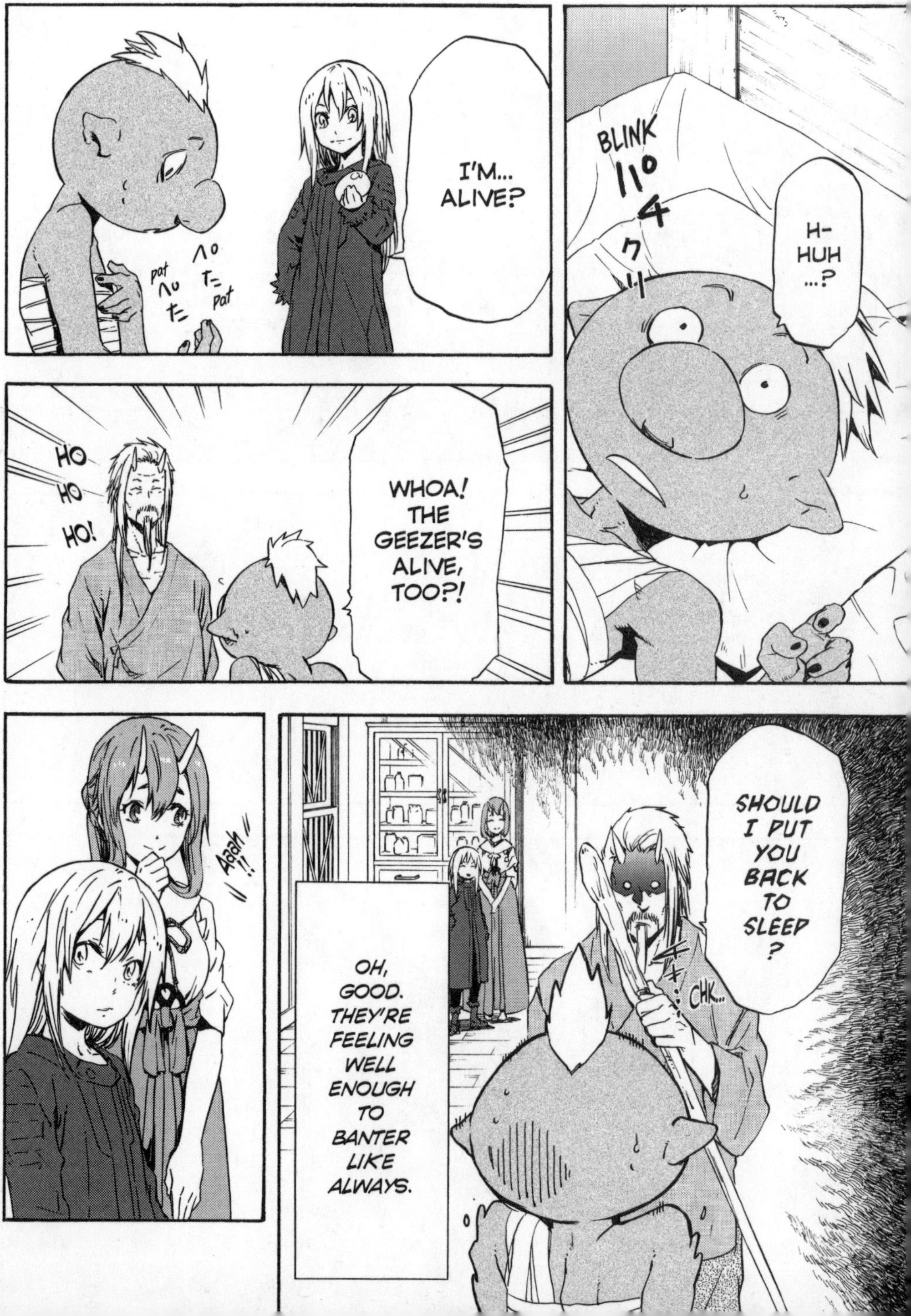
BLINK
H-HUH...?
pat pat
I'M... ALIVE?
HO HO HO!
WHOA! THE GEEZER'S ALIVE, TOO?!
SHOULD I PUT YOU BACK TO SLEEP?
CHK...
OH, GOOD. THEY'RE FEELING WELL ENOUGH TO BANTER LIKE ALWAYS.
Aaah!!

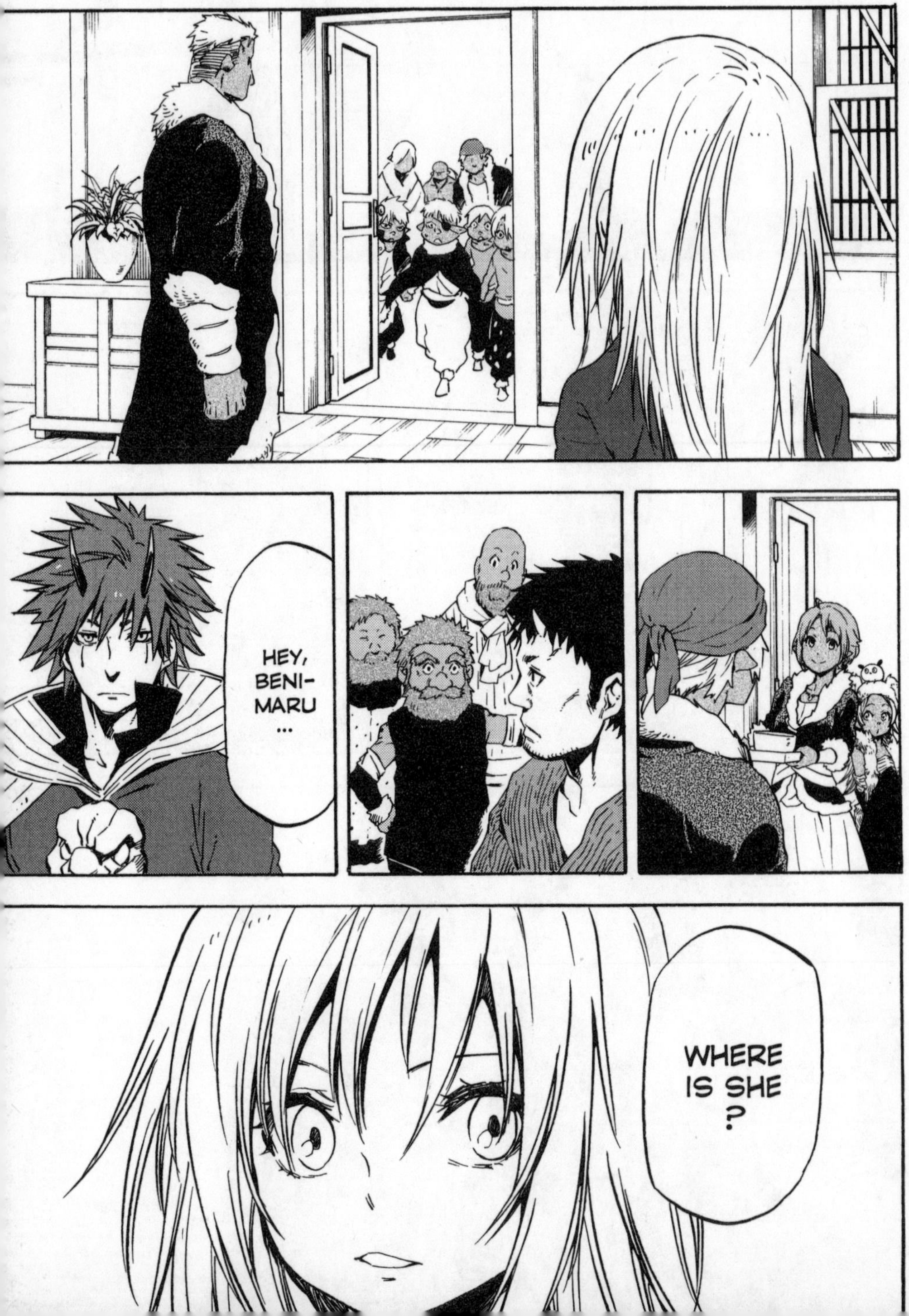
......
HEY, BENI-MARU ...
WHERE IS SHE ?

BENIMARU DIDN'T GIVE ME AN ANSWER.
HE JUST SAID, "FOLLOW ME," AND STARTED WALKING.
WE WENT TO THE SQUARE WHERE THE MONSTERS' BODIES WERE LAID OUT TO REST.
...HERE WE ARE.

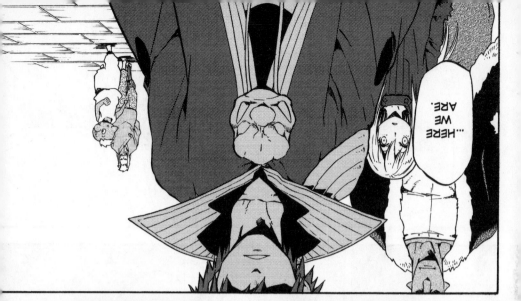

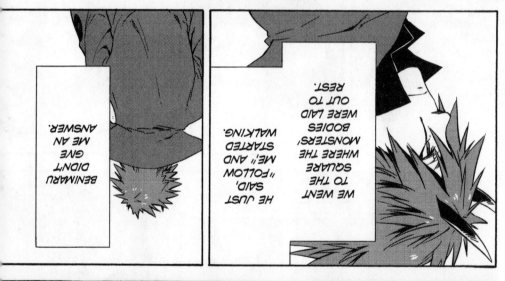

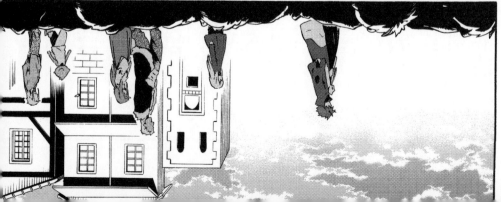

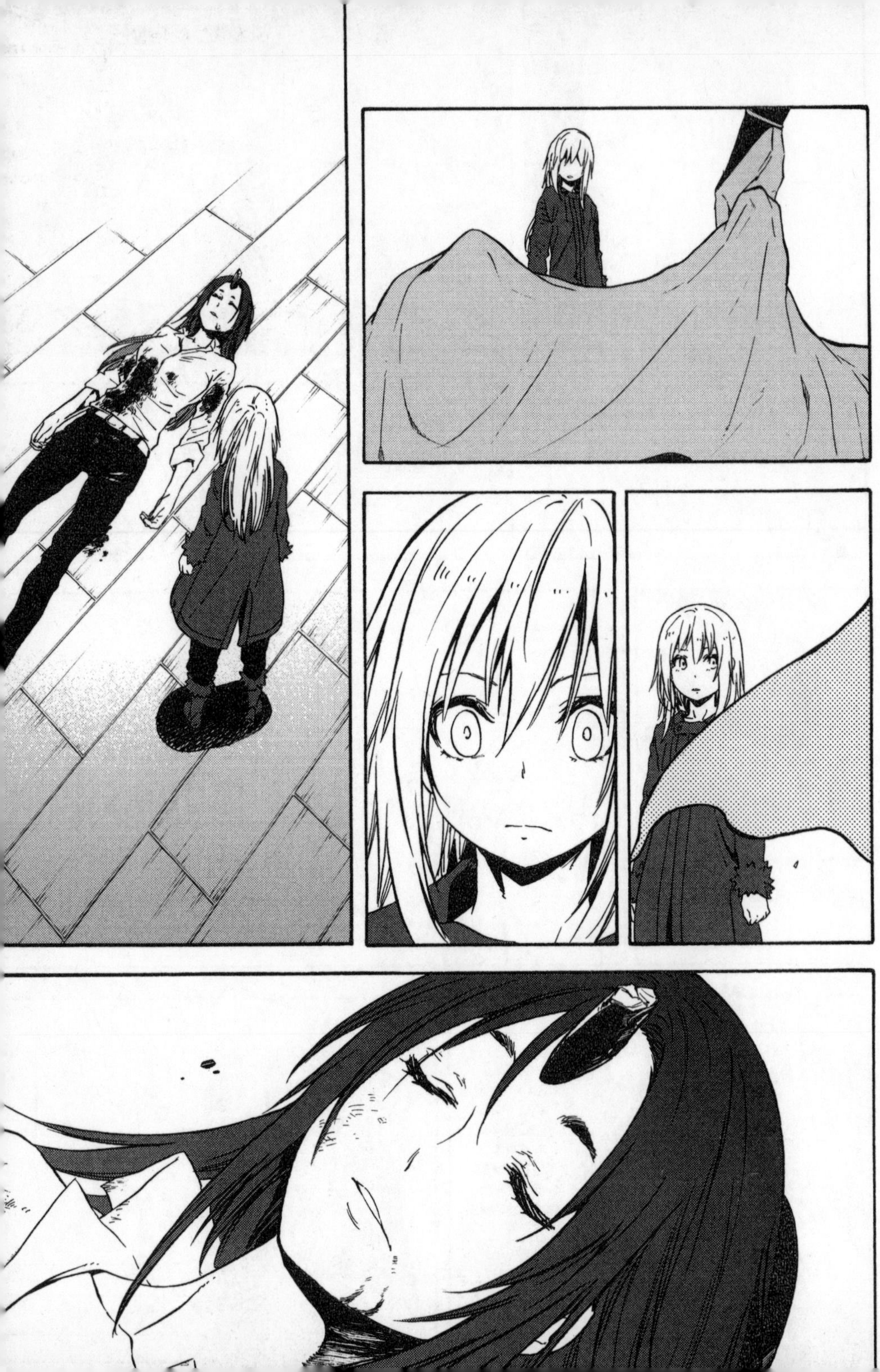

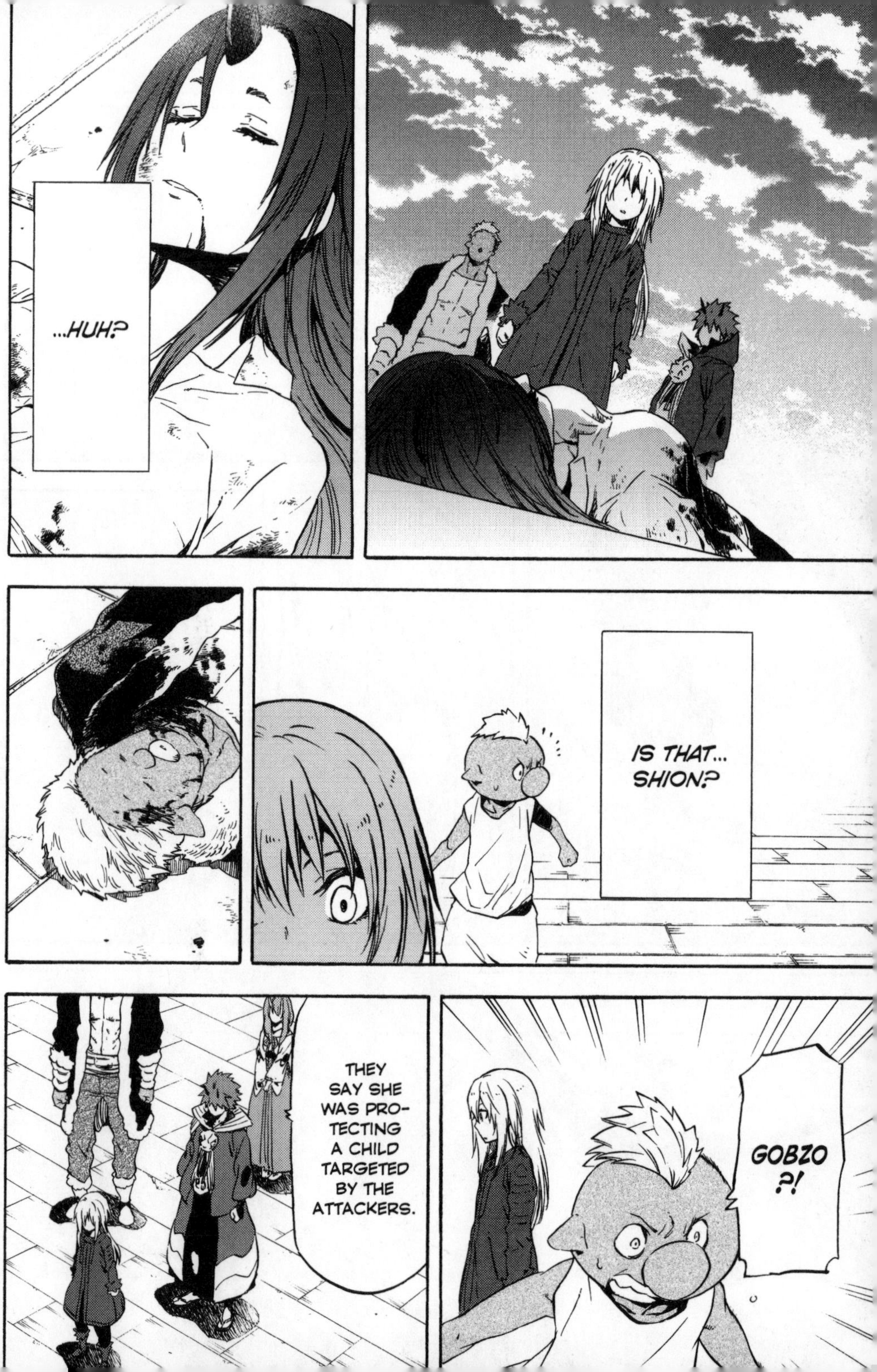
...HUH?
IS THAT... SHION?
GOBZO ?!
THEY SAY SHE WAS PRO-TECTING A CHILD TARGETED BY THE ATTACKERS.

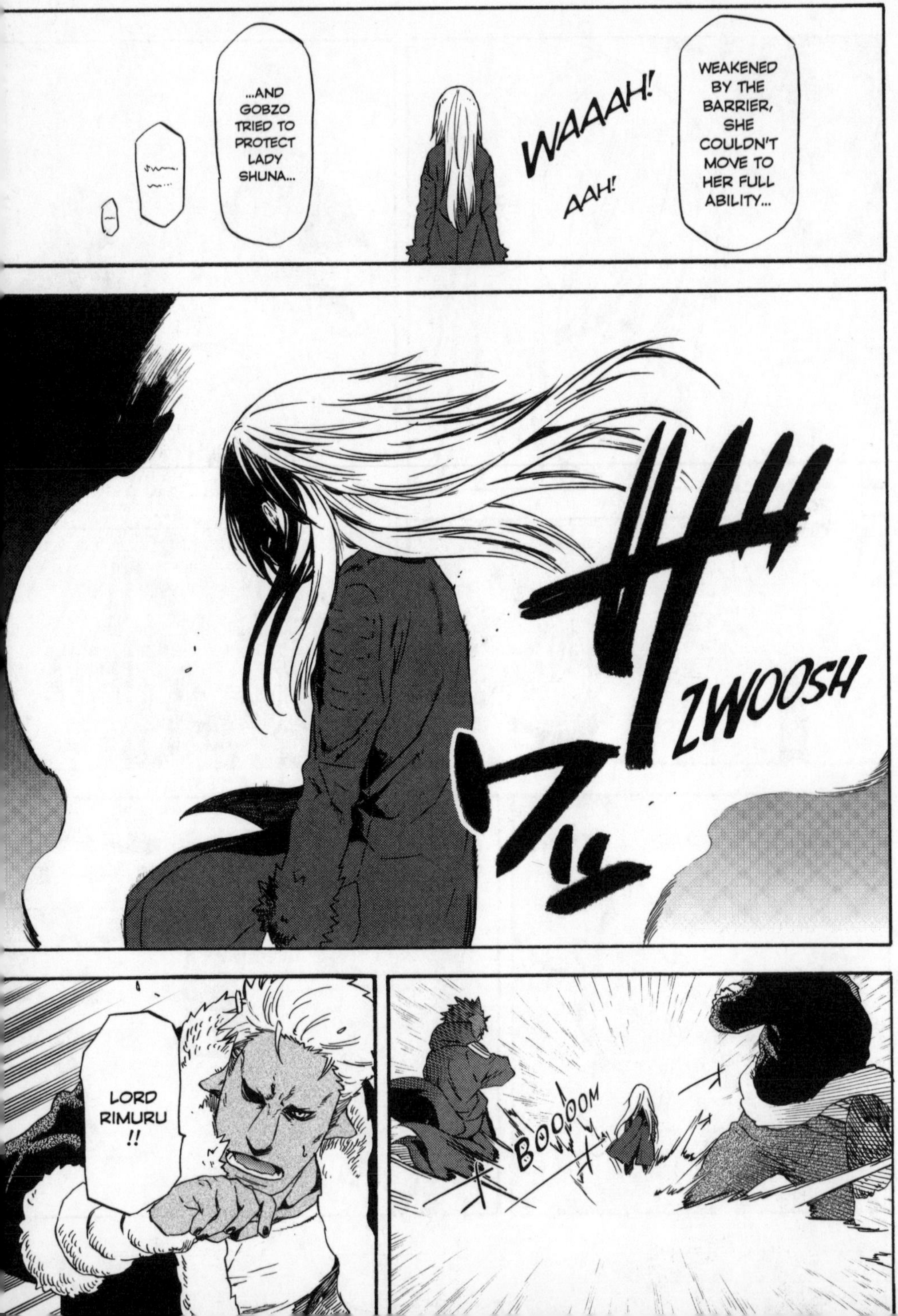
WEAKENED BY THE BARRIER, SHE COULDN'T MOVE TO HER FULL ABILITY...
WAAAH!
AAH!
...AND GOBZO TRIED TO PROTECT LADY SHUNA...
ZWOOSH
BOOOOM
LORD RIMURU !!

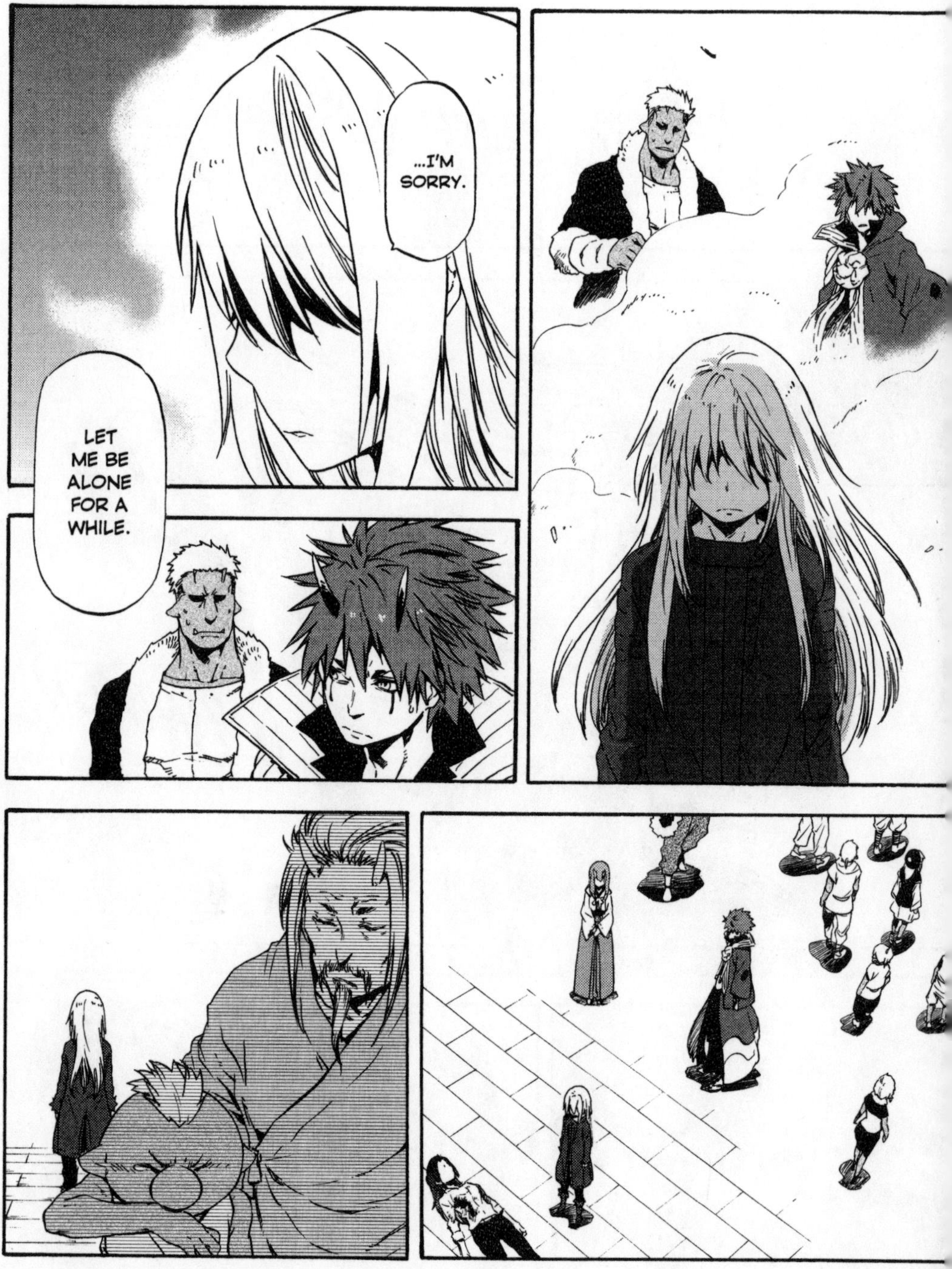
...I'M SORRY.
LET ME BE ALONE FOR A WHILE.

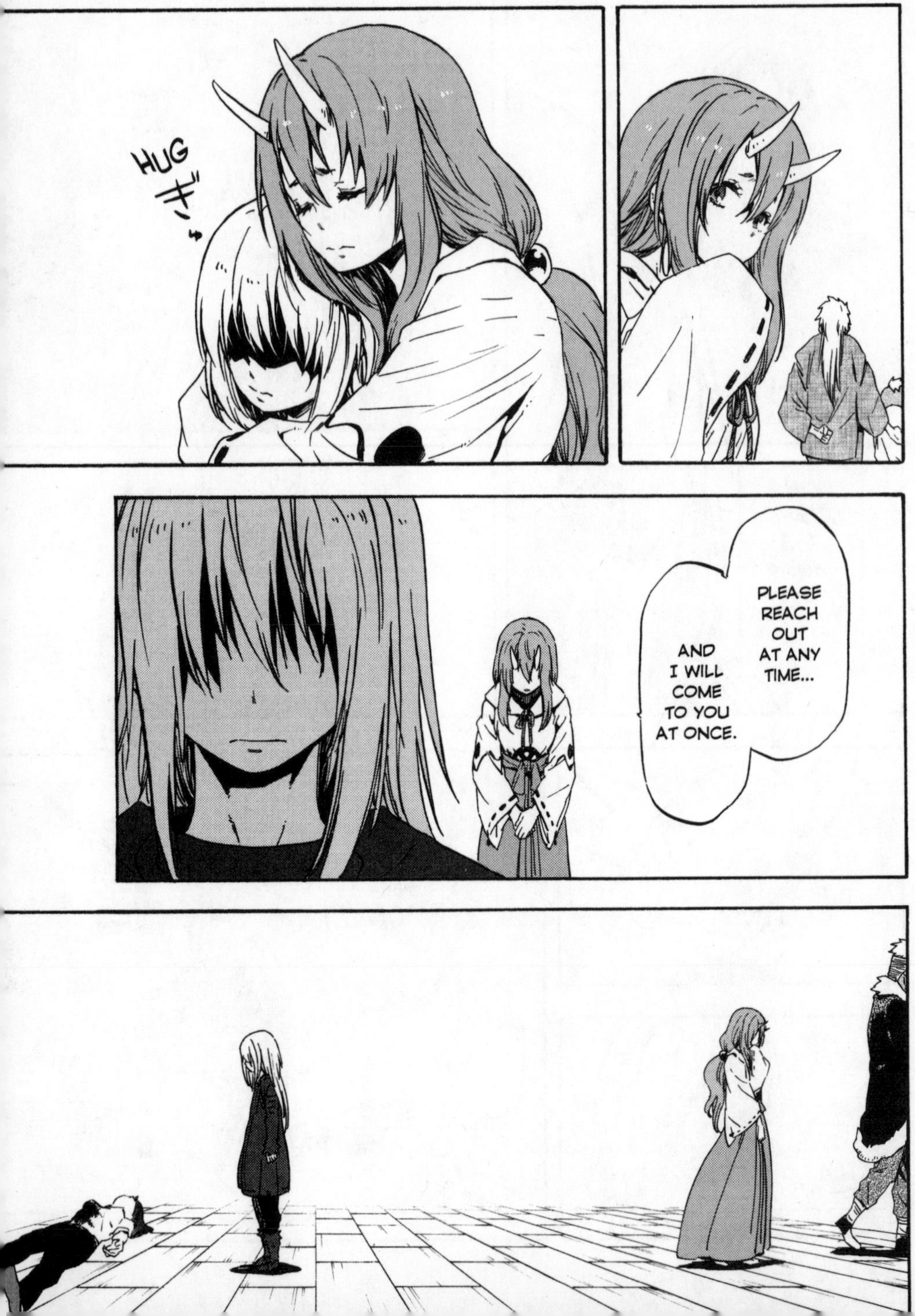
HUG ぎゅ
PLEASE REACH OUT AT ANY TIME...
AND I WILL COME TO YOU AT ONCE.

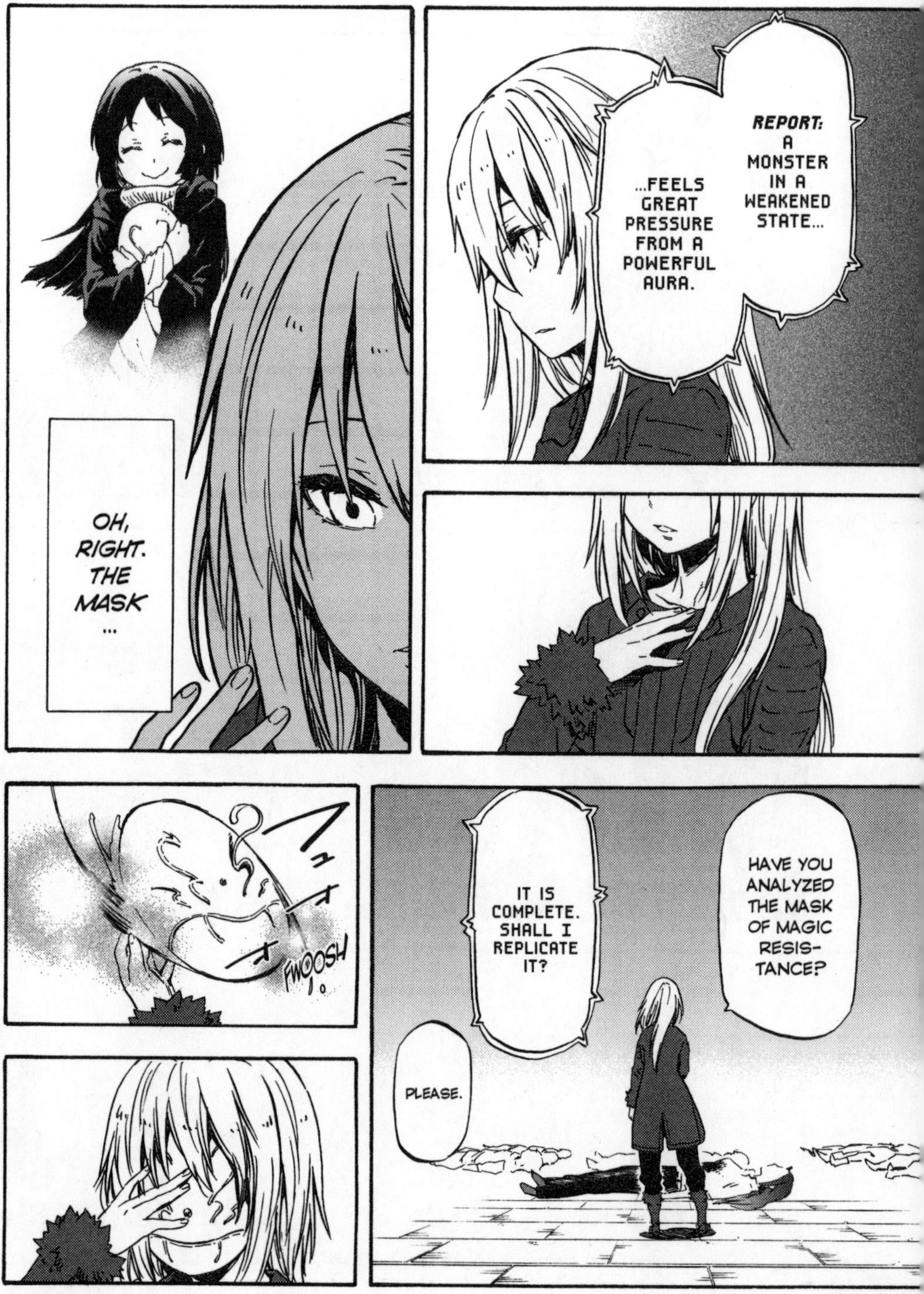
REPORT: A MONSTER IN A WEAKENED STATE...
...FEELS GREAT PRESSURE FROM A POWERFUL AURA.
OH, RIGHT. THE MASK ...
HAVE YOU ANALYZED THE MASK OF MAGIC RESIS-TANCE?
IT IS COMPLETE. SHALL I REPLICATE IT?
PLEASE.
FWOOSH

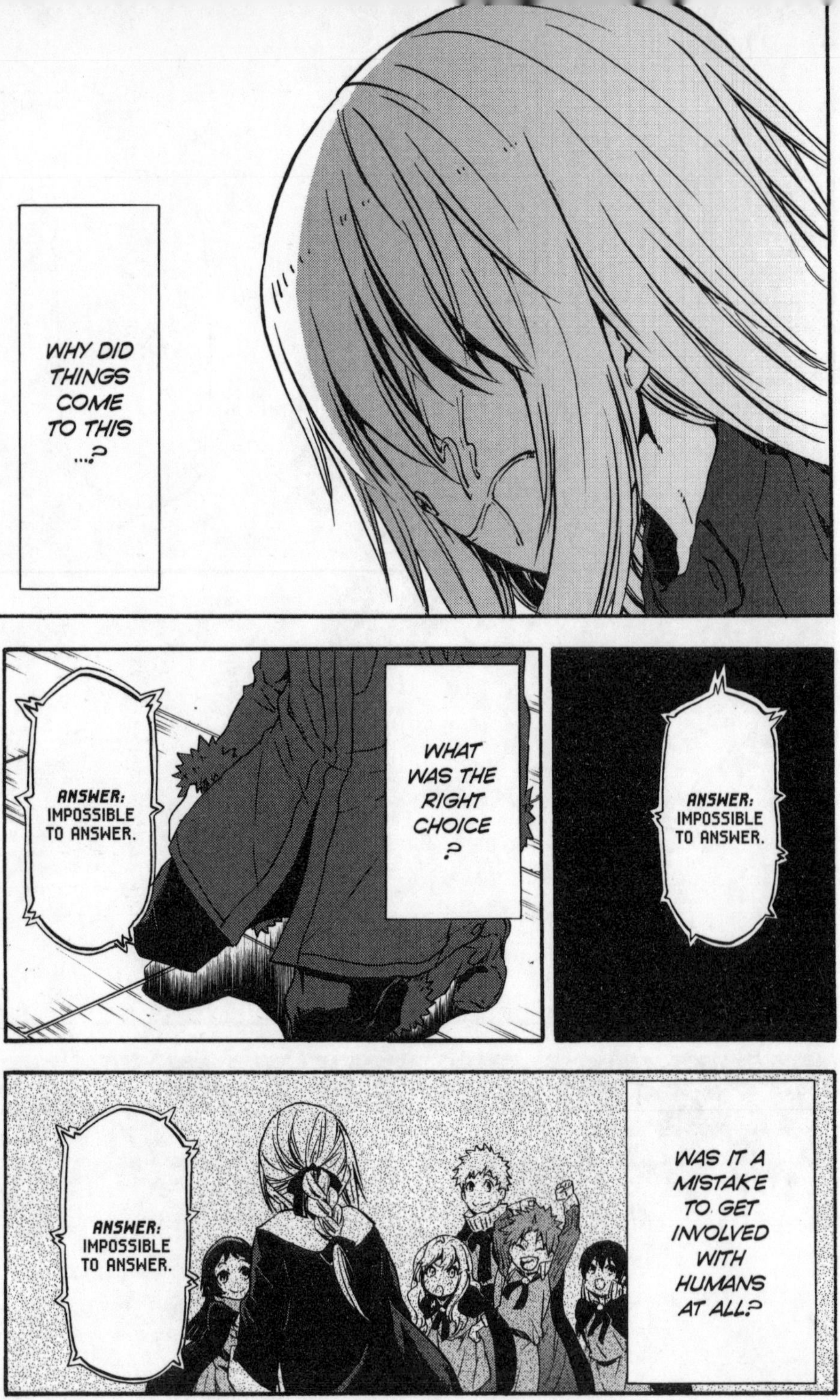
WHY DID THINGS COME TO THIS ...?
ANSWER: IMPOSSIBLE TO ANSWER.
WHAT WAS THE RIGHT CHOICE ?
ANSWER: IMPOSSIBLE TO ANSWER.
WAS IT A MISTAKE TO GET INVOLVED WITH HUMANS AT ALL?
ANSWER: IMPOSSIBLE TO ANSWER.

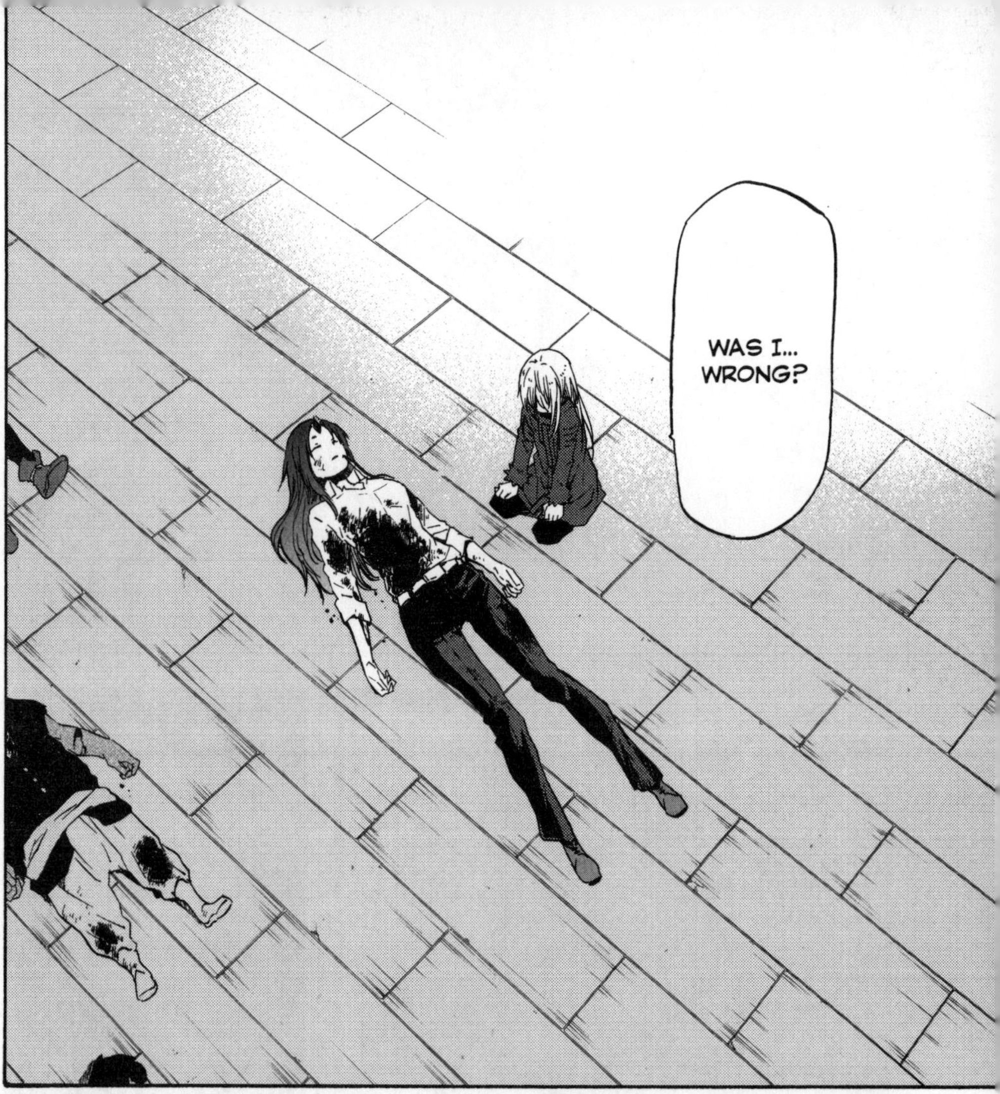
WAS I... WRONG?
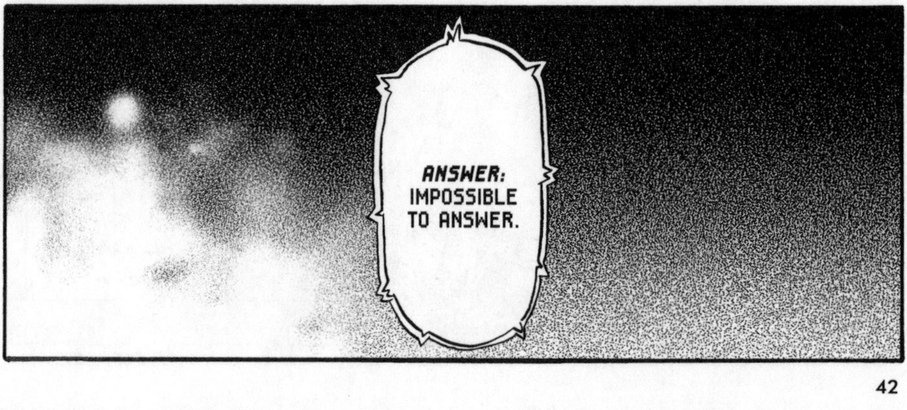
ANSWER: IMPOSSIBLE TO ANSWER.

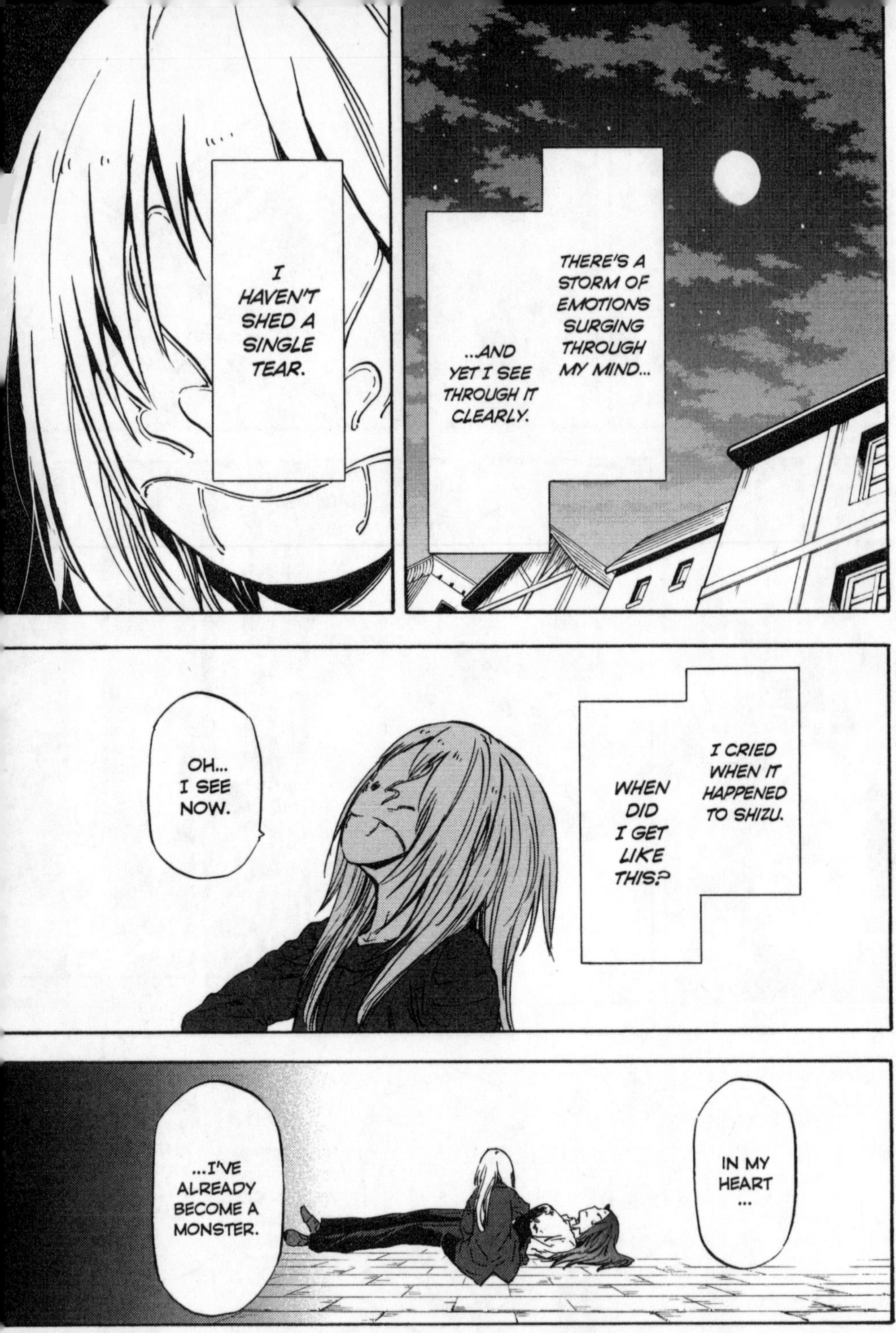
THERE'S A STORM OF EMOTIONS SURGING THROUGH MY MIND...
...AND YET I SEE THROUGH IT CLEARLY.
I HAVEN'T SHED A SINGLE TEAR.
I CRIED WHEN IT HAPPENED TO SHIZU.
WHEN DID I GET LIKE THIS?
OH... I SEE NOW.
IN MY HEART ...
...I'VE ALREADY BECOME A MONSTER.

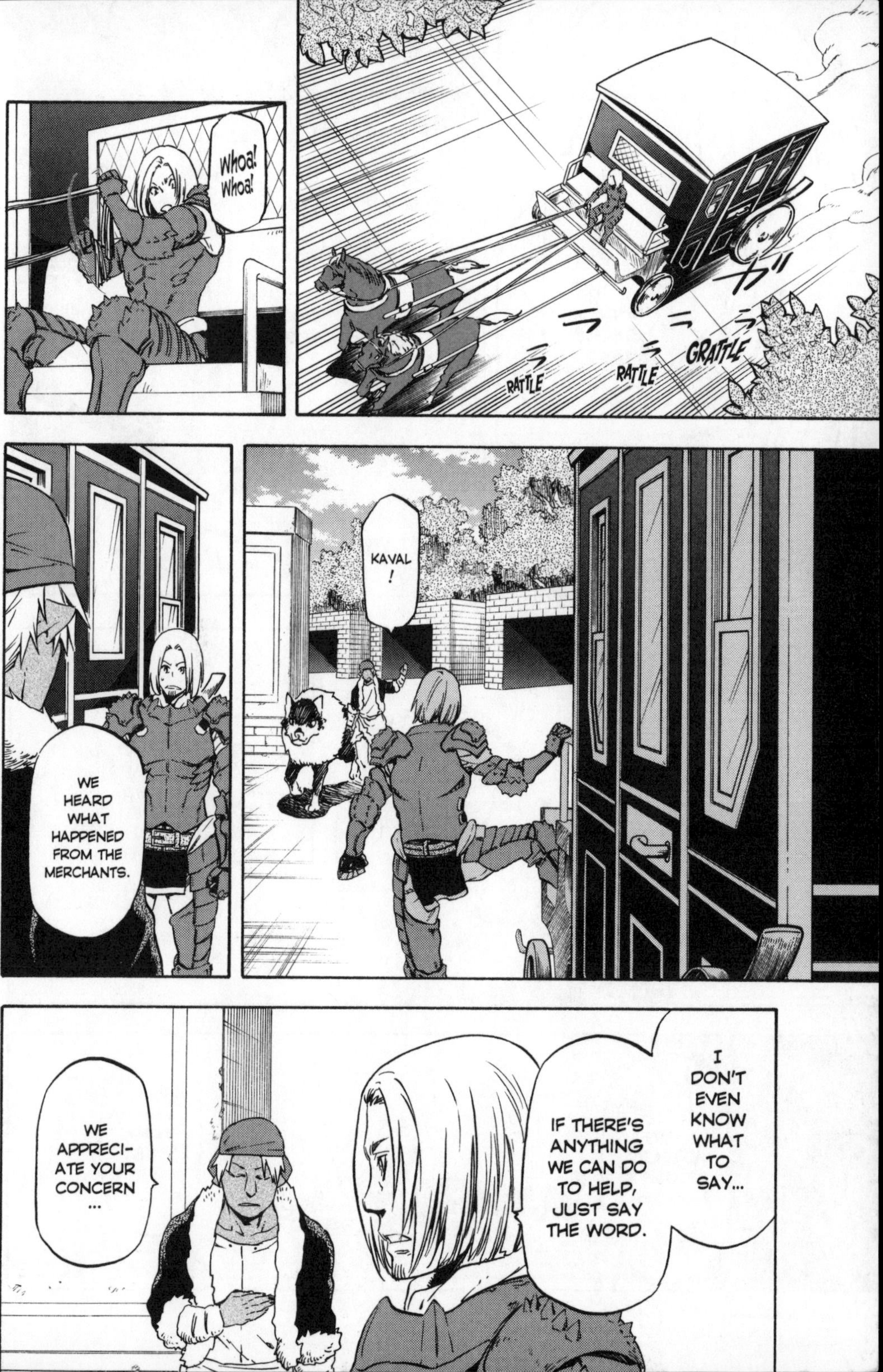
RATTLE
RATTLE
GRATTLE
Whoa! Whoa!
KAVAL!
WE HEARD WHAT HAPPENED FROM THE MERCHANTS.
I DON'T EVEN KNOW WHAT TO SAY...
IF THERE'S ANYTHING WE CAN DO TO HELP, JUST SAY THE WORD.
WE APPRECIATE YOUR CONCERN...

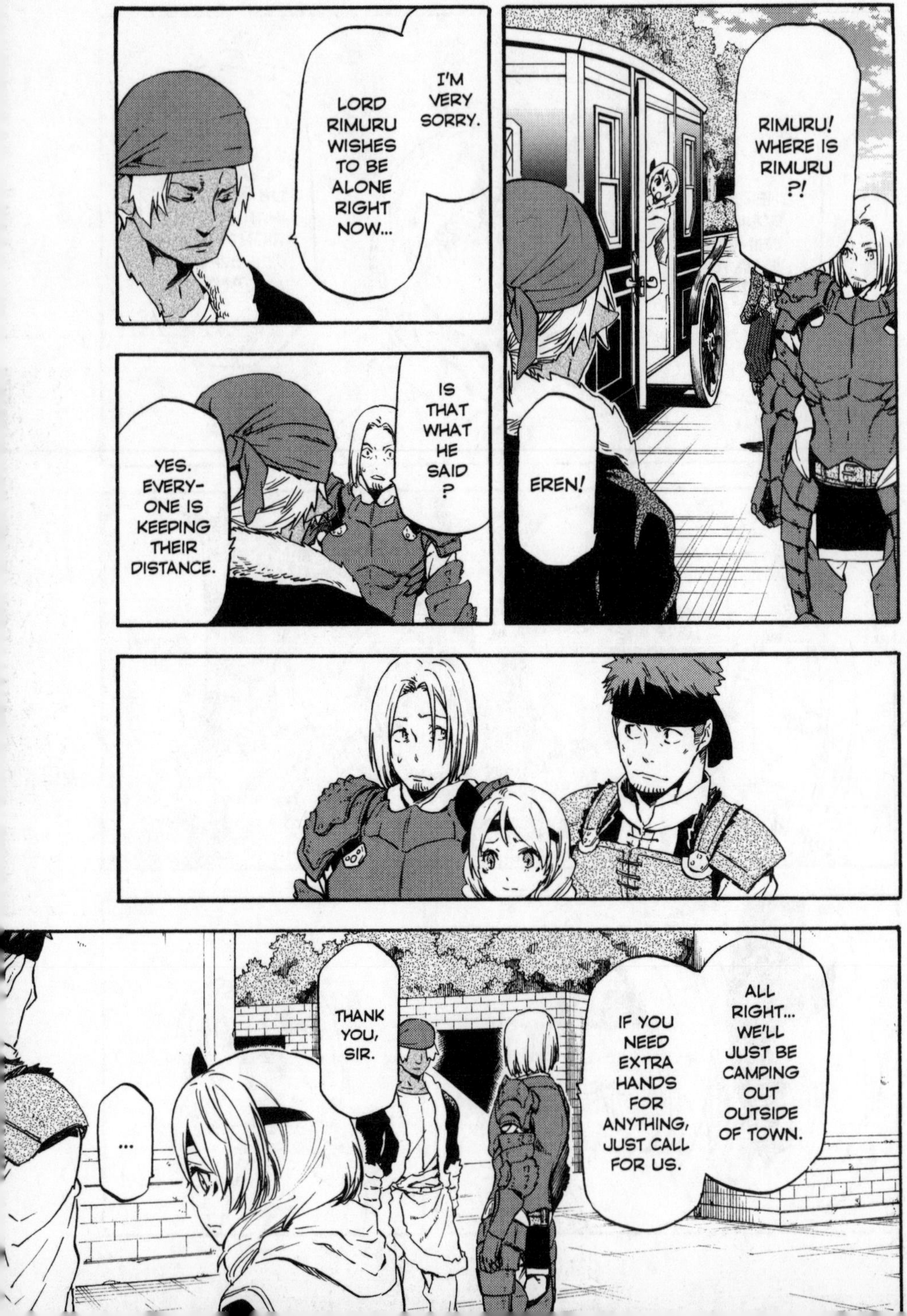
RIMURU! WHERE IS RIMURU ?!
EREN!
I'M VERY SORRY.
LORD RIMURU WISHES TO BE ALONE RIGHT NOW...
IS THAT WHAT HE SAID ?
YES. EVERY-ONE IS KEEPING THEIR DISTANCE.
ALL RIGHT... WE'LL JUST BE CAMPING OUT OUTSIDE OF TOWN.
IF YOU NEED EXTRA HANDS FOR ANYTHING, JUST CALL FOR US.
THANK YOU, SIR.
...

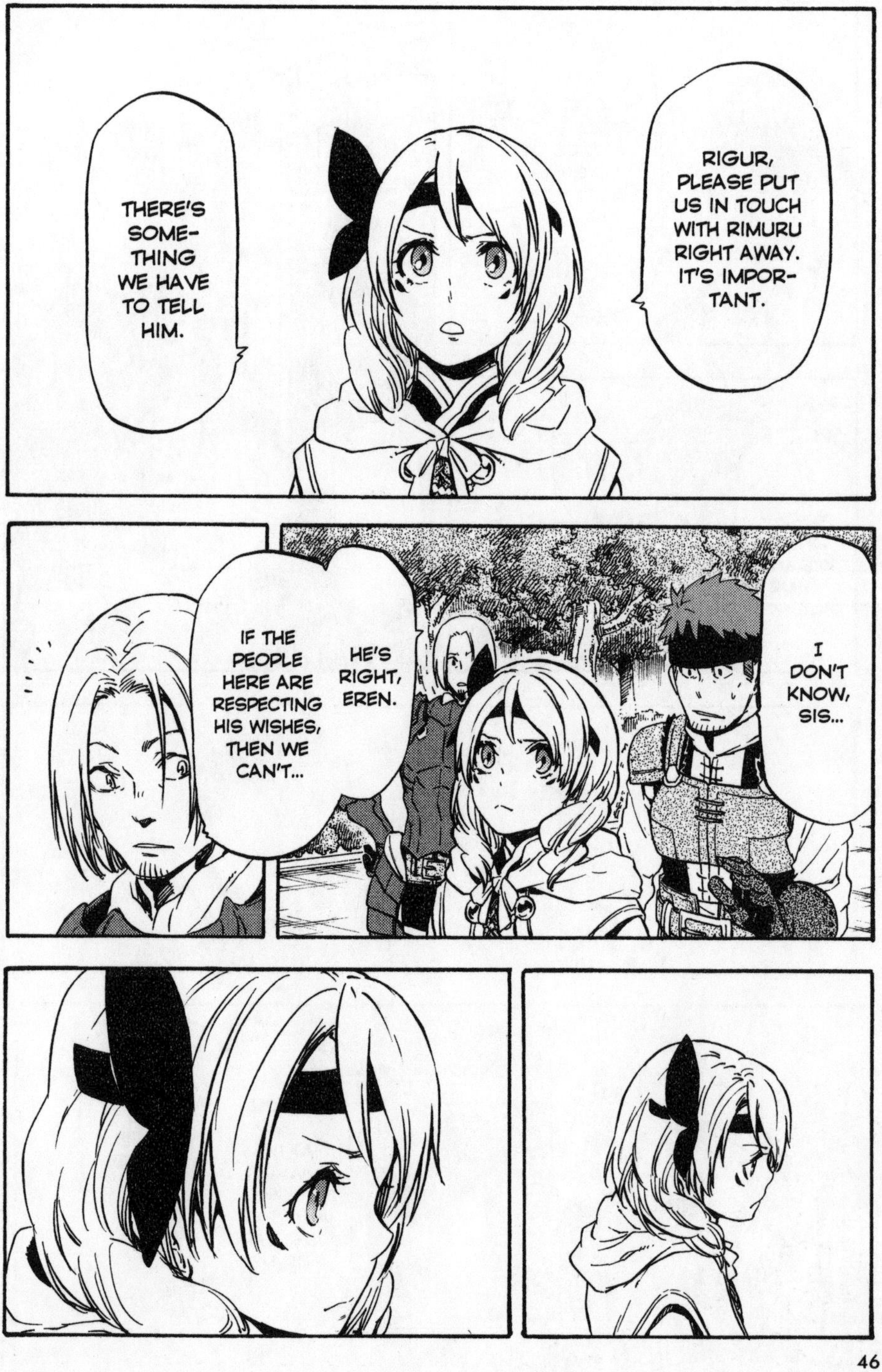
RIGUR, PLEASE PUT US IN TOUCH WITH RIMURU RIGHT AWAY. IT'S IMPORTANT.
THERE'S SOMETHING WE HAVE TO TELL HIM.
I DON'T KNOW, SIS...
HE'S RIGHT, EREN.
IF THE PEOPLE HERE ARE RESPECTING HIS WISHES, THEN WE CAN'T...

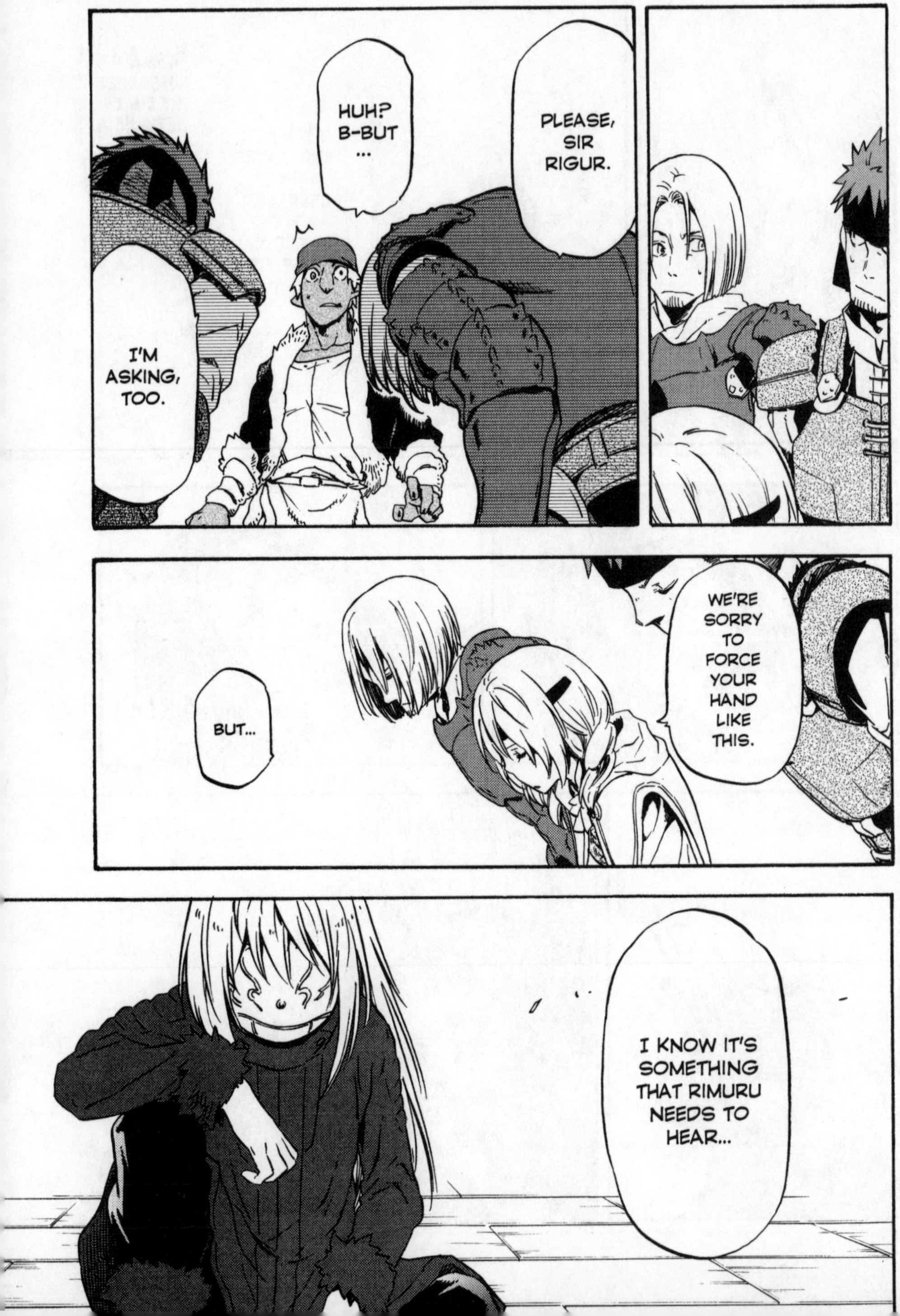
PLEASE, SIR RIGUR.
HUH? B-BUT ...
I'M ASKING, TOO.
WE'RE SORRY TO FORCE YOUR HAND LIKE THIS.
BUT...
I KNOW IT'S SOMETHING THAT RIMURU NEEDS TO HEAR...

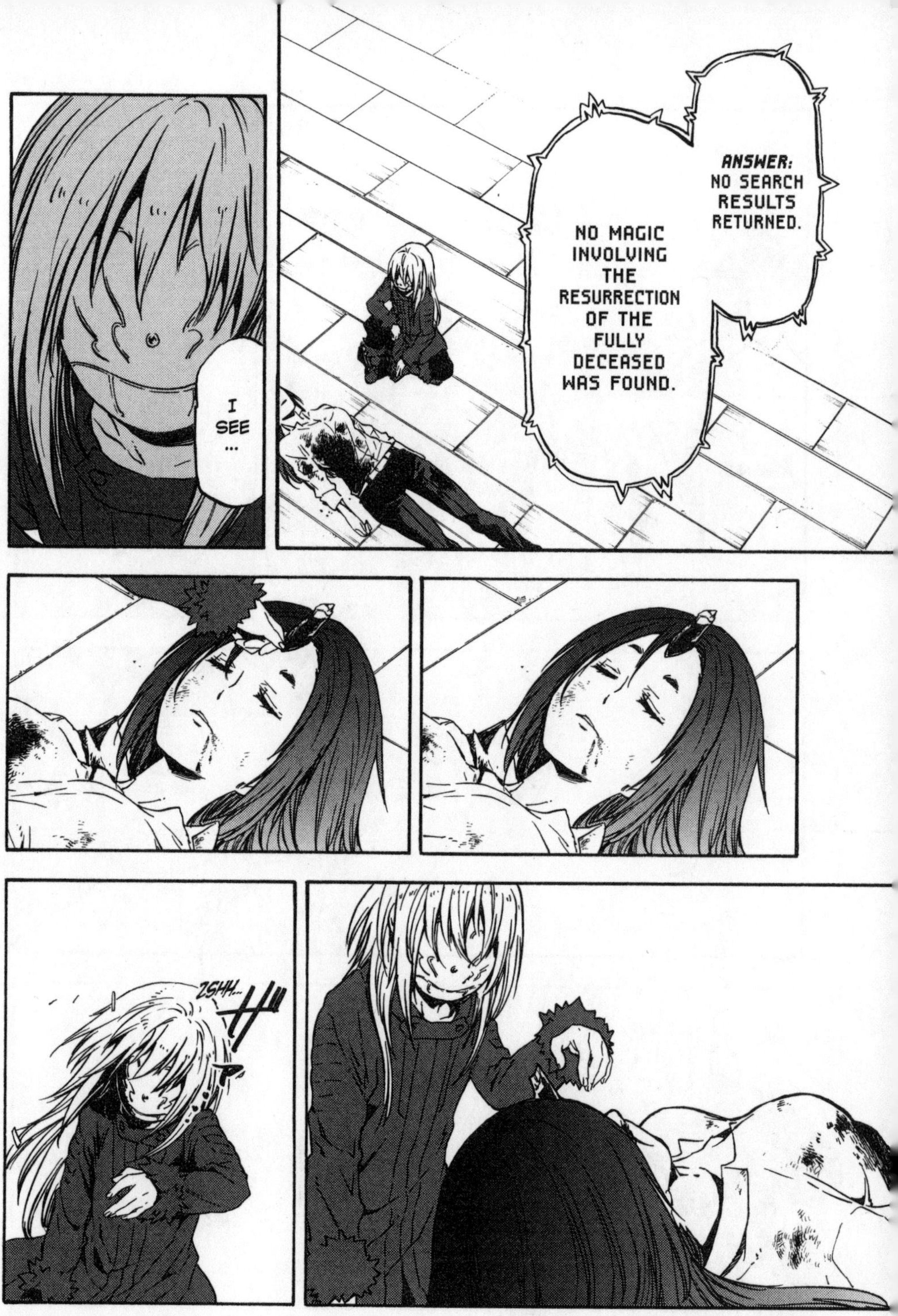
ANSWER: NO SEARCH RESULTS RETURNED.
NO MAGIC INVOLVING THE RESURRECTION OF THE FULLY DECEASED WAS FOUND.
I SEE ...
ZSHH...

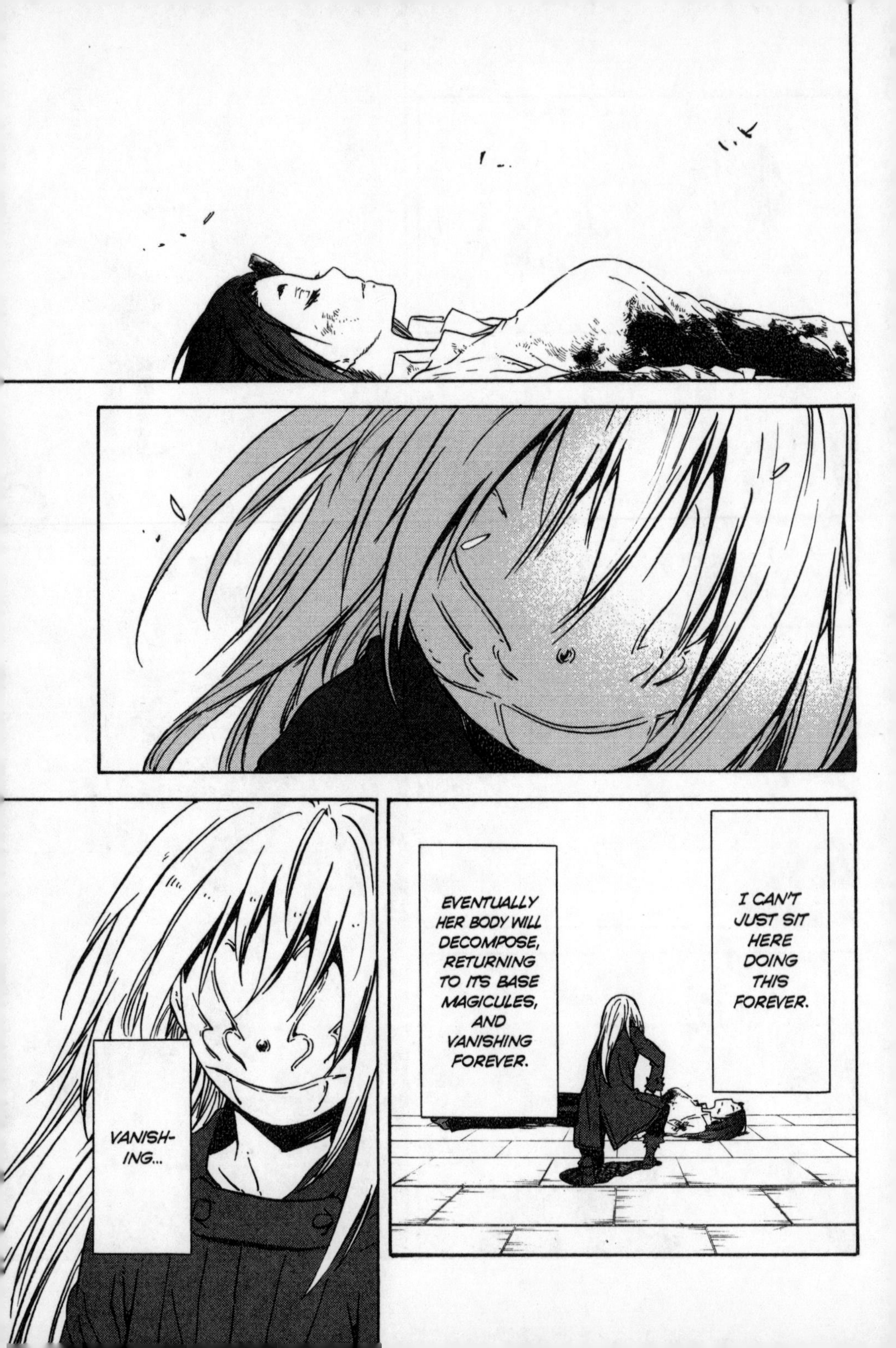
I CAN'T JUST SIT HERE DOING THIS FOREVER.
EVENTUALLY HER BODY WILL DECOMPOSE, RETURNING TO ITS BASE MAGICULES, AND VANISHING FOREVER.
VANISH-ING...

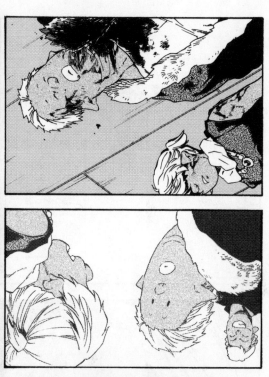

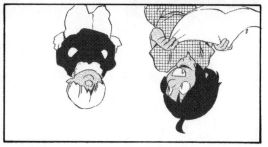

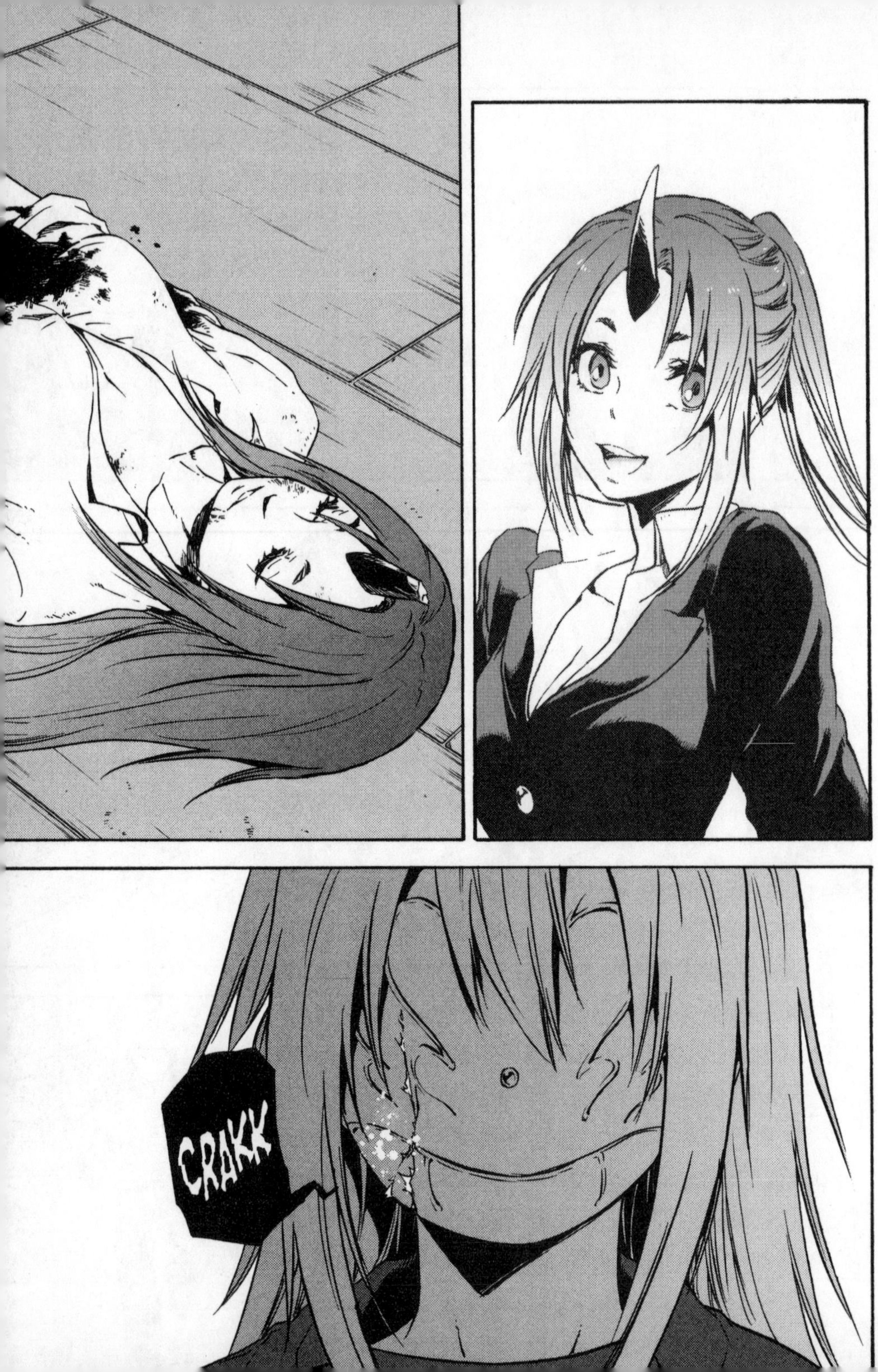
CRAKK

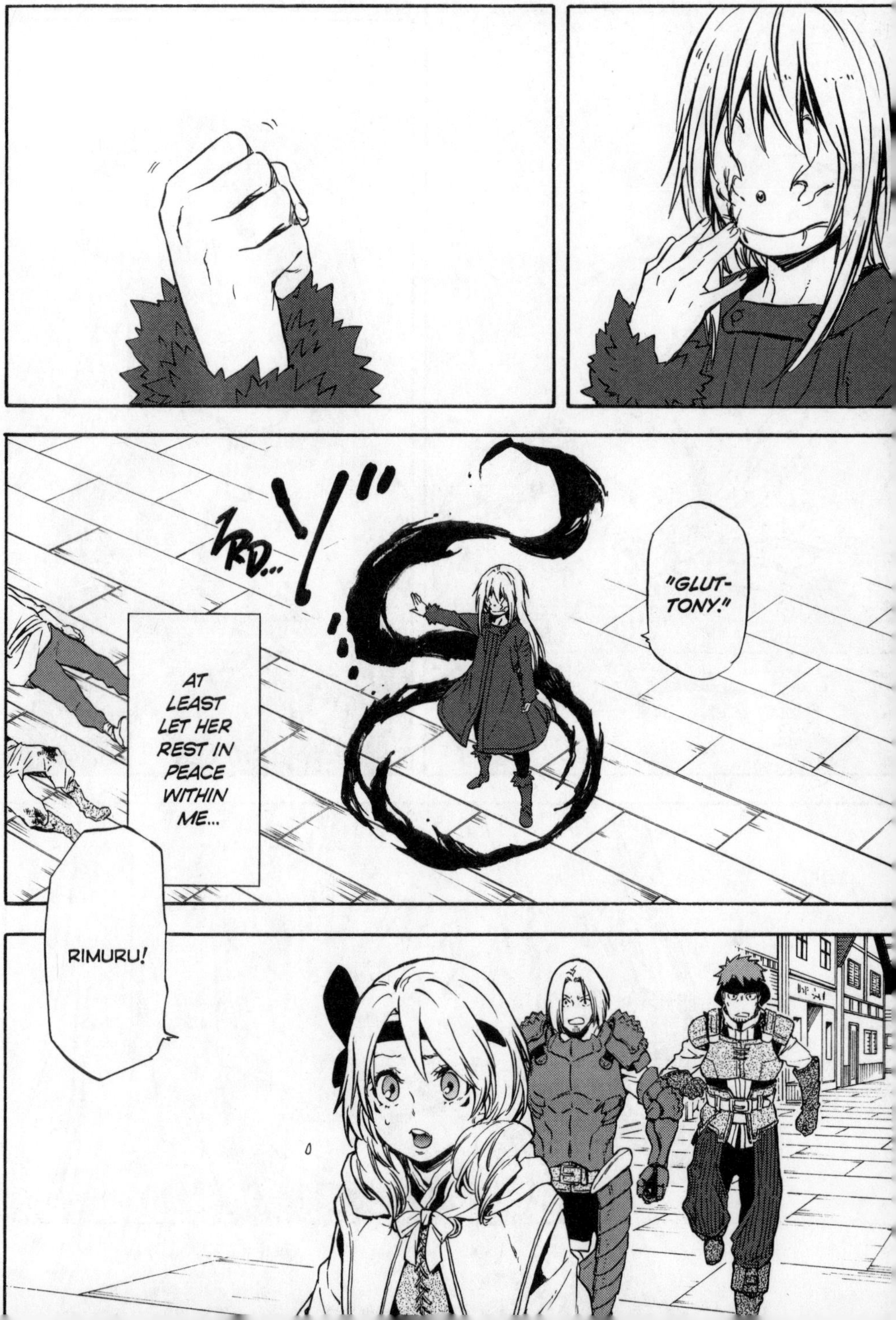
"GLUT-TONY."
AT LEAST LET HER REST IN PEACE WITHIN ME...
RIMURU!

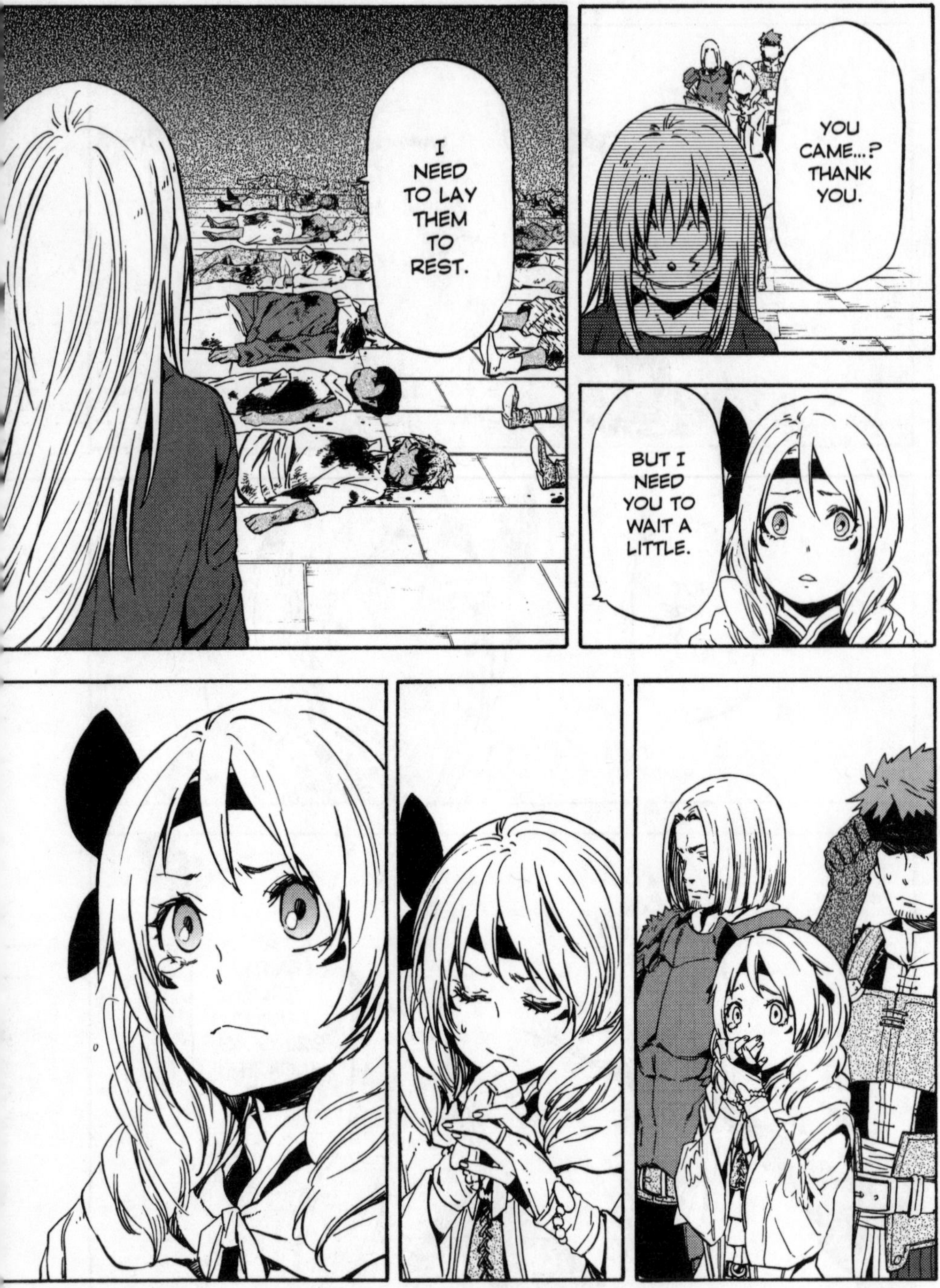
YOU CAME...? THANK YOU.
BUT I NEED YOU TO WAIT A LITTLE.
I NEED TO LAY THEM TO REST.

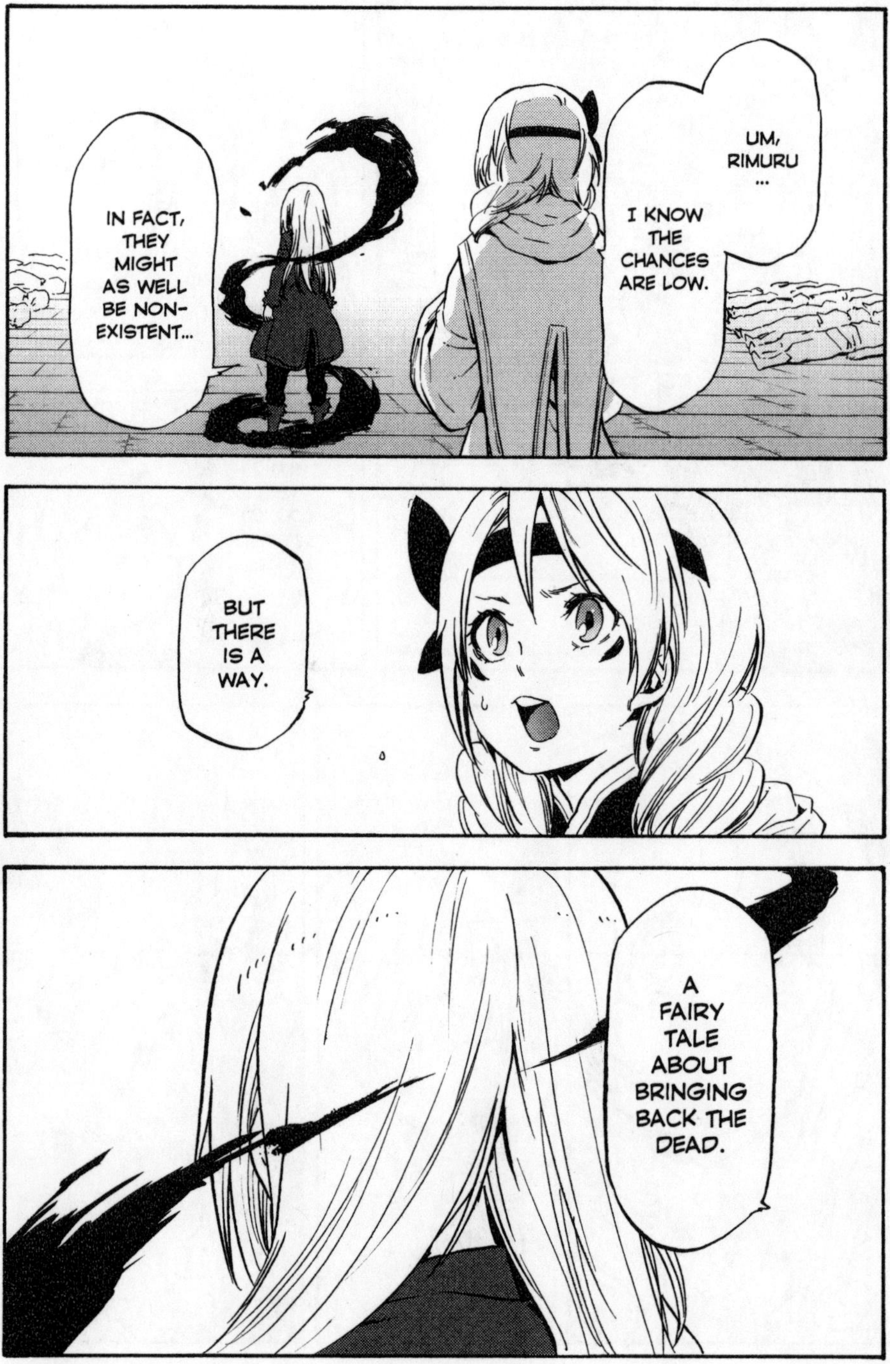
UM, RIMURU ...
I KNOW THE CHANCES ARE LOW.
IN FACT, THEY MIGHT AS WELL BE NON-EXISTENT...
BUT THERE IS A WAY.
A FAIRY TALE ABOUT BRINGING BACK THE DEAD.

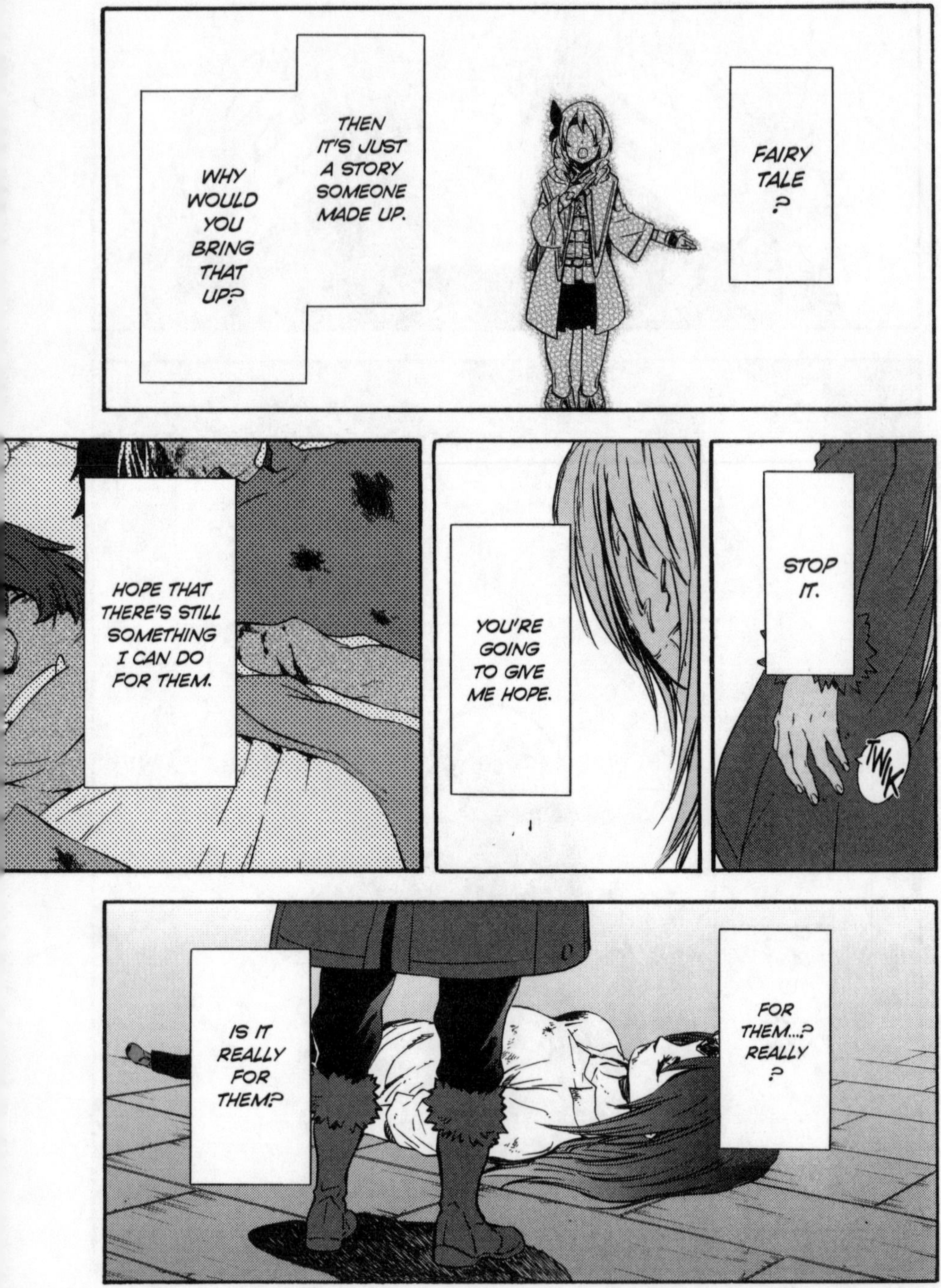
FAIRY TALE ?
THEN IT'S JUST A STORY SOMEONE MADE UP.
WHY WOULD YOU BRING THAT UP?
STOP IT.
TWIK
YOU'RE GOING TO GIVE ME HOPE.
HOPE THAT THERE'S STILL SOMETHING I CAN DO FOR THEM.
FOR THEM...? REALLY ?
IS IT REALLY FOR THEM?

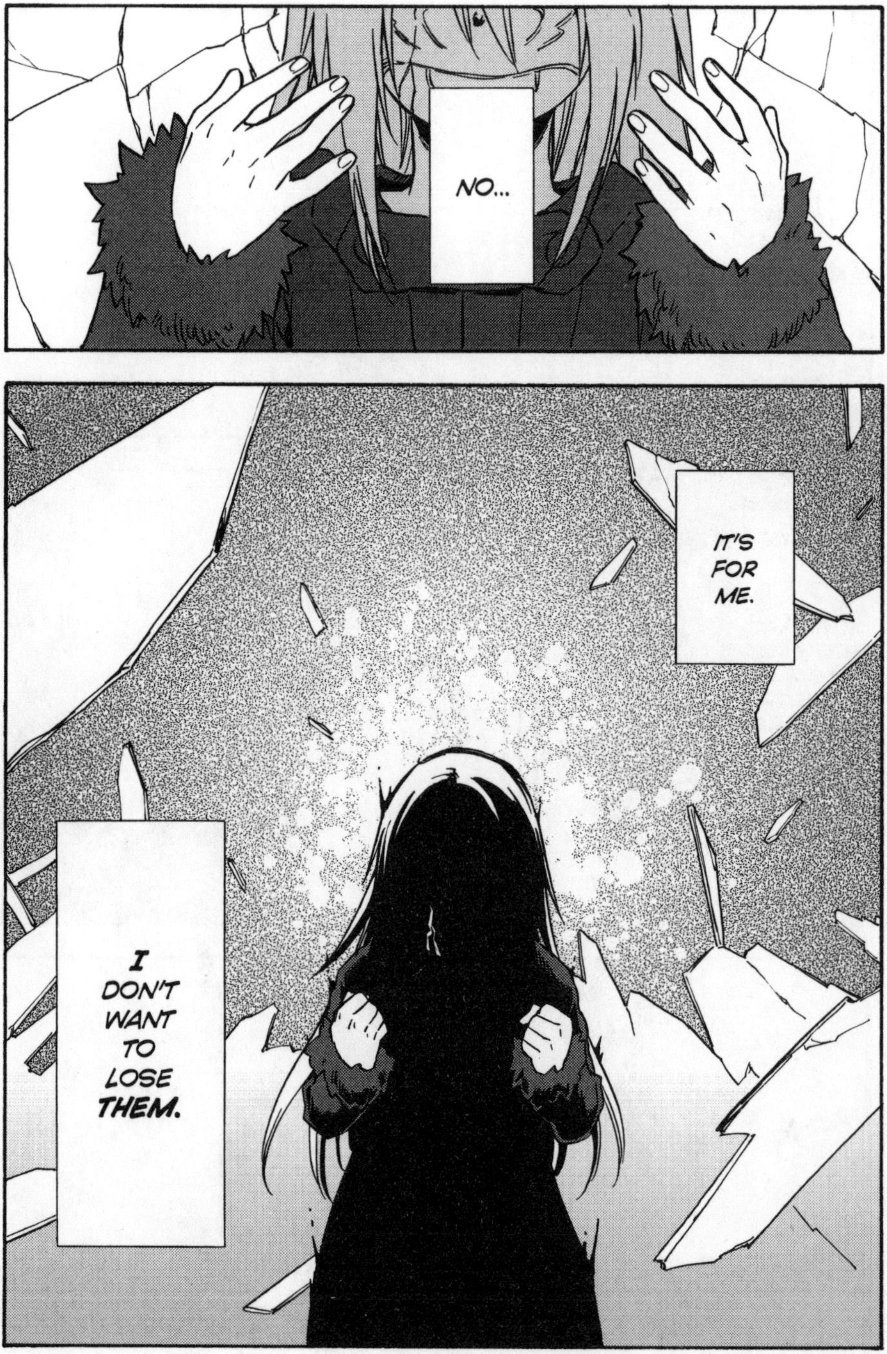
NO...
IT'S FOR ME.
I DON'T WANT TO LOSE THEM.

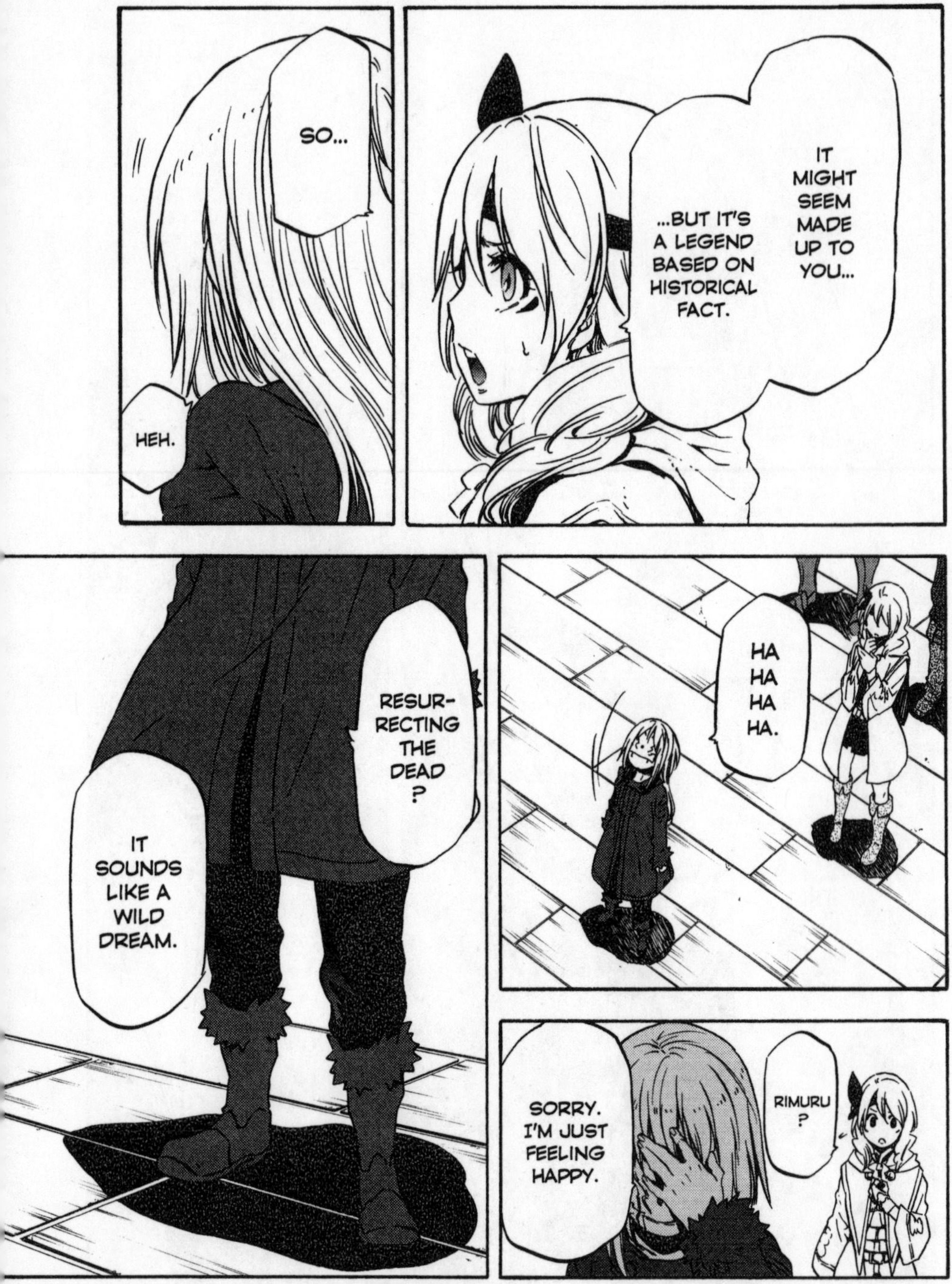
IT MIGHT SEEM MADE UP TO YOU...
...BUT IT'S A LEGEND BASED ON HISTORICAL FACT.
SO...
HEH.
HA HA HA HA.
RESURRECTING THE DEAD?
IT SOUNDS LIKE A WILD DREAM.
RIMURU?
SORRY. I'M JUST FEELING HAPPY.

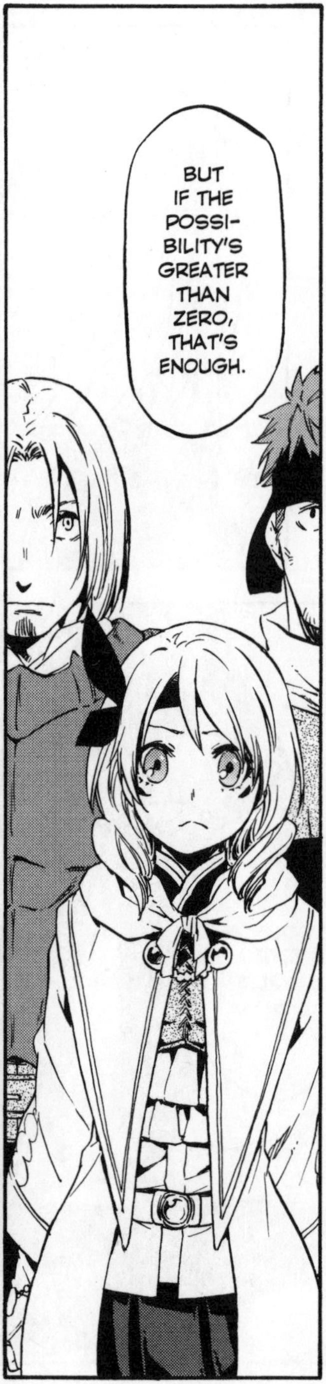
BUT IF THE POSSI- BILITY'S GREATER THAN ZERO, THAT'S ENOUGH.

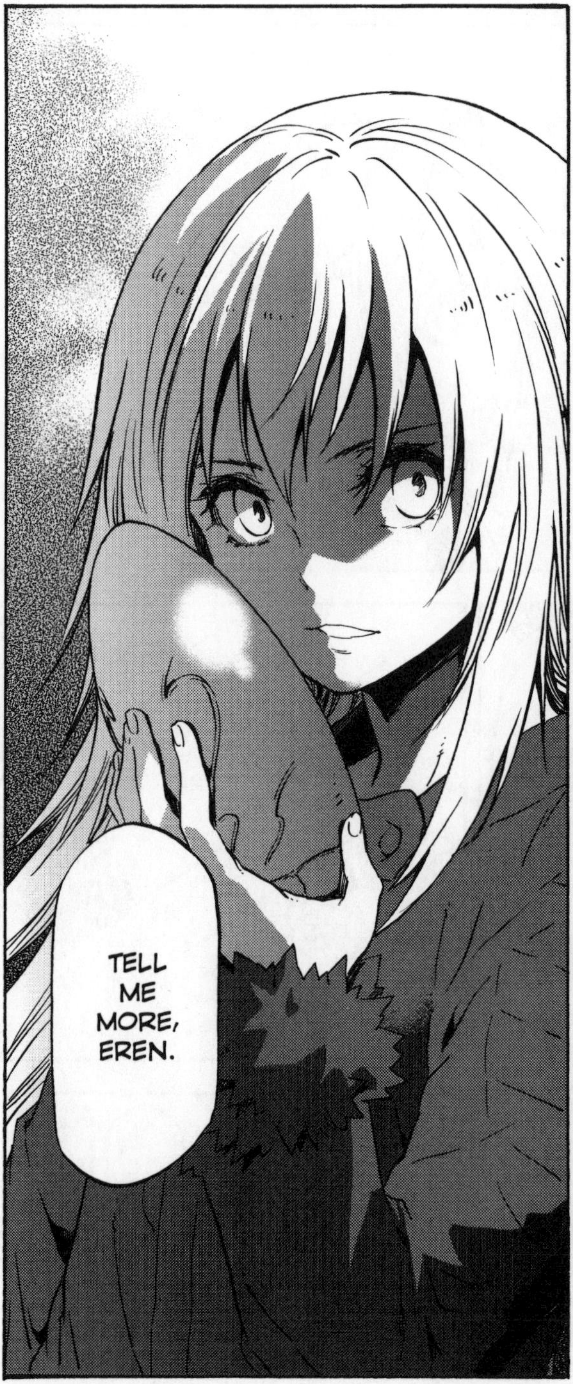
TELL ME MORE, EREN.

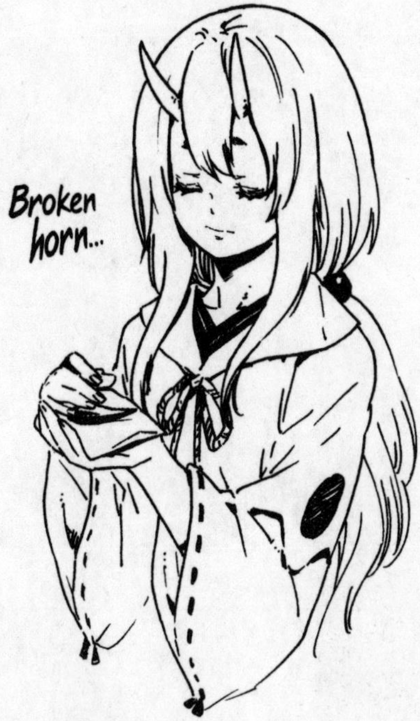
Broken horn...

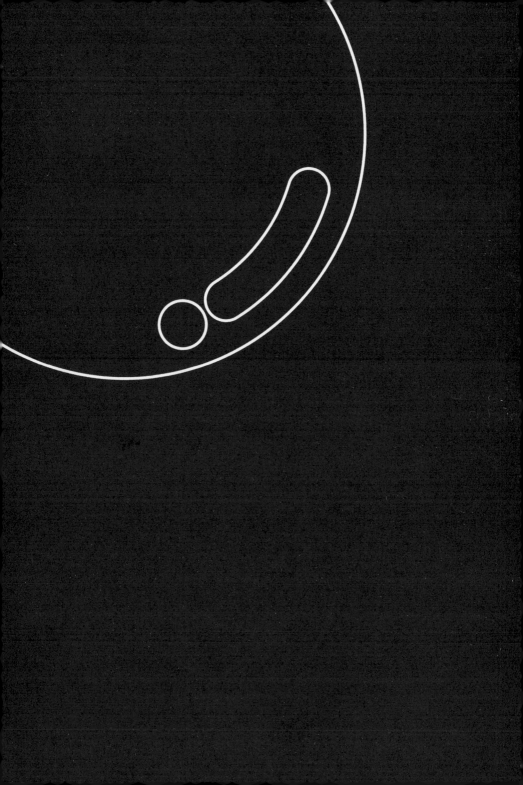

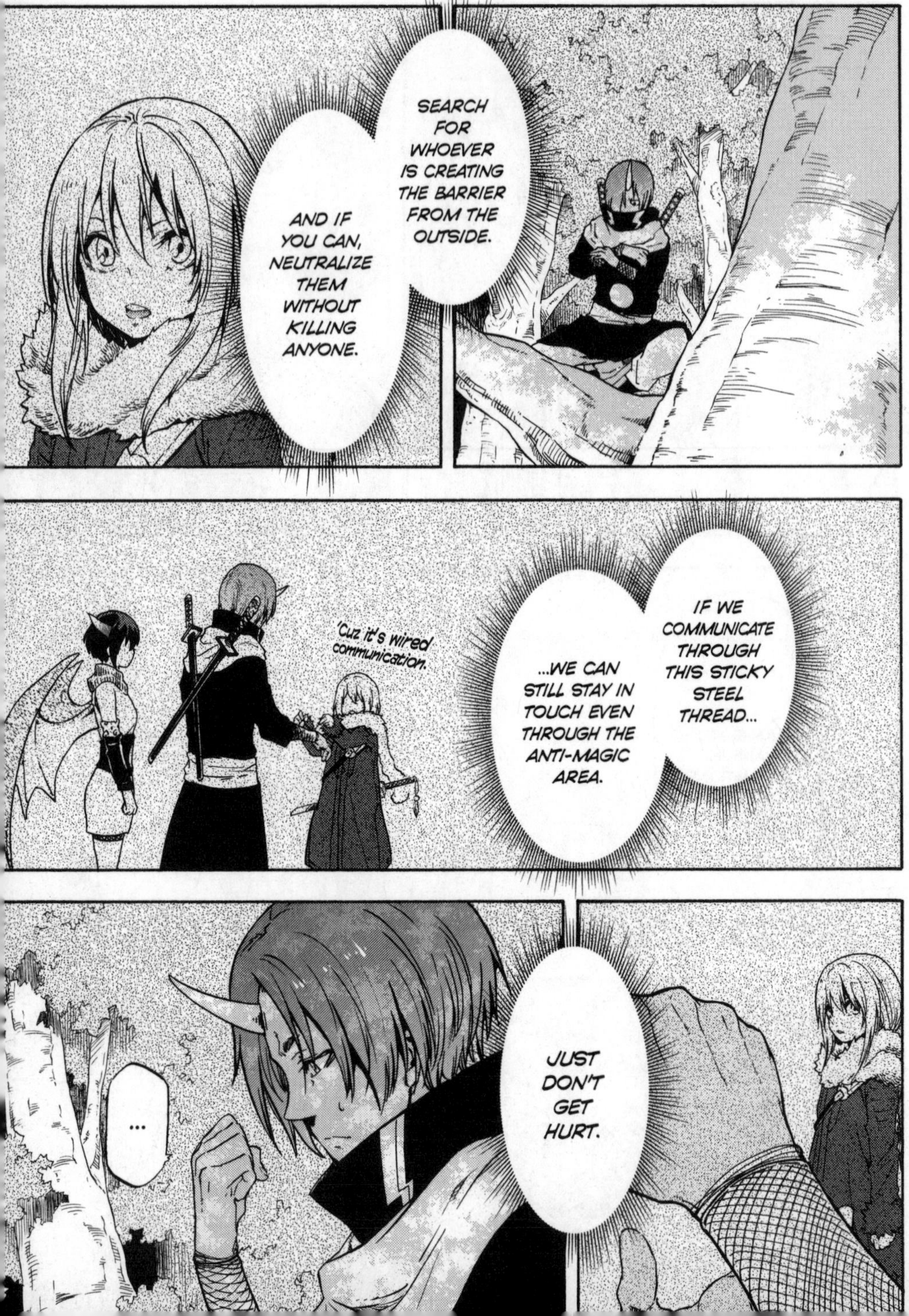
SEARCH FOR WHOEVER IS CREATING THE BARRIER FROM THE OUTSIDE.
AND IF YOU CAN, NEUTRALIZE THEM WITHOUT KILLING ANYONE.
IF WE COMMUNICATE THROUGH THIS STICKY STEEL THREAD...
...WE CAN STILL STAY IN TOUCH EVEN THROUGH THE ANTI-MAGIC AREA.
'Cuz it's wired communication.
JUST DON'T GET HURT.
...

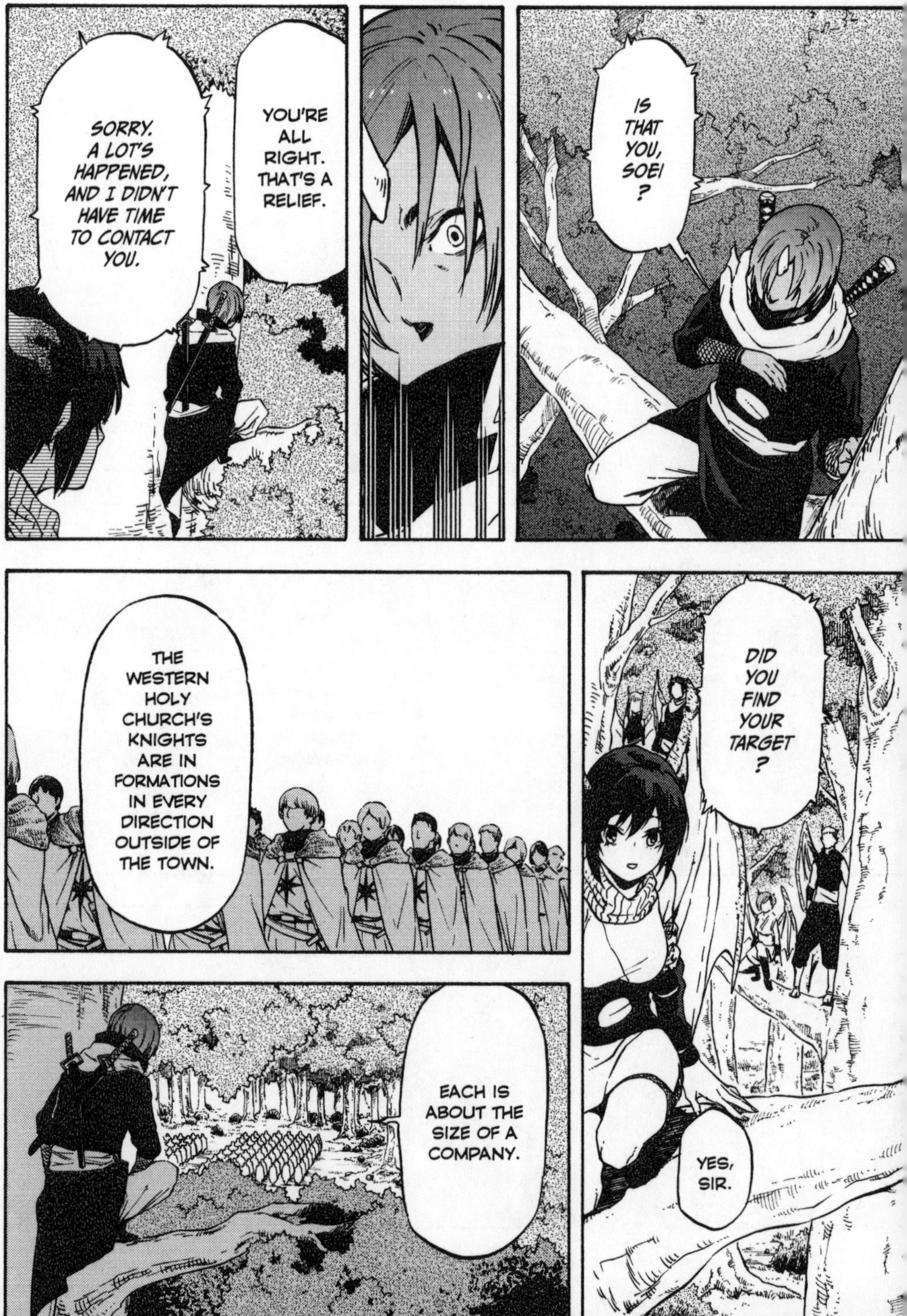
IS THAT YOU, SOEI?
YOU'RE ALL RIGHT. THAT'S A RELIEF.
SORRY. A LOT'S HAPPENED, AND I DIDN'T HAVE TIME TO CONTACT YOU.
DID YOU FIND YOUR TARGET?
YES, SIR.
THE WESTERN HOLY CHURCH'S KNIGHTS ARE IN FORMATIONS IN EVERY DIRECTION OUTSIDE OF THE TOWN.
EACH IS ABOUT THE SIZE OF A COMPANY.

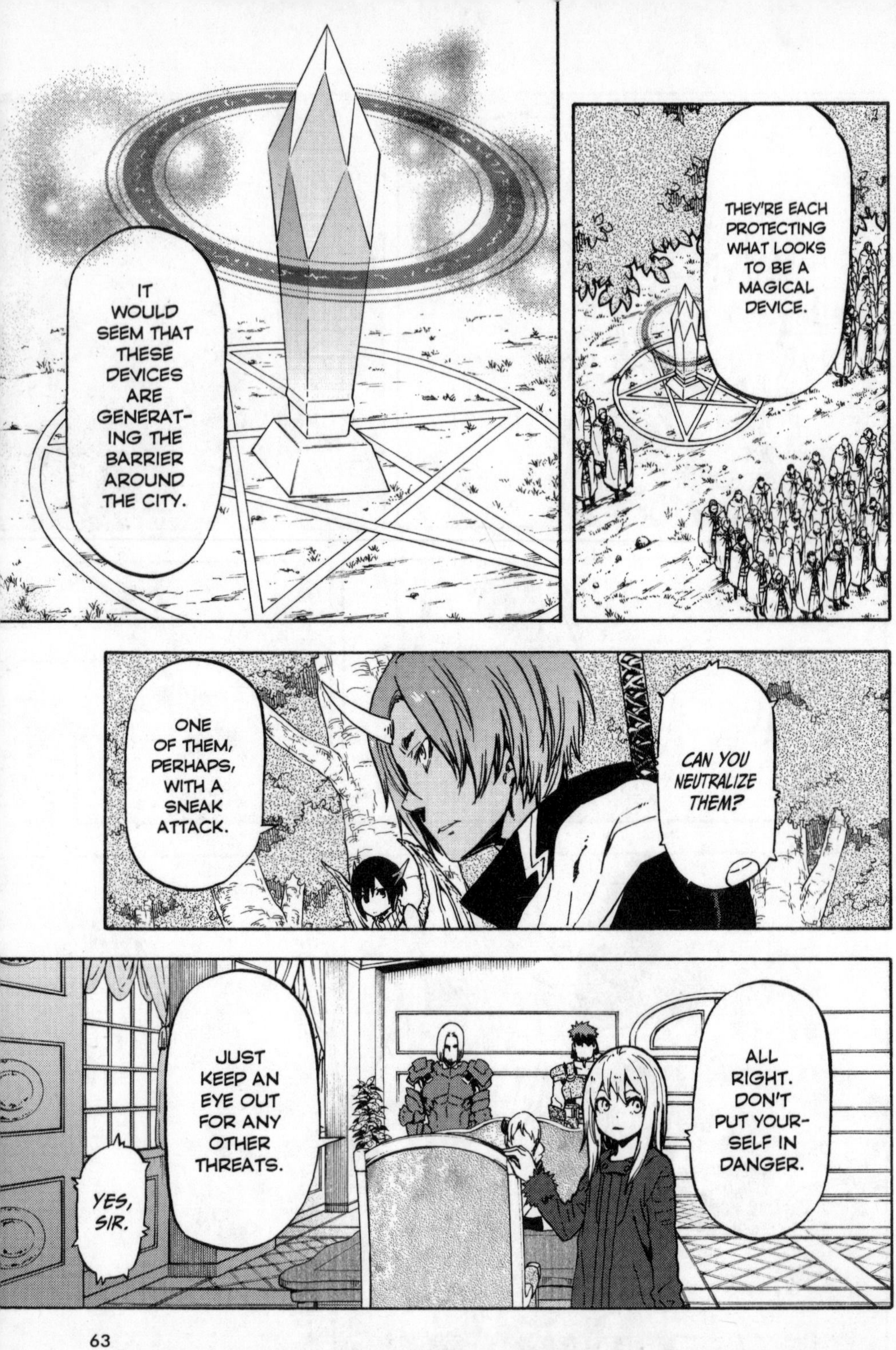
THEY'RE EACH PROTECTING WHAT LOOKS TO BE A MAGICAL DEVICE.
IT WOULD SEEM THAT THESE DEVICES ARE GENERAT-ING THE BARRIER AROUND THE CITY.
CAN YOU NEUTRALIZE THEM?
ONE OF THEM, PERHAPS, WITH A SNEAK ATTACK.
ALL RIGHT. DON'T PUT YOUR-SELF IN DANGER.
JUST KEEP AN EYE OUT FOR ANY OTHER THREATS.
YES, SIR.

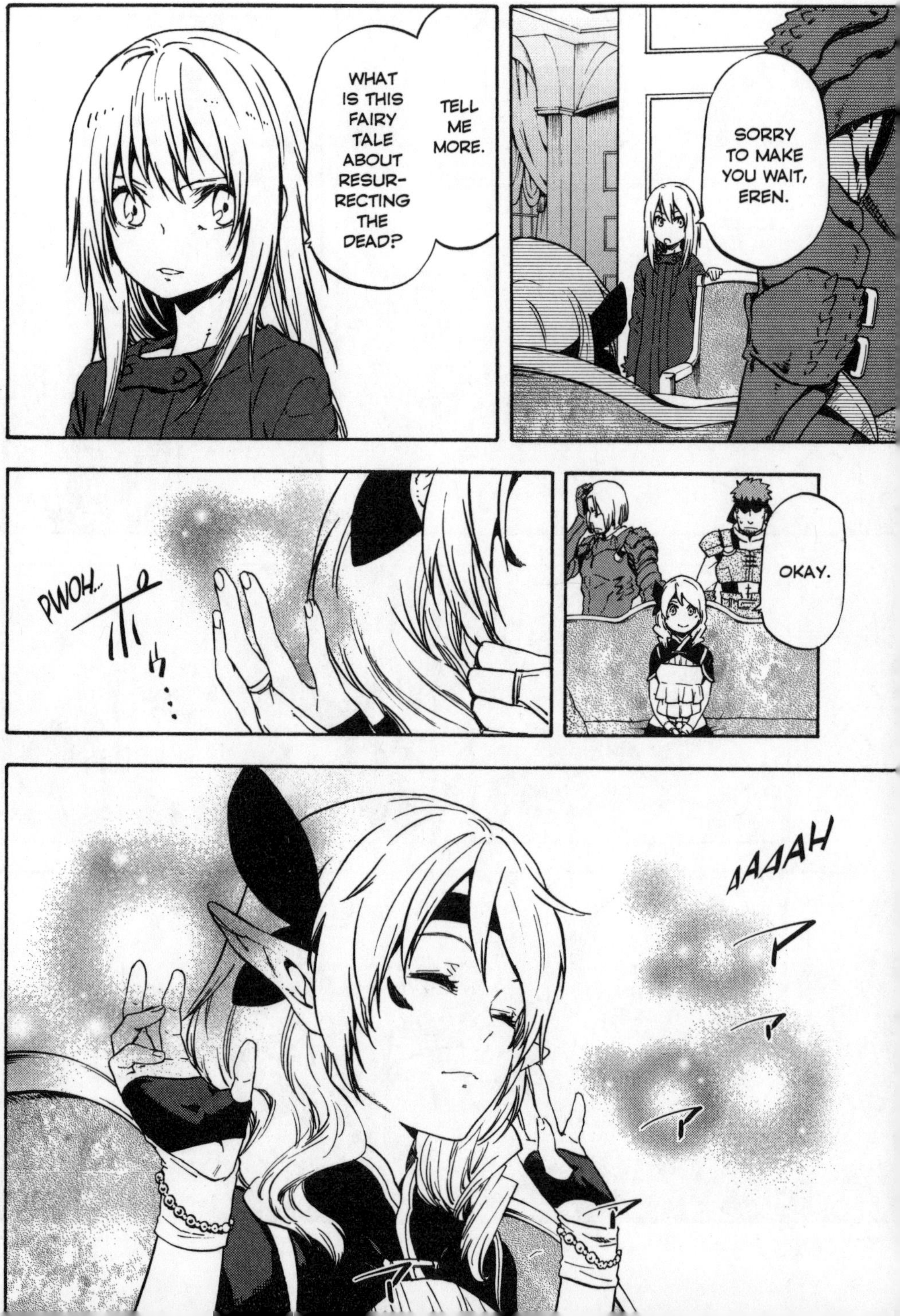
SORRY TO MAKE YOU WAIT, EREN.
WHAT IS THIS FAIRY TALE ABOUT RESURRECTING THE DEAD?
TELL ME MORE.
OKAY.
PWOH...
AAAAH

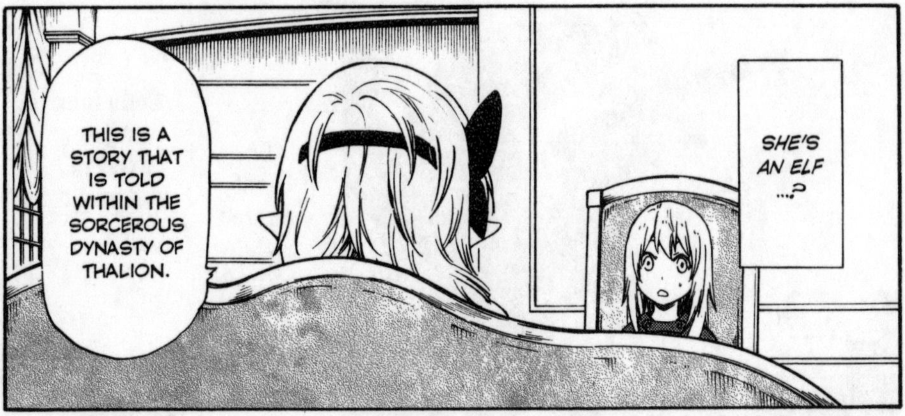
SHE'S AN ELF ...?
THIS IS A STORY THAT IS TOLD WITHIN THE SORCEROUS DYNASTY OF THALION.

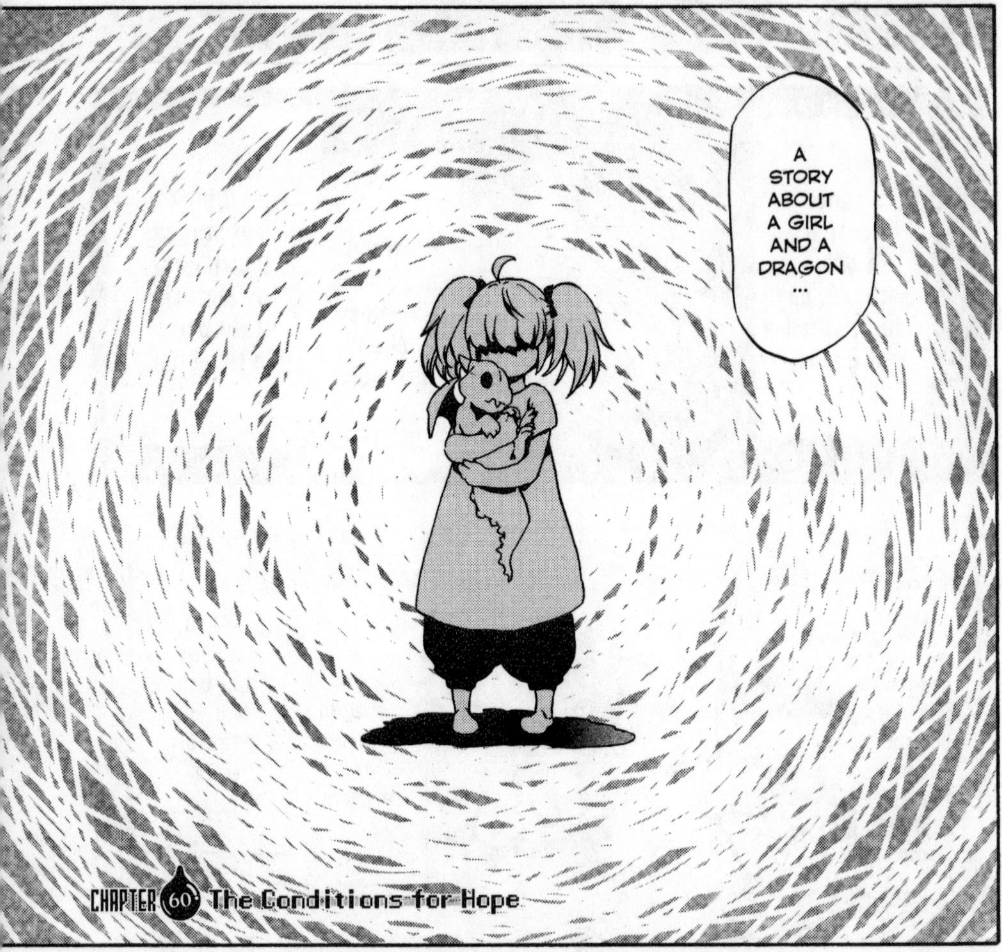
A STORY ABOUT A GIRL AND A DRAGON ...
CHAPTER 60 The Conditions for Hope

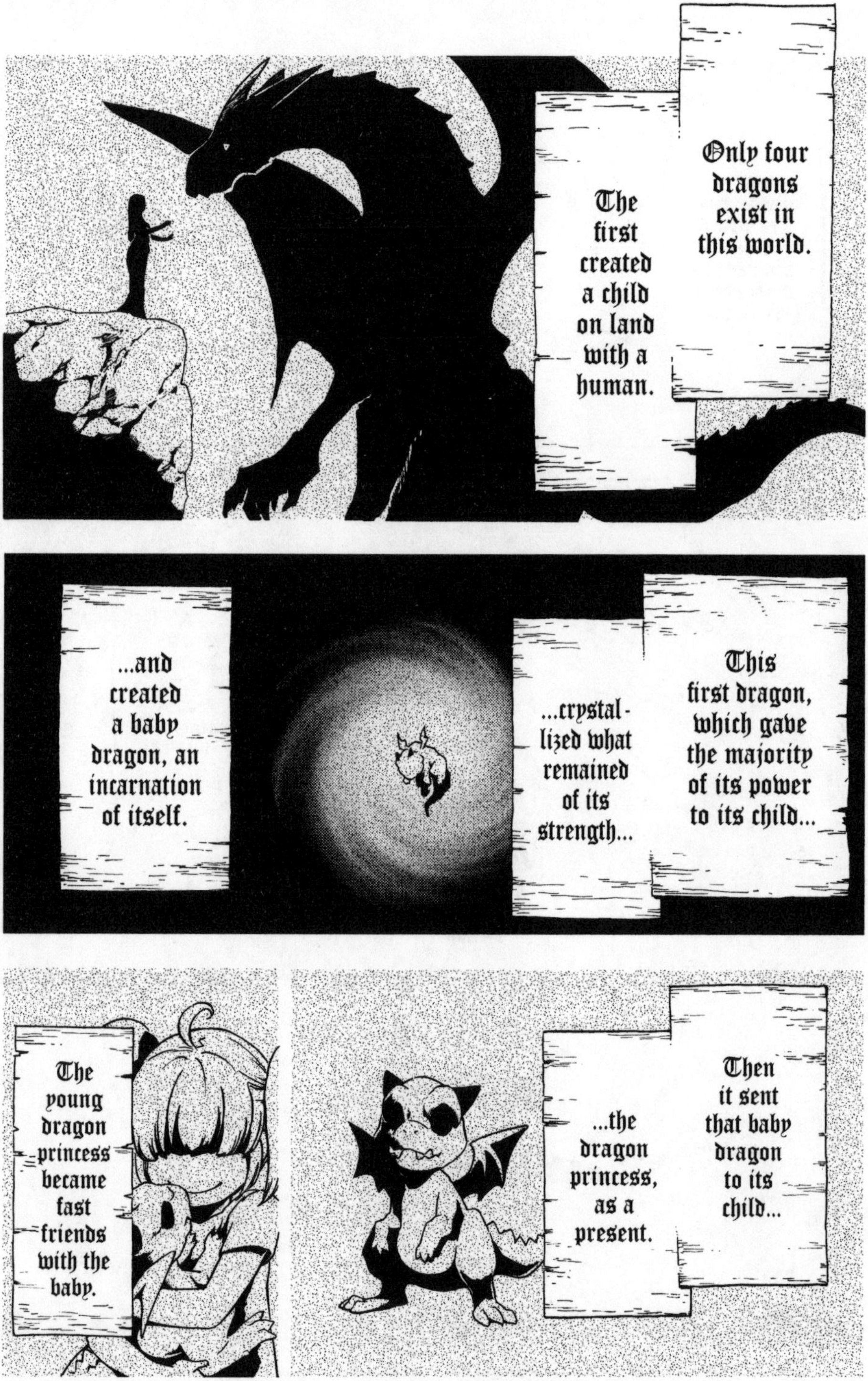
Only four dragons exist in this world.
The first created a child on land with a human.
This first dragon, which gave the majority of its power to its child...
...crystal-lized what remained of its strength...
...and created a baby dragon, an incarnation of itself.
Then it sent that baby dragon to its child...
...the dragon princess, as a present.
The young dragon princess became fast friends with the baby.

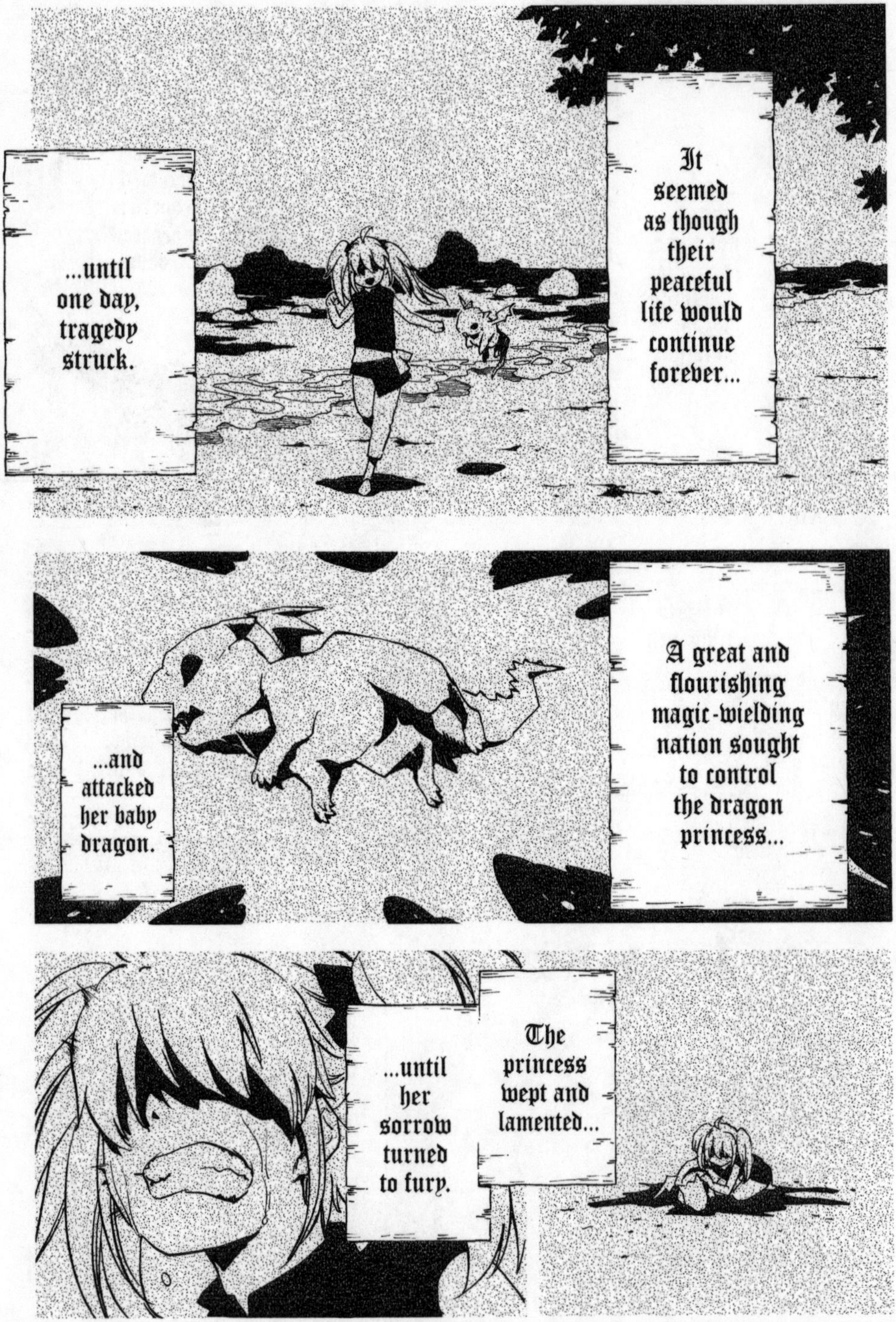
It seemed as though their peaceful life would continue forever...
...until one day, tragedy struck.
A great and flourishing magic-wielding nation sought to control the dragon princess...
...and attacked her baby dragon.
The princess wept and lamented...
...until her sorrow turned to fury.

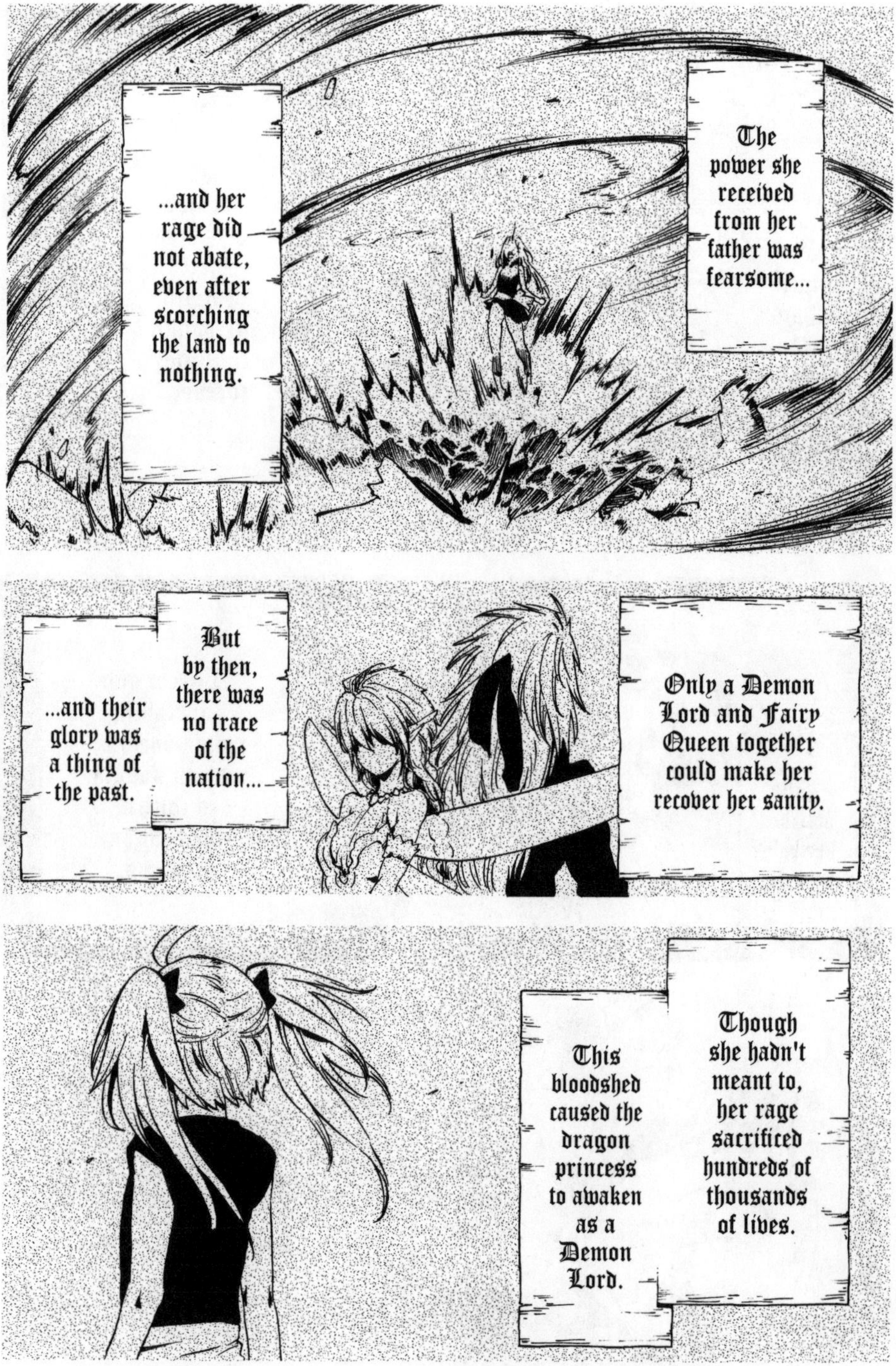
The power she received from her father was fearsome...
...and her rage did not abate, even after scorching the land to nothing.
Only a Demon Lord and Fairy Queen together could make her recover her sanity.
But by then, there was no trace of the nation...
...and their glory was a thing of the past.
Though she hadn't meant to, her rage sacrificed hundreds of thousands of lives.
This bloodshed caused the dragon princess to awaken as a Demon Lord.

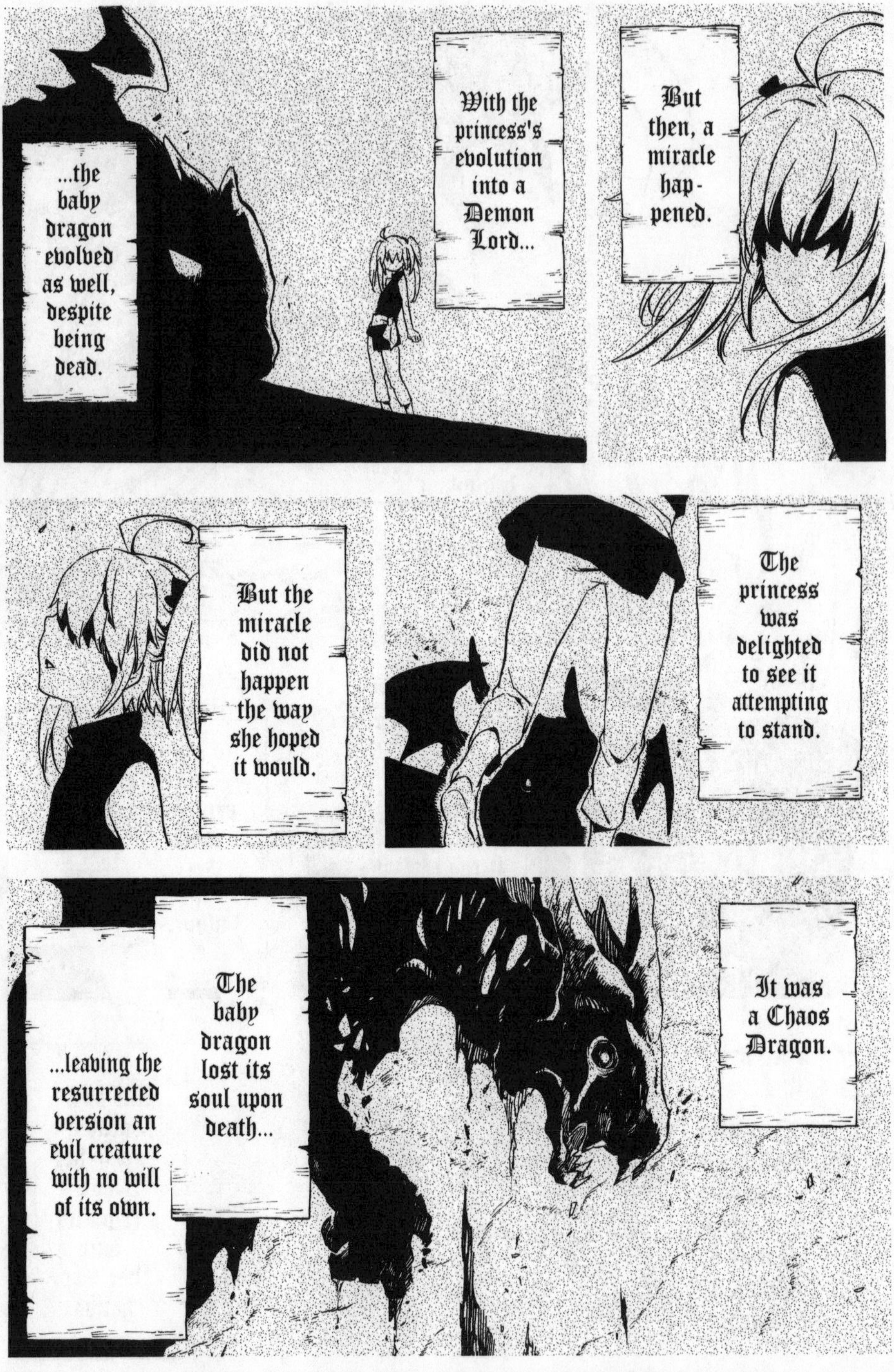
But then, a miracle hap-pened.
With the princess's evolution into a Demon Lord...
...the baby dragon evolved as well, despite being dead.
The princess was delighted to see it attempting to stand.
But the miracle did not happen the way she hoped it would.
It was a Chaos Dragon.
The baby dragon lost its soul upon death...
...leaving the resurrected version an evil creature with no will of its own.

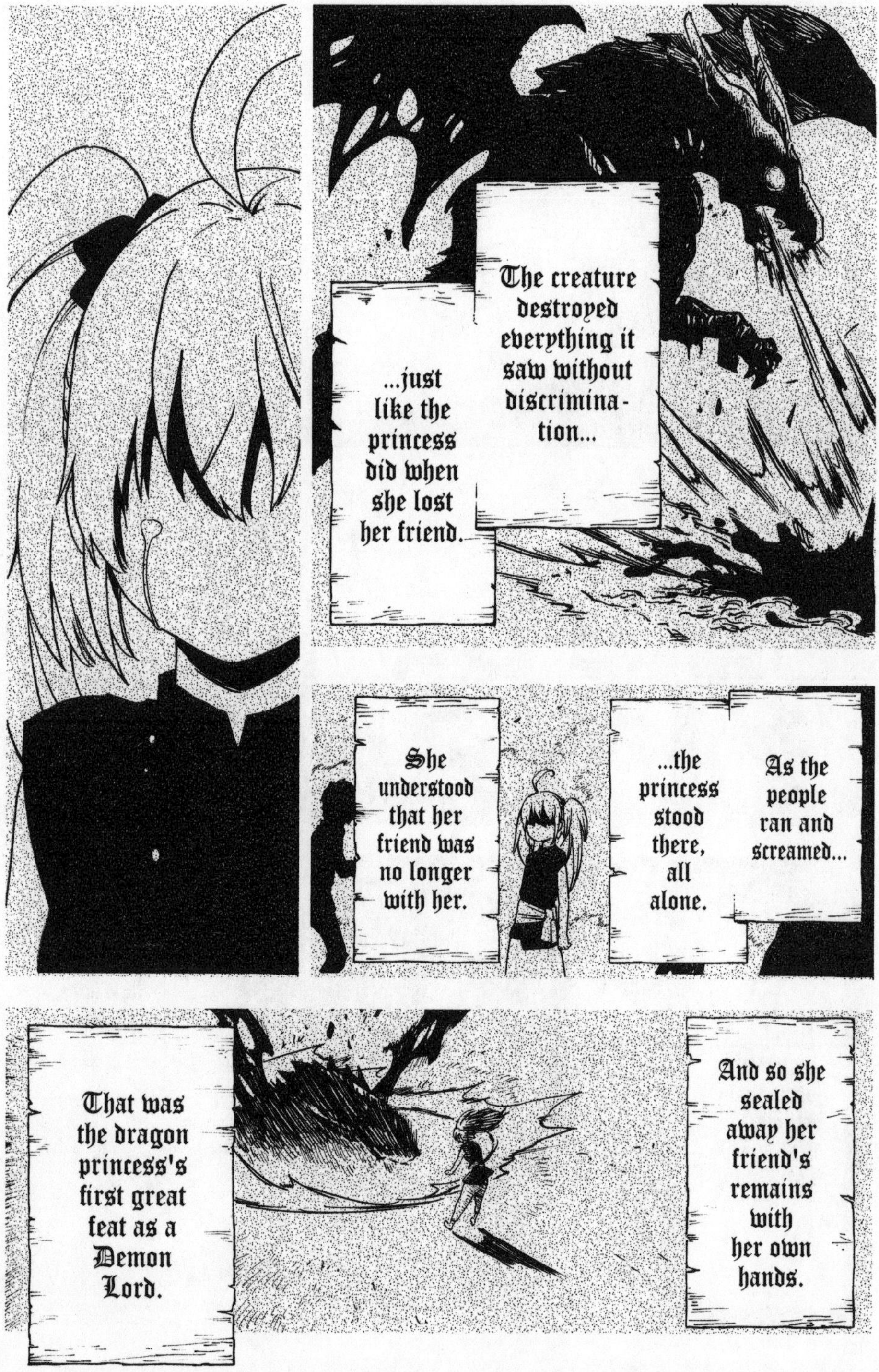
The creature destroyed everything it saw without discrimina-tion...
...just like the princess did when she lost her friend.
As the people ran and screamed...
...the princess stood there, all alone.
She understood that her friend was no longer with her.
And so she sealed away her friend's remains with her own hands.
That was the dragon princess's first great feat as a Demon Lord.

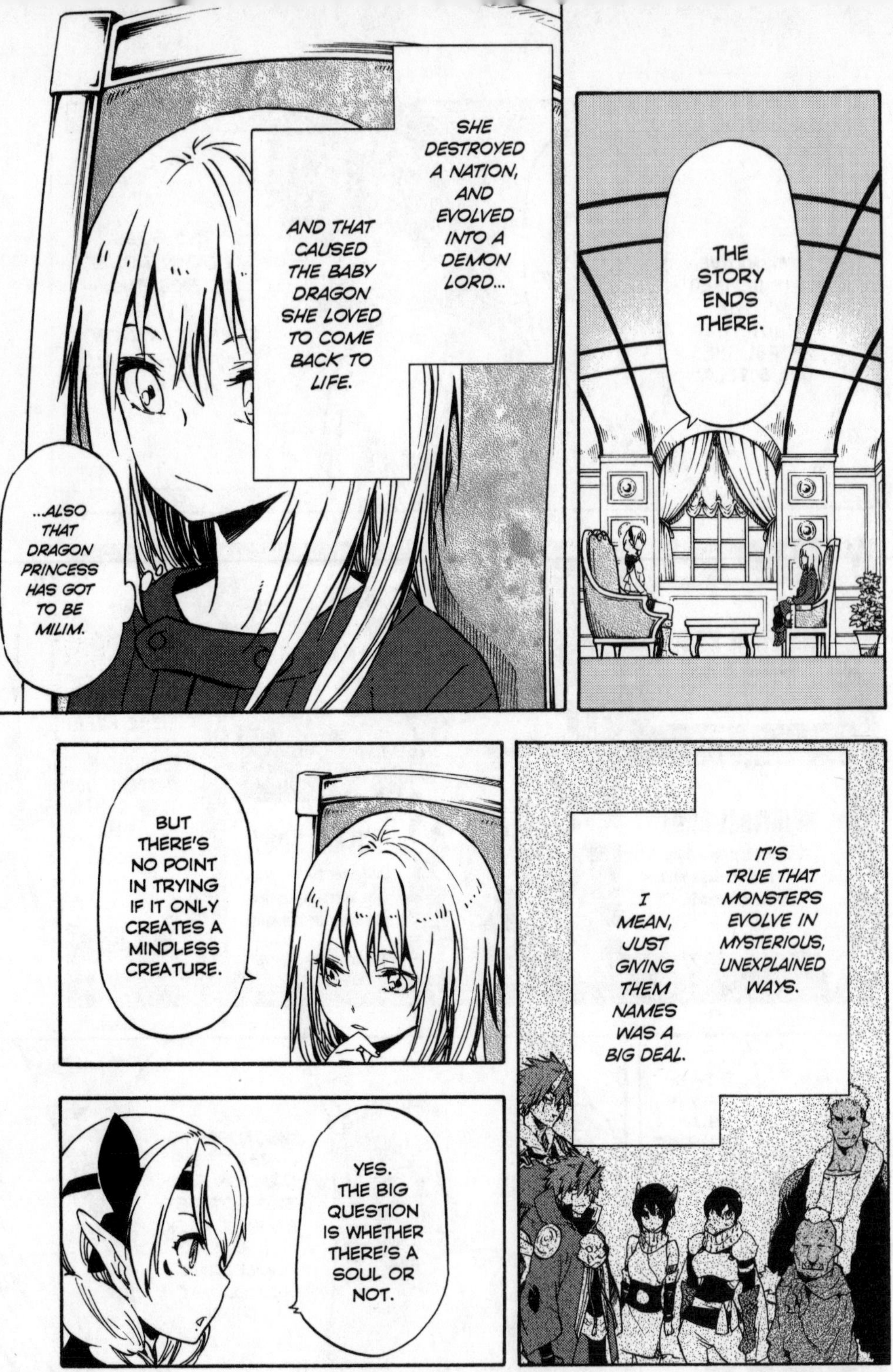
THE STORY ENDS THERE.
SHE DESTROYED A NATION, AND EVOLVED INTO A DEMON LORD...
AND THAT CAUSED THE BABY DRAGON SHE LOVED TO COME BACK TO LIFE.
...
...ALSO THAT DRAGON PRINCESS HAS GOT TO BE MILIM.
IT'S TRUE THAT MONSTERS EVOLVE IN MYSTERIOUS, UNEXPLAINED WAYS.
I MEAN, JUST GIVING THEM NAMES WAS A BIG DEAL.
BUT THERE'S NO POINT IN TRYING IF IT ONLY CREATES A MINDLESS CREATURE.
YES. THE BIG QUESTION IS WHETHER THERE'S A SOUL OR NOT.

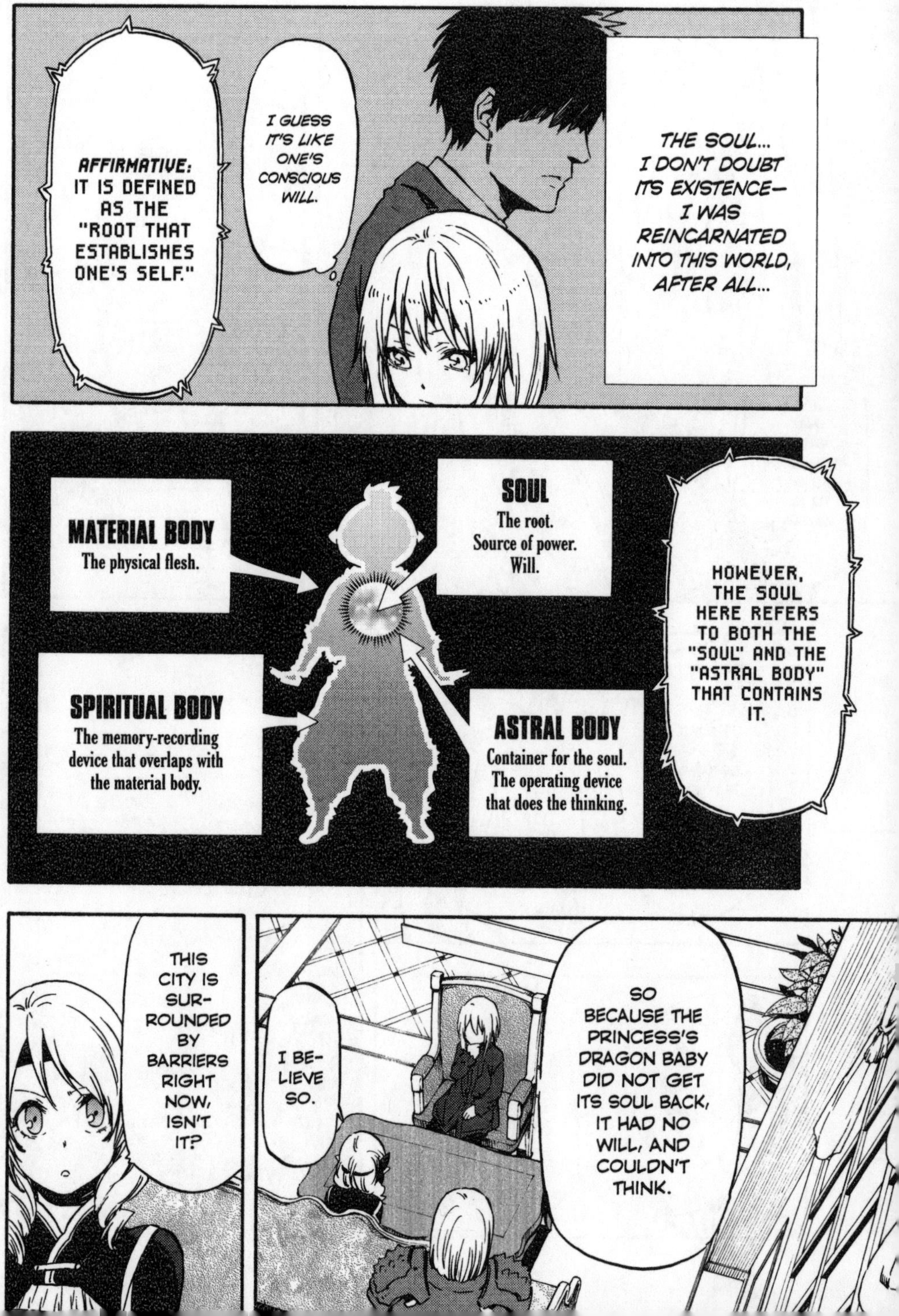
THE SOUL... I DON'T DOUBT ITS EXISTENCE— I WAS REINCARNATED INTO THIS WORLD, AFTER ALL...
I GUESS IT'S LIKE ONE'S CONSCIOUS WILL.
AFFIRMATIVE: IT IS DEFINED AS THE "ROOT THAT ESTABLISHES ONE'S SELF."
SOUL
The root. Source of power. Will.
MATERIAL BODY
The physical flesh.
ASTRAL BODY
Container for the soul. The operating device that does the thinking.
SPIRITUAL BODY
The memory-recording device that overlaps with the material body.
HOWEVER, THE SOUL HERE REFERS TO BOTH THE "SOUL" AND THE "ASTRAL BODY" THAT CONTAINS IT.
SO BECAUSE THE PRINCESS'S DRAGON BABY DID NOT GET ITS SOUL BACK, IT HAD NO WILL, AND COULDN'T THINK.
I BE- LIEVE SO.
THIS CITY IS SUR- ROUNDED BY BARRIERS RIGHT NOW, ISN'T IT?

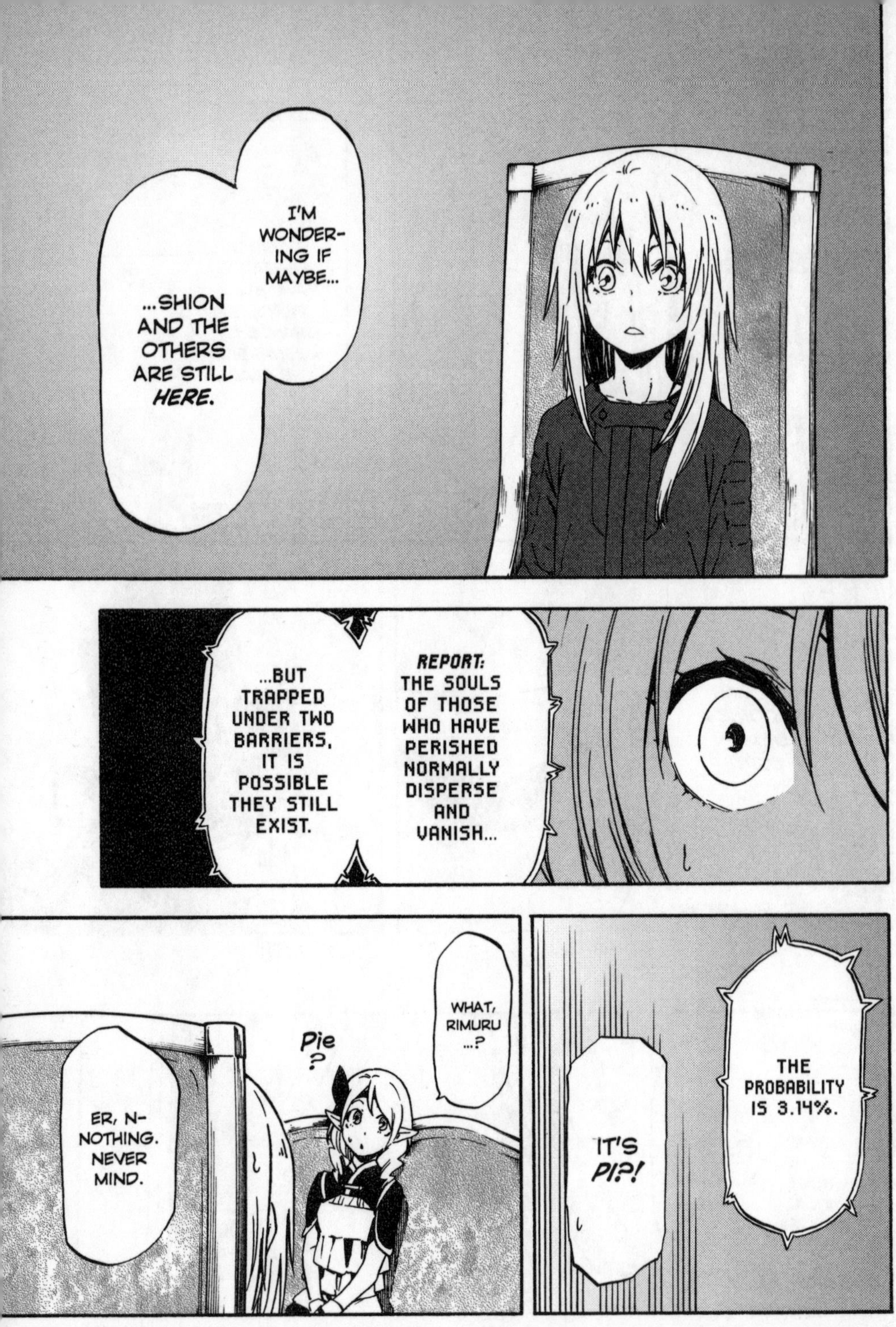
I'M WONDERING IF MAYBE...
...SHION AND THE OTHERS ARE STILL *HERE*.
REPORT: THE SOULS OF THOSE WHO HAVE PERISHED NORMALLY DISPERSE AND VANISH...
...BUT TRAPPED UNDER TWO BARRIERS, IT IS POSSIBLE THEY STILL EXIST.
THE PROBABILITY IS 3.14%.
IT'S *PI?!*
WHAT, RIMURU ...?
Pie?
ER, N-NOTHING. NEVER MIND.

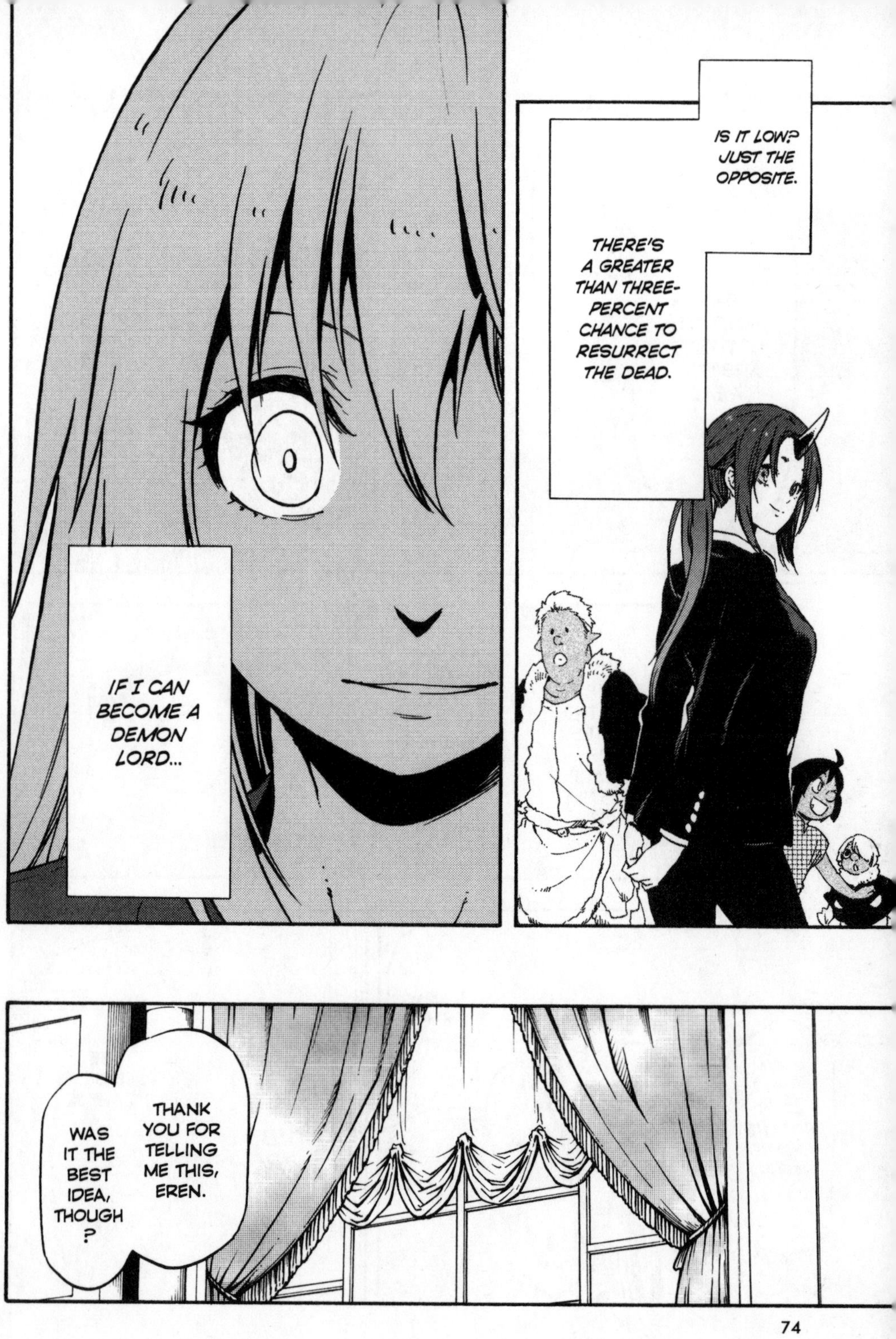
IS IT LOW? JUST THE OPPOSITE.
THERE'S A GREATER THAN THREE-PERCENT CHANCE TO RESURRECT THE DEAD.
...
IF I CAN BECOME A DEMON LORD...
THANK YOU FOR TELLING ME THIS, EREN.
WAS IT THE BEST IDEA, THOUGH?

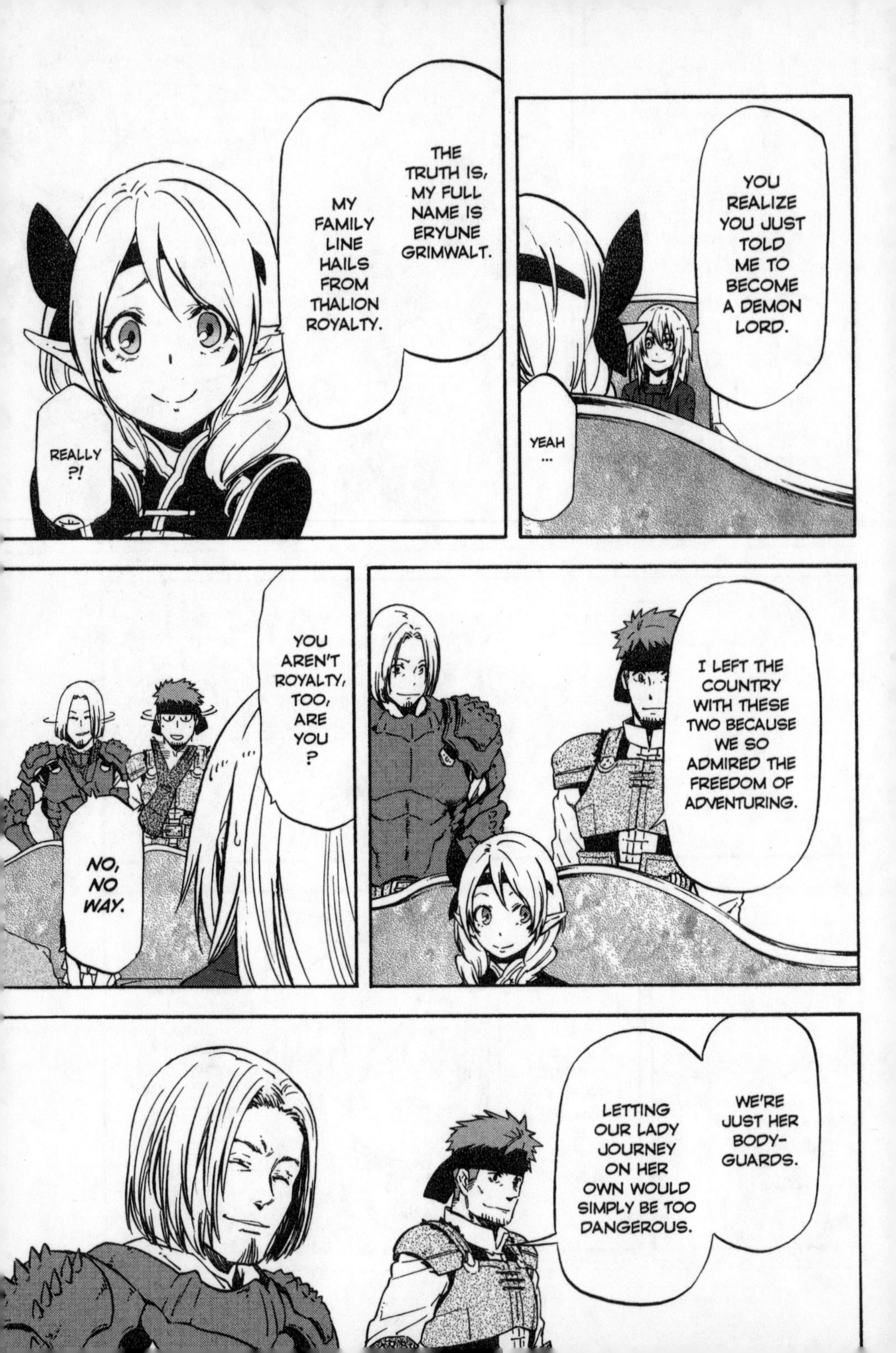
YOU REALIZE YOU JUST TOLD ME TO BECOME A DEMON LORD.
YEAH...
THE TRUTH IS, MY FULL NAME IS ERYUNE GRIMWALT.
MY FAMILY LINE HAILS FROM THALION ROYALTY.
REALLY?!
I LEFT THE COUNTRY WITH THESE TWO BECAUSE WE SO ADMIRED THE FREEDOM OF ADVENTURING.
YOU AREN'T ROYALTY, TOO, ARE YOU?
NO, NO WAY.
WE'RE JUST HER BODY-GUARDS.
LETTING OUR LADY JOURNEY ON HER OWN WOULD SIMPLY BE TOO DANGEROUS.

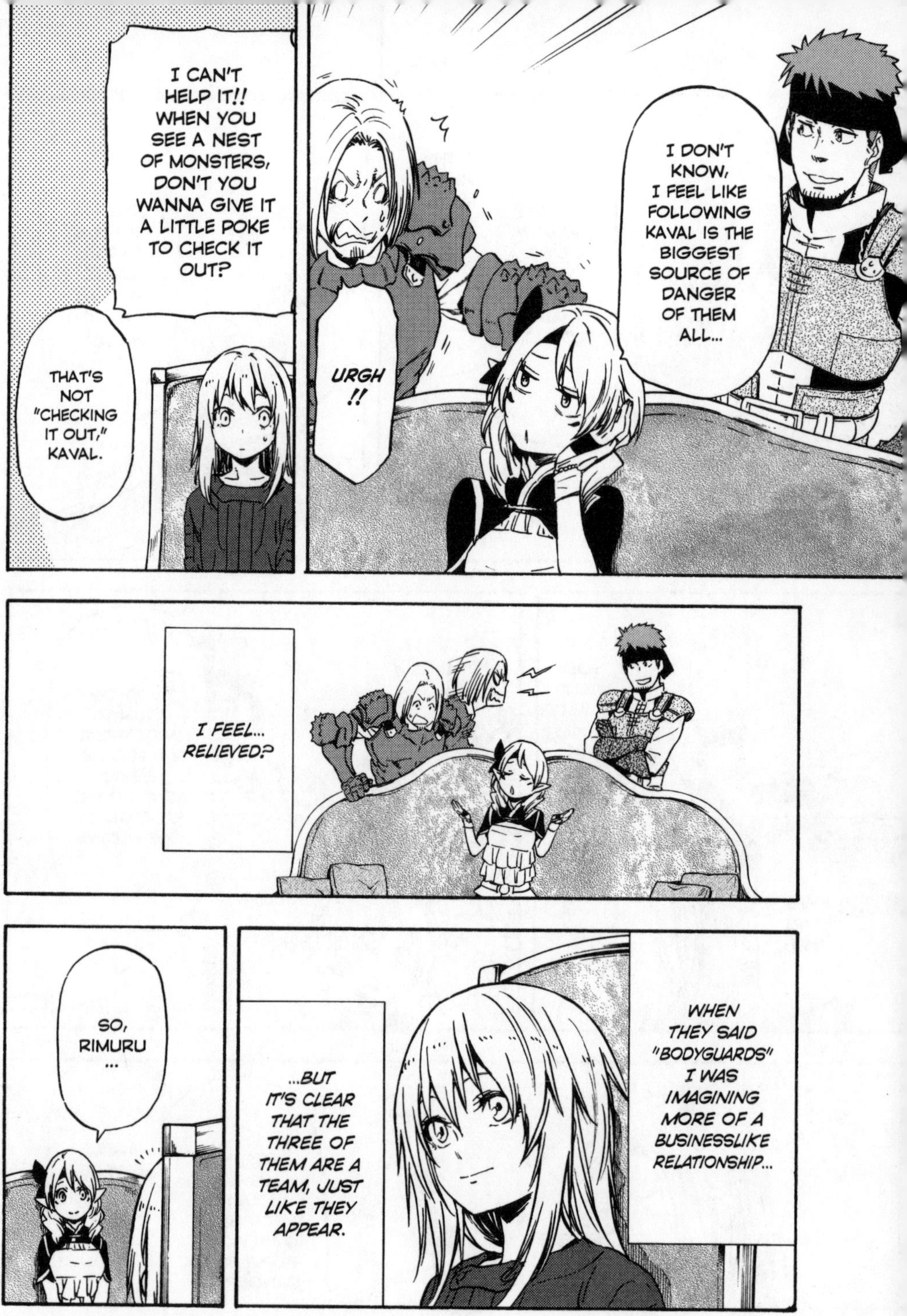
I DON'T KNOW, I FEEL LIKE FOLLOWING KAVAL IS THE BIGGEST SOURCE OF DANGER OF THEM ALL...
URGH !!
I CAN'T HELP IT!! WHEN YOU SEE A NEST OF MONSTERS, DON'T YOU WANNA GIVE IT A LITTLE POKE TO CHECK IT OUT?
THAT'S NOT "CHECKING IT OUT," KAVAL.
I FEEL... RELIEVED?
WHEN THEY SAID "BODYGUARDS" I WAS IMAGINING MORE OF A BUSINESSLIKE RELATIONSHIP...
...BUT IT'S CLEAR THAT THE THREE OF THEM ARE A TEAM, JUST LIKE THEY APPEAR.
SO, RIMURU ...

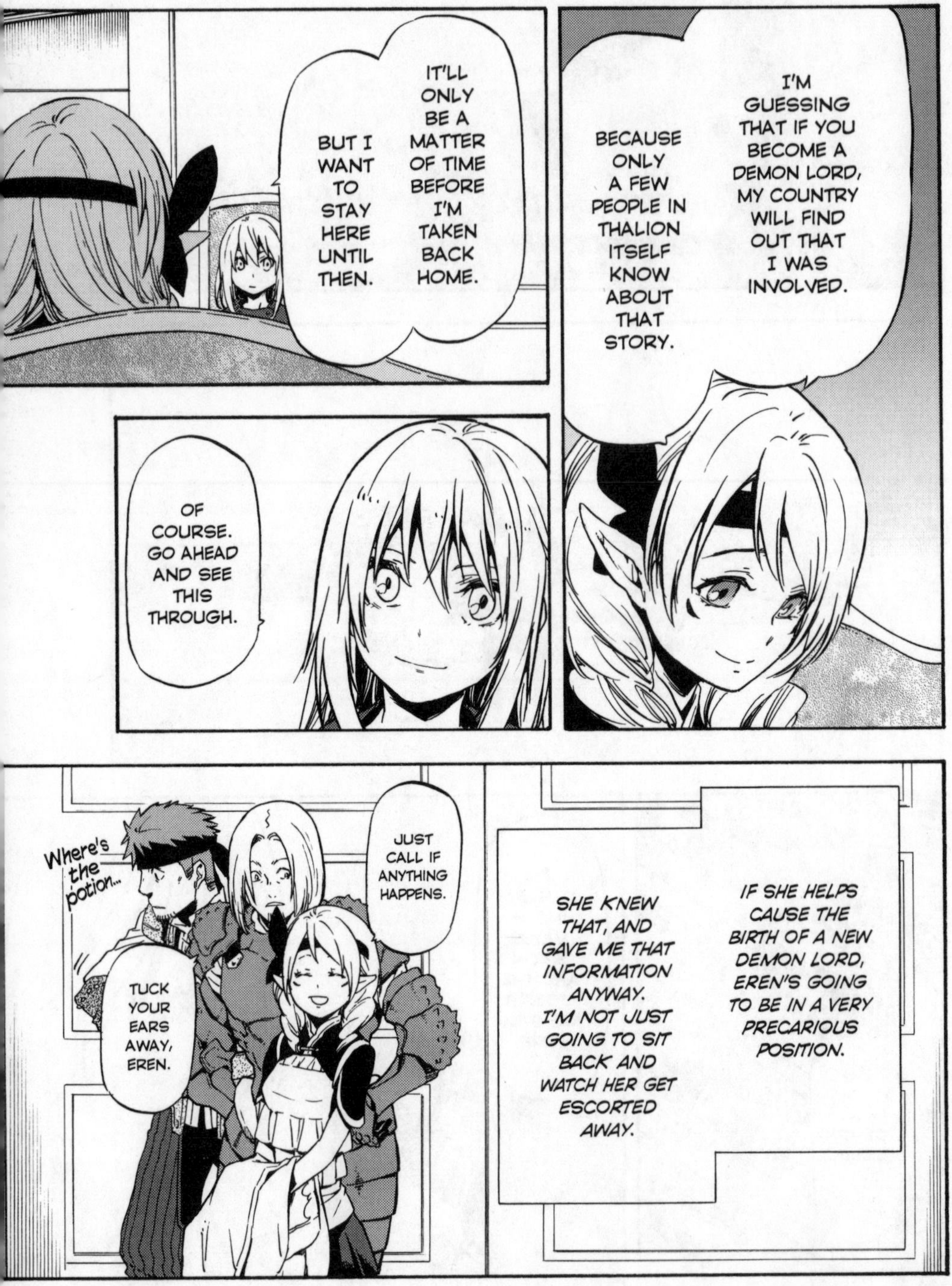
I'M GUESSING THAT IF YOU BECOME A DEMON LORD, MY COUNTRY WILL FIND OUT THAT I WAS INVOLVED.
BECAUSE ONLY A FEW PEOPLE IN THALION ITSELF KNOW ABOUT THAT STORY.
IT'LL ONLY BE A MATTER OF TIME BEFORE I'M TAKEN BACK HOME.
BUT I WANT TO STAY HERE UNTIL THEN.
OF COURSE. GO AHEAD AND SEE THIS THROUGH.
IF SHE HELPS CAUSE THE BIRTH OF A NEW DEMON LORD, EREN'S GOING TO BE IN A VERY PRECARIOUS POSITION.
SHE KNEW THAT, AND GAVE ME THAT INFORMATION ANYWAY. I'M NOT JUST GOING TO SIT BACK AND WATCH HER GET ESCORTED AWAY.
JUST CALL IF ANYTHING HAPPENS.
Where's the potion...
TUCK YOUR EARS AWAY, EREN.

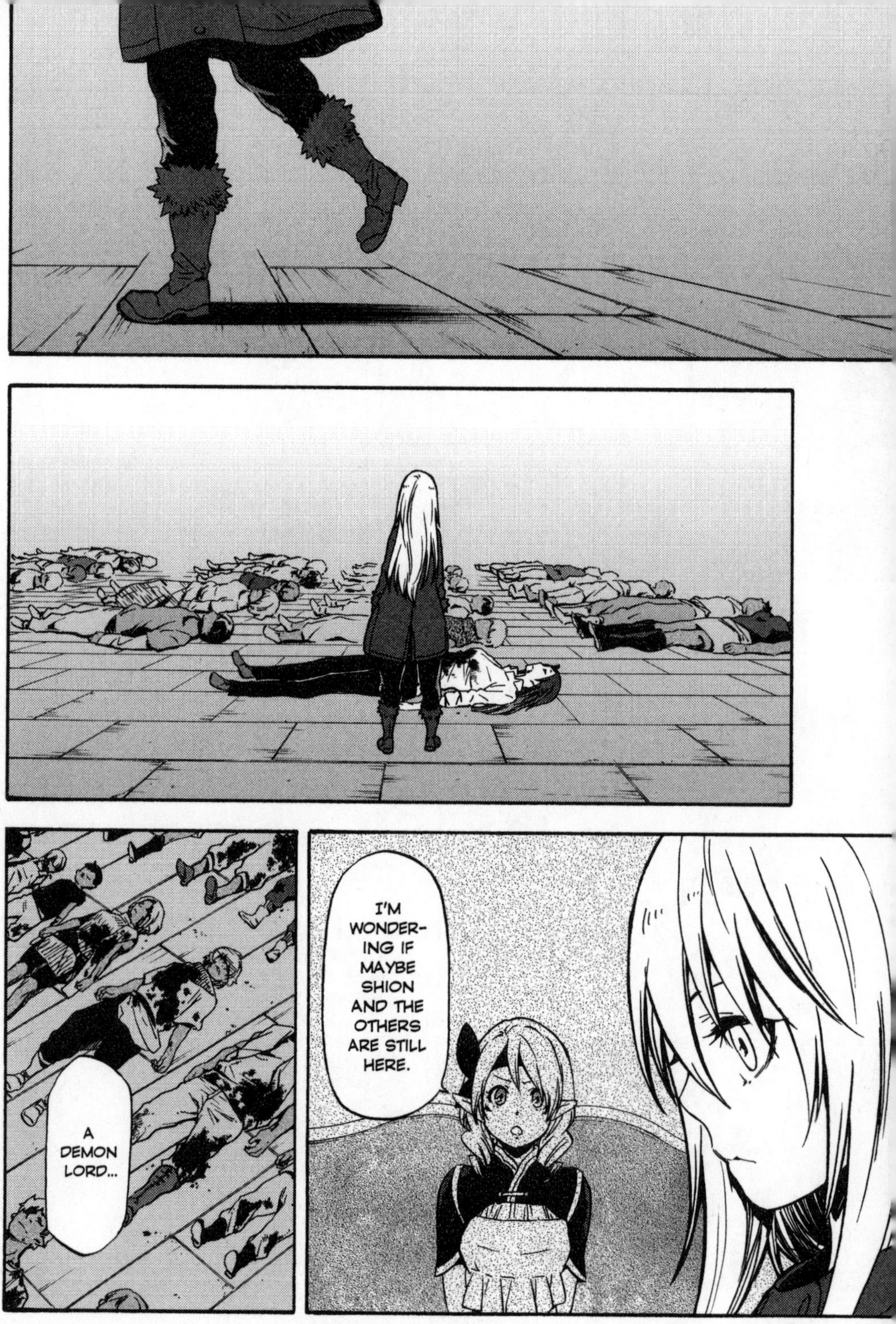
I'M WONDERING IF MAYBE SHION AND THE OTHERS ARE STILL HERE.
A DEMON LORD...

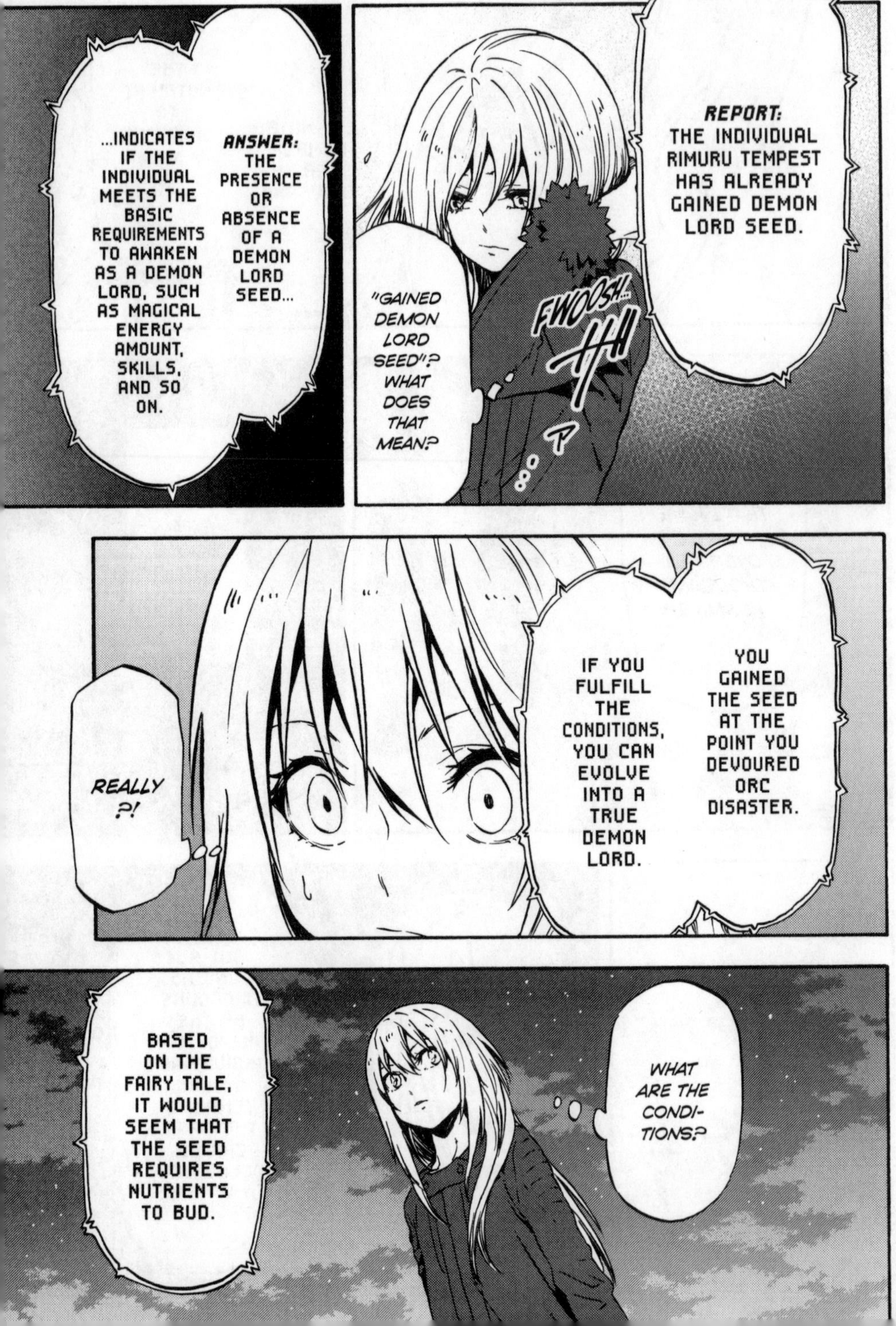
REPORT: THE INDIVIDUAL RIMURU TEMPEST HAS ALREADY GAINED DEMON LORD SEED.
FWOOSH... HH
"GAINED DEMON LORD SEED"? WHAT DOES THAT MEAN?
ANSWER: THE PRESENCE OR ABSENCE OF A DEMON LORD SEED...
...INDICATES IF THE INDIVIDUAL MEETS THE BASIC REQUIREMENTS TO AWAKEN AS A DEMON LORD, SUCH AS MAGICAL ENERGY AMOUNT, SKILLS, AND SO ON.
YOU GAINED THE SEED AT THE POINT YOU DEVOURED ORC DISASTER.
IF YOU FULFILL THE CONDITIONS, YOU CAN EVOLVE INTO A TRUE DEMON LORD.
REALLY ?!
BASED ON THE FAIRY TALE, IT WOULD SEEM THAT THE SEED REQUIRES NUTRIENTS TO BUD.
WHAT ARE THE CONDI-TIONS?

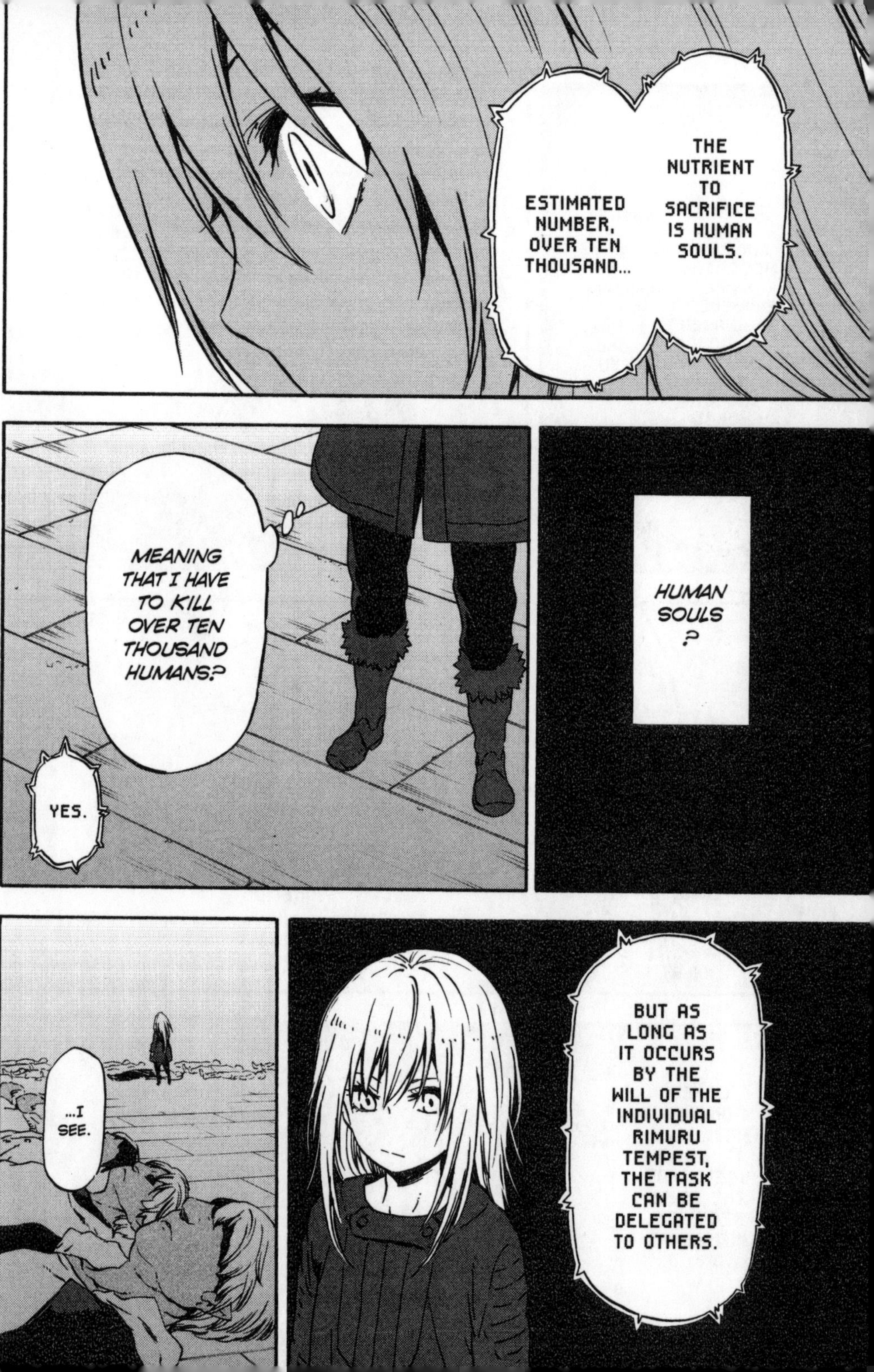
THE NUTRIENT TO SACRIFICE IS HUMAN SOULS.
ESTIMATED NUMBER, OVER TEN THOUSAND...
HUMAN SOULS?
MEANING THAT I HAVE TO KILL OVER TEN THOUSAND HUMANS?
YES.
BUT AS LONG AS IT OCCURS BY THE WILL OF THE INDIVIDUAL RIMURU TEMPEST, THE TASK CAN BE DELEGATED TO OTHERS.
...I SEE.

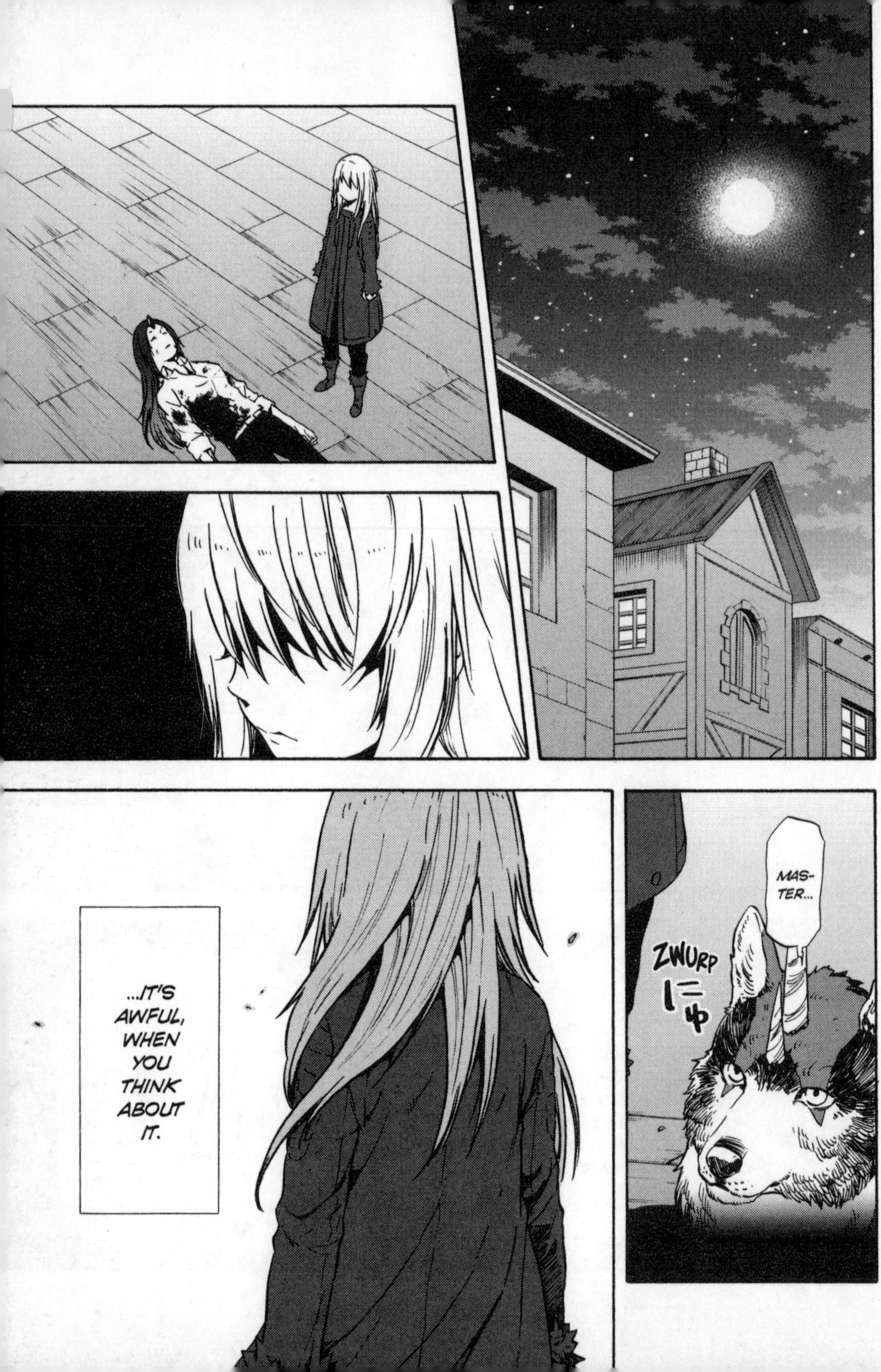
MASTER...
ZWURP
...IT'S AWFUL, WHEN YOU THINK ABOUT IT.

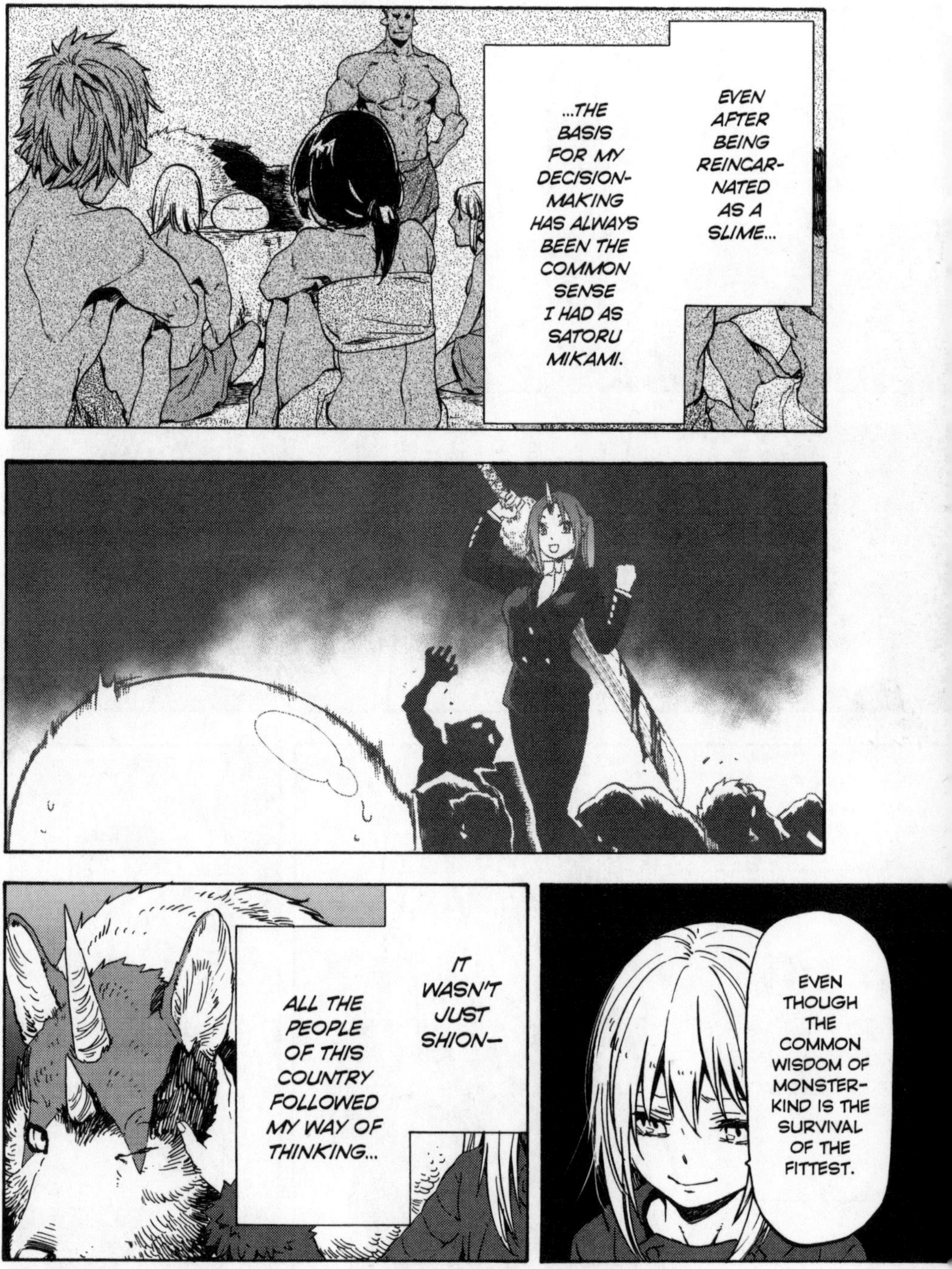
EVEN AFTER BEING REINCARNATED AS A SLIME...
...THE BASIS FOR MY DECISION-MAKING HAS ALWAYS BEEN THE COMMON SENSE I HAD AS SATORU MIKAMI.
EVEN THOUGH THE COMMON WISDOM OF MONSTERKIND IS THE SURVIVAL OF THE FITTEST.
IT WASN'T JUST SHION—
ALL THE PEOPLE OF THIS COUNTRY FOLLOWED MY WAY OF THINKING...

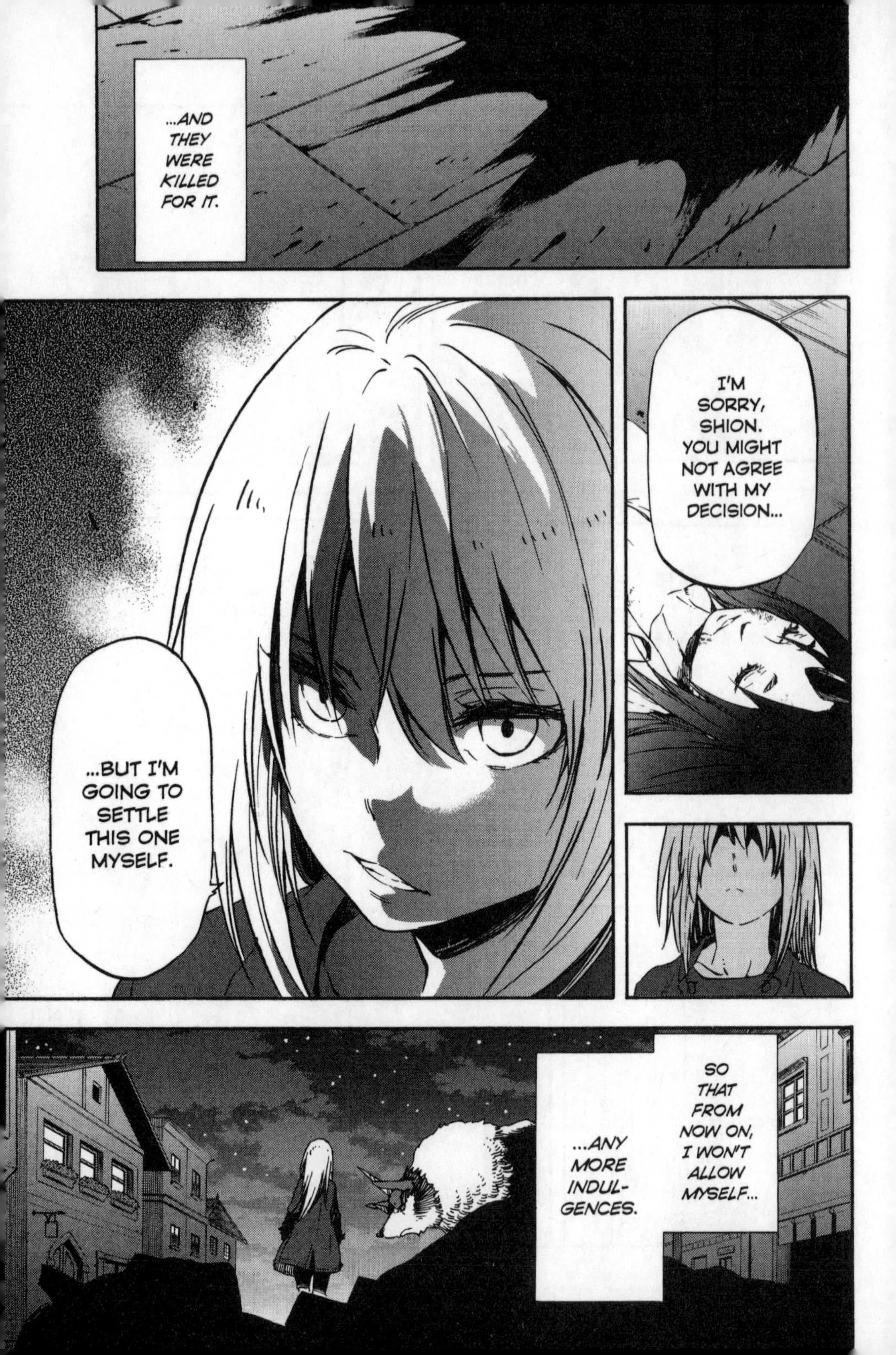
...AND THEY WERE KILLED FOR IT.
I'M SORRY, SHION. YOU MIGHT NOT AGREE WITH MY DECISION...
...BUT I'M GOING TO SETTLE THIS ONE MYSELF.
SO THAT FROM NOW ON, I WON'T ALLOW MYSELF...
...ANY MORE INDUL-GENCES.

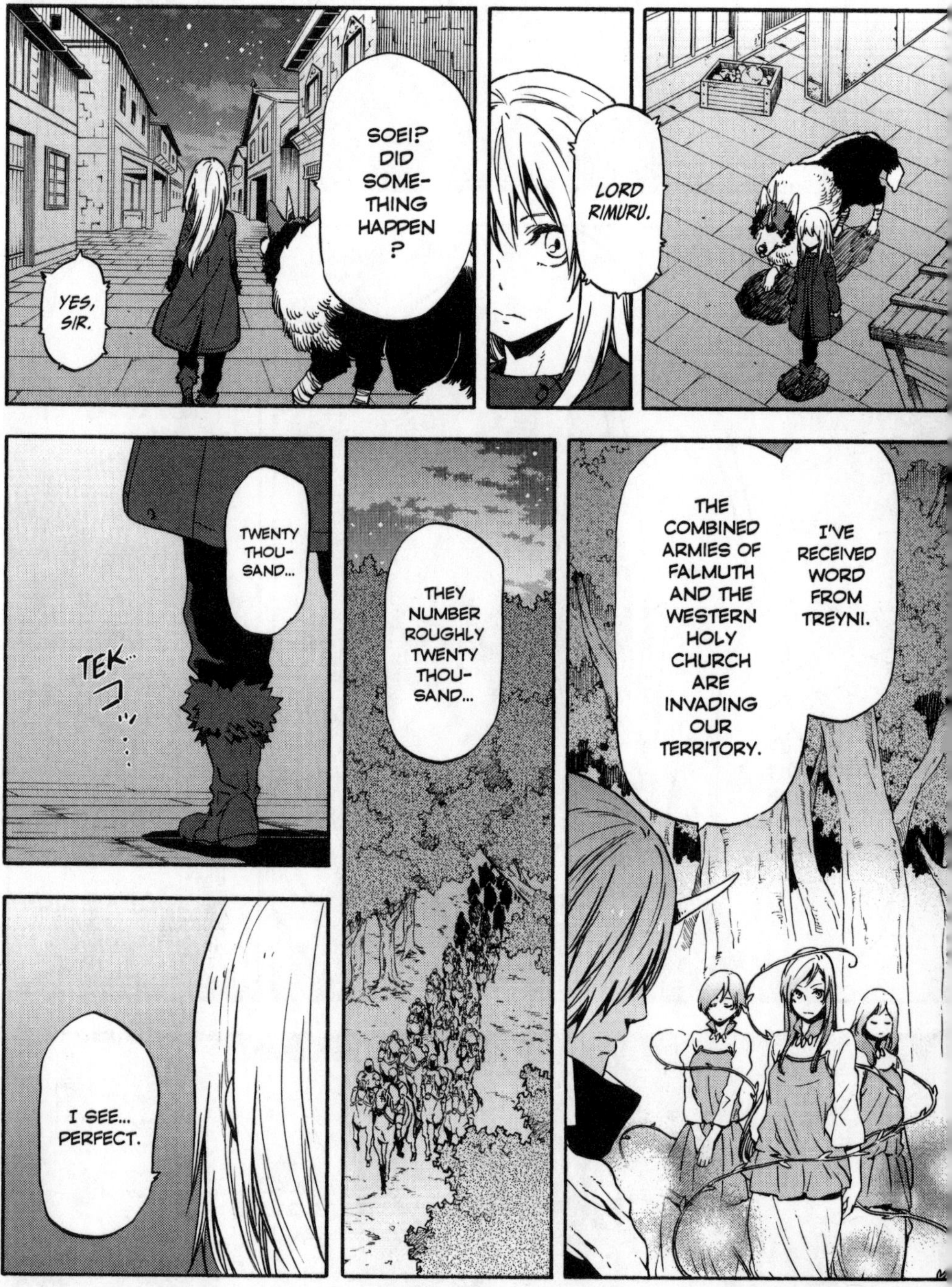
LORD RIMURU.
SOEI? DID SOMETHING HAPPEN?
YES, SIR.
I'VE RECEIVED WORD FROM TREYNI.
THE COMBINED ARMIES OF FALMUTH AND THE WESTERN HOLY CHURCH ARE INVADING OUR TERRITORY.
THEY NUMBER ROUGHLY TWENTY THOUSAND...
TWENTY THOUSAND...
TEK...
コッ...
I SEE... PERFECT.

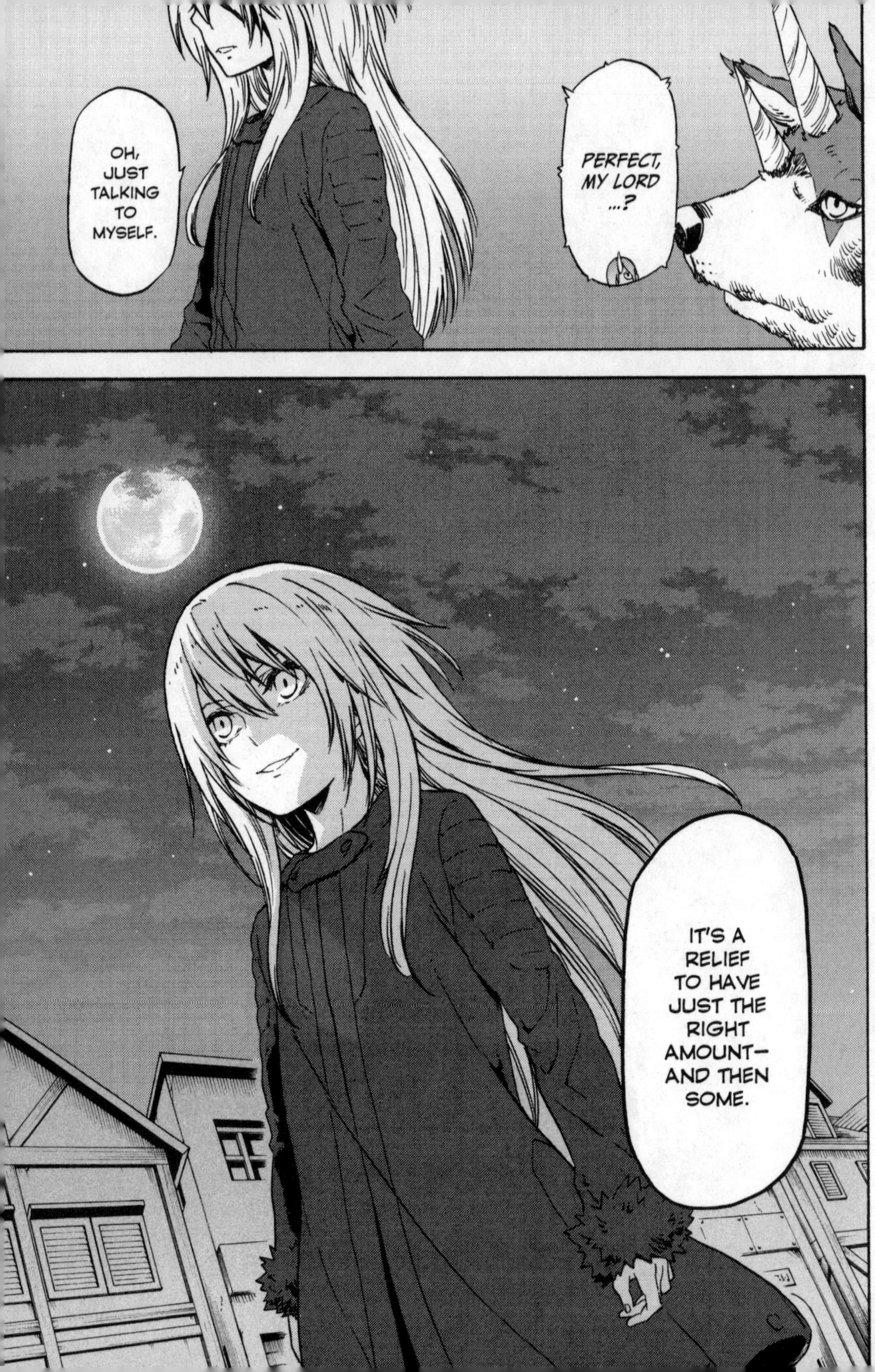
PERFECT, MY LORD ...?
OH, JUST TALKING TO MYSELF.
IT'S A RELIEF TO HAVE JUST THE RIGHT AMOUNT—AND THEN SOME.

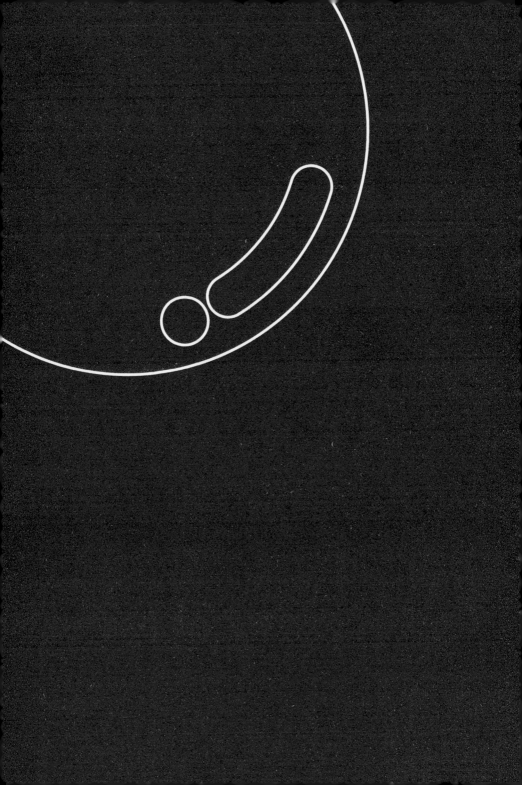

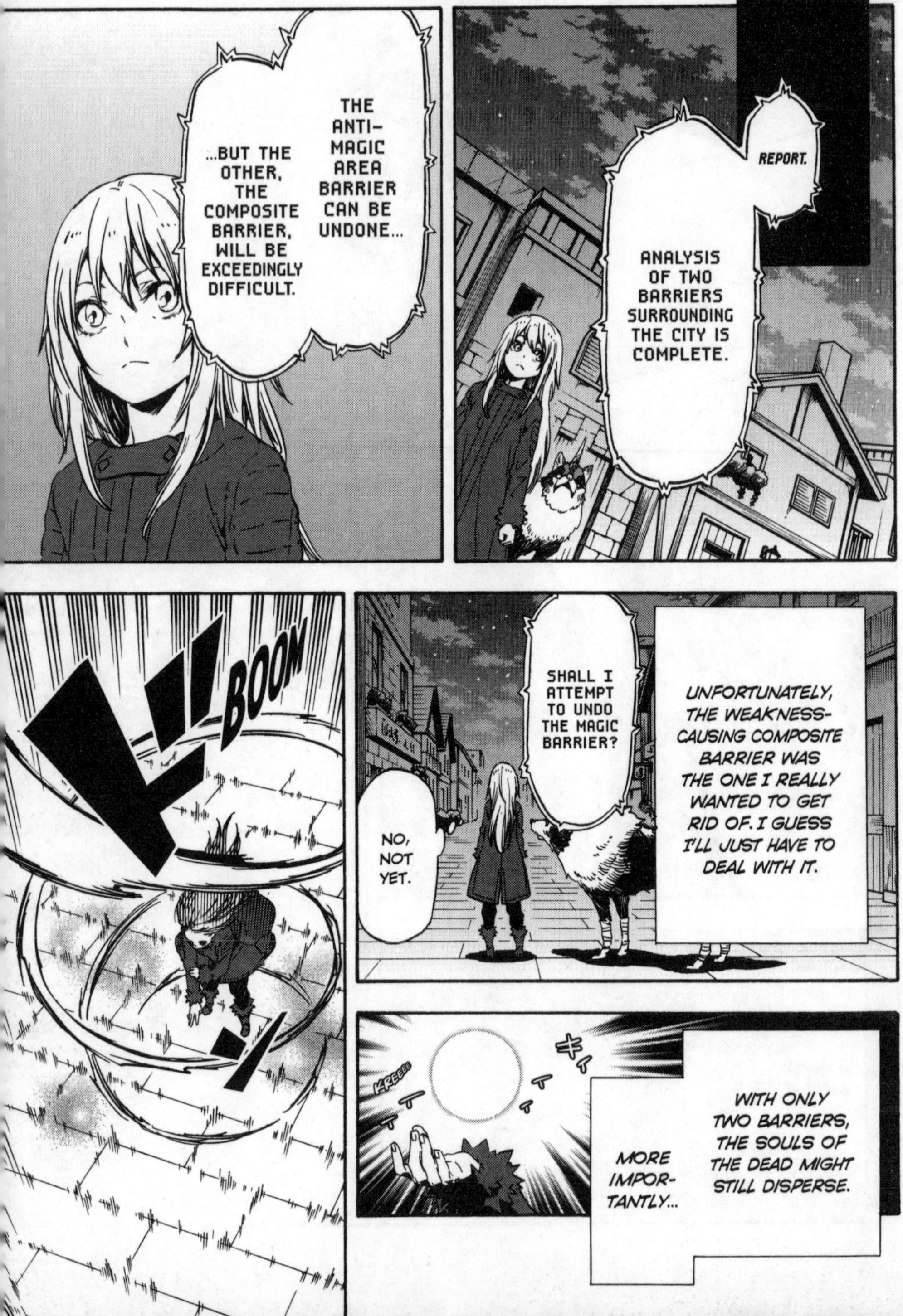
REPORT.
ANALYSIS OF TWO BARRIERS SURROUNDING THE CITY IS COMPLETE.
THE ANTI-MAGIC AREA BARRIER CAN BE UNDONE...
...BUT THE OTHER, THE COMPOSITE BARRIER, WILL BE EXCEEDINGLY DIFFICULT.
SHALL I ATTEMPT TO UNDO THE MAGIC BARRIER?
UNFORTUNATELY, THE WEAKNESS-CAUSING COMPOSITE BARRIER WAS THE ONE I REALLY WANTED TO GET RID OF. I GUESS I'LL JUST HAVE TO DEAL WITH IT.
NO, NOT YET.
キィ
K-REEEE
WITH ONLY TWO BARRIERS, THE SOULS OF THE DEAD MIGHT STILL DISPERSE.
MORE IMPORTANTLY...
BOOM

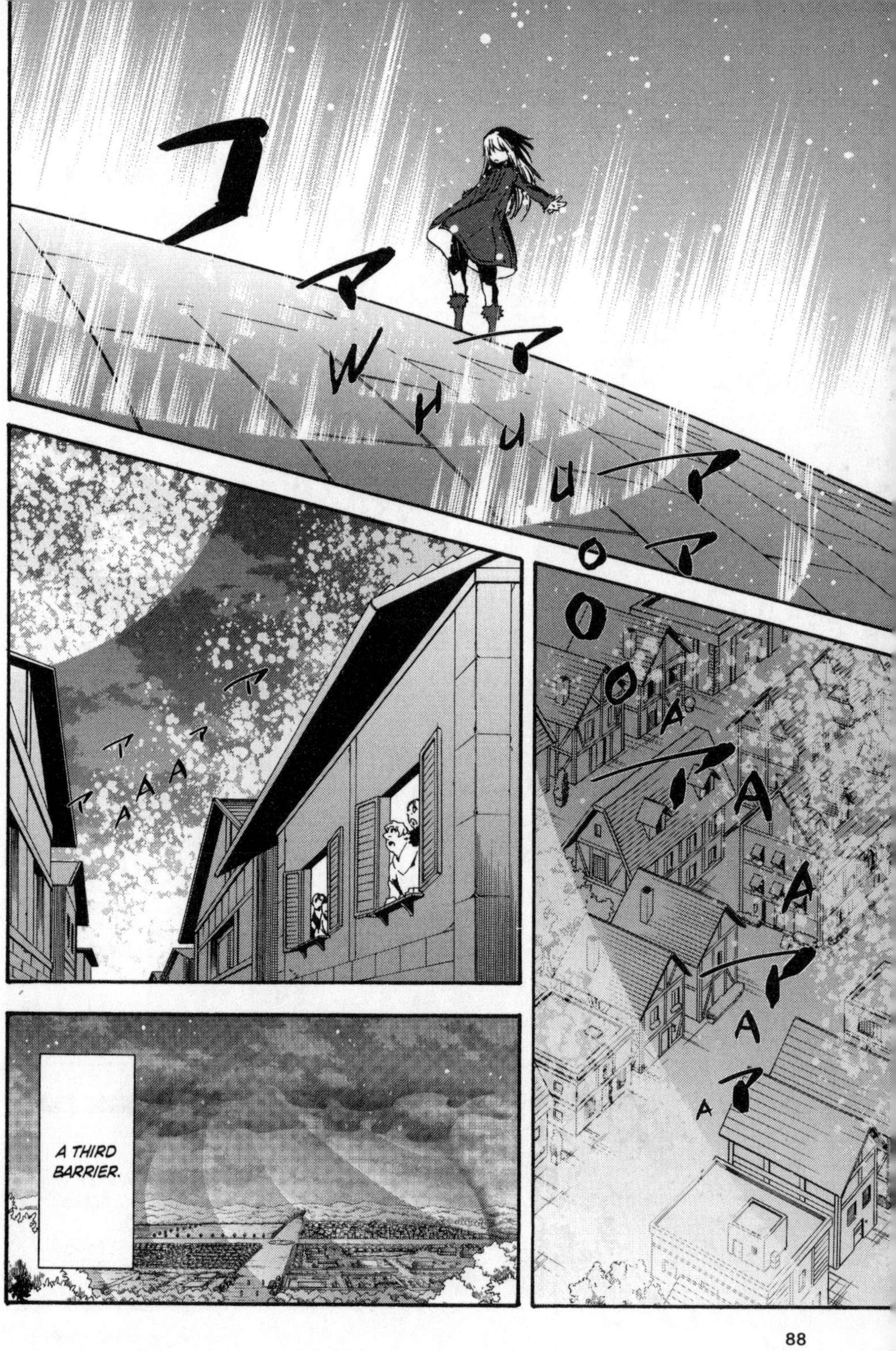

Whuuoooaaaaa
aaaa
A THIRD BARRIER.

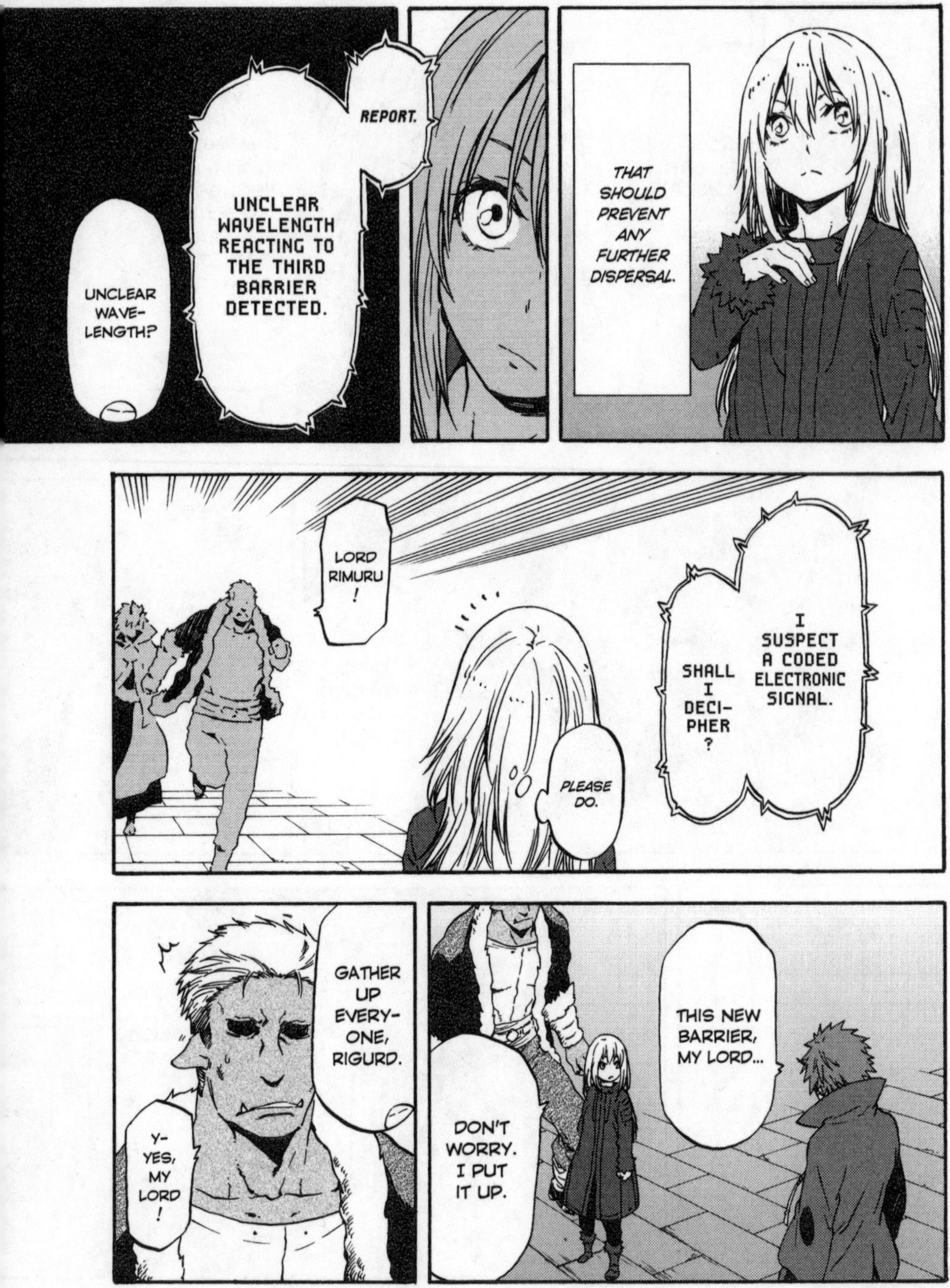
THAT SHOULD PREVENT ANY FURTHER DISPERSAL.
REPORT.
UNCLEAR WAVELENGTH REACTING TO THE THIRD BARRIER DETECTED.
UNCLEAR WAVE-LENGTH?
I SUSPECT A CODED ELECTRONIC SIGNAL.
SHALL I DECI-PHER?
PLEASE DO.
LORD RIMURU!
THIS NEW BARRIER, MY LORD...
DON'T WORRY. I PUT IT UP.
GATHER UP EVERY-ONE, RIGURD.
Y-YES, MY LORD!

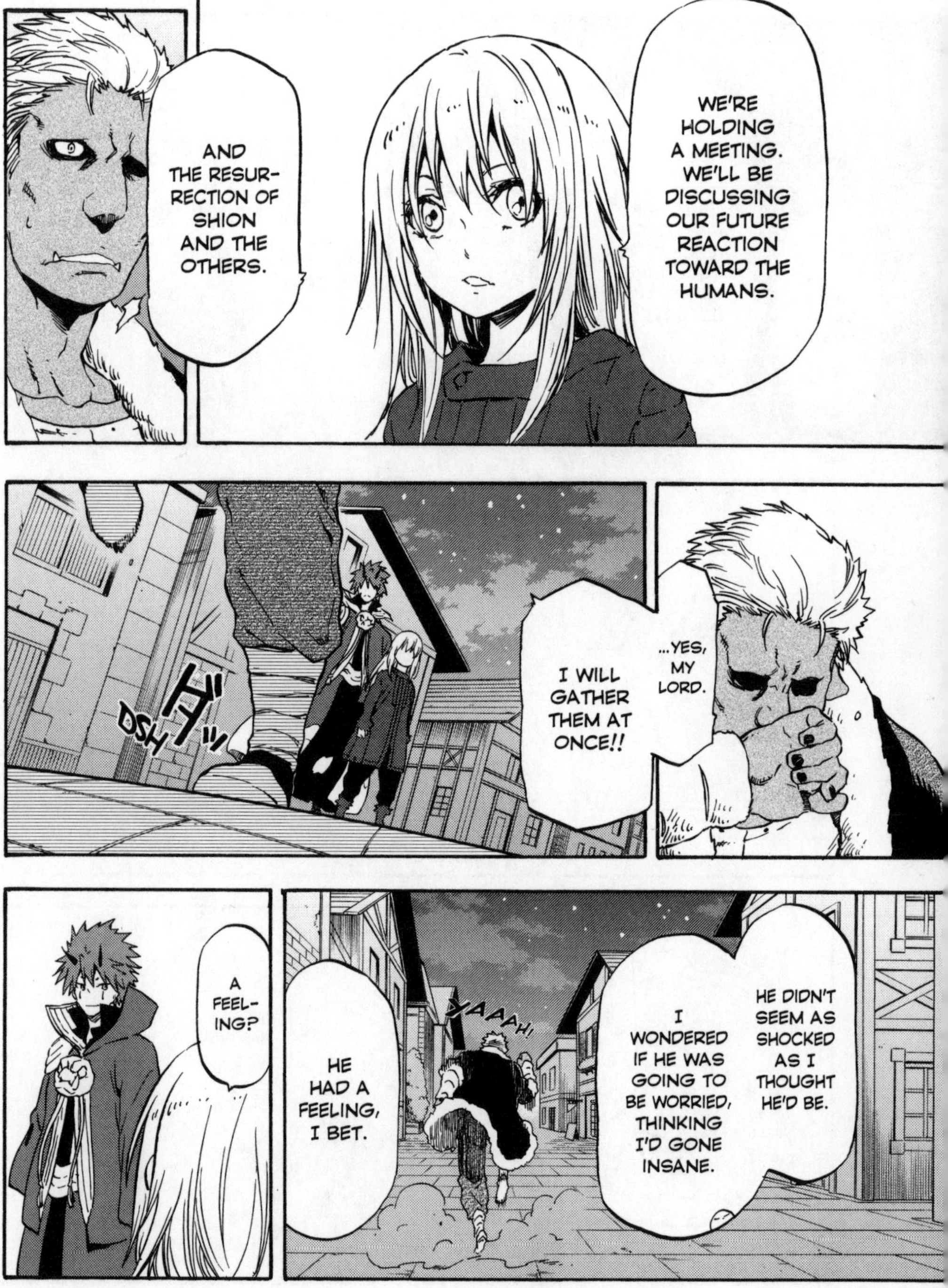
WE'RE HOLDING A MEETING. WE'LL BE DISCUSSING OUR FUTURE REACTION TOWARD THE HUMANS.
AND THE RESURRECTION OF SHION AND THE OTHERS.
...YES, MY LORD.
I WILL GATHER THEM AT ONCE!!
DSH
HE DIDN'T SEEM AS SHOCKED AS I THOUGHT HE'D BE.
I WONDERED IF HE WAS GOING TO BE WORRIED, THINKING I'D GONE INSANE.
YAAAH!
HE HAD A FEELING, I BET.
A FEELING?

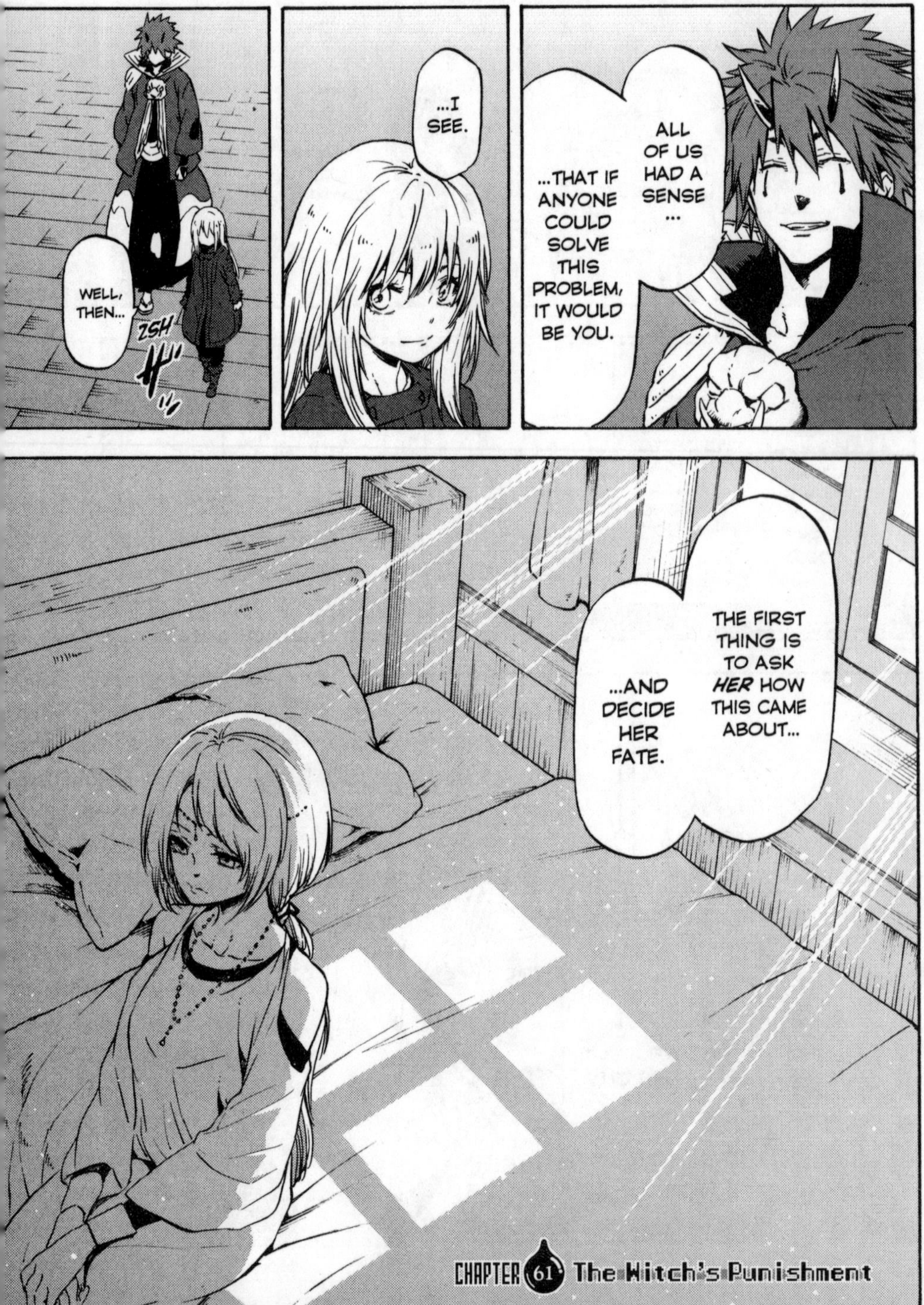
ALL OF US HAD A SENSE ...
...THAT IF ANYONE COULD SOLVE THIS PROBLEM, IT WOULD BE YOU.
...I SEE.
WELL, THEN...
ZSH
THE FIRST THING IS TO ASK *HER* HOW THIS CAME ABOUT...
...AND DECIDE HER FATE.
CHAPTER 61 The Witch's Punishment

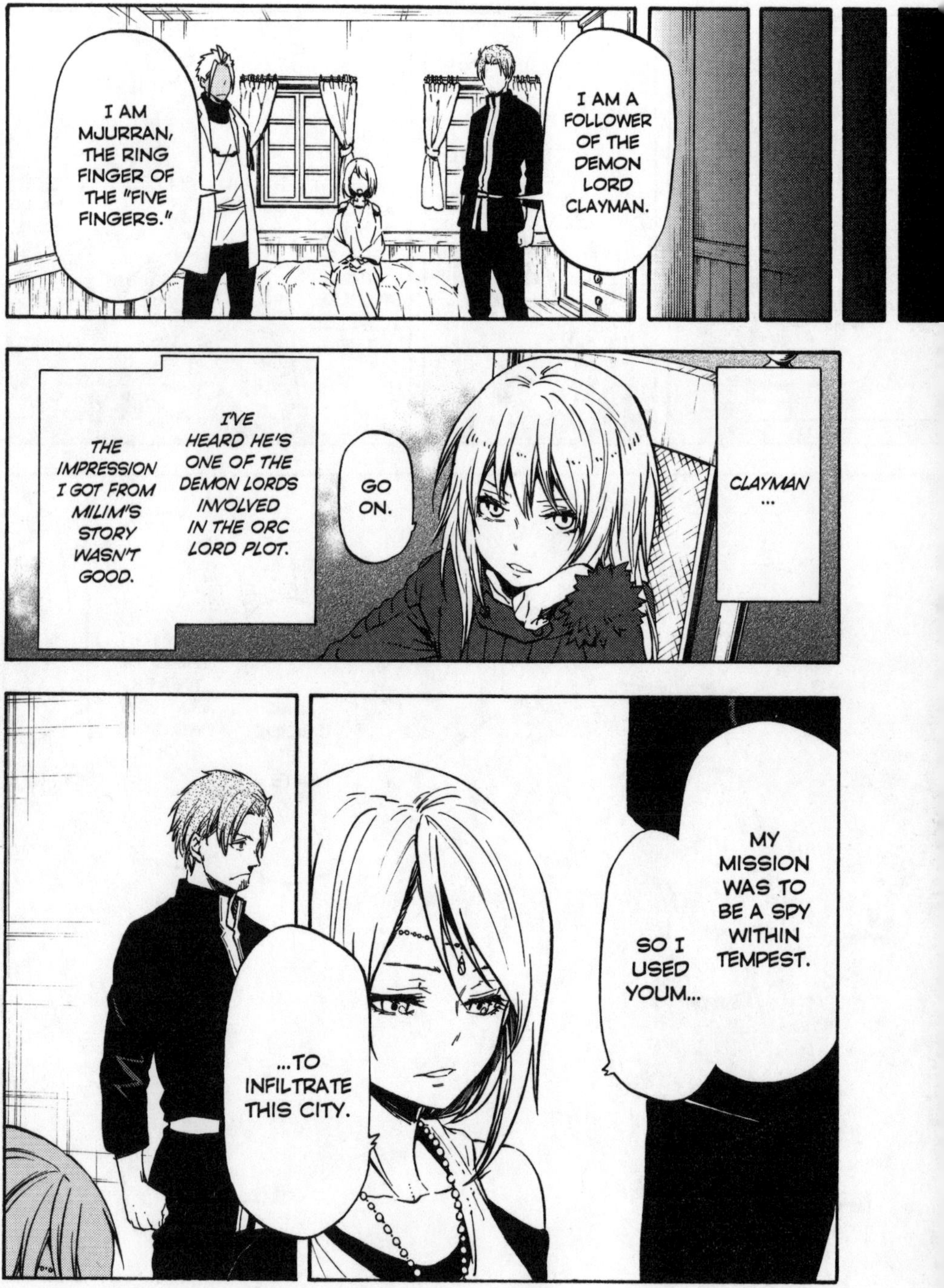
I AM A FOLLOWER OF THE DEMON LORD CLAYMAN.
I AM MJURRAN, THE RING FINGER OF THE "FIVE FINGERS."
CLAYMAN ...
GO ON.
I'VE HEARD HE'S ONE OF THE DEMON LORDS INVOLVED IN THE ORC LORD PLOT.
THE IMPRESSION I GOT FROM MILIM'S STORY WASN'T GOOD.
MY MISSION WAS TO BE A SPY WITHIN TEMPEST.
SO I USED YOUM...
...TO INFILTRATE THIS CITY.

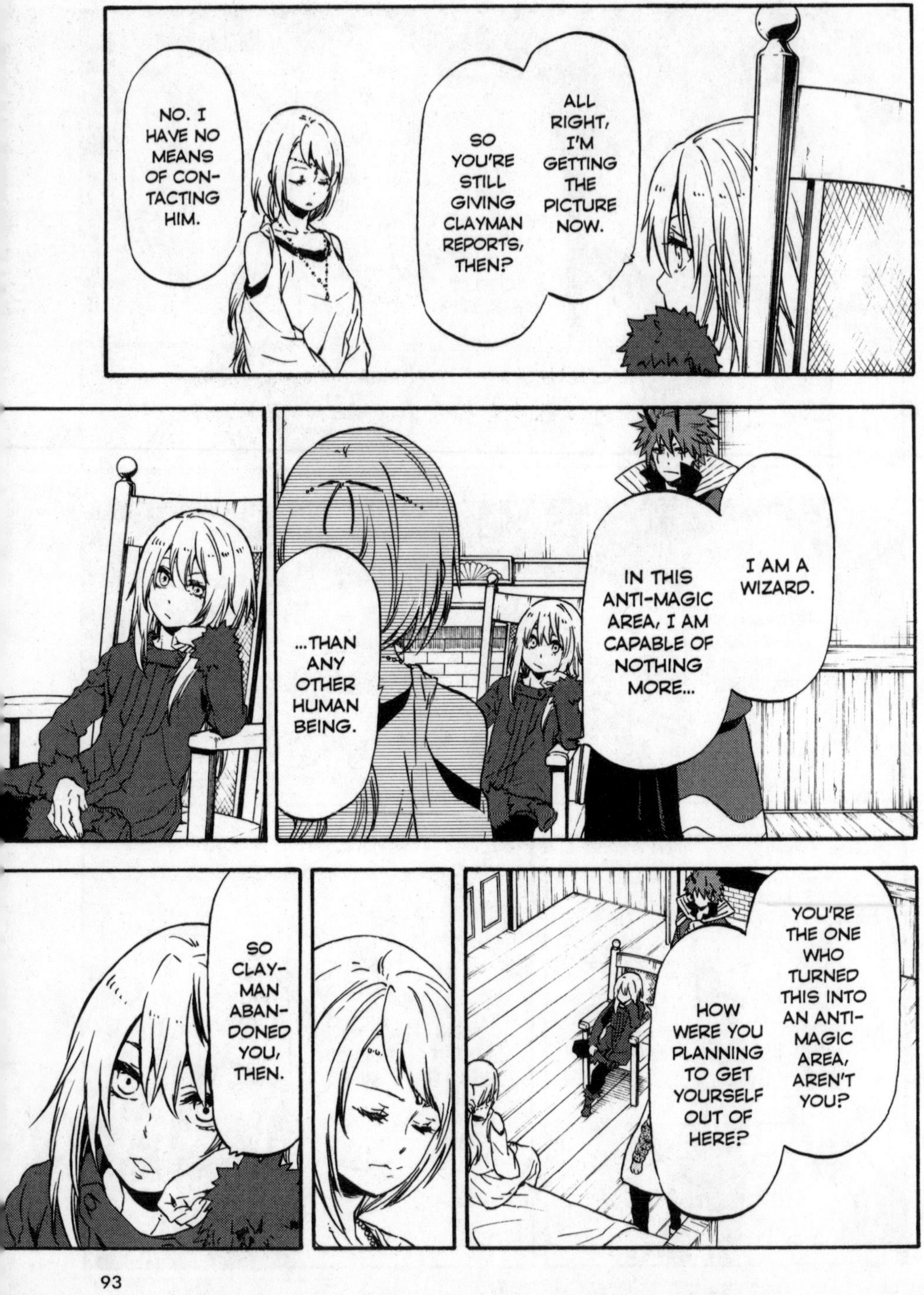
ALL RIGHT, I'M GETTING THE PICTURE NOW.
SO YOU'RE STILL GIVING CLAYMAN REPORTS, THEN?
NO. I HAVE NO MEANS OF CONTACTING HIM.
I AM A WIZARD.
IN THIS ANTI-MAGIC AREA, I AM CAPABLE OF NOTHING MORE...
...THAN ANY OTHER HUMAN BEING.
YOU'RE THE ONE WHO TURNED THIS INTO AN ANTI-MAGIC AREA, AREN'T YOU?
HOW WERE YOU PLANNING TO GET YOURSELF OUT OF HERE?
SO CLAYMAN ABANDONED YOU, THEN.

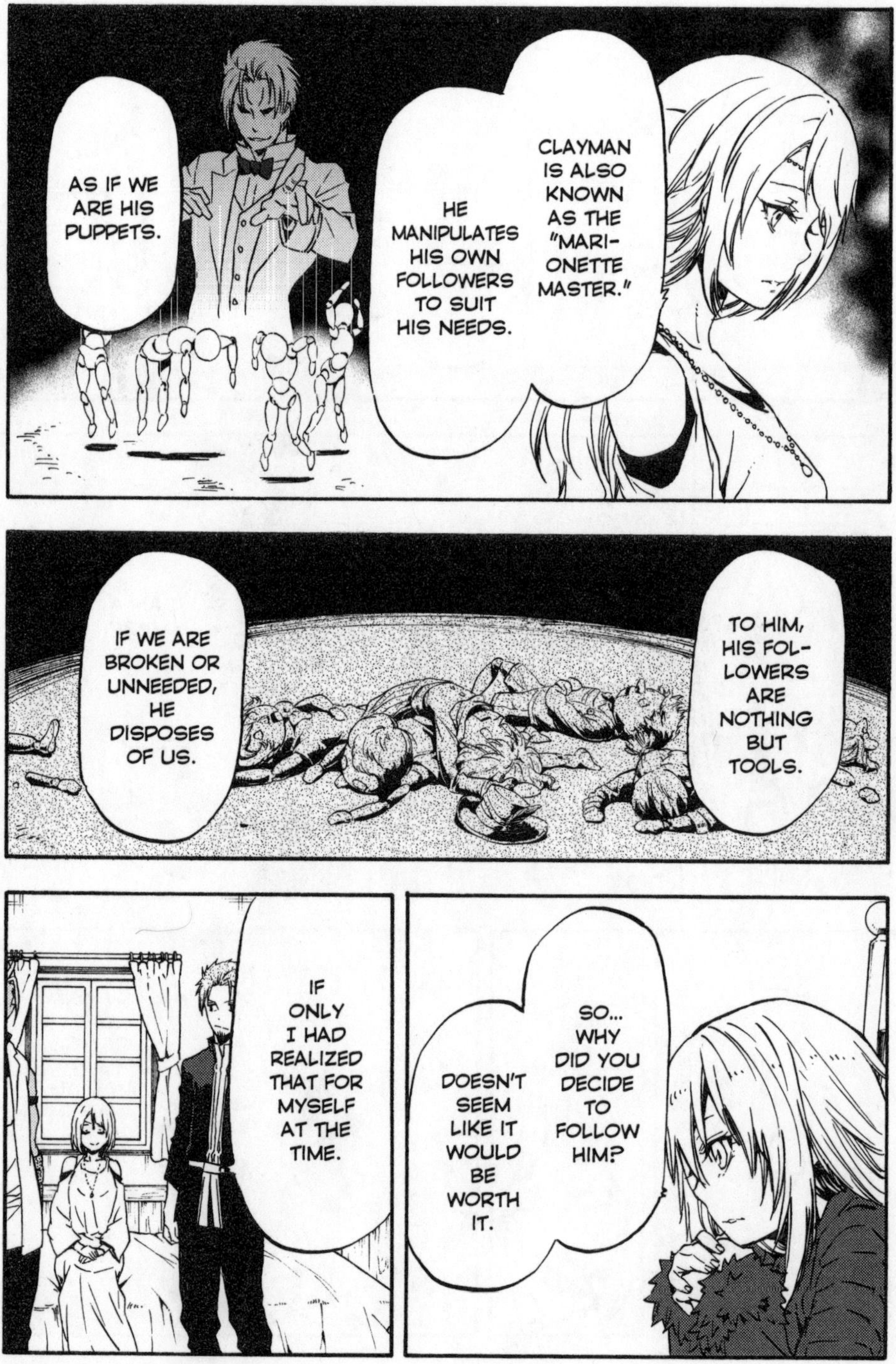
CLAYMAN IS ALSO KNOWN AS THE "MARI-ONETTE MASTER."
HE MANIPULATES HIS OWN FOLLOWERS TO SUIT HIS NEEDS.
AS IF WE ARE HIS PUPPETS.
TO HIM, HIS FOL-LOWERS ARE NOTHING BUT TOOLS.
IF WE ARE BROKEN OR UNNEEDED, HE DISPOSES OF US.
SO... WHY DID YOU DECIDE TO FOLLOW HIM?
DOESN'T SEEM LIKE IT WOULD BE WORTH IT.
IF ONLY I HAD REALIZED THAT FOR MYSELF AT THE TIME.

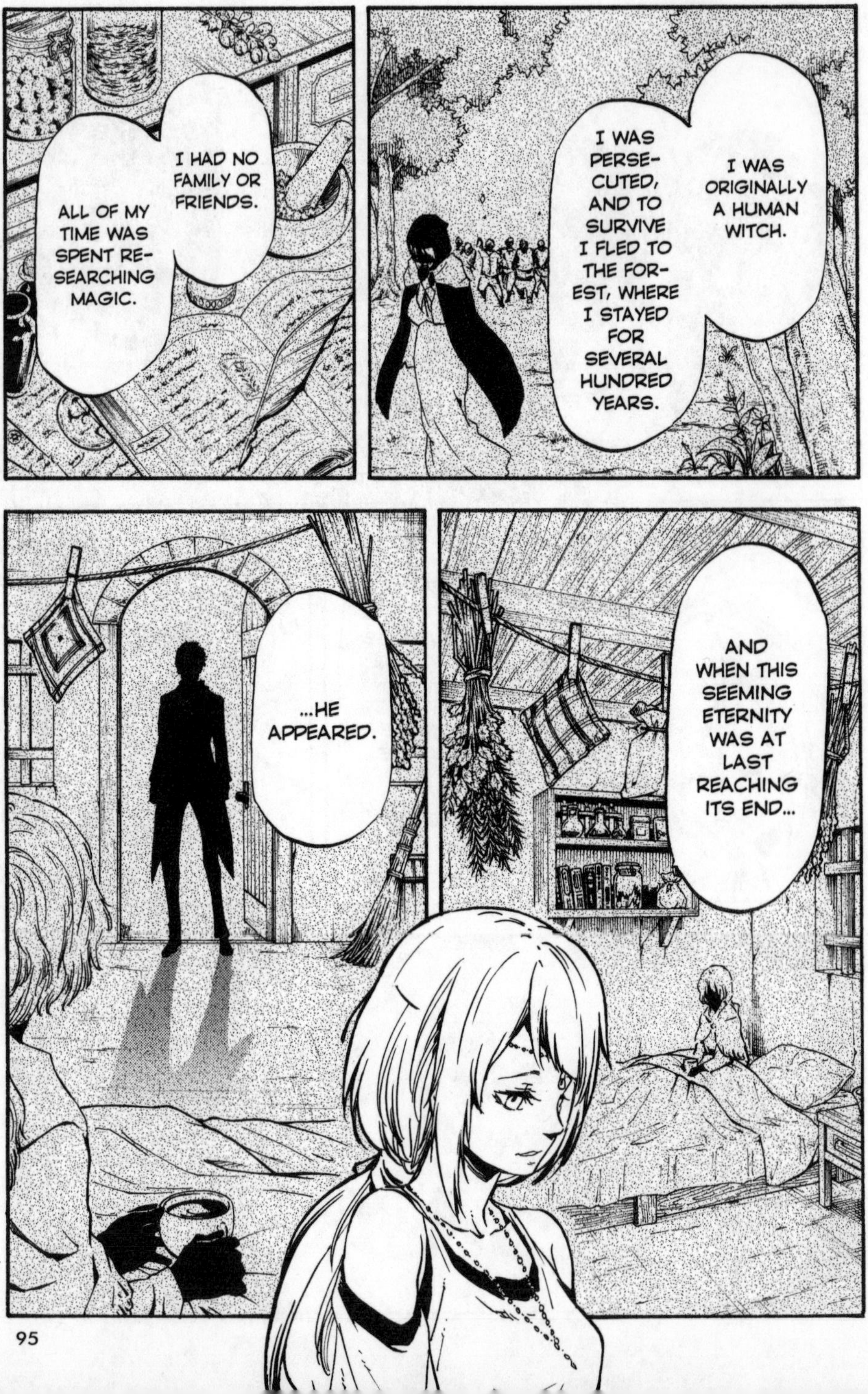
I WAS ORIGINALLY A HUMAN WITCH.
I WAS PERSE-CUTED, AND TO SURVIVE I FLED TO THE FOR-EST, WHERE I STAYED FOR SEVERAL HUNDRED YEARS.
I HAD NO FAMILY OR FRIENDS.
ALL OF MY TIME WAS SPENT RE-SEARCHING MAGIC.
AND WHEN THIS SEEMING ETERNITY WAS AT LAST REACHING ITS END...
...HE APPEARED.

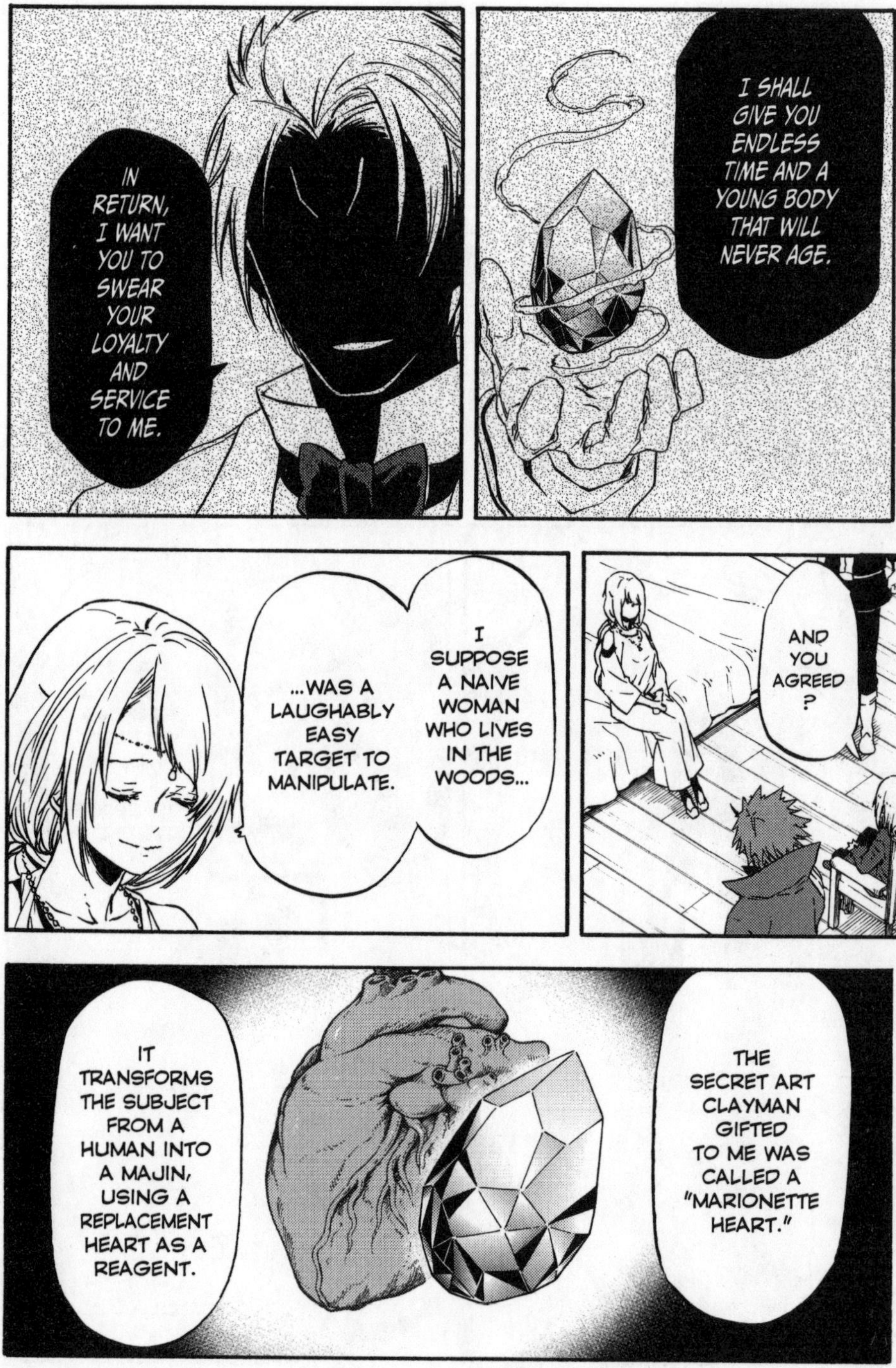
I SHALL GIVE YOU ENDLESS TIME AND A YOUNG BODY THAT WILL NEVER AGE.
IN RETURN, I WANT YOU TO SWEAR YOUR LOYALTY AND SERVICE TO ME.
AND YOU AGREED?
I SUPPOSE A NAIVE WOMAN WHO LIVES IN THE WOODS...
...WAS A LAUGHABLY EASY TARGET TO MANIPULATE.
THE SECRET ART CLAYMAN GIFTED TO ME WAS CALLED A "MARIONETTE HEART."
IT TRANSFORMS THE SUBJECT FROM A HUMAN INTO A MAJIN, USING A REPLACEMENT HEART AS A REAGENT.

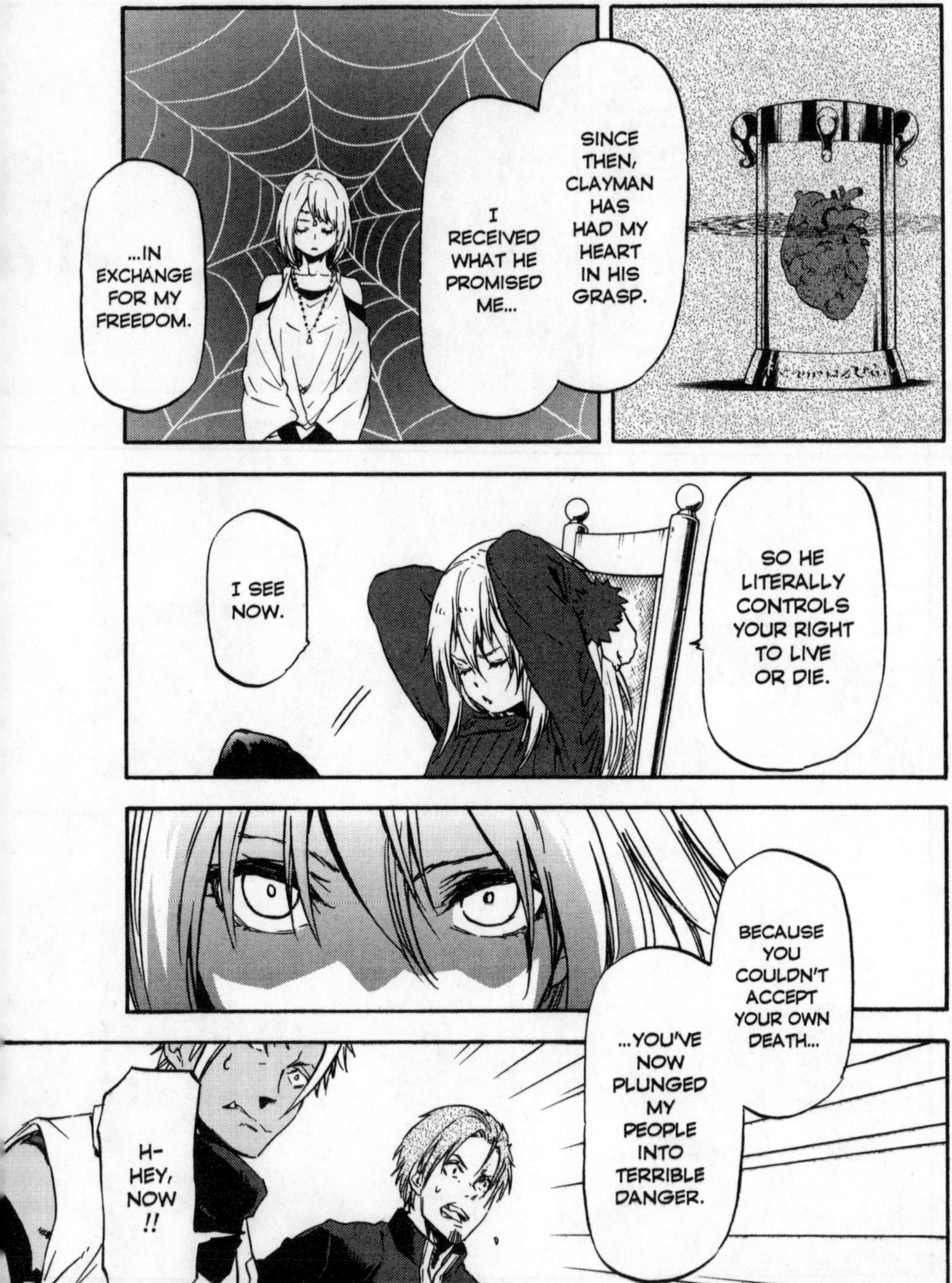
SINCE THEN, CLAYMAN HAS HAD MY HEART IN HIS GRASP.
I RECEIVED WHAT HE PROMISED ME...
...IN EXCHANGE FOR MY FREEDOM.
SO HE LITERALLY CONTROLS YOUR RIGHT TO LIVE OR DIE.
I SEE NOW.
BECAUSE YOU COULDN'T ACCEPT YOUR OWN DEATH...
...YOU'VE NOW PLUNGED MY PEOPLE INTO TERRIBLE DANGER.
H-HEY, NOW!!

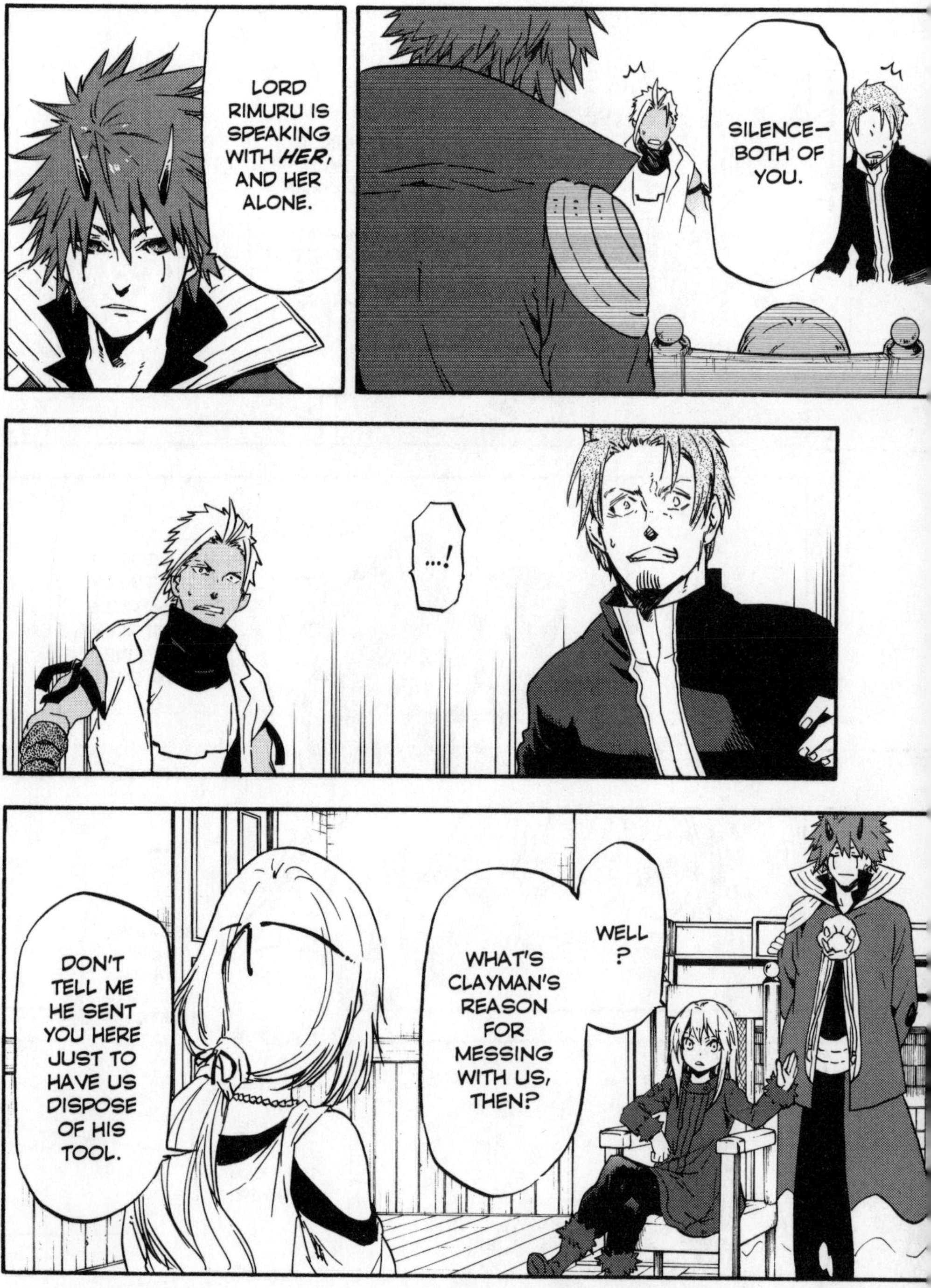
SILENCE—BOTH OF YOU.
LORD RIMURU IS SPEAKING WITH *HER*, AND HER ALONE.
...!
WELL?
WHAT'S CLAYMAN'S REASON FOR MESSING WITH US, THEN?
DON'T TELL ME HE SENT YOU HERE JUST TO HAVE US DISPOSE OF HIS TOOL.

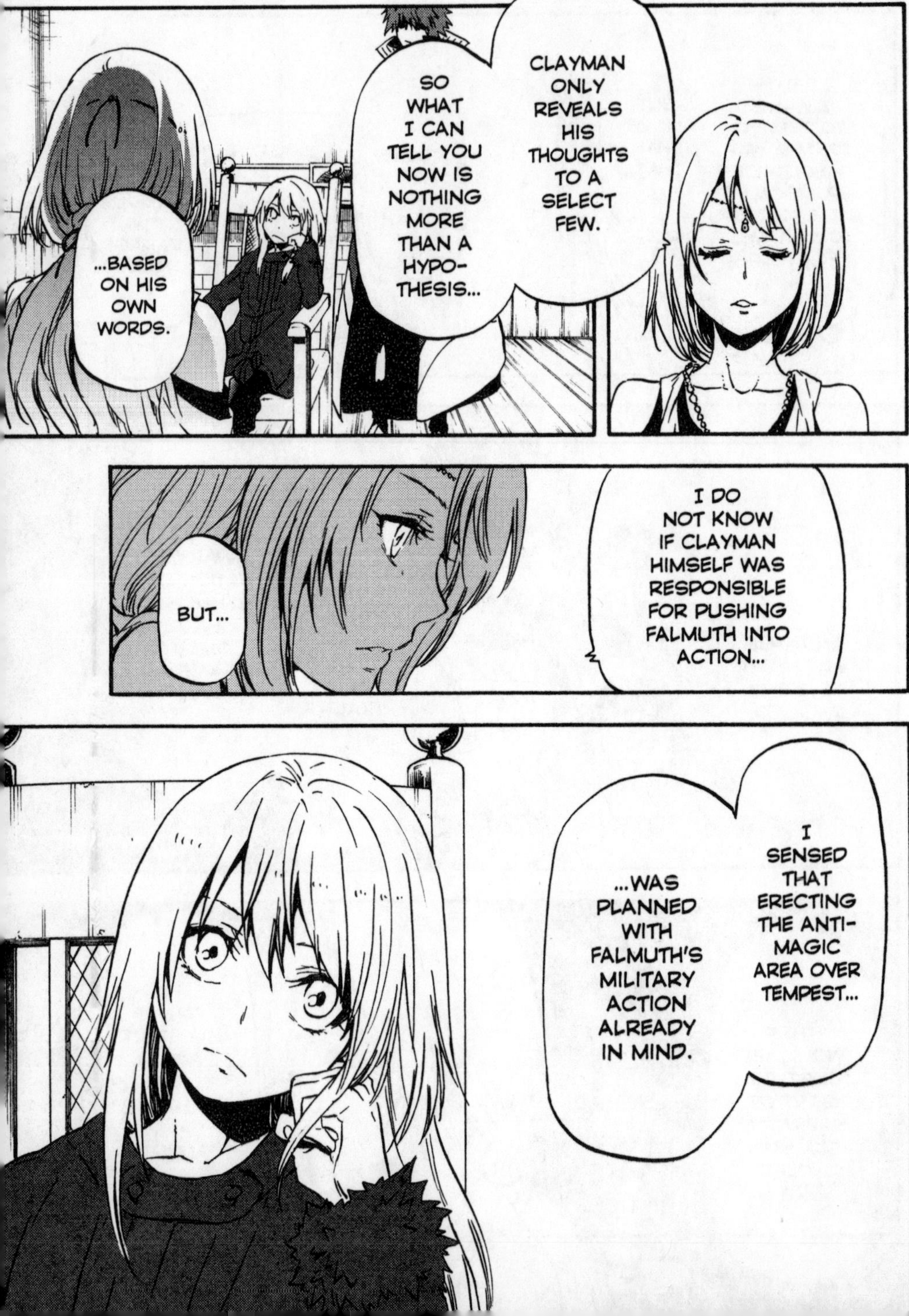
CLAYMAN ONLY REVEALS HIS THOUGHTS TO A SELECT FEW.
SO WHAT I CAN TELL YOU NOW IS NOTHING MORE THAN A HYPO-THESIS...
...BASED ON HIS OWN WORDS.
I DO NOT KNOW IF CLAYMAN HIMSELF WAS RESPONSIBLE FOR PUSHING FALMUTH INTO ACTION...
BUT...
I SENSED THAT ERECTING THE ANTI-MAGIC AREA OVER TEMPEST...
...WAS PLANNED WITH FALMUTH'S MILITARY ACTION ALREADY IN MIND.

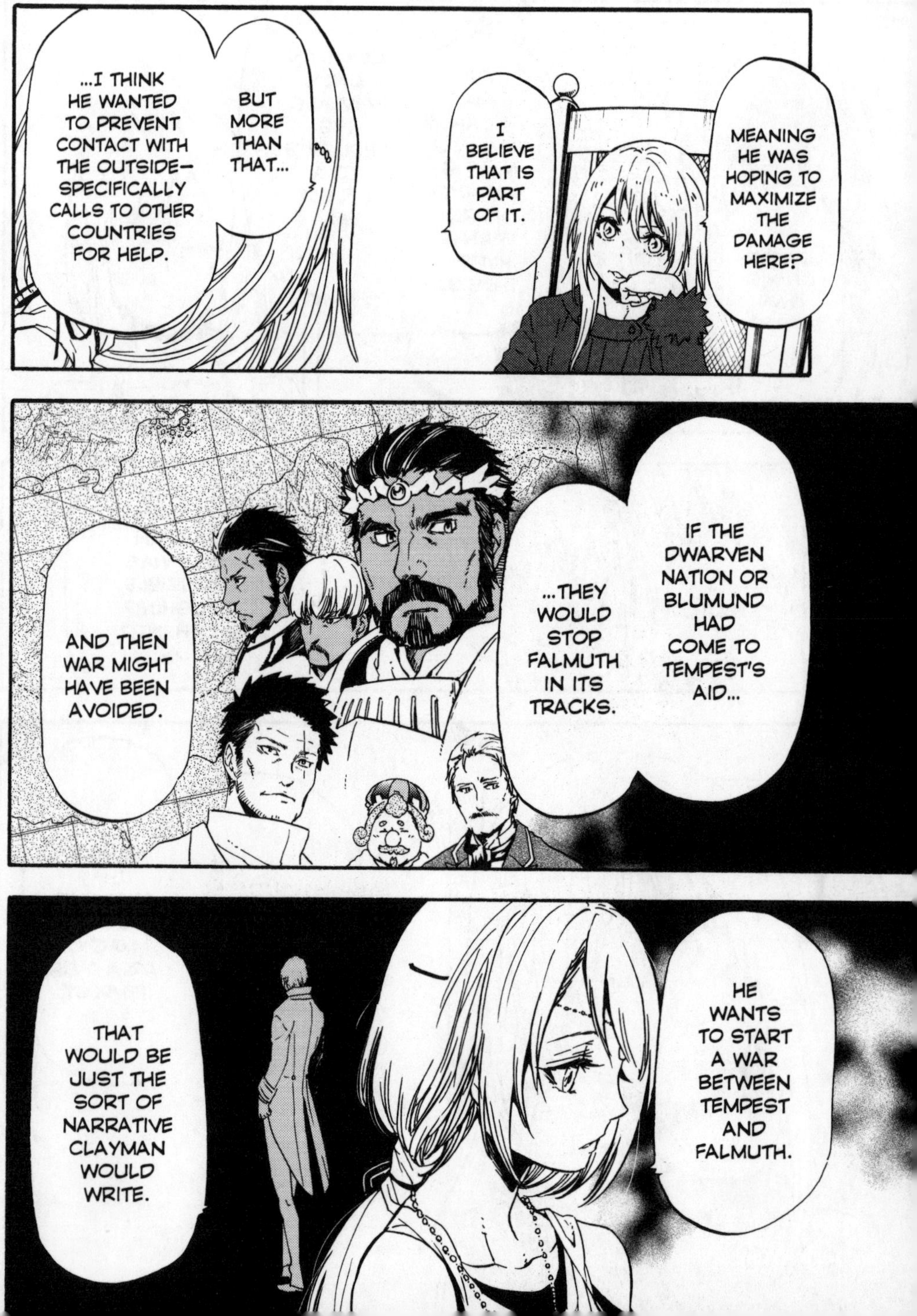
MEANING HE WAS HOPING TO MAXIMIZE THE DAMAGE HERE?
I BELIEVE THAT IS PART OF IT.
BUT MORE THAN THAT...
...I THINK HE WANTED TO PREVENT CONTACT WITH THE OUTSIDE—SPECIFICALLY CALLS TO OTHER COUNTRIES FOR HELP.
IF THE DWARVEN NATION OR BLUMUND HAD COME TO TEMPEST'S AID...
...THEY WOULD STOP FALMUTH IN ITS TRACKS.
AND THEN WAR MIGHT HAVE BEEN AVOIDED.
HE WANTS TO START A WAR BETWEEN TEMPEST AND FALMUTH.
THAT WOULD BE JUST THE SORT OF NARRATIVE CLAYMAN WOULD WRITE.

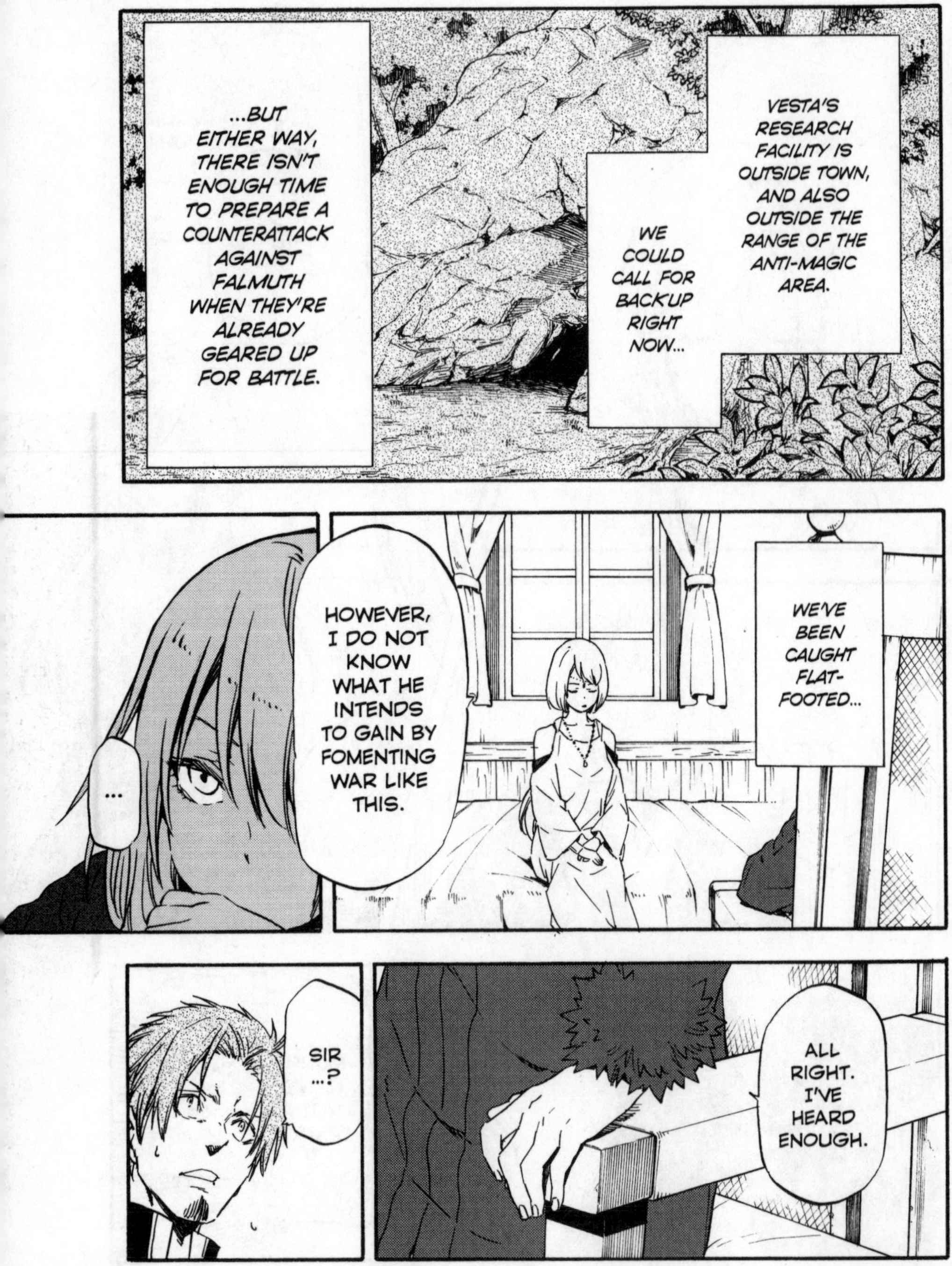
VESTA'S RESEARCH FACILITY IS OUTSIDE TOWN, AND ALSO OUTSIDE THE RANGE OF THE ANTI-MAGIC AREA.
WE COULD CALL FOR BACKUP RIGHT NOW...
...BUT EITHER WAY, THERE ISN'T ENOUGH TIME TO PREPARE A COUNTERATTACK AGAINST FALMUTH WHEN THEY'RE ALREADY GEARED UP FOR BATTLE.
WE'VE BEEN CAUGHT FLAT-FOOTED...
HOWEVER, I DO NOT KNOW WHAT HE INTENDS TO GAIN BY FOMENTING WAR LIKE THIS.
...
ALL RIGHT. I'VE HEARD ENOUGH.
SIR ...?

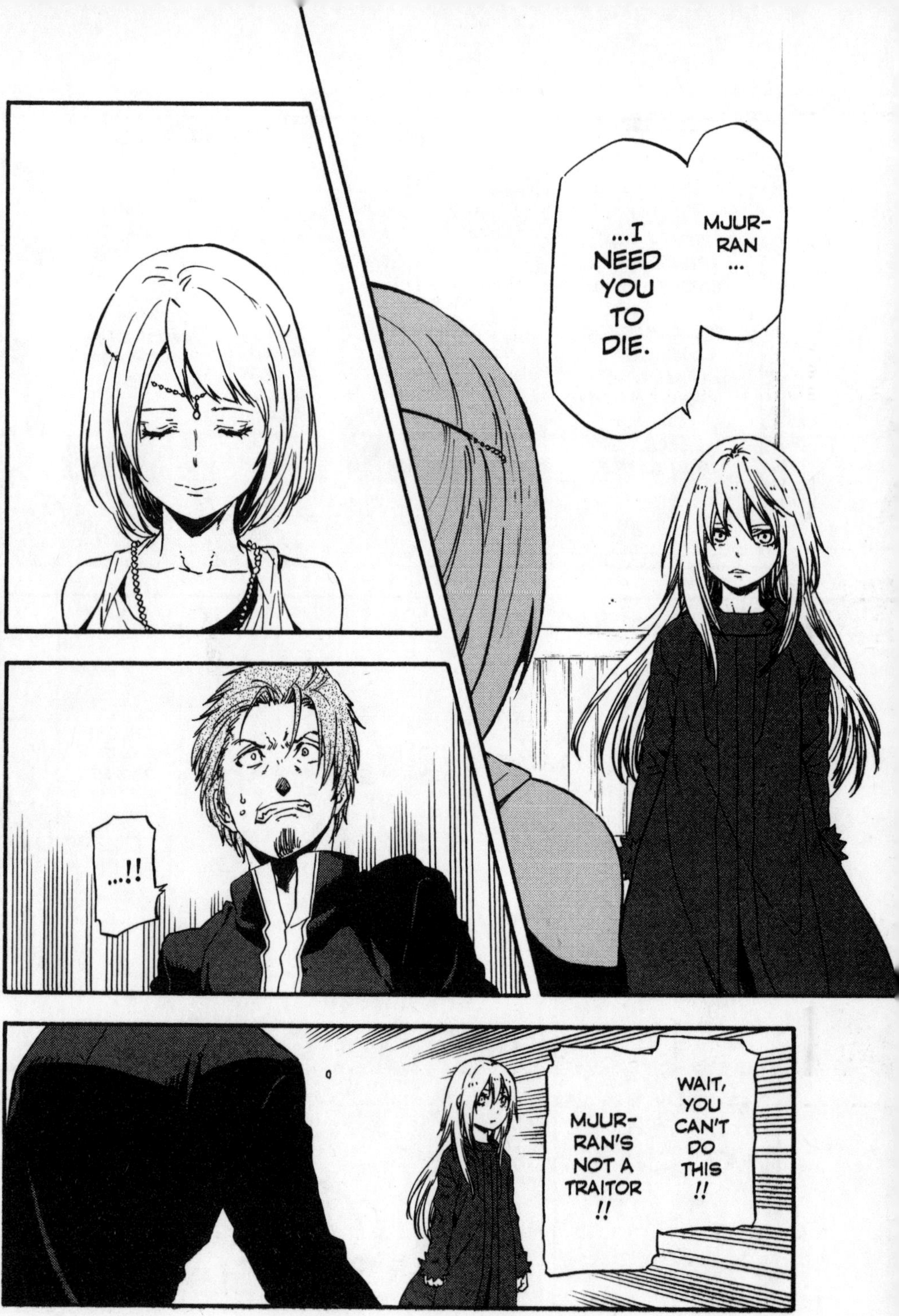
MJUR-RAN...
...I NEED YOU TO DIE.
...!!
WAIT, YOU CAN'T DO THIS!!
MJUR-RAN'S NOT A TRAITOR!!

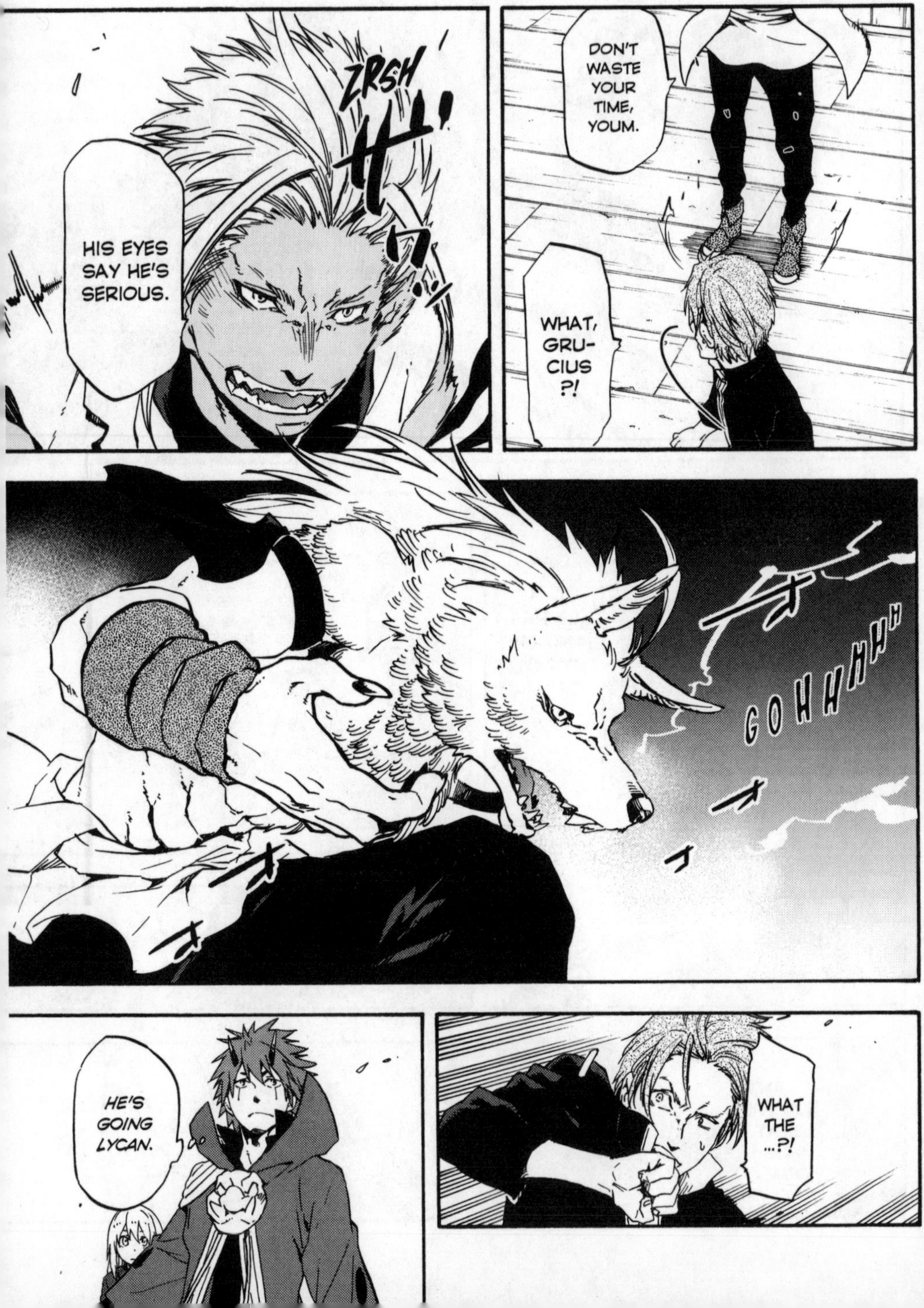
DON'T WASTE YOUR TIME, YOUM.
WHAT, GRU-CIUS ?!
ZRSH
HIS EYES SAY HE'S SERIOUS.
GOHHHHHH
WHAT THE ...?!
HE'S GOING LYCAN.

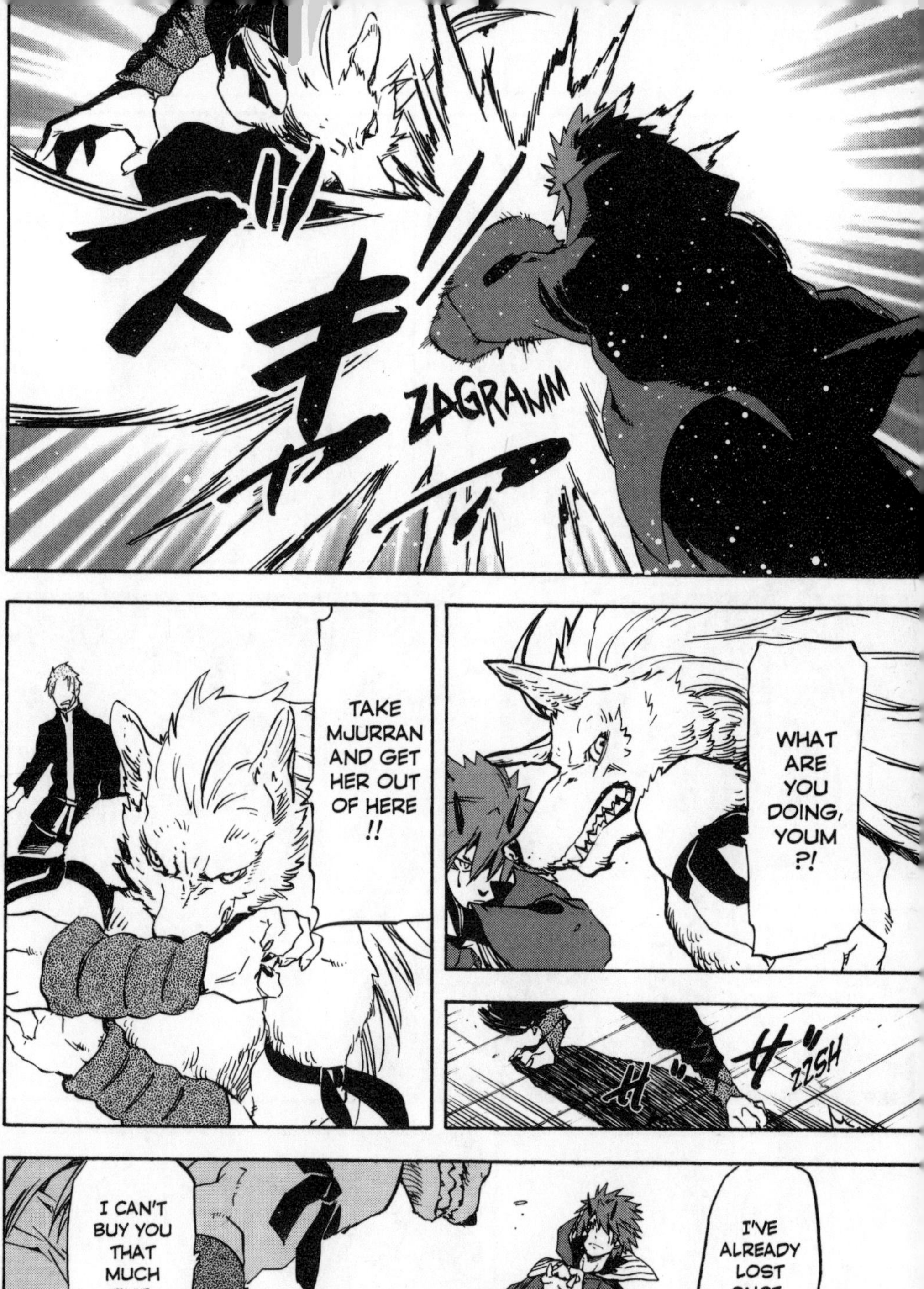
ZAGRAMM
WHAT ARE YOU DOING, YOUM ?!
ZZSH
TAKE MJURRAN AND GET HER OUT OF HERE !!
I'VE ALREADY LOST ONCE...
I CAN'T BUY YOU THAT MUCH TIME.

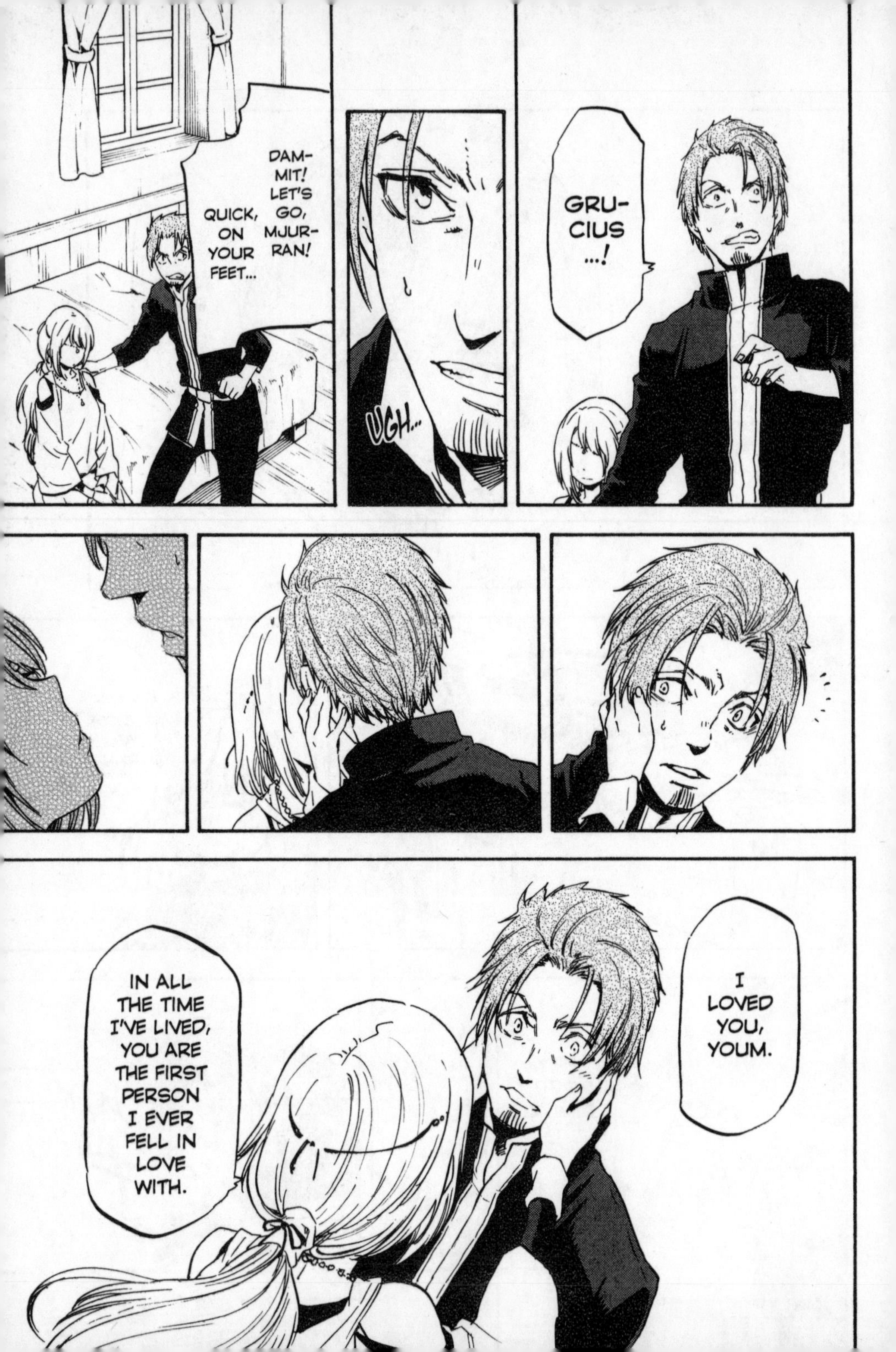
GRU-CIUS ...!
UGH...
DAM-MIT! LET'S GO, MJUR-RAN!
QUICK, ON YOUR FEET...
I LOVED YOU, YOUM.
IN ALL THE TIME I'VE LIVED, YOU ARE THE FIRST PERSON I EVER FELL IN LOVE WITH.

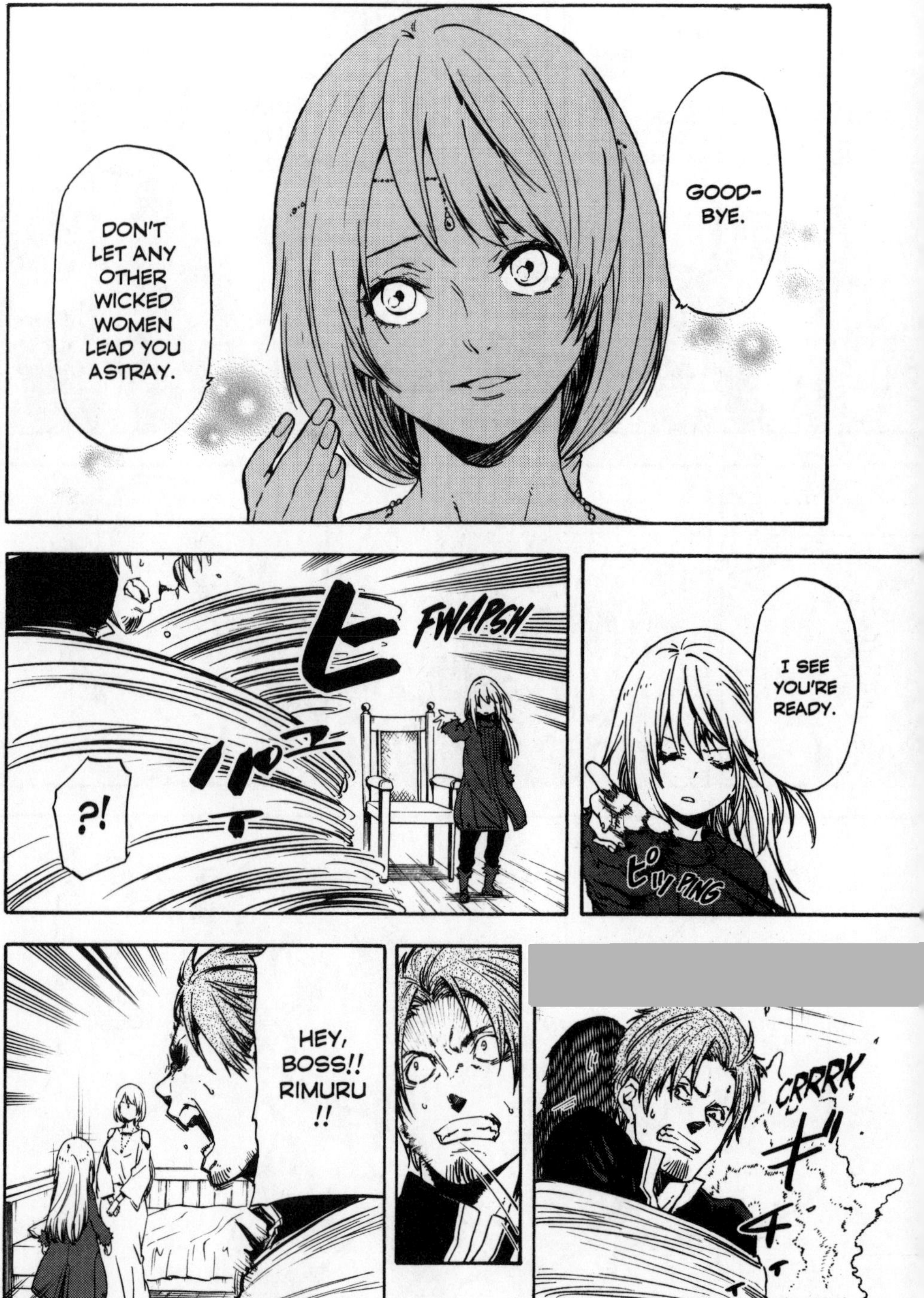
GOOD-BYE.
DON'T LET ANY OTHER WICKED WOMEN LEAD YOU ASTRAY.
I SEE YOU'RE READY.
PING
FWAPSH
?!
CRRRK
HEY, BOSS!! RIMURU!!

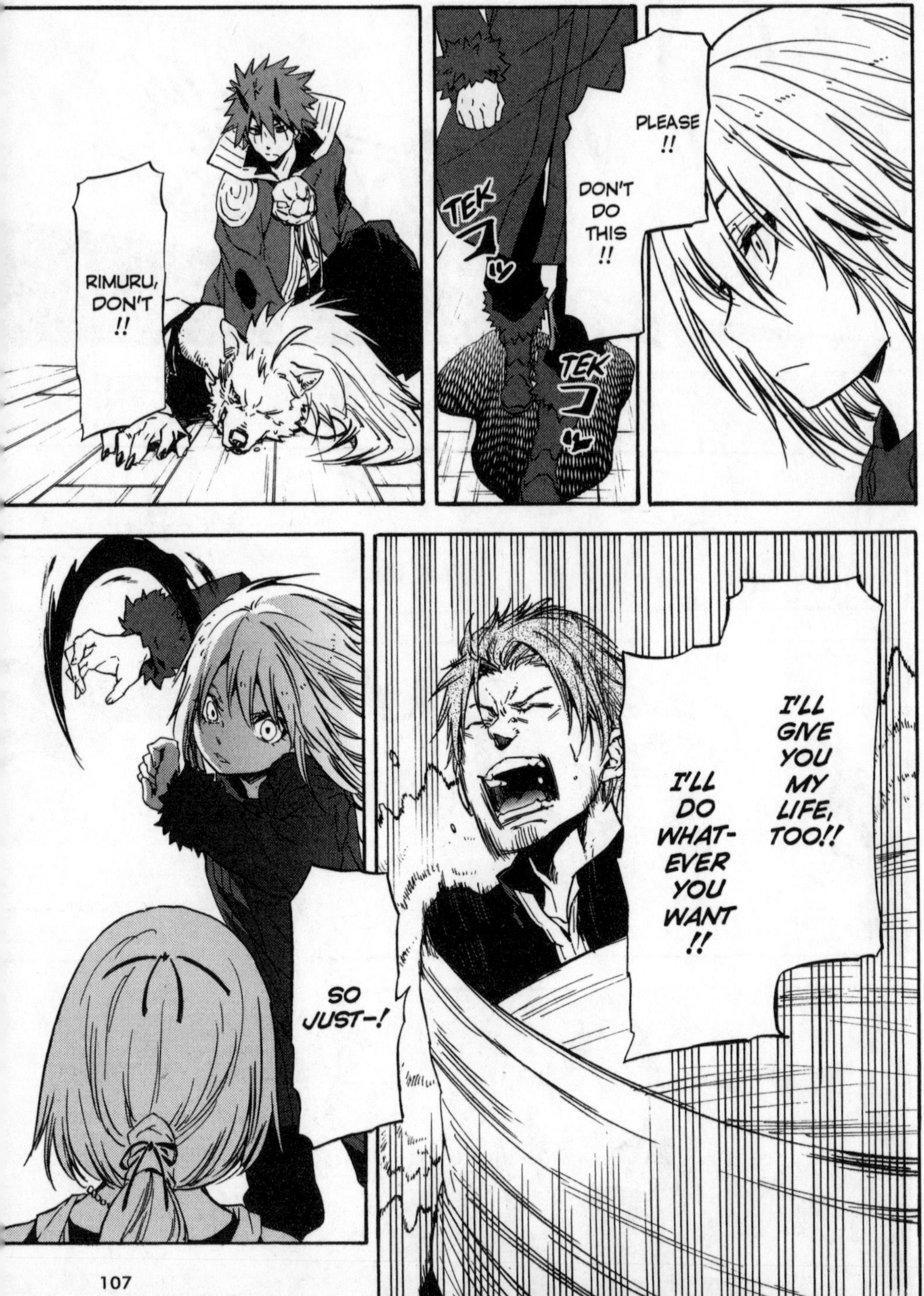
PLEASE!!
DON'T DO THIS!!
TEK
TEK
RIMURU, DON'T!!
I'LL GIVE YOU MY LIFE, TOO!!
I'LL DO WHAT-EVER YOU WANT!!
SO JUST-!

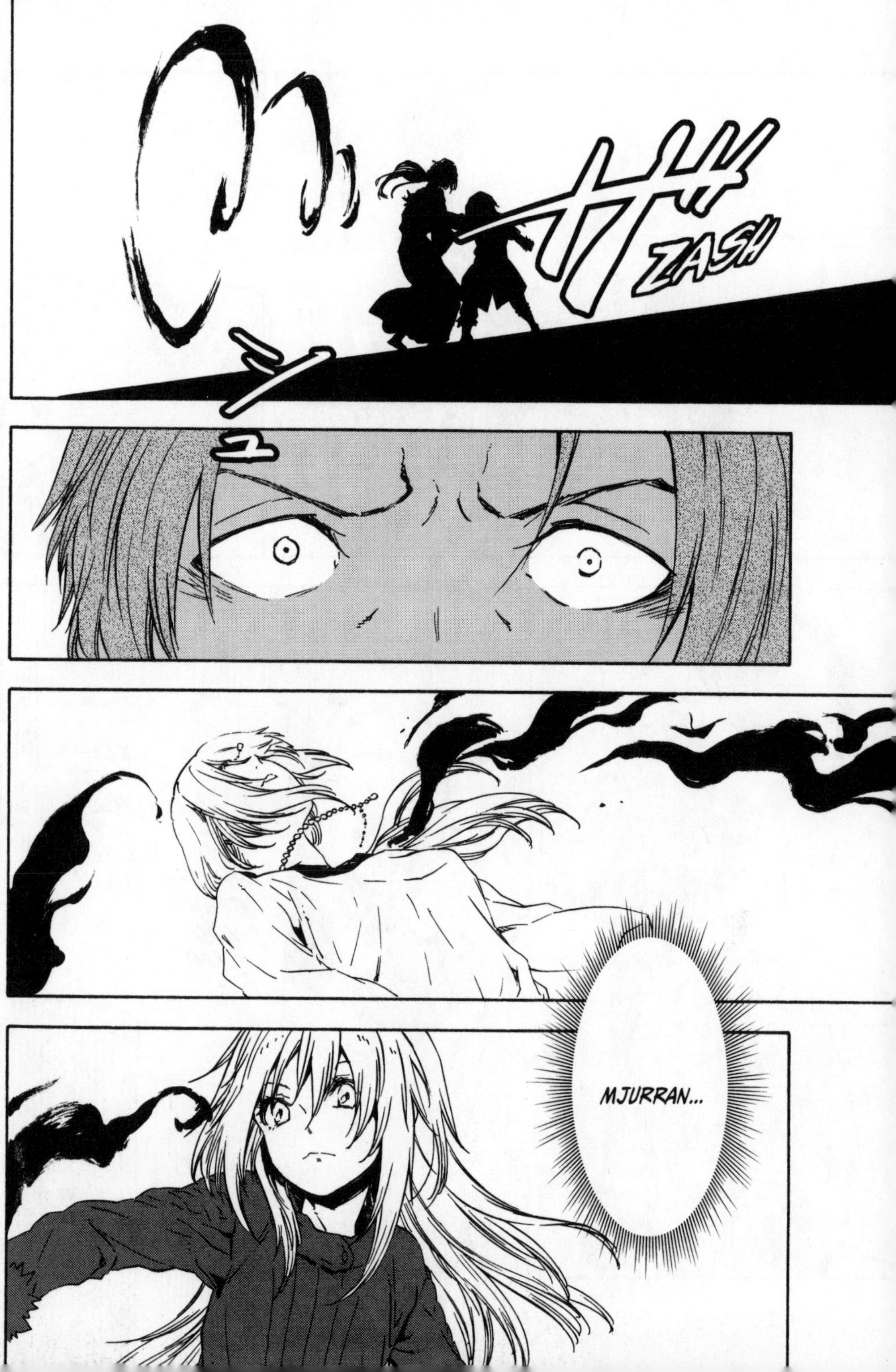
ZASH
MJURRAN...

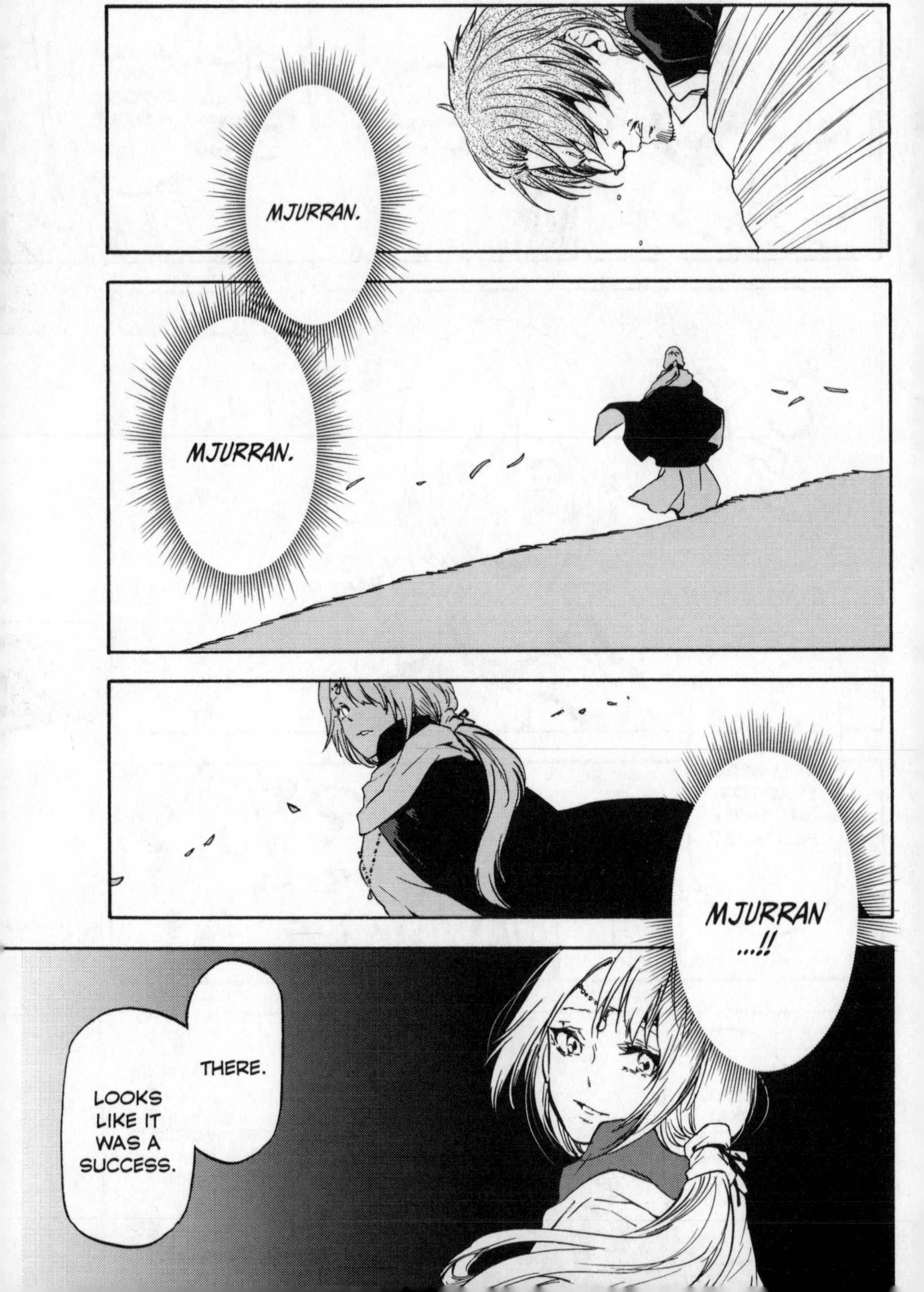
MJURRAN.
MJURRAN.
MJURRAN ...!!
THERE.
LOOKS LIKE IT WAS A SUCCESS.

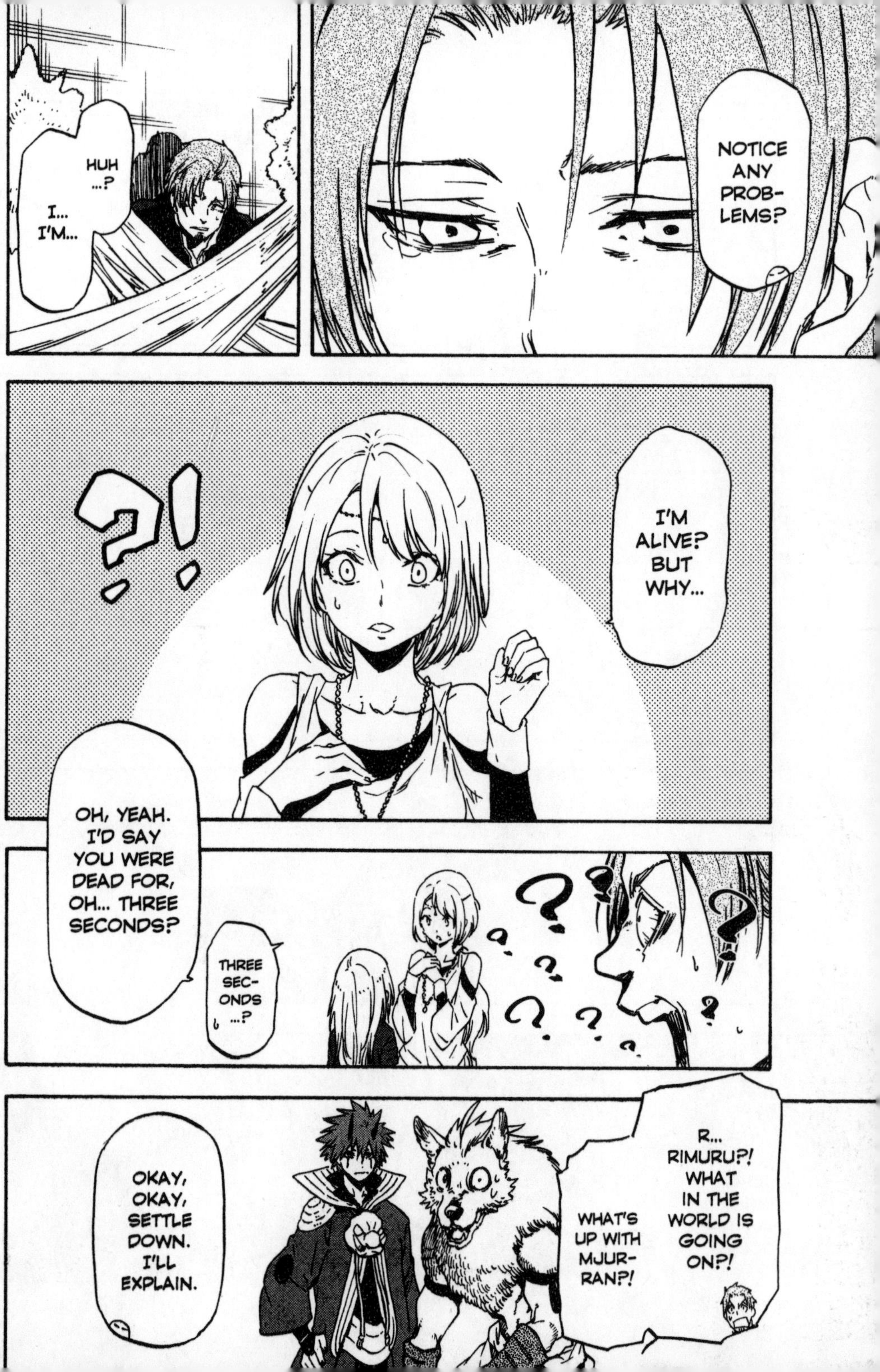
NOTICE ANY PROB-LEMS?
HUH ...?
I... I'M...
I'M ALIVE? BUT WHY...
?!
OH, YEAH. I'D SAY YOU WERE DEAD FOR, OH... THREE SECONDS?
THREE SEC-ONDS ...?
R... RIMURU?! WHAT IN THE WORLD IS GOING ON?!
WHAT'S UP WITH MJUR-RAN?!
OKAY, OKAY, SETTLE DOWN. I'LL EXPLAIN.

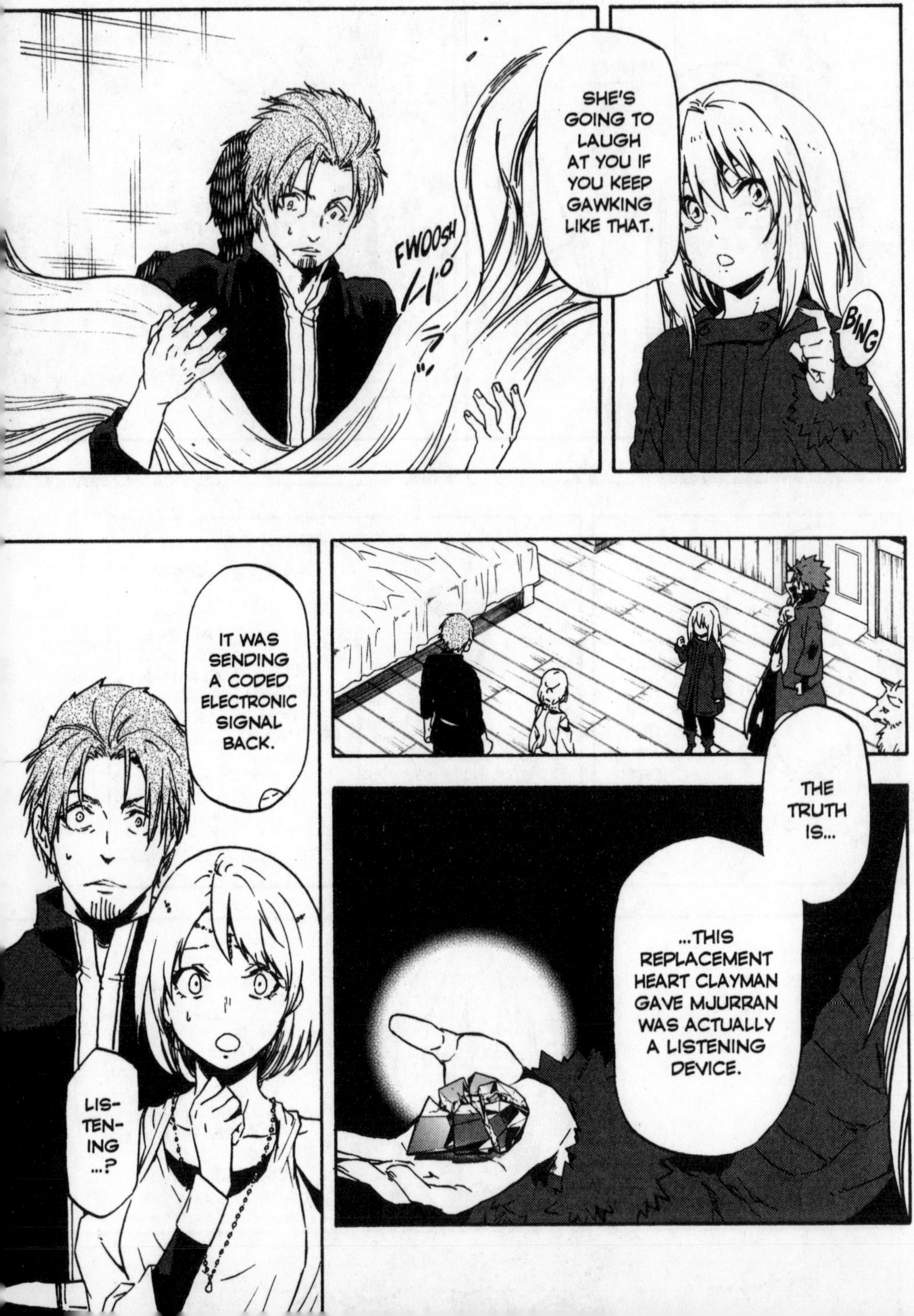
SHE'S GOING TO LAUGH AT YOU IF YOU KEEP GAWKING LIKE THAT.
BING
FWOOSH
THE TRUTH IS...
...THIS REPLACEMENT HEART CLAYMAN GAVE MJURRAN WAS ACTUALLY A LISTENING DEVICE.
IT WAS SENDING A CODED ELECTRONIC SIGNAL BACK.
LIS-TEN-ING ...?

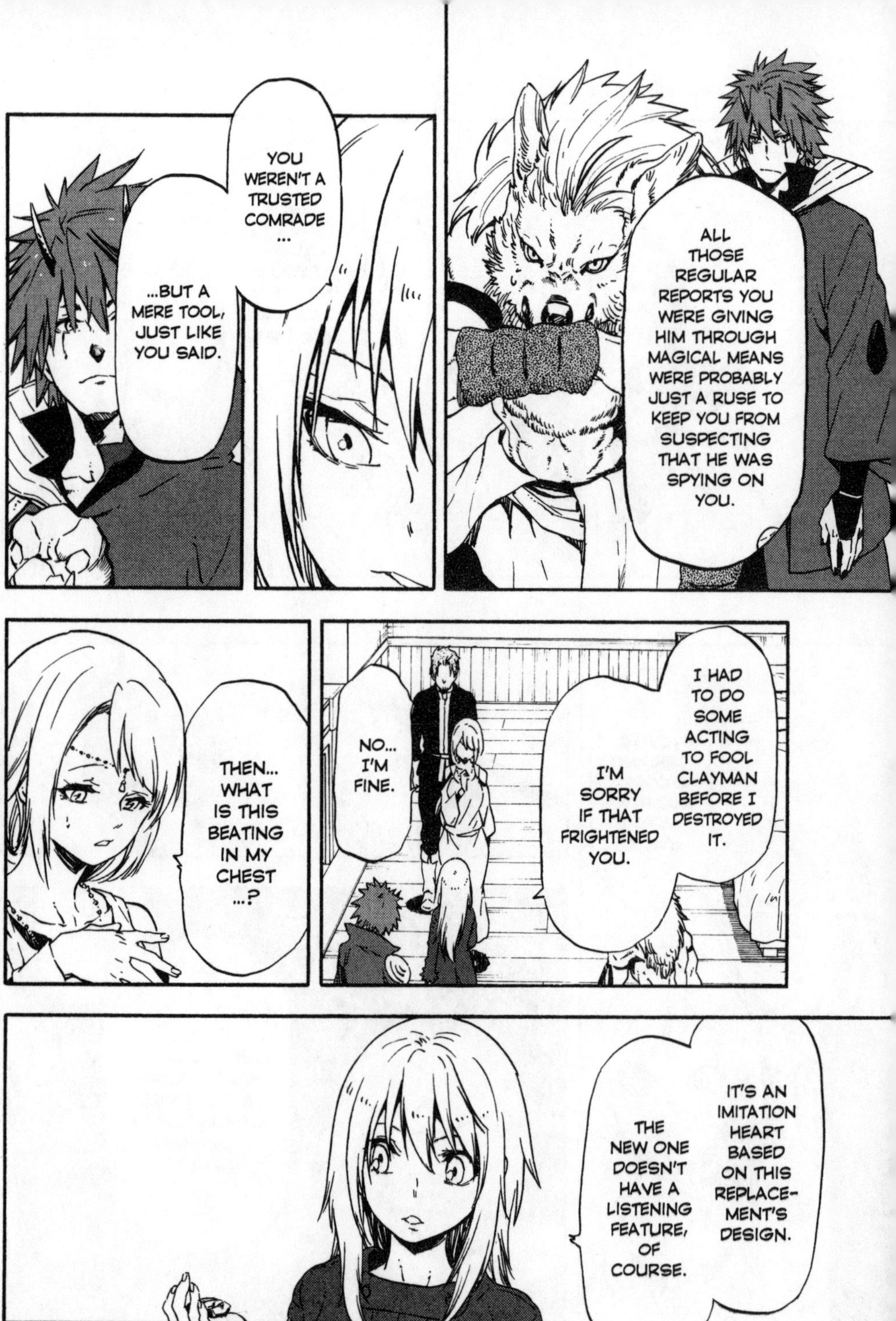
ALL THOSE REGULAR REPORTS YOU WERE GIVING HIM THROUGH MAGICAL MEANS WERE PROBABLY JUST A RUSE TO KEEP YOU FROM SUSPECTING THAT HE WAS SPYING ON YOU.
YOU WEREN'T A TRUSTED COMRADE ...
...BUT A MERE TOOL, JUST LIKE YOU SAID.
I HAD TO DO SOME ACTING TO FOOL CLAYMAN BEFORE I DESTROYED IT.
I'M SORRY IF THAT FRIGHTENED YOU.
NO... I'M FINE.
THEN... WHAT IS THIS BEATING IN MY CHEST ...?
IT'S AN IMITATION HEART BASED ON THIS REPLACEMENT'S DESIGN.
THE NEW ONE DOESN'T HAVE A LISTENING FEATURE, OF COURSE.

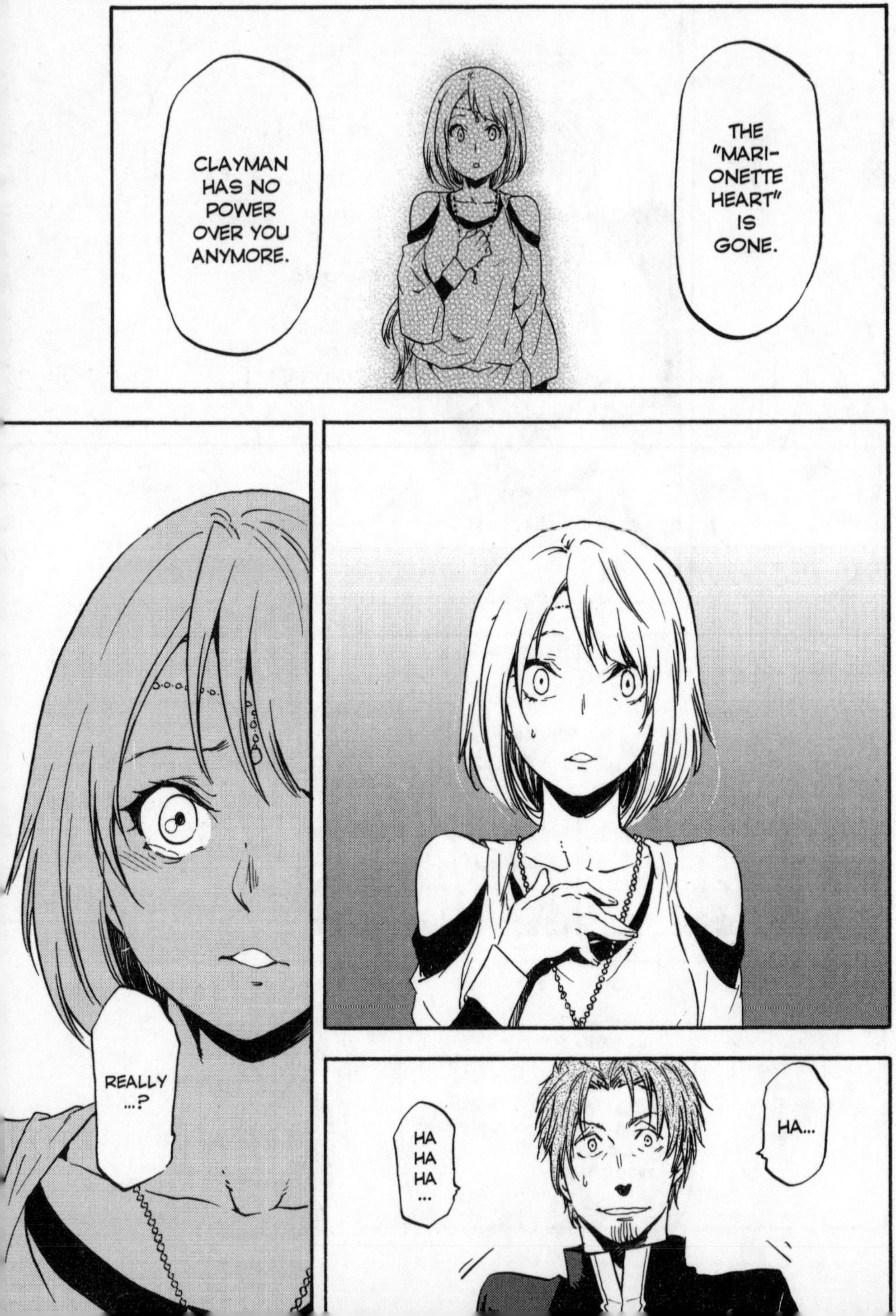
THE "MARI-ONETTE HEART" IS GONE.
CLAYMAN HAS NO POWER OVER YOU ANYMORE.
HA...
HA HA HA ...
REALLY ...?

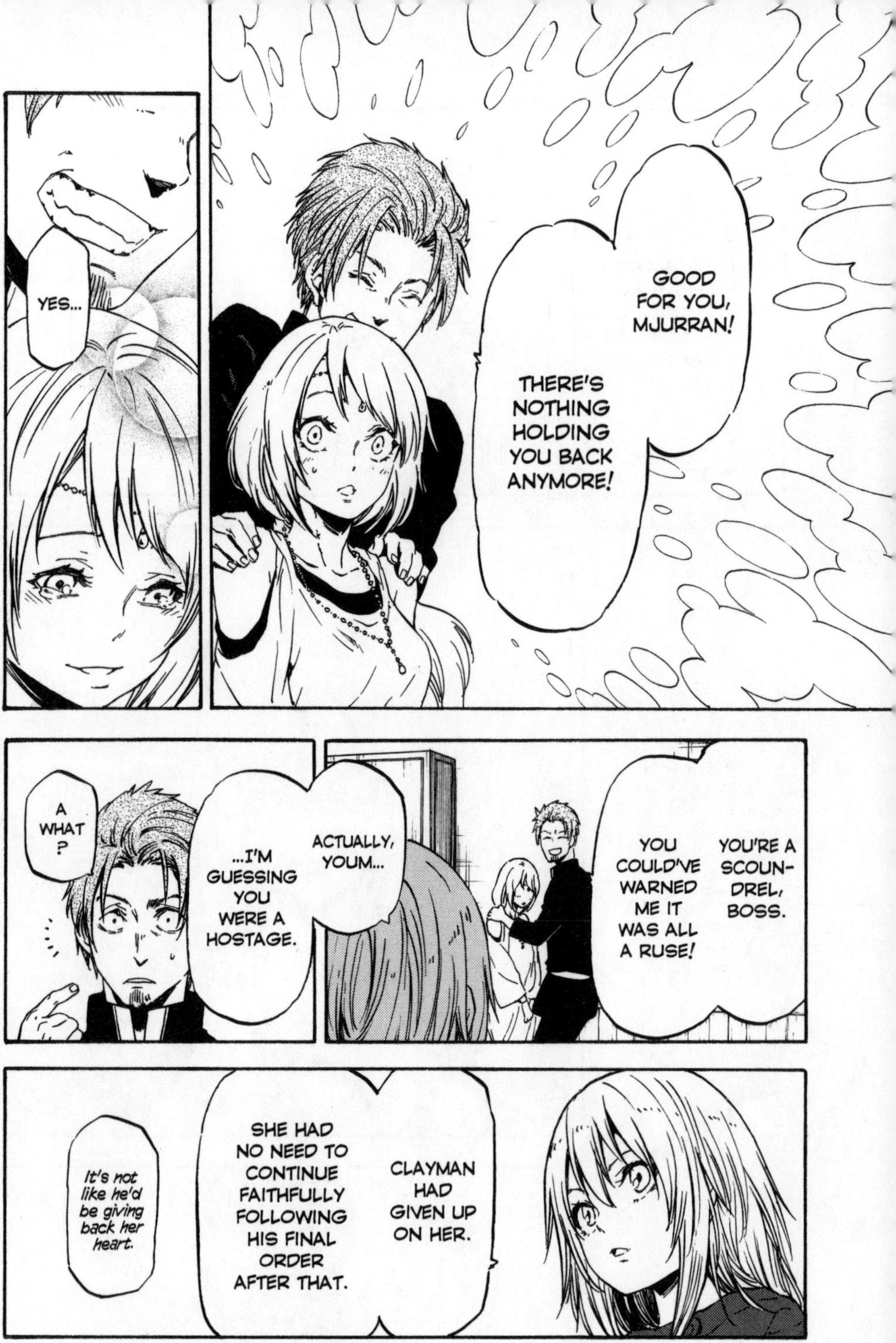
GOOD FOR YOU, MJURRAN!
THERE'S NOTHING HOLDING YOU BACK ANYMORE!
YES...
YOU'RE A SCOUN-DREL, BOSS.
YOU COULD'VE WARNED ME IT WAS ALL A RUSE!
ACTUALLY, YOUM...
...I'M GUESSING YOU WERE A HOSTAGE.
A WHAT?
CLAYMAN HAD GIVEN UP ON HER.
SHE HAD NO NEED TO CONTINUE FAITHFULLY FOLLOWING HIS FINAL ORDER AFTER THAT.
It's not like he'd be giving back her heart.

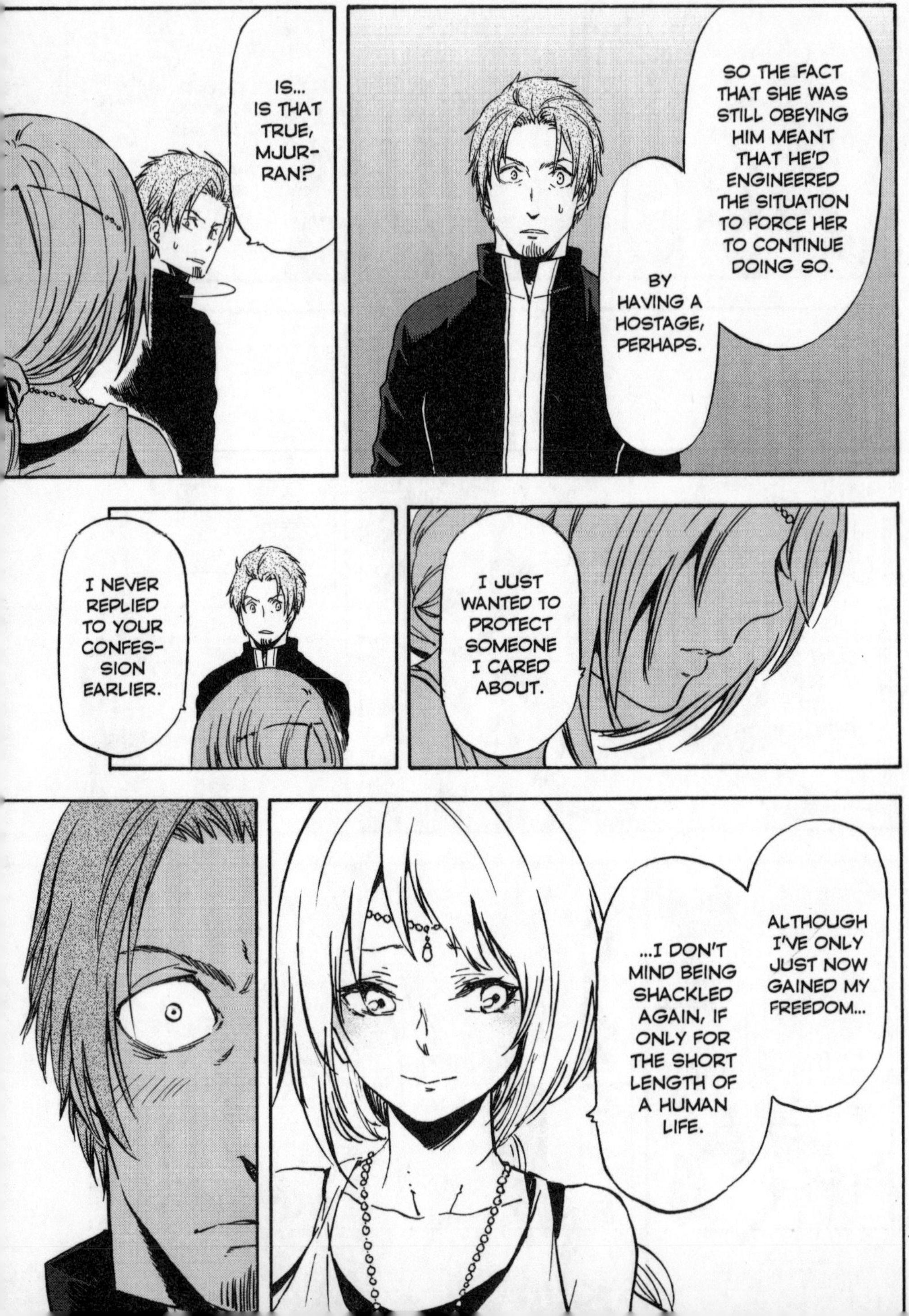
SO THE FACT THAT SHE WAS STILL OBEYING HIM MEANT THAT HE'D ENGINEERED THE SITUATION TO FORCE HER TO CONTINUE DOING SO.
BY HAVING A HOSTAGE, PERHAPS.
IS... IS THAT TRUE, MJURRAN?
I JUST WANTED TO PROTECT SOMEONE I CARED ABOUT.
I NEVER REPLIED TO YOUR CONFESSION EARLIER.
ALTHOUGH I'VE ONLY JUST NOW GAINED MY FREEDOM...
...I DON'T MIND BEING SHACKLED AGAIN, IF ONLY FOR THE SHORT LENGTH OF A HUMAN LIFE.

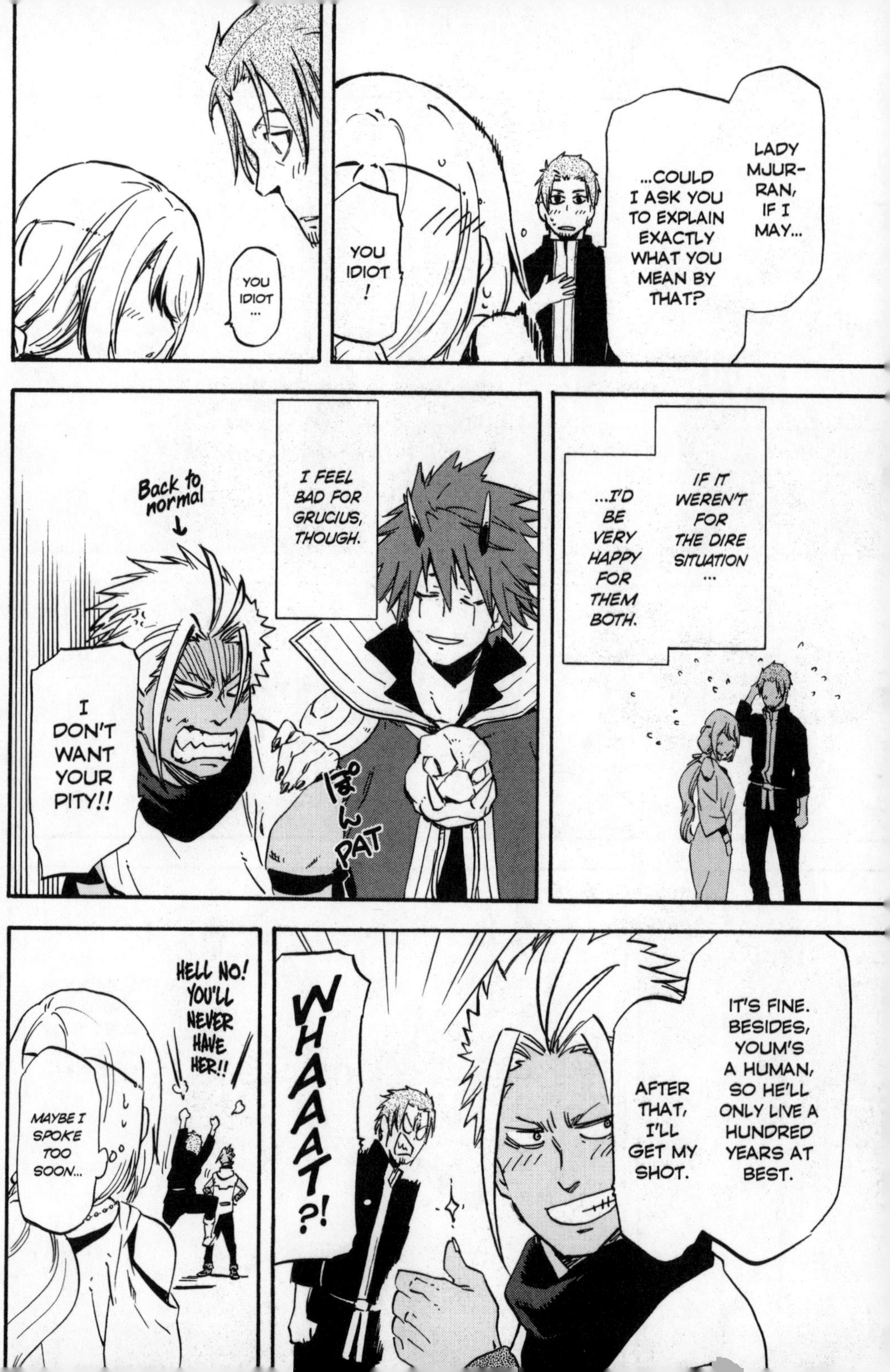
LADY MJUR-RAN, IF I MAY...
...COULD I ASK YOU TO EXPLAIN EXACTLY WHAT YOU MEAN BY THAT?
YOU IDIOT!
YOU IDIOT...
IF IT WEREN'T FOR THE DIRE SITUATION...
...I'D BE VERY HAPPY FOR THEM BOTH.
I FEEL BAD FOR GRUCIUS, THOUGH.
Back to normal
I DON'T WANT YOUR PITY!!
ぽん PAT
IT'S FINE. BESIDES, YOUM'S A HUMAN, SO HE'LL ONLY LIVE A HUNDRED YEARS AT BEST.
AFTER THAT, I'LL GET MY SHOT.
WHAAAT?!
HELL NO! YOU'LL NEVER HAVE HER!!
MAYBE I SPOKE TOO SOON...

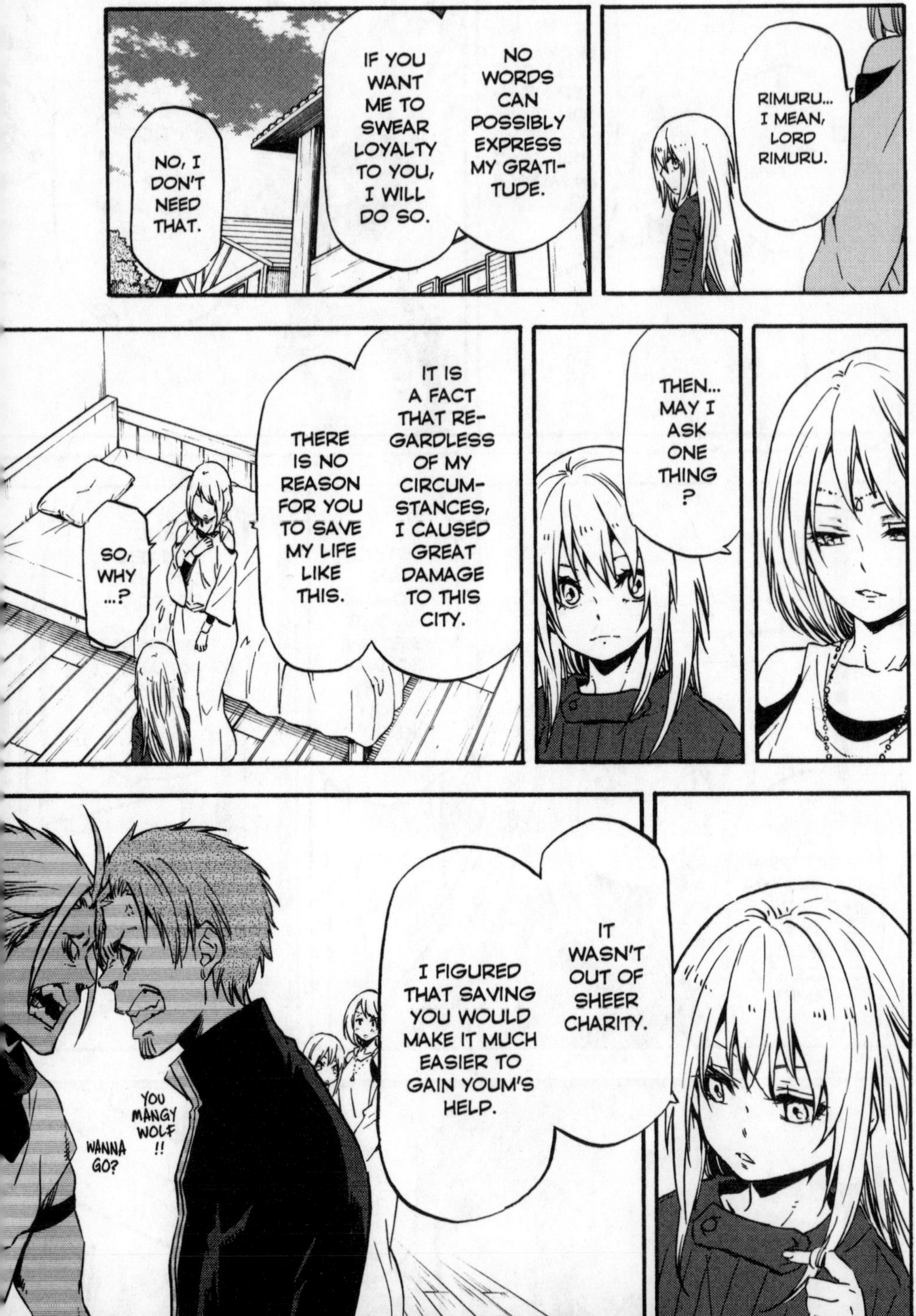
RIMURU... I MEAN, LORD RIMURU.
NO WORDS CAN POSSIBLY EXPRESS MY GRATI-TUDE.
IF YOU WANT ME TO SWEAR LOYALTY TO YOU, I WILL DO SO.
NO, I DON'T NEED THAT.
THEN... MAY I ASK ONE THING ?
IT IS A FACT THAT RE-GARDLESS OF MY CIRCUM-STANCES, I CAUSED GREAT DAMAGE TO THIS CITY.
THERE IS NO REASON FOR YOU TO SAVE MY LIFE LIKE THIS.
SO, WHY ...?
IT WASN'T OUT OF SHEER CHARITY.
I FIGURED THAT SAVING YOU WOULD MAKE IT MUCH EASIER TO GAIN YOUM'S HELP.
YOU MANGY WOLF !!
WANNA GO?

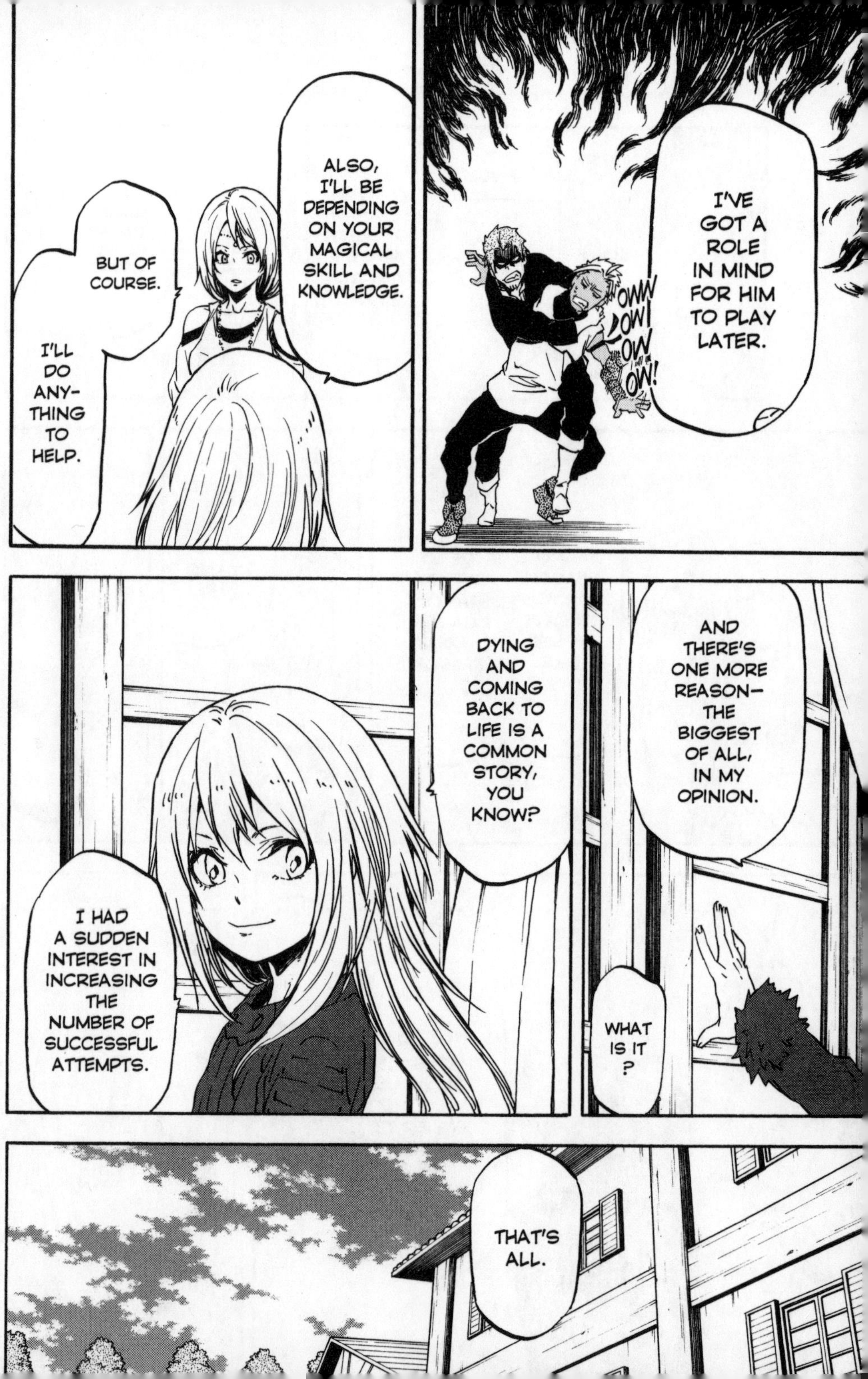
I'VE GOT A ROLE IN MIND FOR HIM TO PLAY LATER.
OWW! OW! OW! OW!
ALSO, I'LL BE DEPENDING ON YOUR MAGICAL SKILL AND KNOWLEDGE.
BUT OF COURSE.
I'LL DO ANY-THING TO HELP.
AND THERE'S ONE MORE REASON—THE BIGGEST OF ALL, IN MY OPINION.
WHAT IS IT ?
DYING AND COMING BACK TO LIFE IS A COMMON STORY, YOU KNOW?
I HAD A SUDDEN INTEREST IN INCREASING THE NUMBER OF SUCCESSFUL ATTEMPTS.
THAT'S ALL.

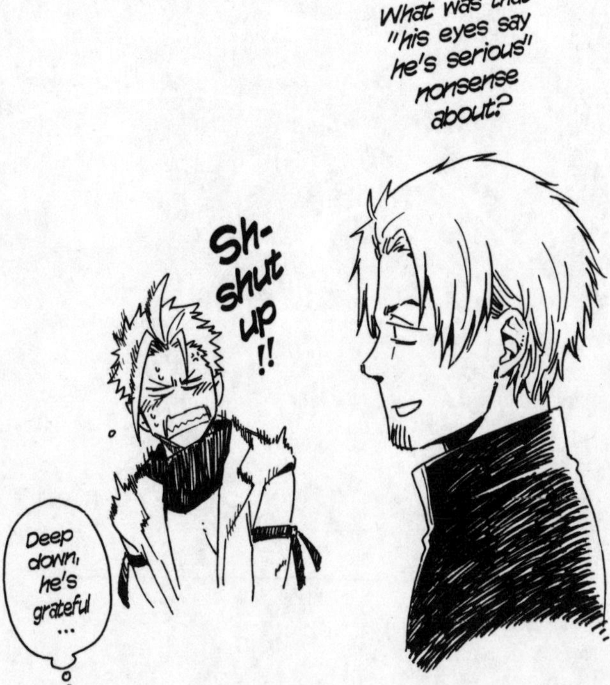
What was that "his eyes say he's serious" nonsense about?
Sh-shut up!!
Deep down, he's grateful...

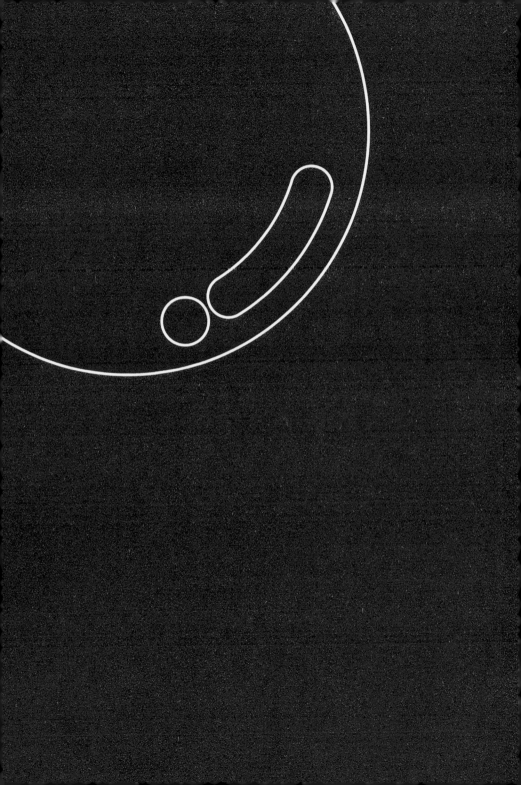

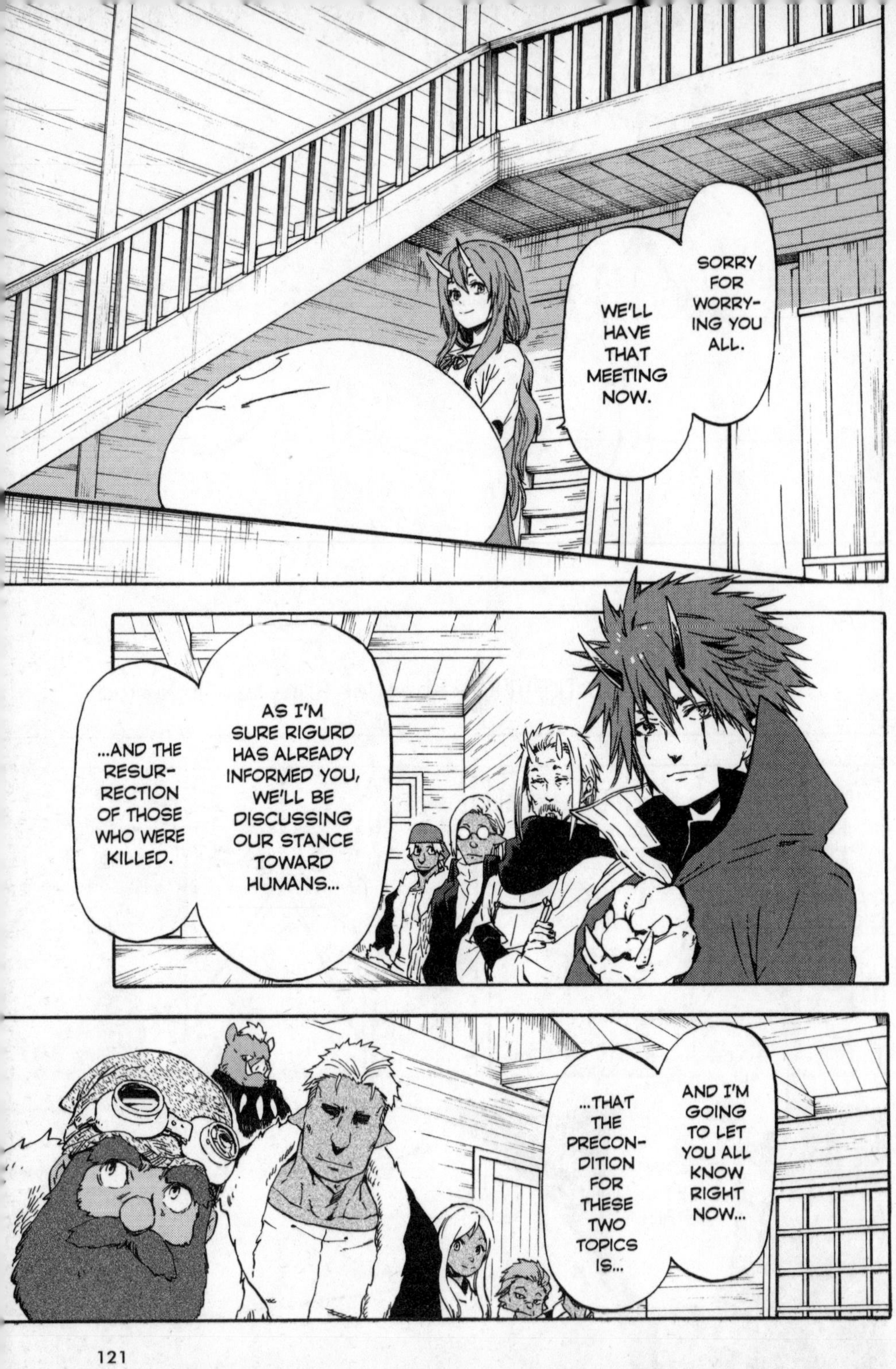
SORRY FOR WORRYING YOU ALL.
WE'LL HAVE THAT MEETING NOW.
AS I'M SURE RIGURD HAS ALREADY INFORMED YOU, WE'LL BE DISCUSSING OUR STANCE TOWARD HUMANS...
...AND THE RESURRECTION OF THOSE WHO WERE KILLED.
AND I'M GOING TO LET YOU ALL KNOW RIGHT NOW...
...THAT THE PRECONDITION FOR THESE TWO TOPICS IS...

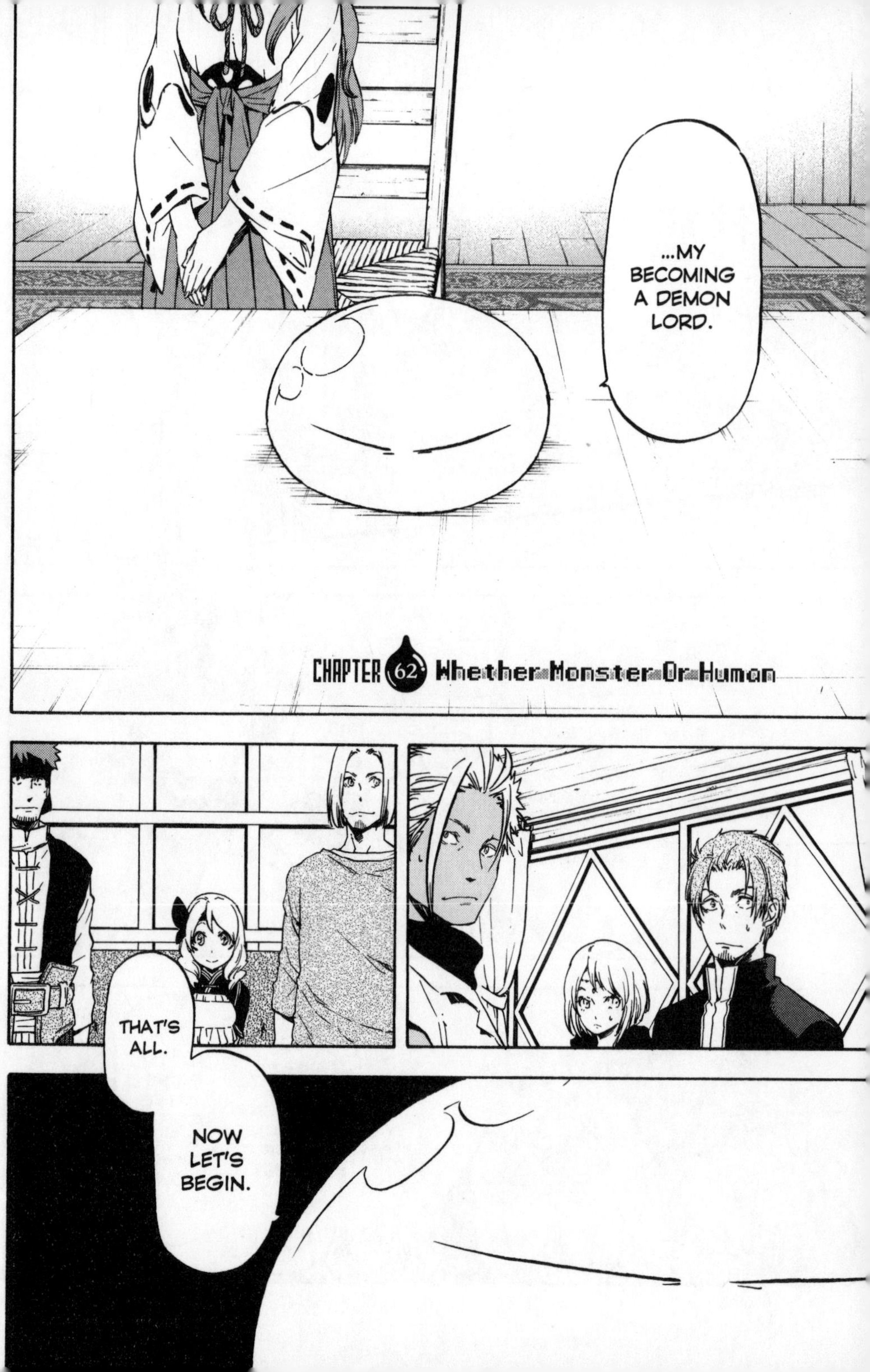
...MY BECOMING A DEMON LORD.
CHAPTER 62 Whether Monster Or Human
THAT'S ALL.
NOW LET'S BEGIN.

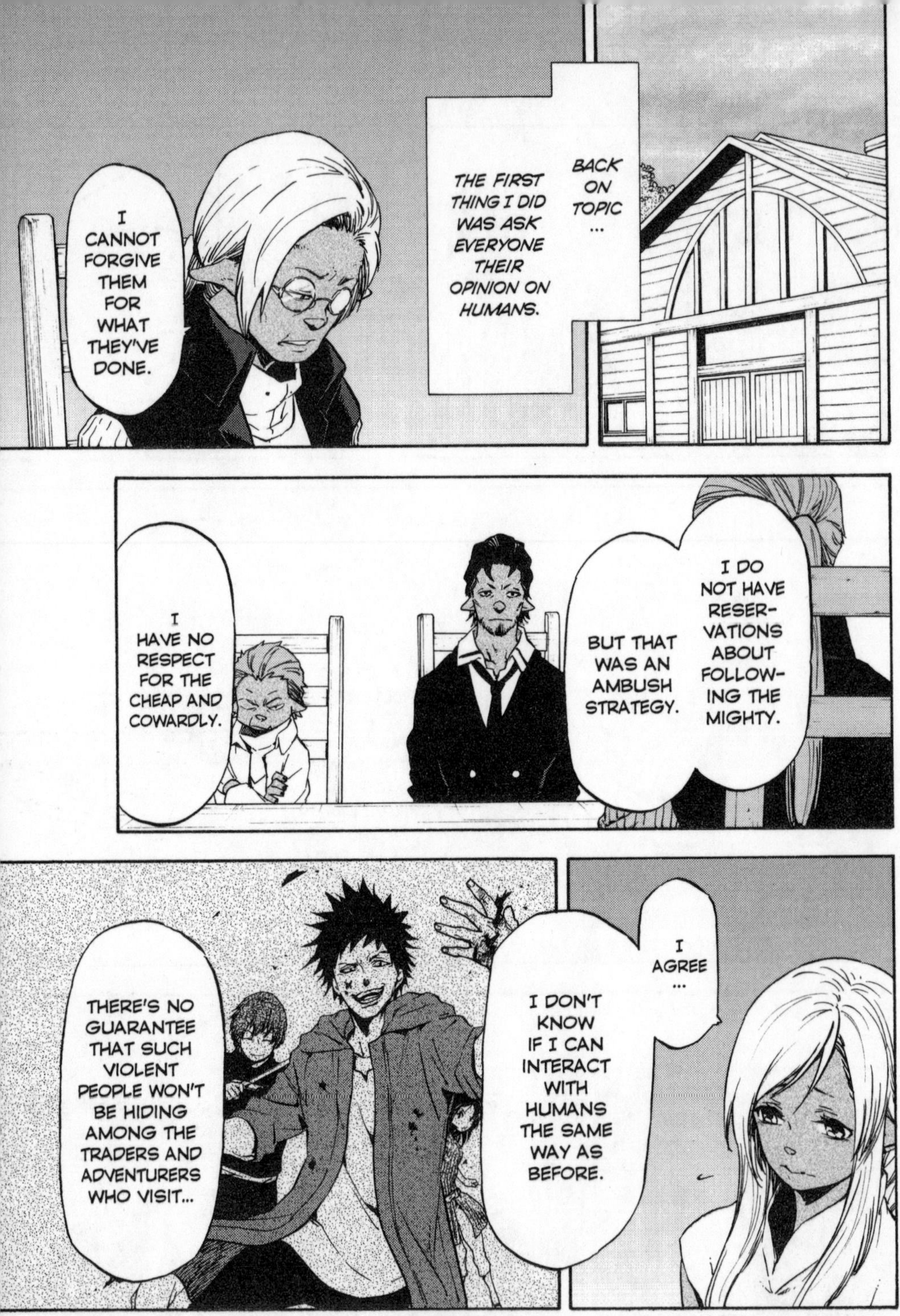
BACK ON TOPIC ...
THE FIRST THING I DID WAS ASK EVERYONE THEIR OPINION ON HUMANS.
I CANNOT FORGIVE THEM FOR WHAT THEY'VE DONE.
I DO NOT HAVE RESER-VATIONS ABOUT FOLLOW-ING THE MIGHTY.
BUT THAT WAS AN AMBUSH STRATEGY.
I HAVE NO RESPECT FOR THE CHEAP AND COWARDLY.
I AGREE ...
I DON'T KNOW IF I CAN INTERACT WITH HUMANS THE SAME WAY AS BEFORE.
THERE'S NO GUARANTEE THAT SUCH VIOLENT PEOPLE WON'T BE HIDING AMONG THE TRADERS AND ADVENTURERS WHO VISIT...

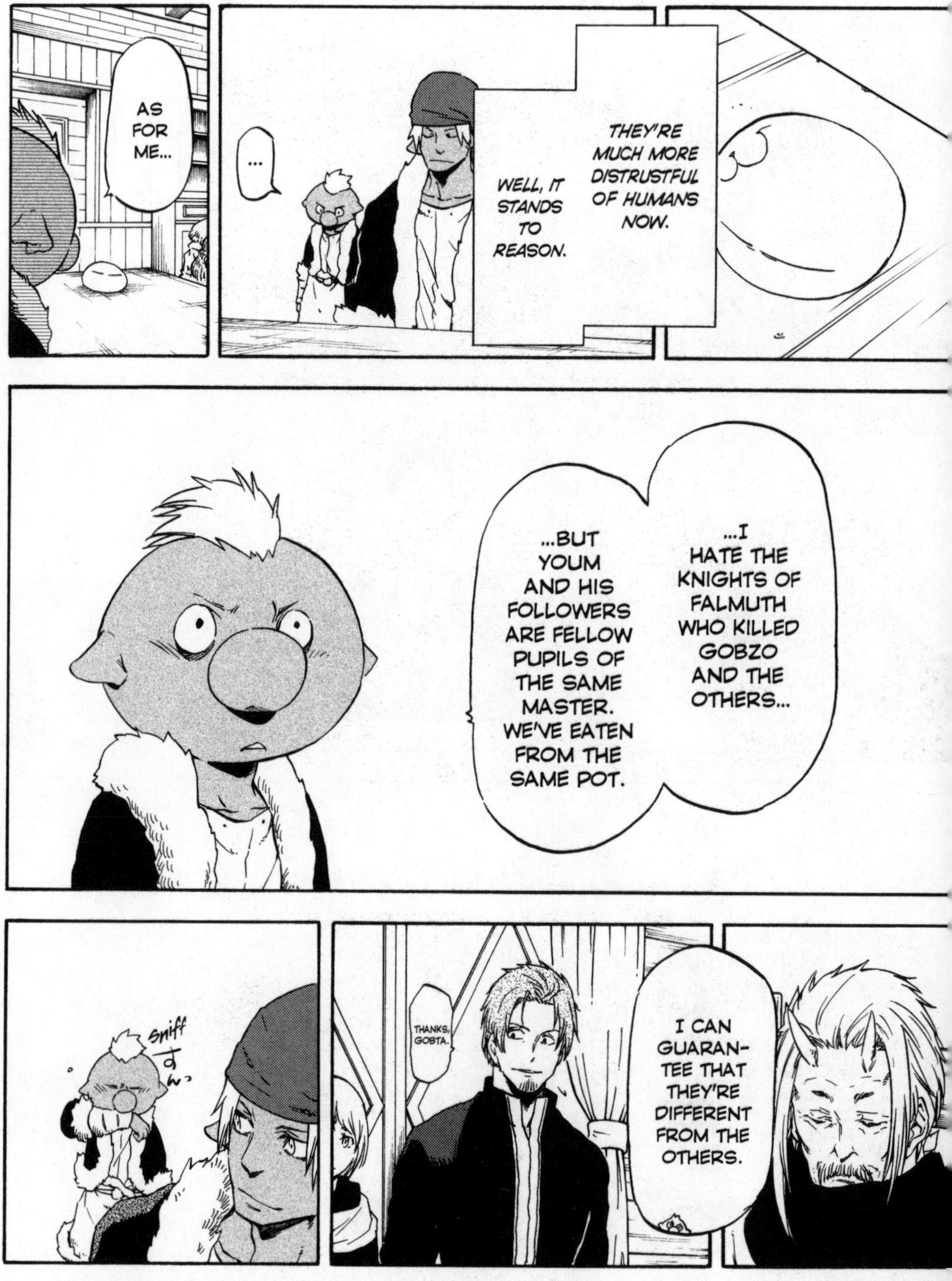
THEY'RE MUCH MORE DISTRUSTFUL OF HUMANS NOW.
WELL, IT STANDS TO REASON.
...
AS FOR ME...
...I HATE THE KNIGHTS OF FALMUTH WHO KILLED GOBZO AND THE OTHERS...
...BUT YOUM AND HIS FOLLOWERS ARE FELLOW PUPILS OF THE SAME MASTER. WE'VE EATEN FROM THE SAME POT.
I CAN GUARANTEE THAT THEY'RE DIFFERENT FROM THE OTHERS.
THANKS, GOBTA.
Sniff
すんっ

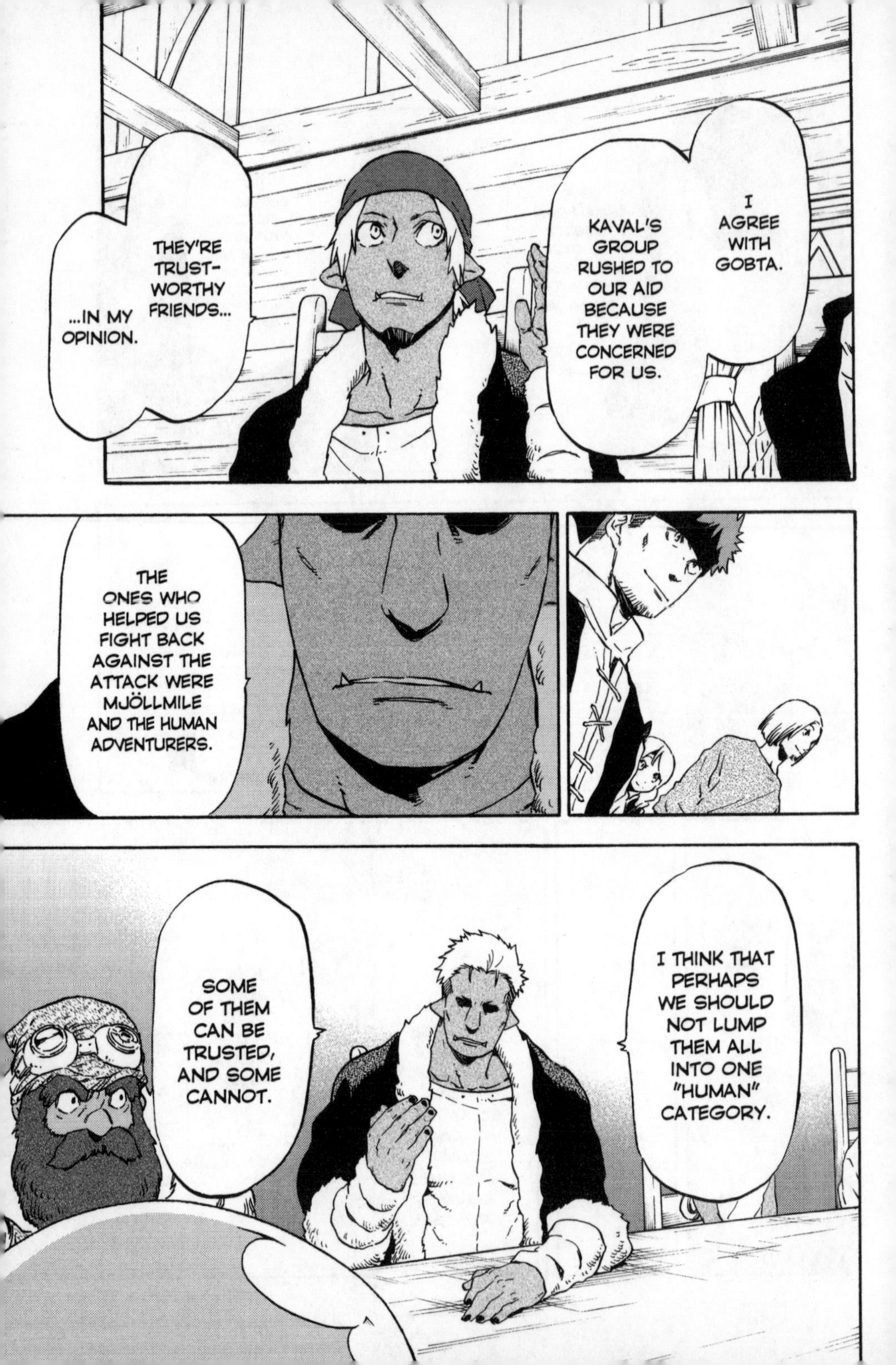
I AGREE WITH GOBTA.
KAVAL'S GROUP RUSHED TO OUR AID BECAUSE THEY WERE CONCERNED FOR US.
THEY'RE TRUST-WORTHY FRIENDS...
...IN MY OPINION.
THE ONES WHO HELPED US FIGHT BACK AGAINST THE ATTACK WERE MJÖLLMILE AND THE HUMAN ADVENTURERS.
I THINK THAT PERHAPS WE SHOULD NOT LUMP THEM ALL INTO ONE "HUMAN" CATEGORY.
SOME OF THEM CAN BE TRUSTED, AND SOME CANNOT.

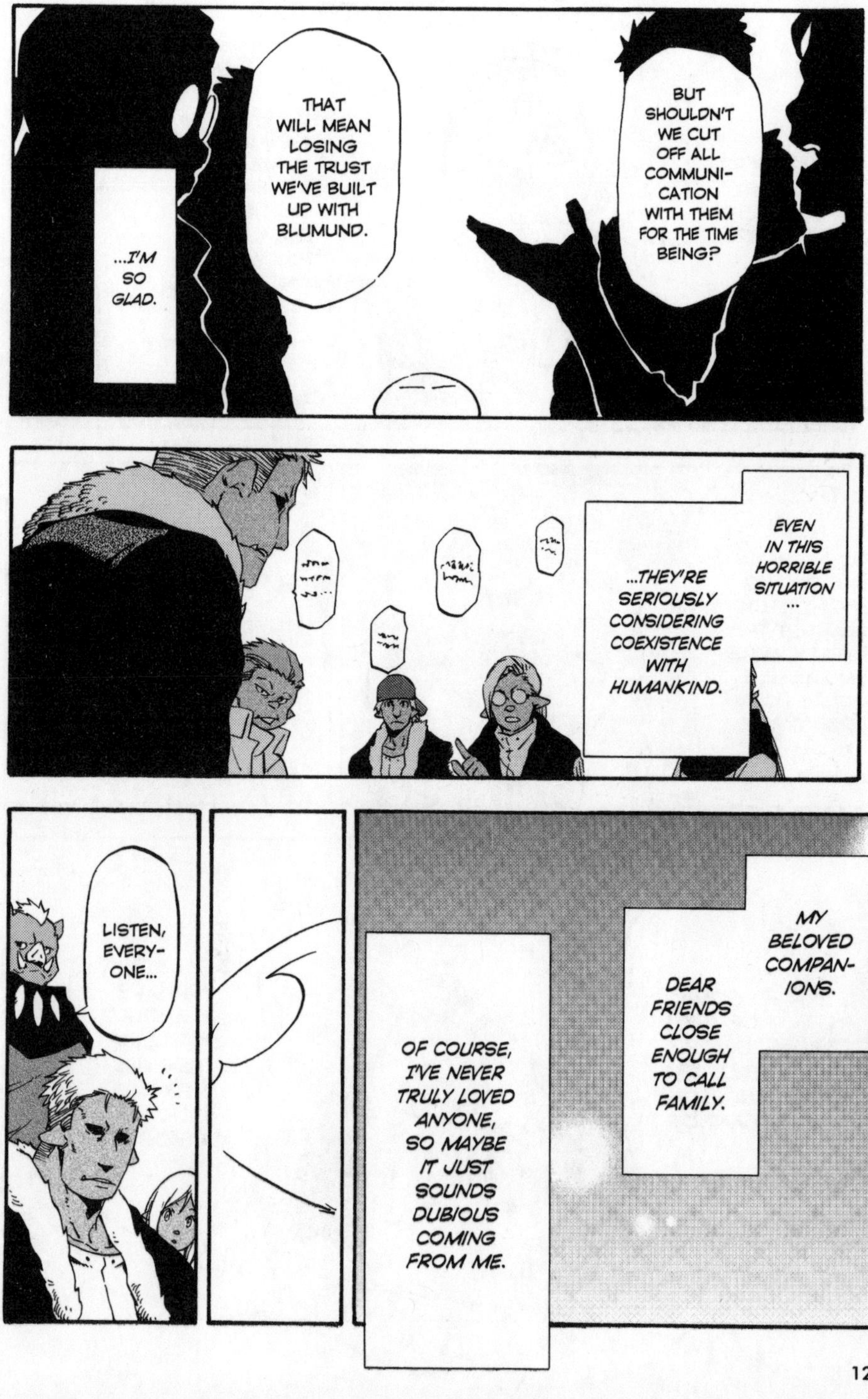

BUT SHOULDN'T WE CUT OFF ALL COMMUNICATION WITH THEM FOR THE TIME BEING?
THAT WILL MEAN LOSING THE TRUST WE'VE BUILT UP WITH BLUMUND.
...I'M SO GLAD.
EVEN IN THIS HORRIBLE SITUATION...
...THEY'RE SERIOUSLY CONSIDERING COEXISTENCE WITH HUMANKIND.
MY BELOVED COMPANIONS.
DEAR FRIENDS CLOSE ENOUGH TO CALL FAMILY.
OF COURSE, I'VE NEVER TRULY LOVED ANYONE, SO MAYBE IT JUST SOUNDS DUBIOUS COMING FROM ME.
LISTEN, EVERYONE...

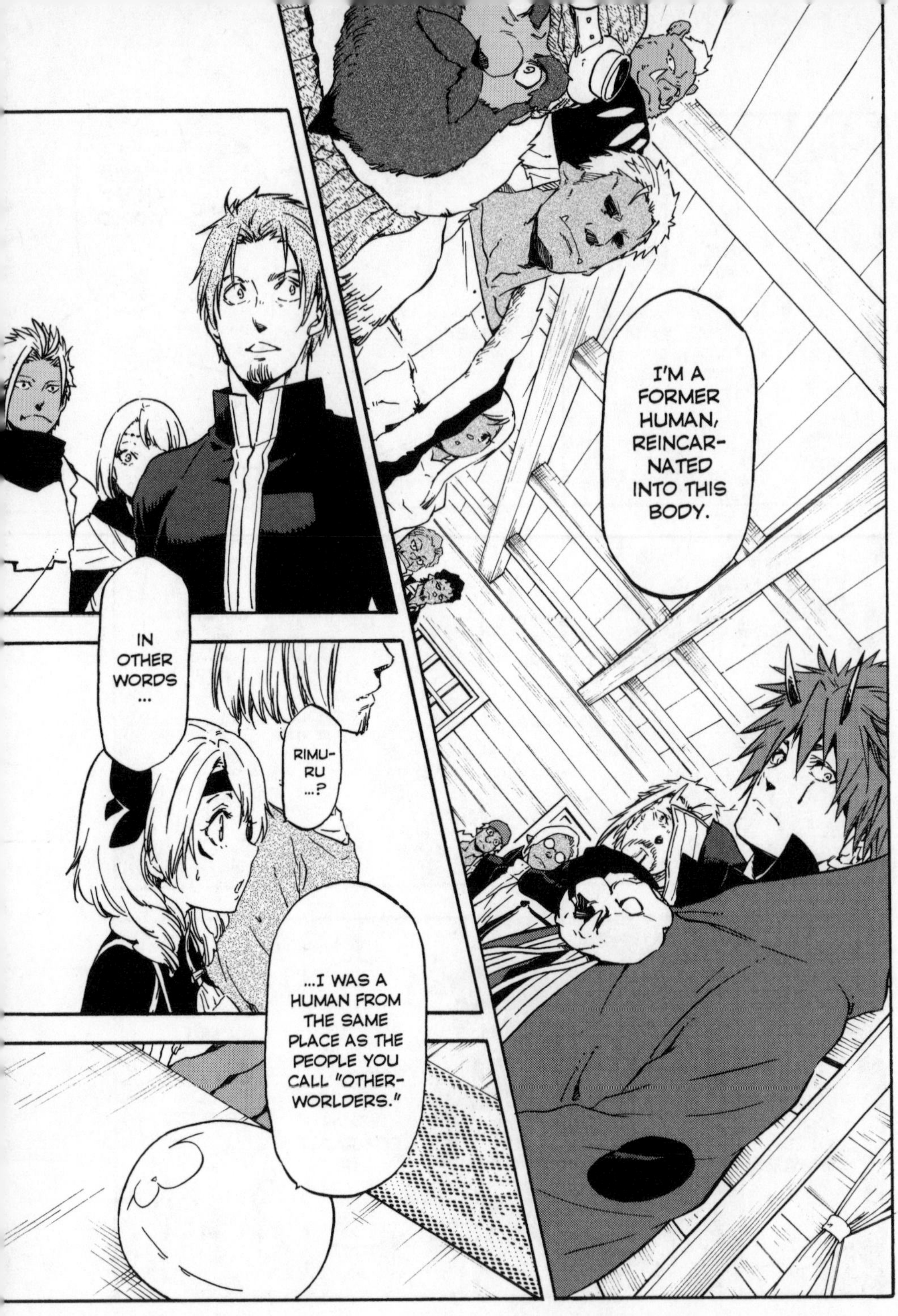
I'M A FORMER HUMAN, REINCARNATED INTO THIS BODY.
IN OTHER WORDS ...
RIMURU ...?
...I WAS A HUMAN FROM THE SAME PLACE AS THE PEOPLE YOU CALL "OTHERWORLDERS."

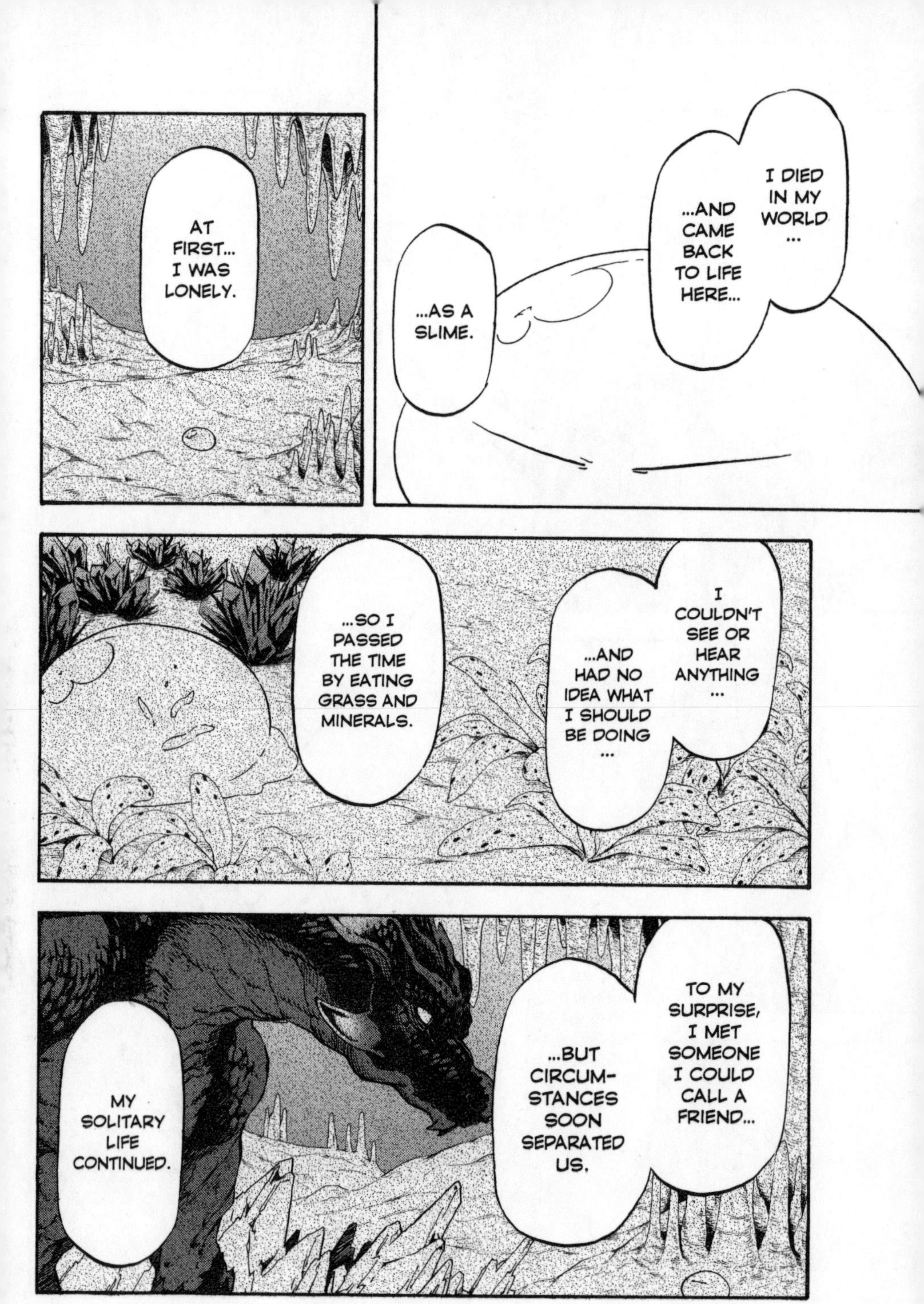
I DIED IN MY WORLD ...
...AND CAME BACK TO LIFE HERE...
...AS A SLIME.
AT FIRST... I WAS LONELY.
I COULDN'T SEE OR HEAR ANYTHING ...
...AND HAD NO IDEA WHAT I SHOULD BE DOING ...
...SO I PASSED THE TIME BY EATING GRASS AND MINERALS.
TO MY SURPRISE, I MET SOMEONE I COULD CALL A FRIEND...
...BUT CIRCUM-STANCES SOON SEPARATED US.
MY SOLITARY LIFE CONTINUED.

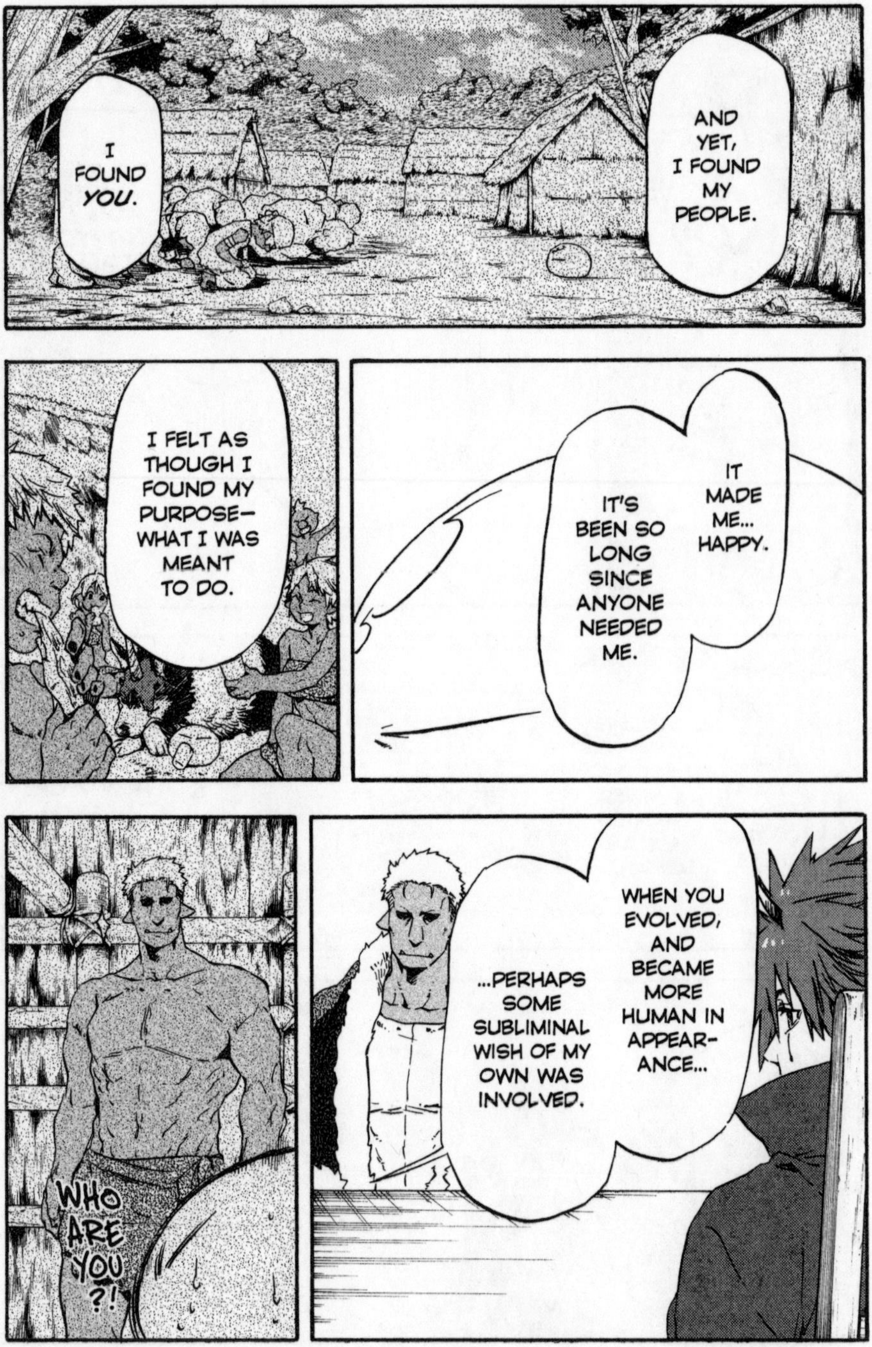
AND YET, I FOUND MY PEOPLE.
I FOUND *YOU*.
IT MADE ME... HAPPY.
IT'S BEEN SO LONG SINCE ANYONE NEEDED ME.
I FELT AS THOUGH I FOUND MY PURPOSE—WHAT I WAS MEANT TO DO.
WHEN YOU EVOLVED, AND BECAME MORE HUMAN IN APPEAR-ANCE...
...PERHAPS SOME SUBLIMINAL WISH OF MY OWN WAS INVOLVED.
WHO ARE YOU ?!

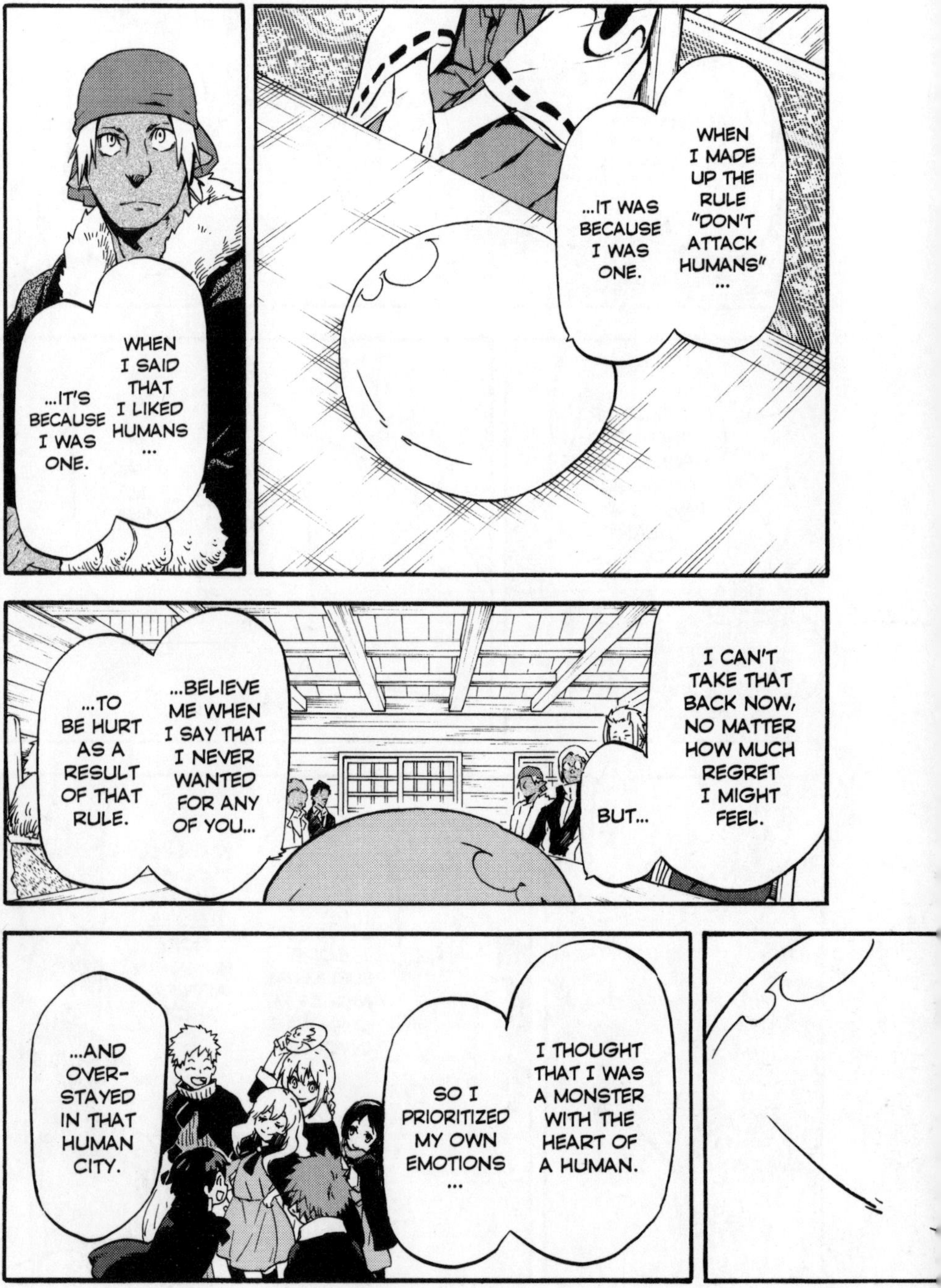
WHEN I MADE UP THE RULE "DON'T ATTACK HUMANS"...
...IT WAS BECAUSE I WAS ONE.
WHEN I SAID THAT I LIKED HUMANS...
...IT'S BECAUSE I WAS ONE.
I CAN'T TAKE THAT BACK NOW, NO MATTER HOW MUCH REGRET I MIGHT FEEL.
BUT...
...BELIEVE ME WHEN I SAY THAT I NEVER WANTED FOR ANY OF YOU...
...TO BE HURT AS A RESULT OF THAT RULE.
I THOUGHT THAT I WAS A MONSTER WITH THE HEART OF A HUMAN.
SO I PRIORITIZED MY OWN EMOTIONS...
...AND OVER-STAYED IN THAT HUMAN CITY.

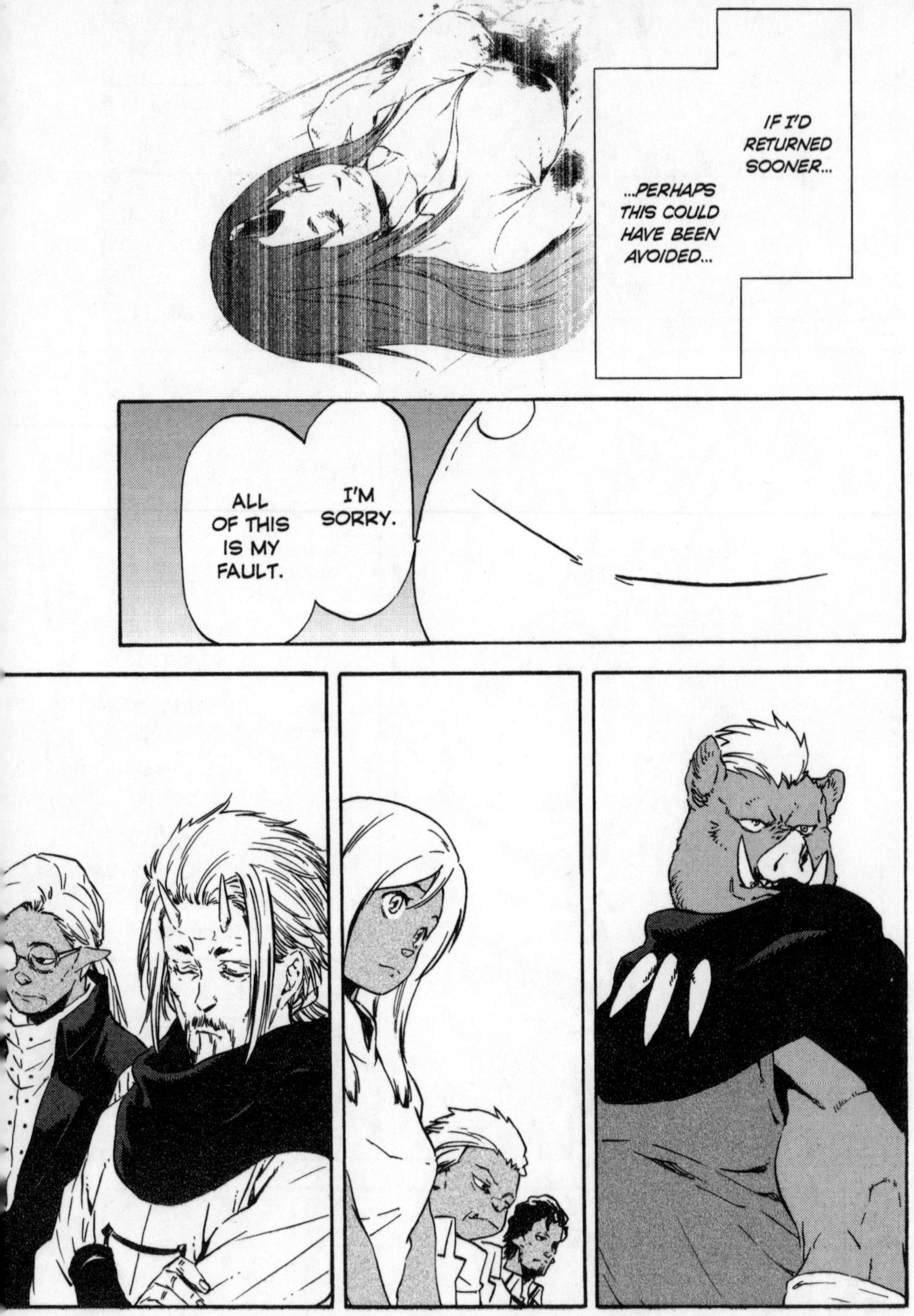
IF I'D RETURNED SOONER...
...PERHAPS THIS COULD HAVE BEEN AVOIDED...
I'M SORRY.
ALL OF THIS IS MY FAULT.

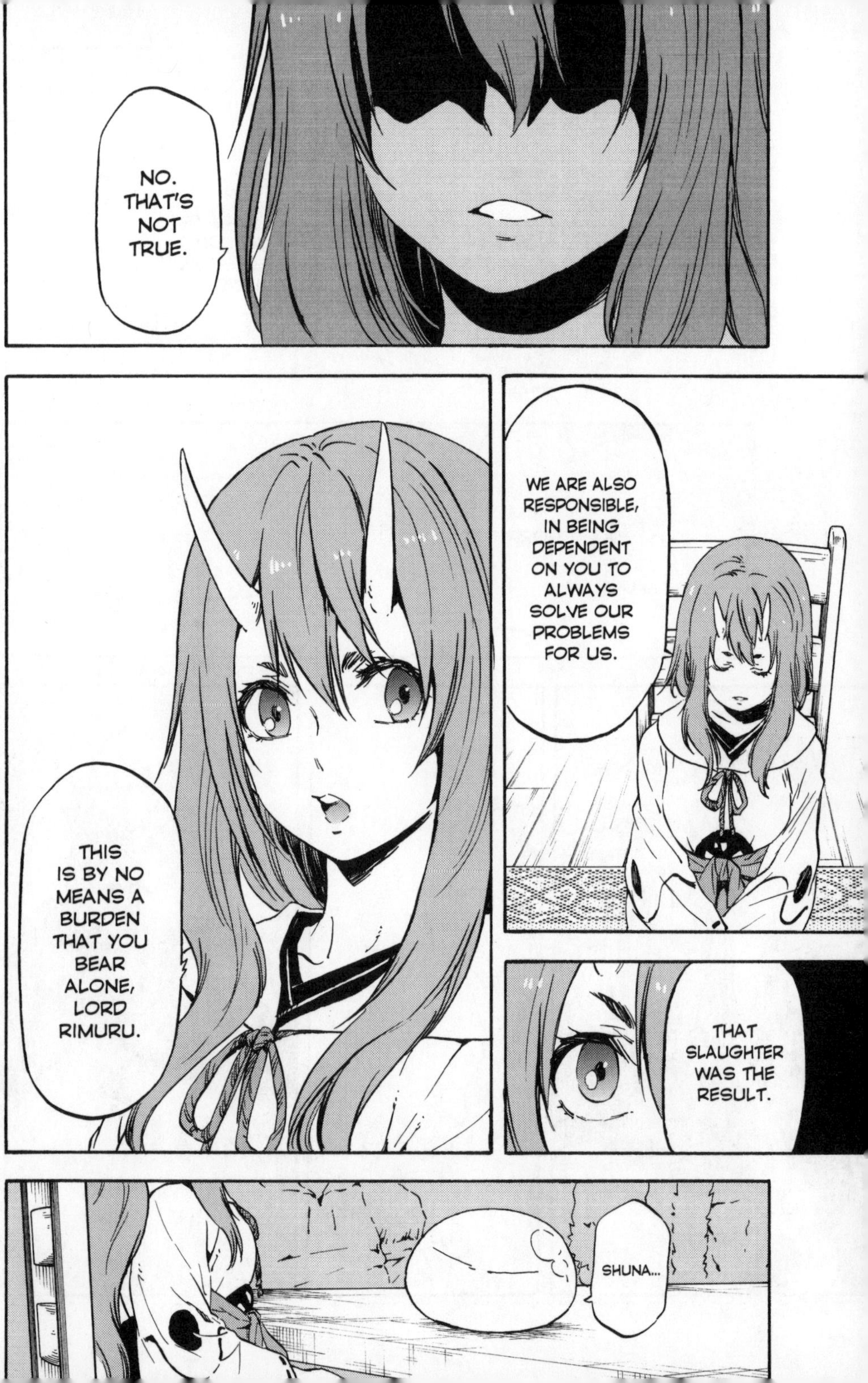
NO. THAT'S NOT TRUE.
WE ARE ALSO RESPONSIBLE, IN BEING DEPENDENT ON YOU TO ALWAYS SOLVE OUR PROBLEMS FOR US.
THAT SLAUGHTER WAS THE RESULT.
THIS IS BY NO MEANS A BURDEN THAT YOU BEAR ALONE, LORD RIMURU.
SHUNA...

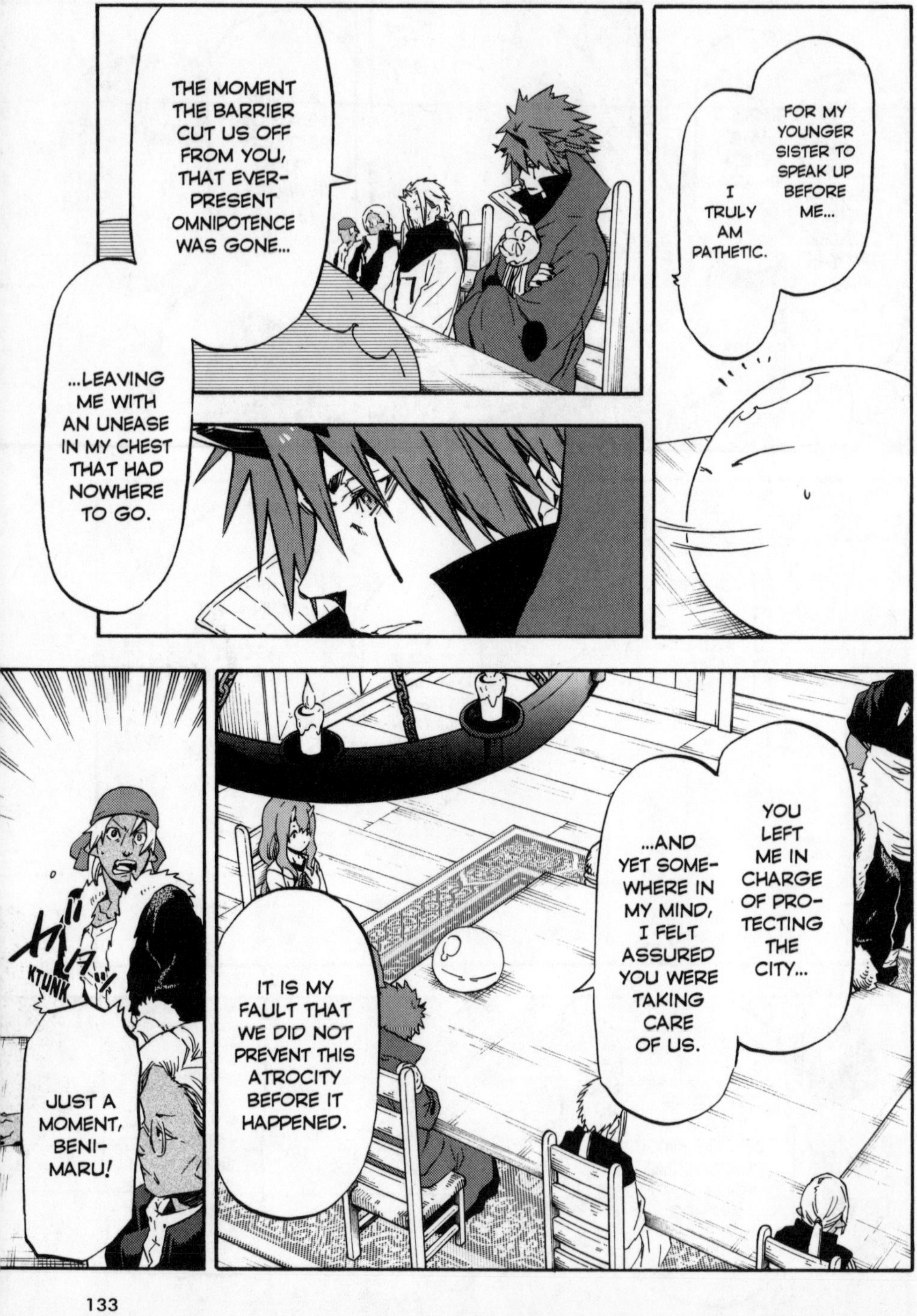
FOR MY YOUNGER SISTER TO SPEAK UP BEFORE ME...
I TRULY AM PATHETIC.
THE MOMENT THE BARRIER CUT US OFF FROM YOU, THAT EVER-PRESENT OMNIPOTENCE WAS GONE...
...LEAVING ME WITH AN UNEASE IN MY CHEST THAT HAD NOWHERE TO GO.
YOU LEFT ME IN CHARGE OF PRO-TECTING THE CITY...
...AND YET SOME-WHERE IN MY MIND, I FELT ASSURED YOU WERE TAKING CARE OF US.
IT IS MY FAULT THAT WE DID NOT PREVENT THIS ATROCITY BEFORE IT HAPPENED.
KTUNK
JUST A MOMENT, BENI-MARU!

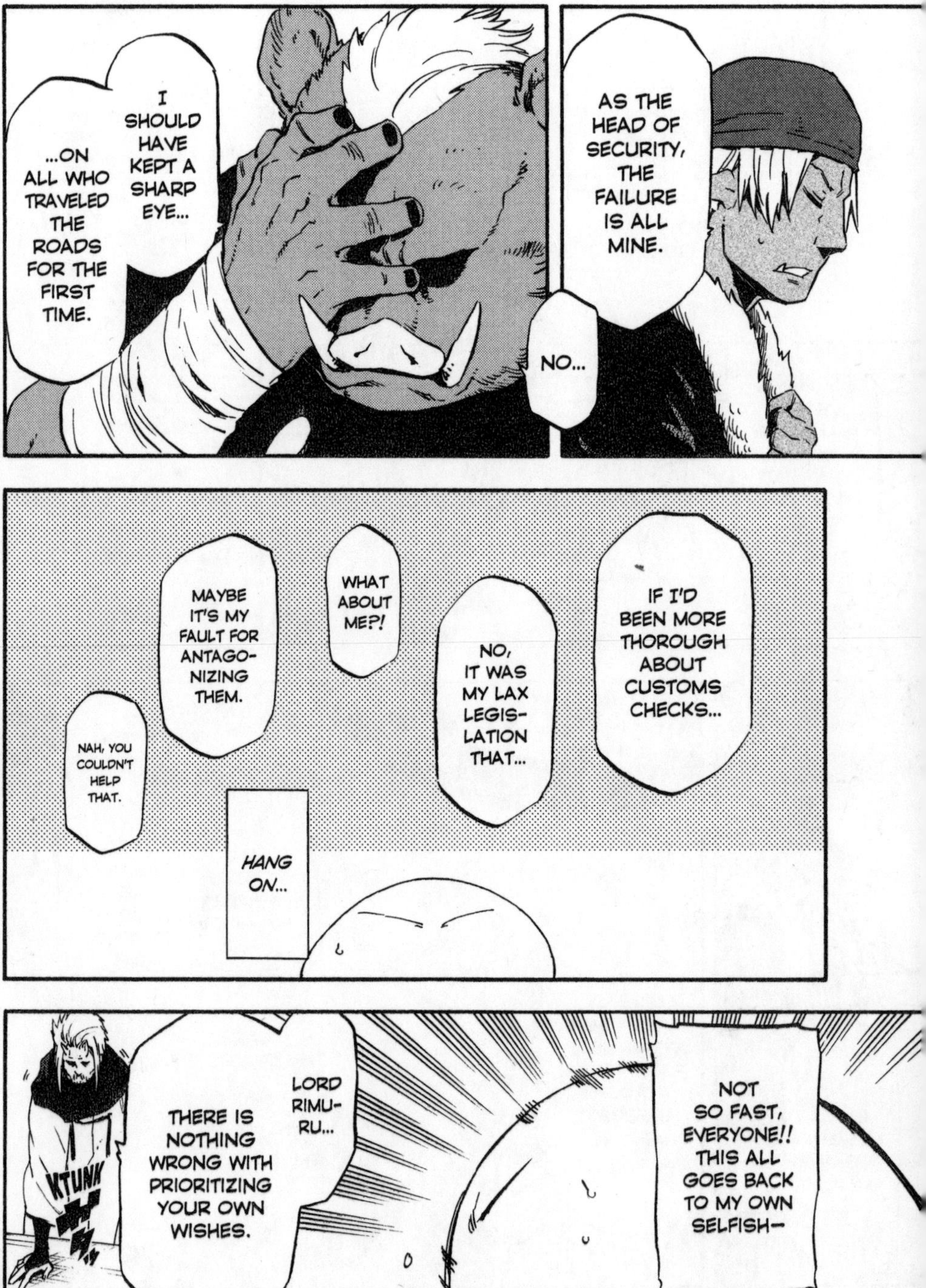

AS THE HEAD OF SECURITY, THE FAILURE IS ALL MINE.
NO...
I SHOULD HAVE KEPT A SHARP EYE...
...ON ALL WHO TRAVELED THE ROADS FOR THE FIRST TIME.
IF I'D BEEN MORE THOROUGH ABOUT CUSTOMS CHECKS...
NO, IT WAS MY LAX LEGIS-LATION THAT...
WHAT ABOUT ME?!
MAYBE IT'S MY FAULT FOR ANTAGO-NIZING THEM.
NAH, YOU COULDN'T HELP THAT.
HANG ON...
NOT SO FAST, EVERYONE!! THIS ALL GOES BACK TO MY OWN SELFISH—
LORD RIMU-RU...
THERE IS NOTHING WRONG WITH PRIORITIZING YOUR OWN WISHES.
KTUNK

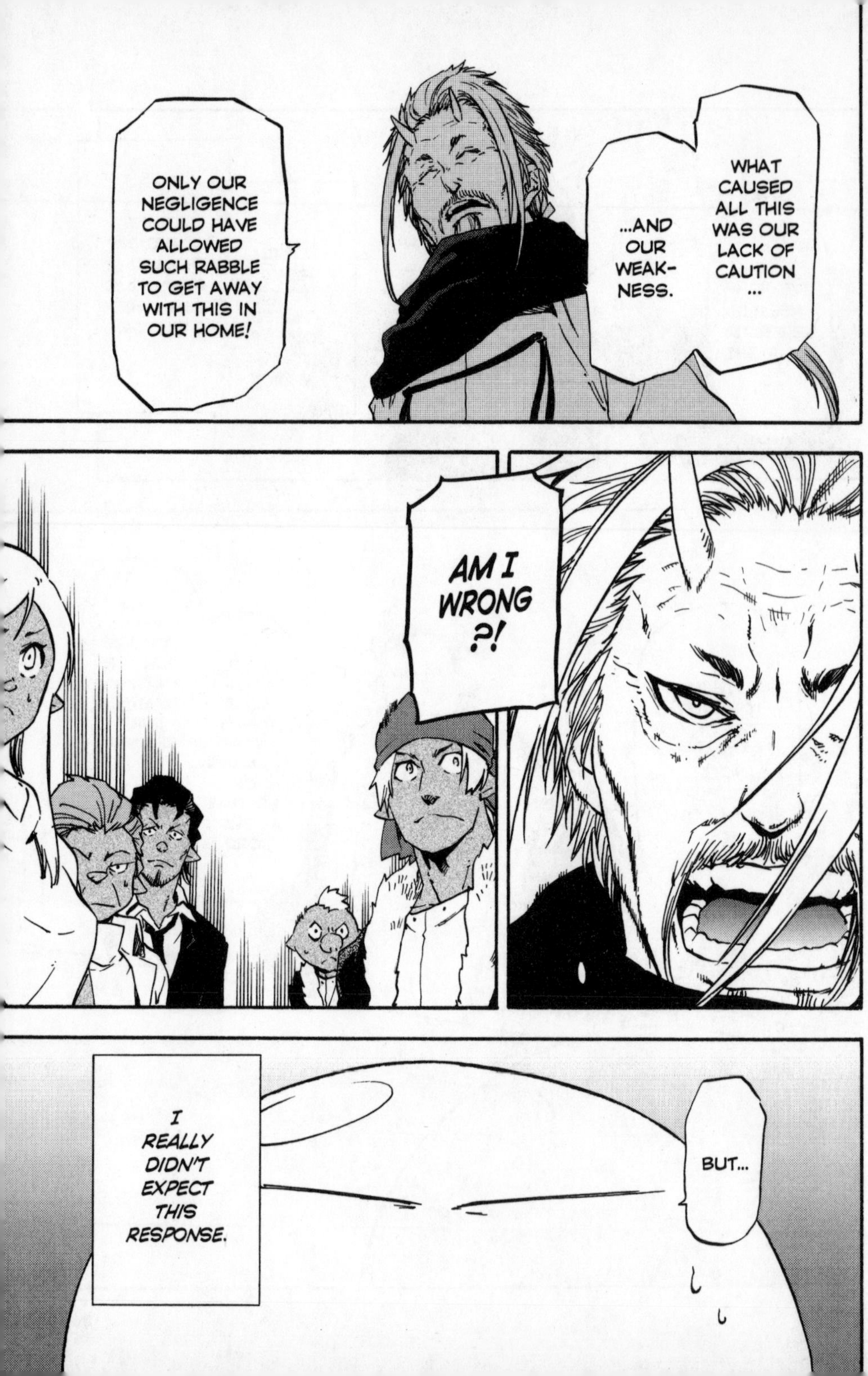
WHAT CAUSED ALL THIS WAS OUR LACK OF CAUTION ...
...AND OUR WEAK-NESS.
ONLY OUR NEGLIGENCE COULD HAVE ALLOWED SUCH RABBLE TO GET AWAY WITH THIS IN OUR HOME!
AM I WRONG ?!
BUT...
I REALLY DIDN'T EXPECT THIS RESPONSE.

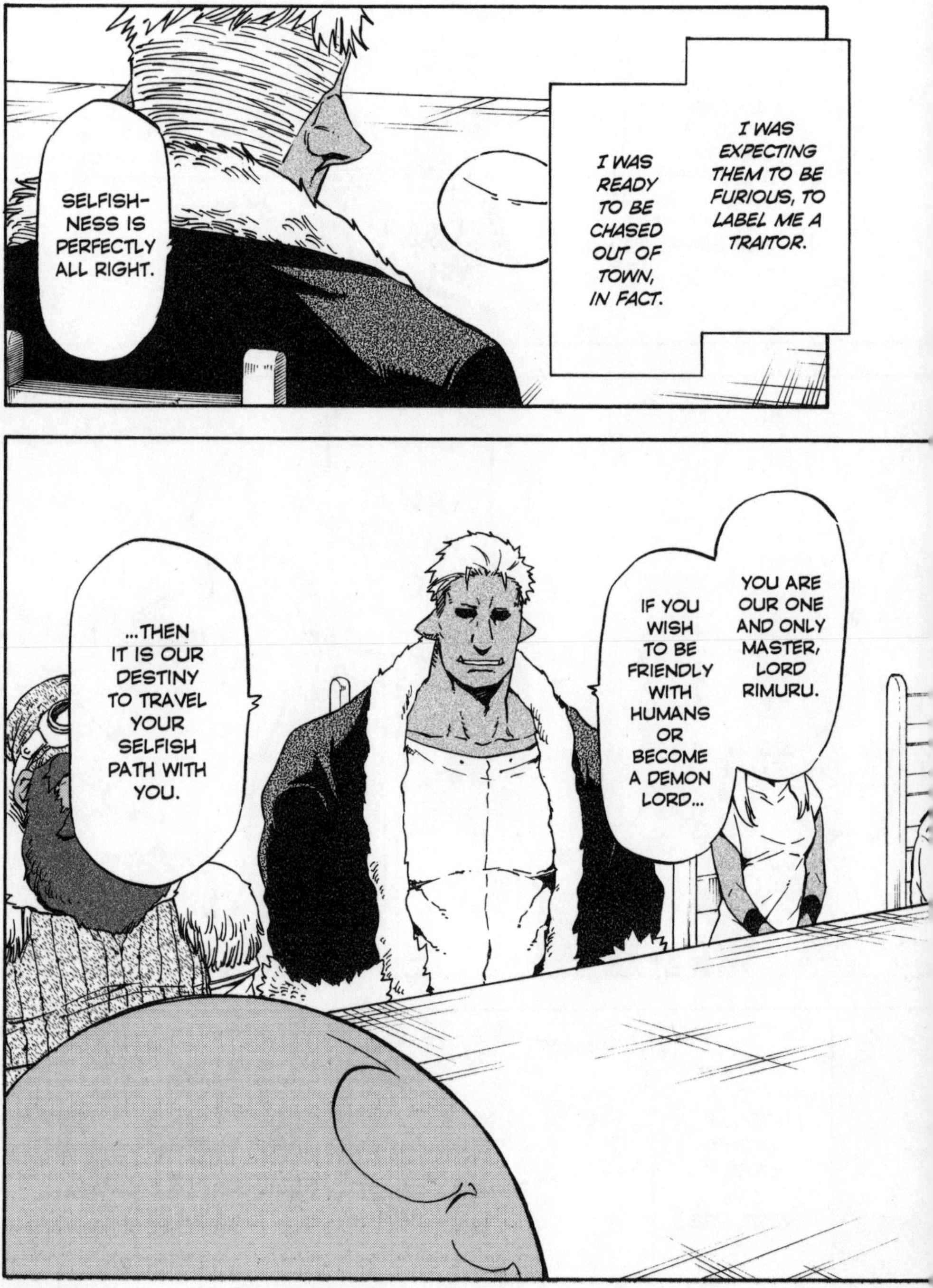
I WAS EXPECTING THEM TO BE FURIOUS, TO LABEL ME A TRAITOR.
I WAS READY TO BE CHASED OUT OF TOWN, IN FACT.
SELFISHNESS IS PERFECTLY ALL RIGHT.
YOU ARE OUR ONE AND ONLY MASTER, LORD RIMURU.
IF YOU WISH TO BE FRIENDLY WITH HUMANS OR BECOME A DEMON LORD...
...THEN IT IS OUR DESTINY TO TRAVEL YOUR SELFISH PATH WITH YOU.

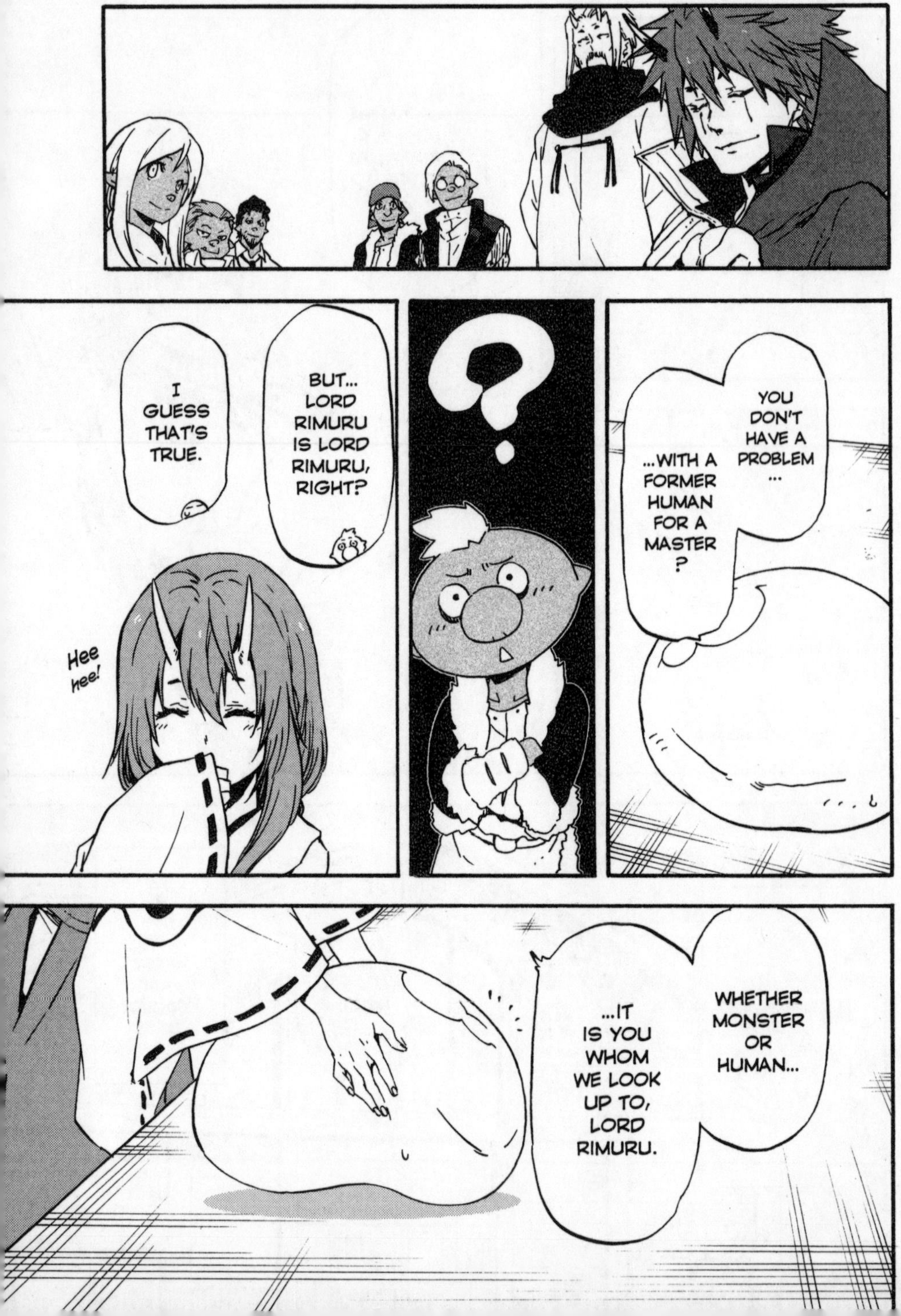
YOU DON'T HAVE A PROBLEM ...
...WITH A FORMER HUMAN FOR A MASTER ?
BUT... LORD RIMURU IS LORD RIMURU, RIGHT?
I GUESS THAT'S TRUE.
Hee hee!
WHETHER MONSTER OR HUMAN...
...IT IS YOU WHOM WE LOOK UP TO, LORD RIMURU.

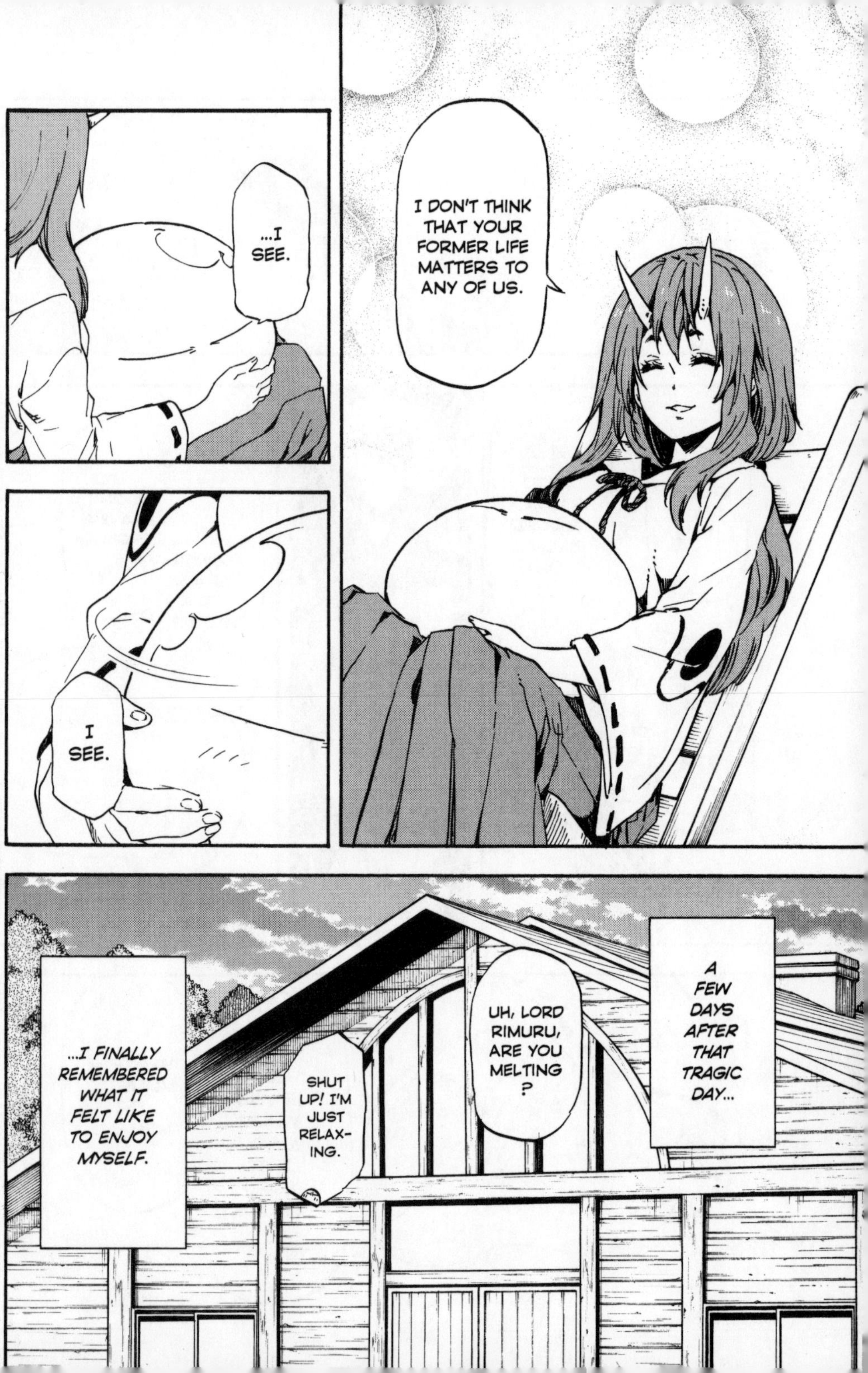
I DON'T THINK THAT YOUR FORMER LIFE MATTERS TO ANY OF US.
...I SEE.
I SEE.
A FEW DAYS AFTER THAT TRAGIC DAY...
UH, LORD RIMURU, ARE YOU MELTING ?
SHUT UP! I'M JUST RELAX-ING.
...I FINALLY REMEMBERED WHAT IT FELT LIKE TO ENJOY MYSELF.

Satoru Mikami

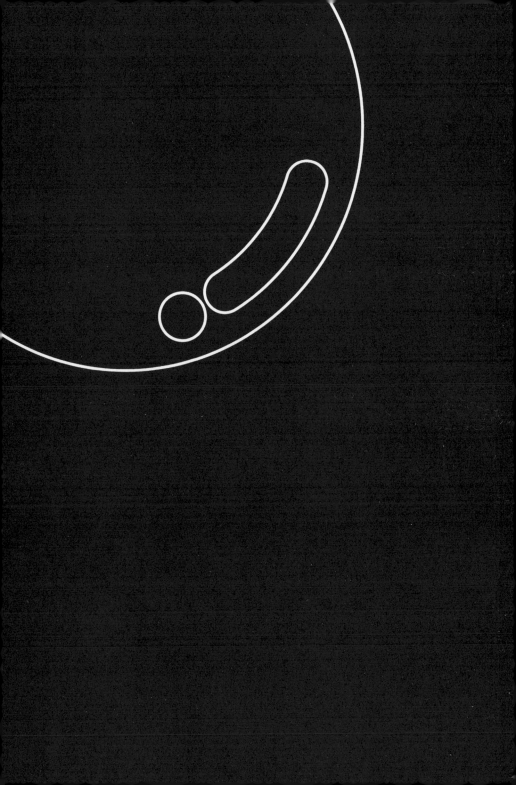

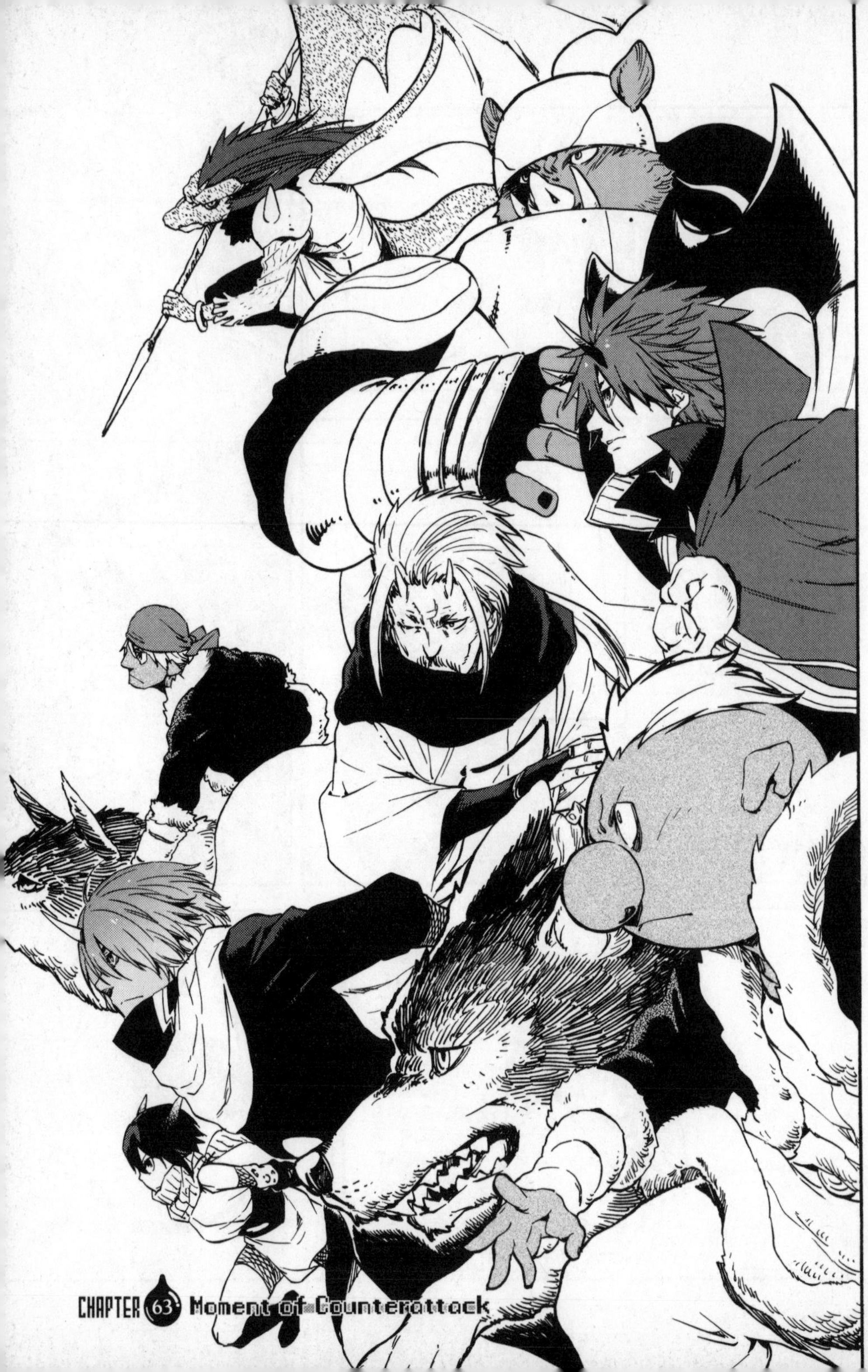
CHAPTER 63 Moment of Counterattack

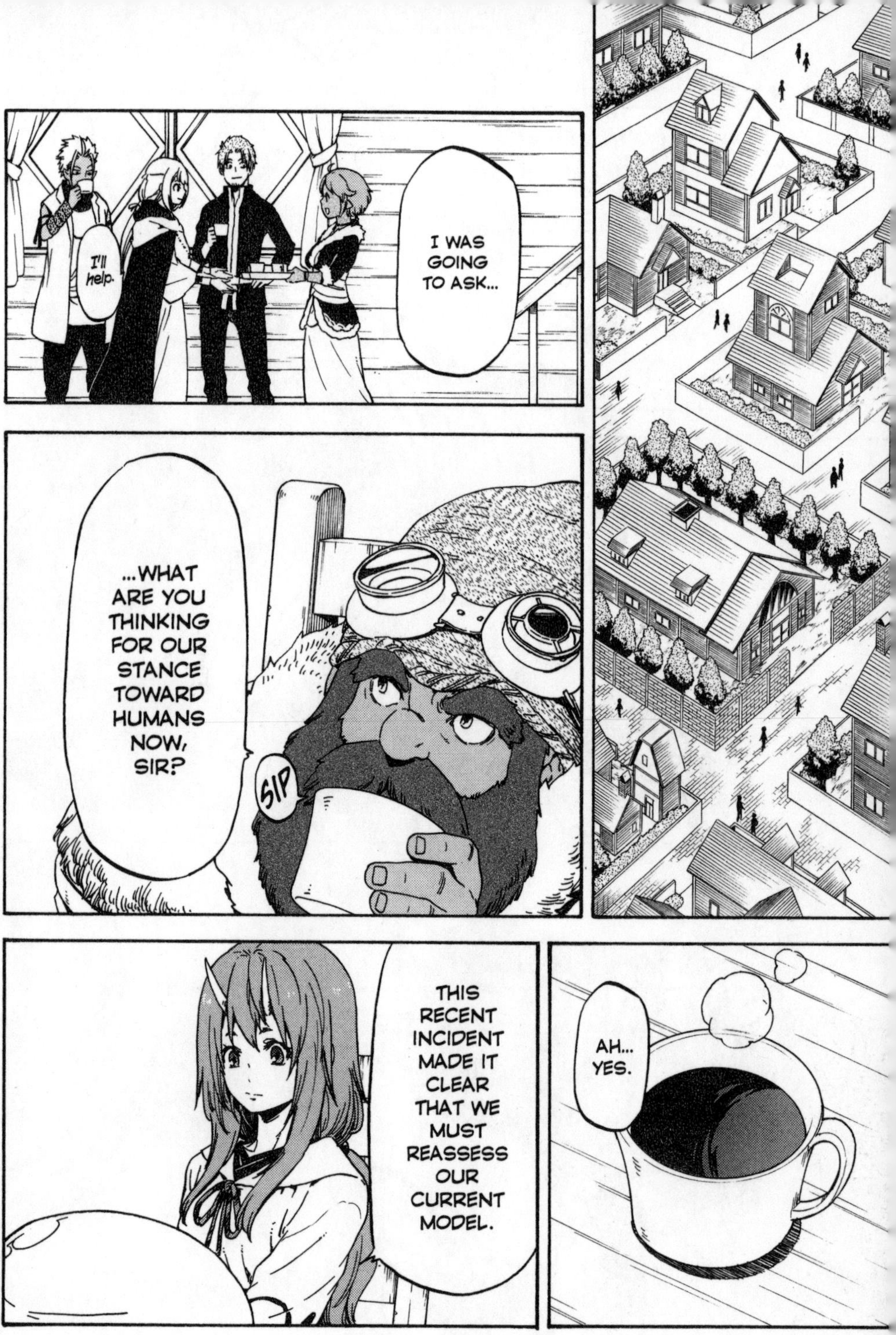
I WAS GOING TO ASK...
I'll help.
...WHAT ARE YOU THINKING FOR OUR STANCE TOWARD HUMANS NOW, SIR?
SIP
AH... YES.
THIS RECENT INCIDENT MADE IT CLEAR THAT WE MUST REASSESS OUR CURRENT MODEL.

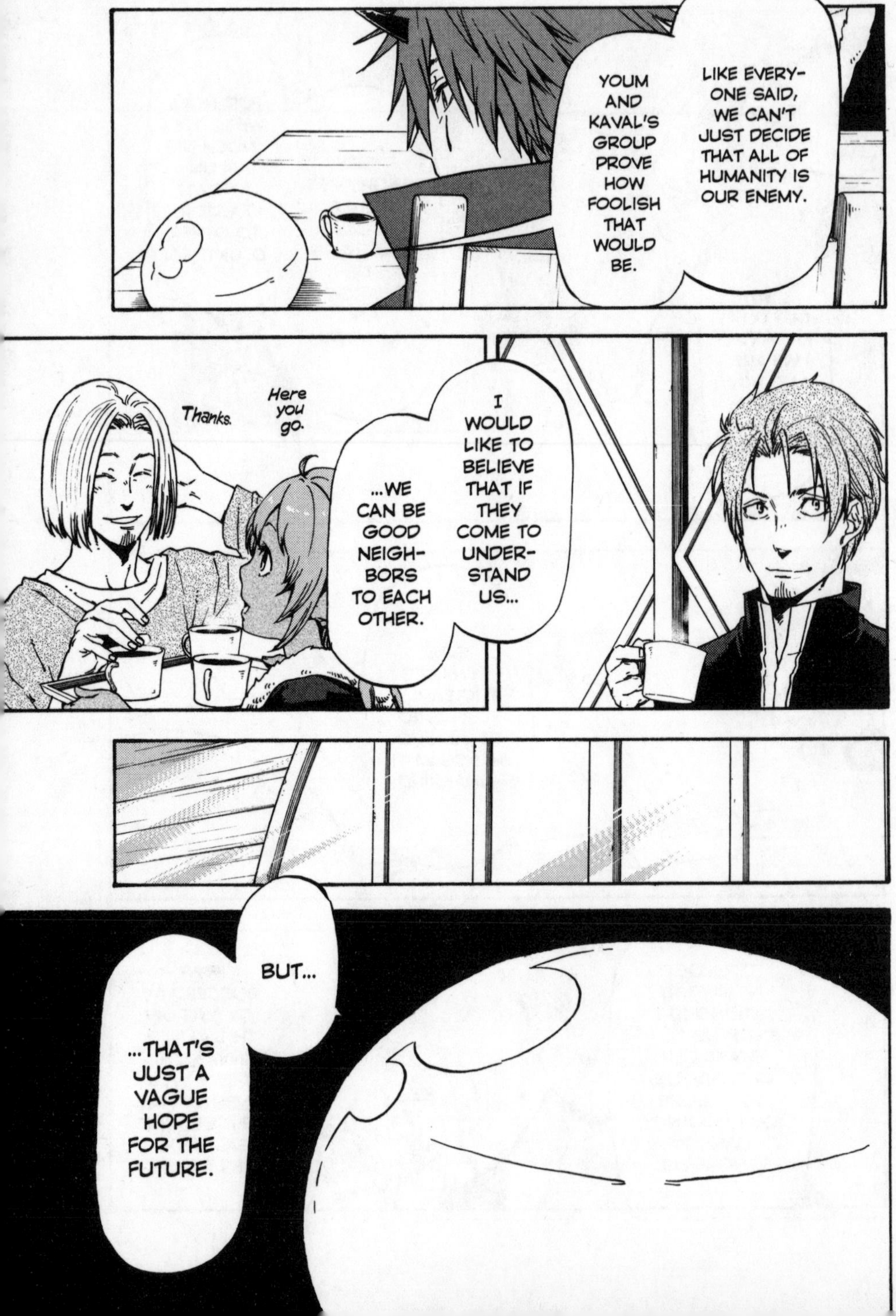
LIKE EVERYONE SAID, WE CAN'T JUST DECIDE THAT ALL OF HUMANITY IS OUR ENEMY.
YOUM AND KAVAL'S GROUP PROVE HOW FOOLISH THAT WOULD BE.
I WOULD LIKE TO BELIEVE THAT IF THEY COME TO UNDERSTAND US...
...WE CAN BE GOOD NEIGHBORS TO EACH OTHER.
Here you go.
Thanks.
BUT...
...THAT'S JUST A VAGUE HOPE FOR THE FUTURE.

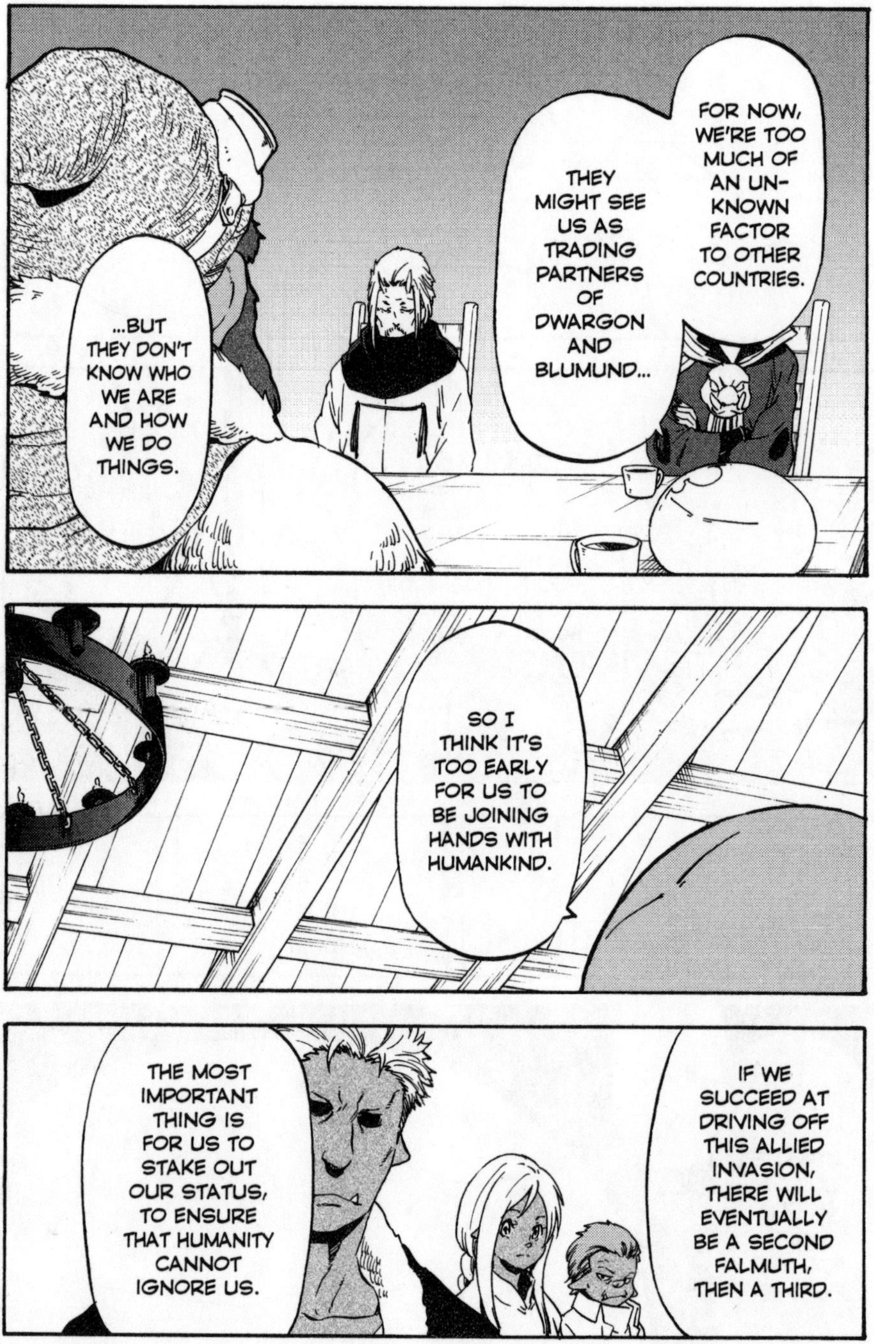
FOR NOW, WE'RE TOO MUCH OF AN UN-KNOWN FACTOR TO OTHER COUNTRIES.
THEY MIGHT SEE US AS TRADING PARTNERS OF DWARGON AND BLUMUND...
...BUT THEY DON'T KNOW WHO WE ARE AND HOW WE DO THINGS.
SO I THINK IT'S TOO EARLY FOR US TO BE JOINING HANDS WITH HUMANKIND.
IF WE SUCCEED AT DRIVING OFF THIS ALLIED INVASION, THERE WILL EVENTUALLY BE A SECOND FALMUTH, THEN A THIRD.
THE MOST IMPORTANT THING IS FOR US TO STAKE OUT OUR STATUS, TO ENSURE THAT HUMANITY CANNOT IGNORE US.

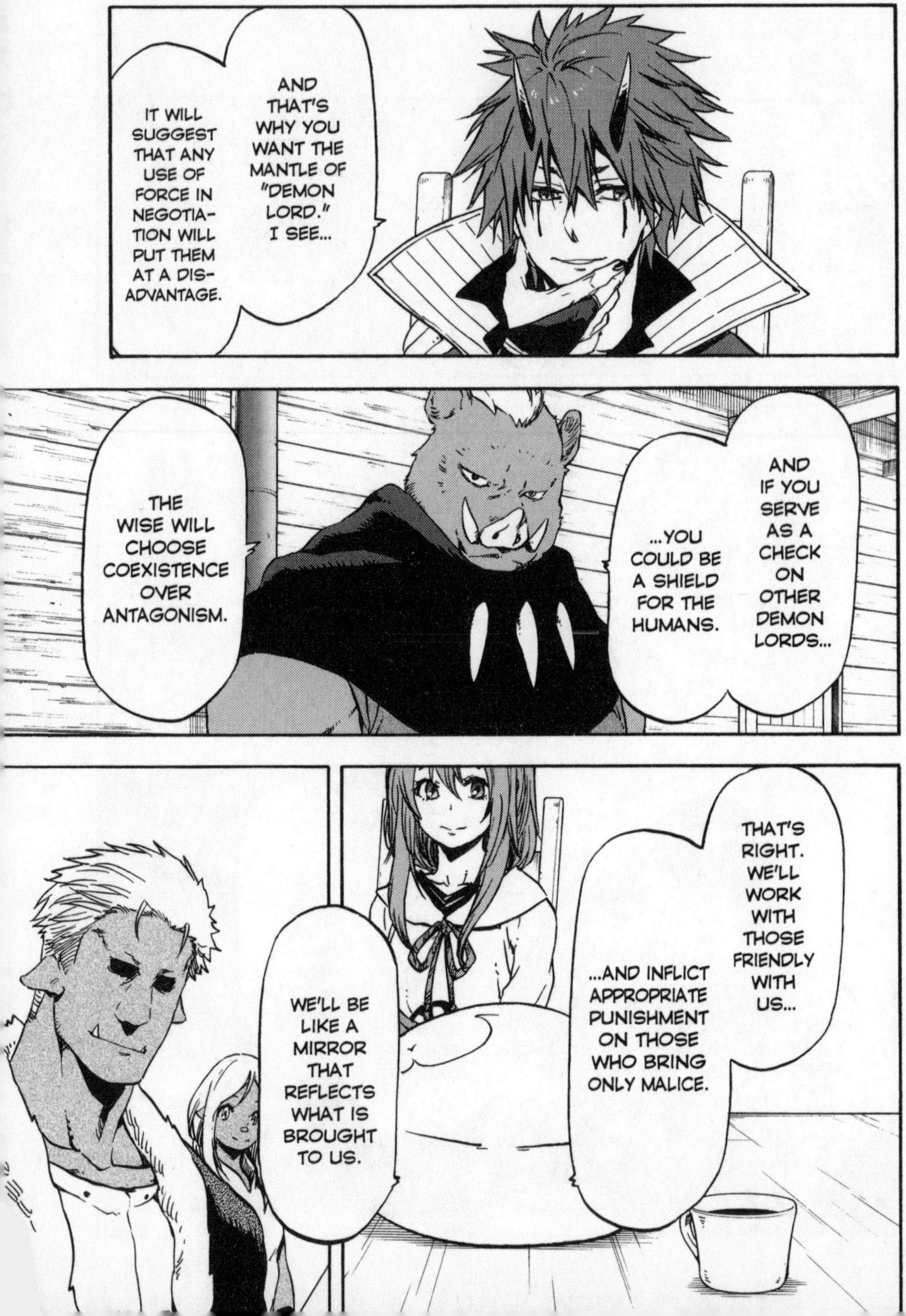
AND THAT'S WHY YOU WANT THE MANTLE OF "DEMON LORD." I SEE...
IT WILL SUGGEST THAT ANY USE OF FORCE IN NEGOTIATION WILL PUT THEM AT A DISADVANTAGE.
AND IF YOU SERVE AS A CHECK ON OTHER DEMON LORDS...
...YOU COULD BE A SHIELD FOR THE HUMANS.
THE WISE WILL CHOOSE COEXISTENCE OVER ANTAGONISM.
THAT'S RIGHT. WE'LL WORK WITH THOSE FRIENDLY WITH US...
...AND INFLICT APPROPRIATE PUNISHMENT ON THOSE WHO BRING ONLY MALICE.
WE'LL BE LIKE A MIRROR THAT REFLECTS WHAT IS BROUGHT TO US.

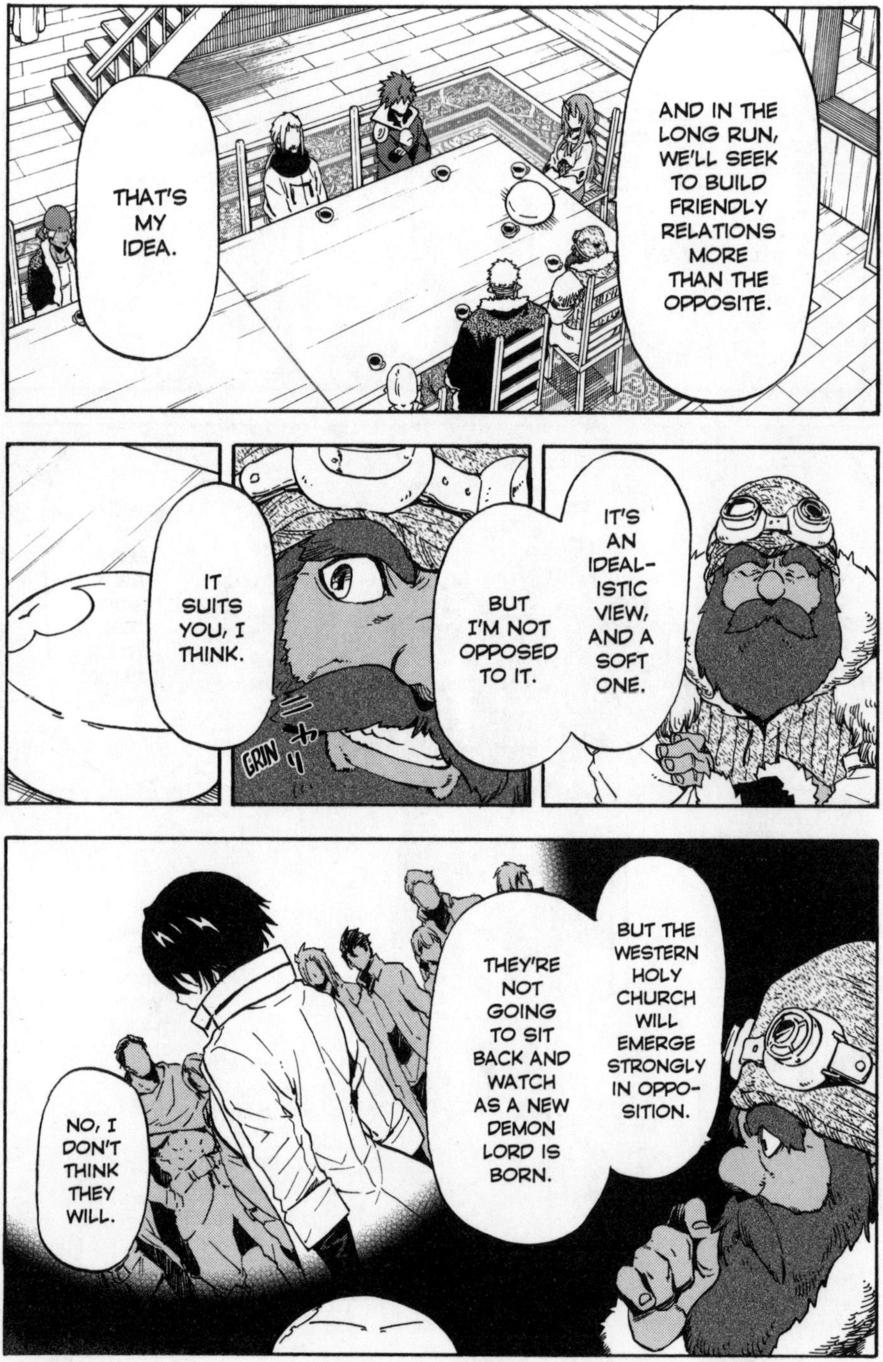
AND IN THE LONG RUN, WE'LL SEEK TO BUILD FRIENDLY RELATIONS MORE THAN THE OPPOSITE.
THAT'S MY IDEA.
IT'S AN IDEAL-ISTIC VIEW, AND A SOFT ONE.
BUT I'M NOT OPPOSED TO IT.
GRIN
IT SUITS YOU, I THINK.
BUT THE WESTERN HOLY CHURCH WILL EMERGE STRONGLY IN OPPO-SITION.
THEY'RE NOT GOING TO SIT BACK AND WATCH AS A NEW DEMON LORD IS BORN.
NO, I DON'T THINK THEY WILL.

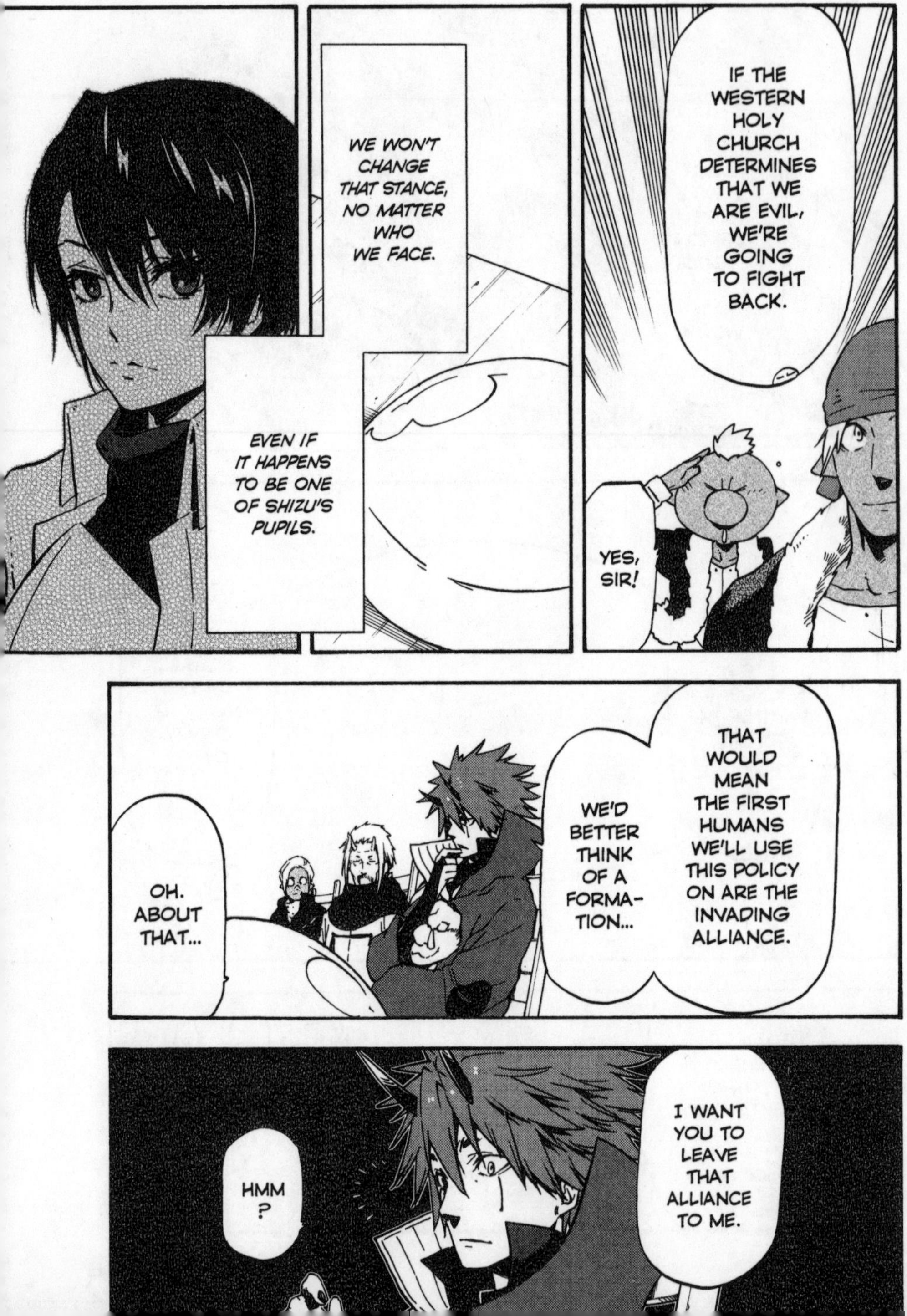
IF THE WESTERN HOLY CHURCH DETERMINES THAT WE ARE EVIL, WE'RE GOING TO FIGHT BACK.
YES, SIR!
WE WON'T CHANGE THAT STANCE, NO MATTER WHO WE FACE.
EVEN IF IT HAPPENS TO BE ONE OF SHIZU'S PUPILS.
THAT WOULD MEAN THE FIRST HUMANS WE'LL USE THIS POLICY ON ARE THE INVADING ALLIANCE.
WE'D BETTER THINK OF A FORMA-TION...
OH. ABOUT THAT...
I WANT YOU TO LEAVE THAT ALLIANCE TO ME.
HMM ?

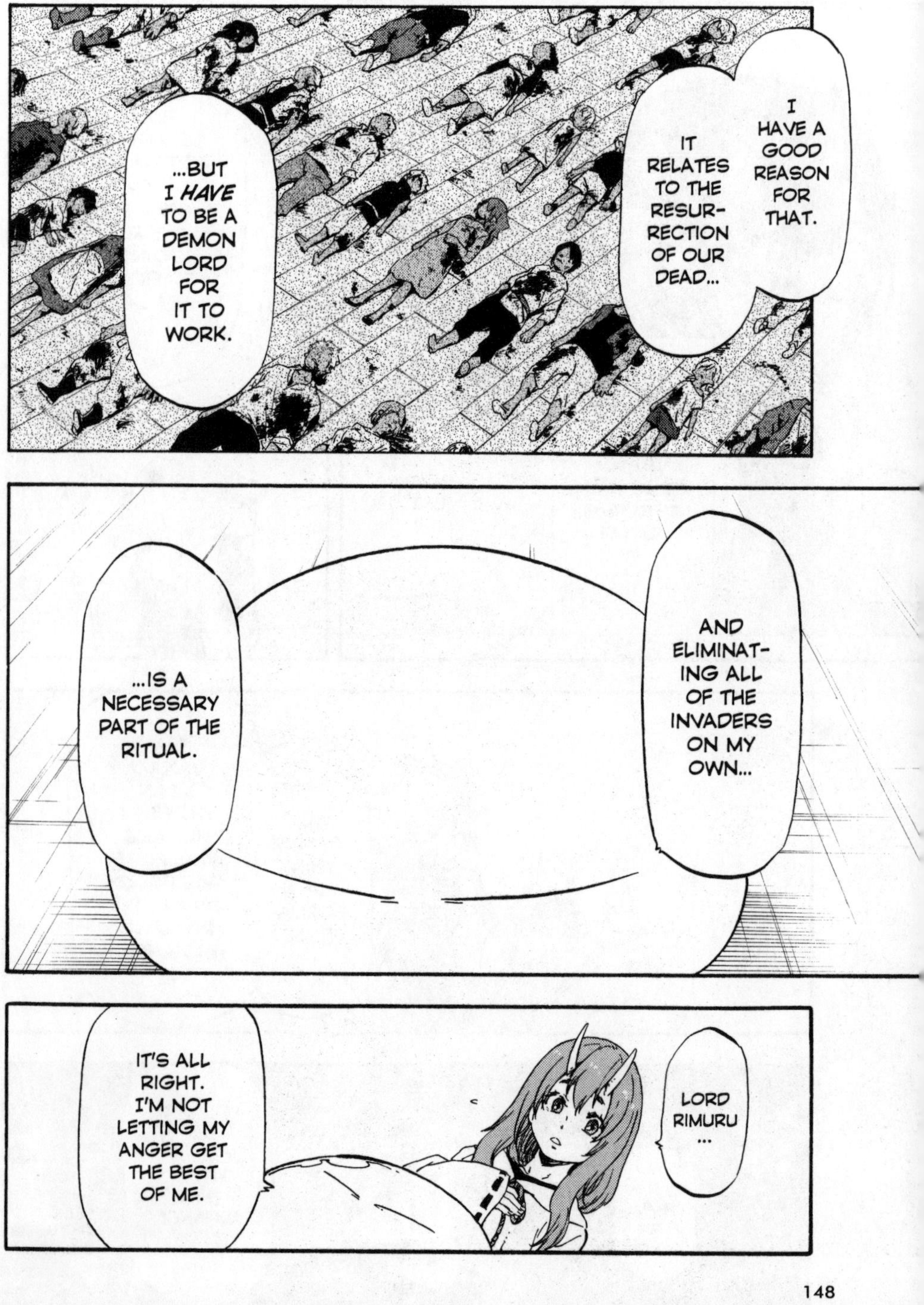
I HAVE A GOOD REASON FOR THAT.
IT RELATES TO THE RESUR-RECTION OF OUR DEAD...
...BUT I *HAVE* TO BE A DEMON LORD FOR IT TO WORK.
AND ELIMINAT-ING ALL OF THE INVADERS ON MY OWN...
...IS A NECESSARY PART OF THE RITUAL.
LORD RIMURU ...
IT'S ALL RIGHT. I'M NOT LETTING MY ANGER GET THE BEST OF ME.

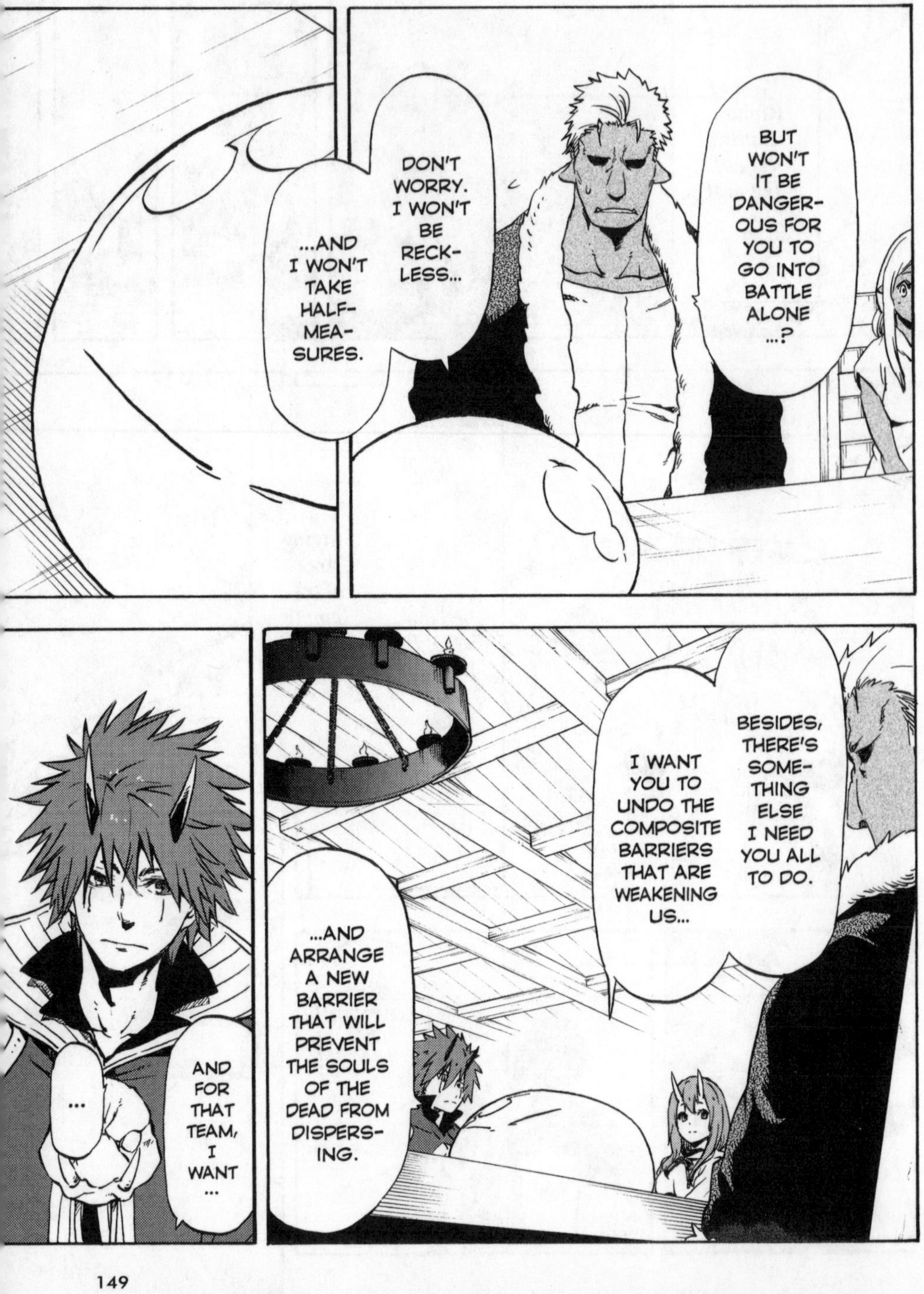
BUT WON'T IT BE DANGEROUS FOR YOU TO GO INTO BATTLE ALONE ...?
DON'T WORRY. I WON'T BE RECKLESS...
...AND I WON'T TAKE HALF-MEASURES.
BESIDES, THERE'S SOMETHING ELSE I NEED YOU ALL TO DO.
I WANT YOU TO UNDO THE COMPOSITE BARRIERS THAT ARE WEAKENING US...
...AND ARRANGE A NEW BARRIER THAT WILL PREVENT THE SOULS OF THE DEAD FROM DISPERSING.
AND FOR THAT TEAM, I WANT ...
...

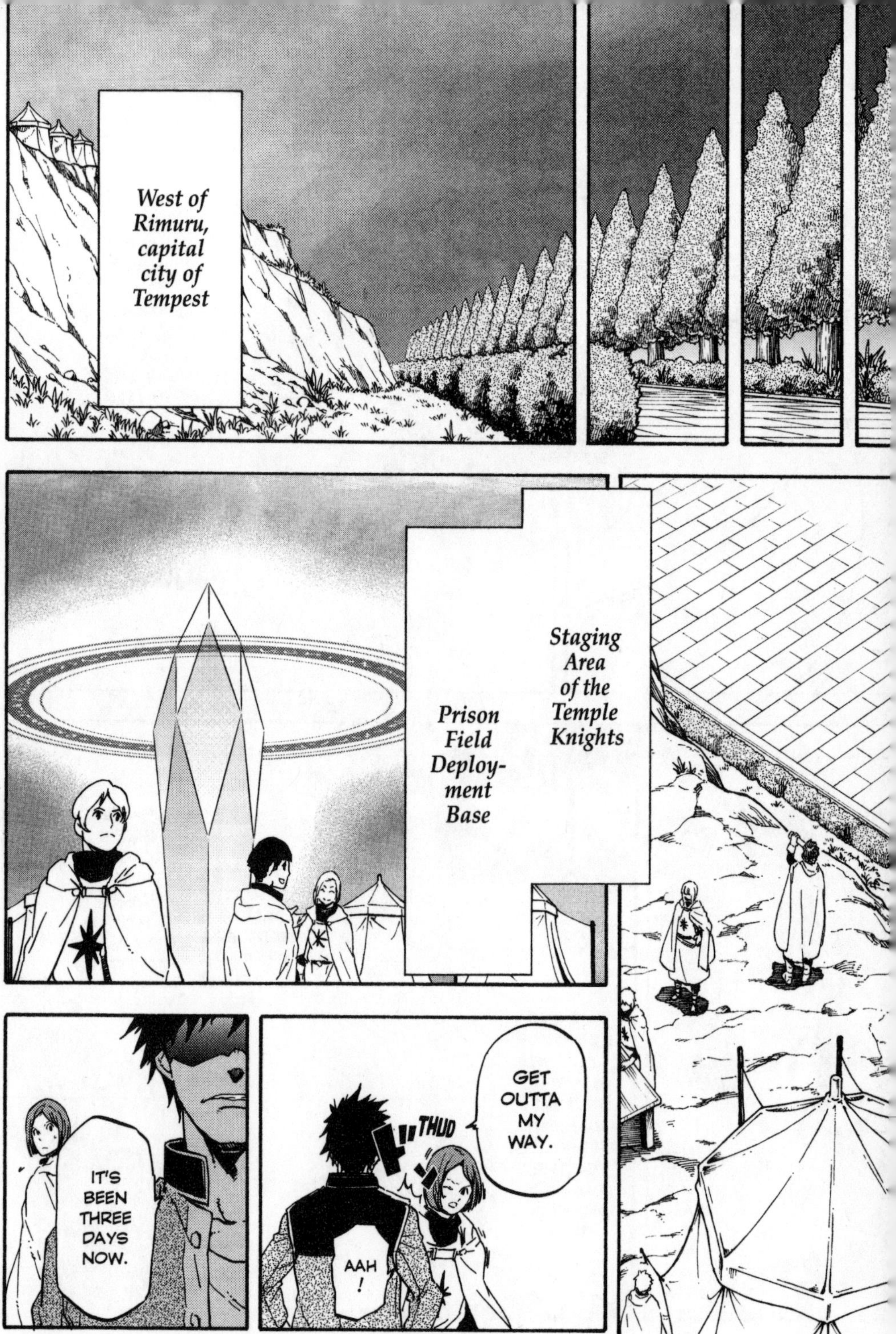
West of Rimuru, capital city of Tempest
Staging Area of the Temple Knights
Prison Field Deployment Base
GET OUTTA MY WAY.
THUD
AAH!
IT'S BEEN THREE DAYS NOW.

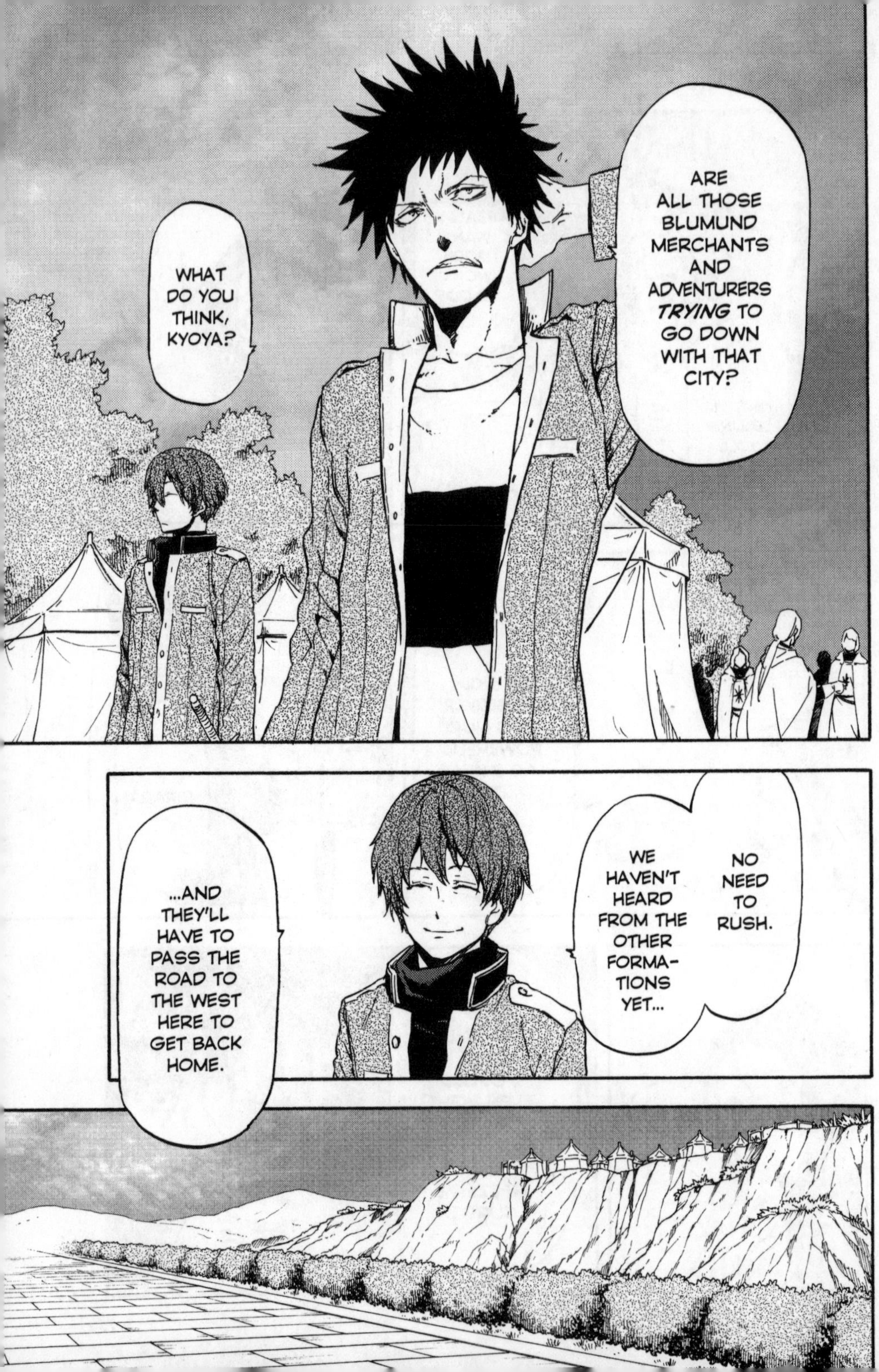
ARE ALL THOSE BLUMUND MERCHANTS AND ADVENTURERS *TRYING* TO GO DOWN WITH THAT CITY?
WHAT DO YOU THINK, KYOYA?
NO NEED TO RUSH.
WE HAVEN'T HEARD FROM THE OTHER FORMA-TIONS YET...
...AND THEY'LL HAVE TO PASS THE ROAD TO THE WEST HERE TO GET BACK HOME.

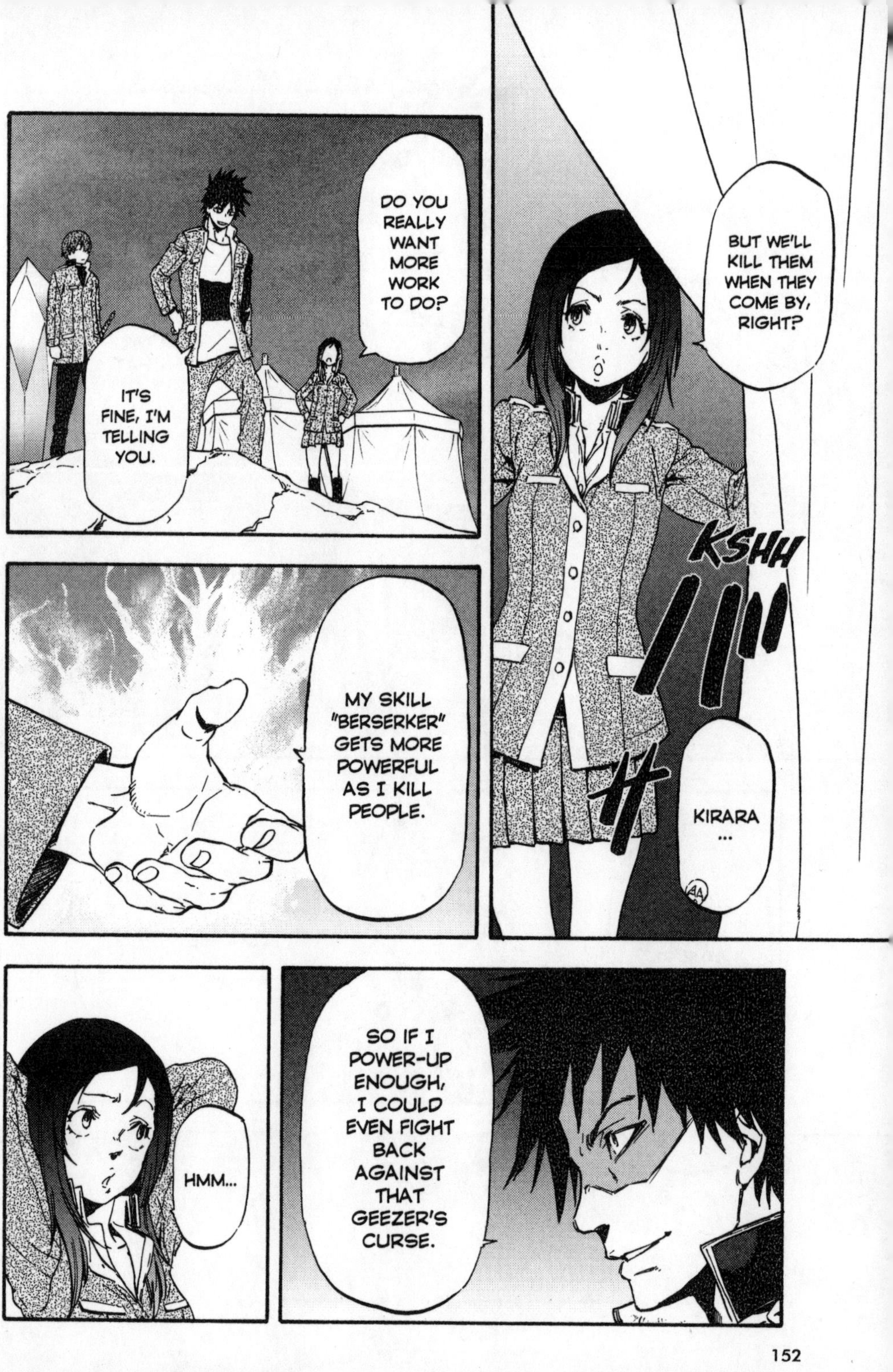
BUT WE'LL KILL THEM WHEN THEY COME BY, RIGHT?
KSHH
KIRARA ...
DO YOU REALLY WANT MORE WORK TO DO?
IT'S FINE, I'M TELLING YOU.
MY SKILL "BERSERKER" GETS MORE POWERFUL AS I KILL PEOPLE.
SO IF I POWER-UP ENOUGH, I COULD EVEN FIGHT BACK AGAINST THAT GEEZER'S CURSE.
HMM...

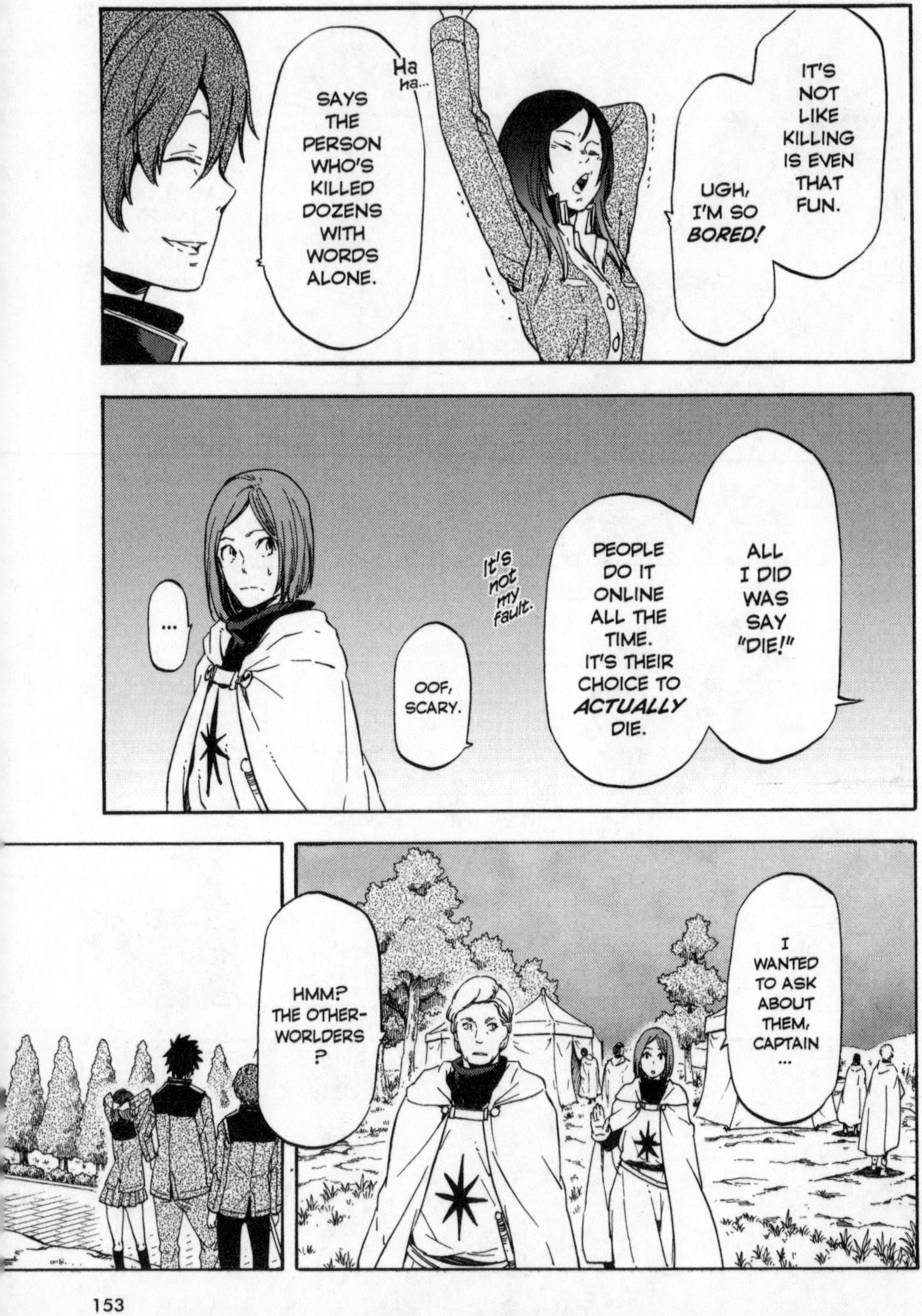
IT'S NOT LIKE KILLING IS EVEN THAT FUN.
UGH, I'M SO *BORED!*
Ha ha...
SAYS THE PERSON WHO'S KILLED DOZENS WITH WORDS ALONE.
ALL I DID WAS SAY "DIE!"
PEOPLE DO IT ONLINE ALL THE TIME. IT'S THEIR CHOICE TO *ACTUALLY* DIE.
It's not my fault.
OOF, SCARY.
...
I WANTED TO ASK ABOUT THEM, CAPTAIN ...
HMM? THE OTHER-WORLDERS ?

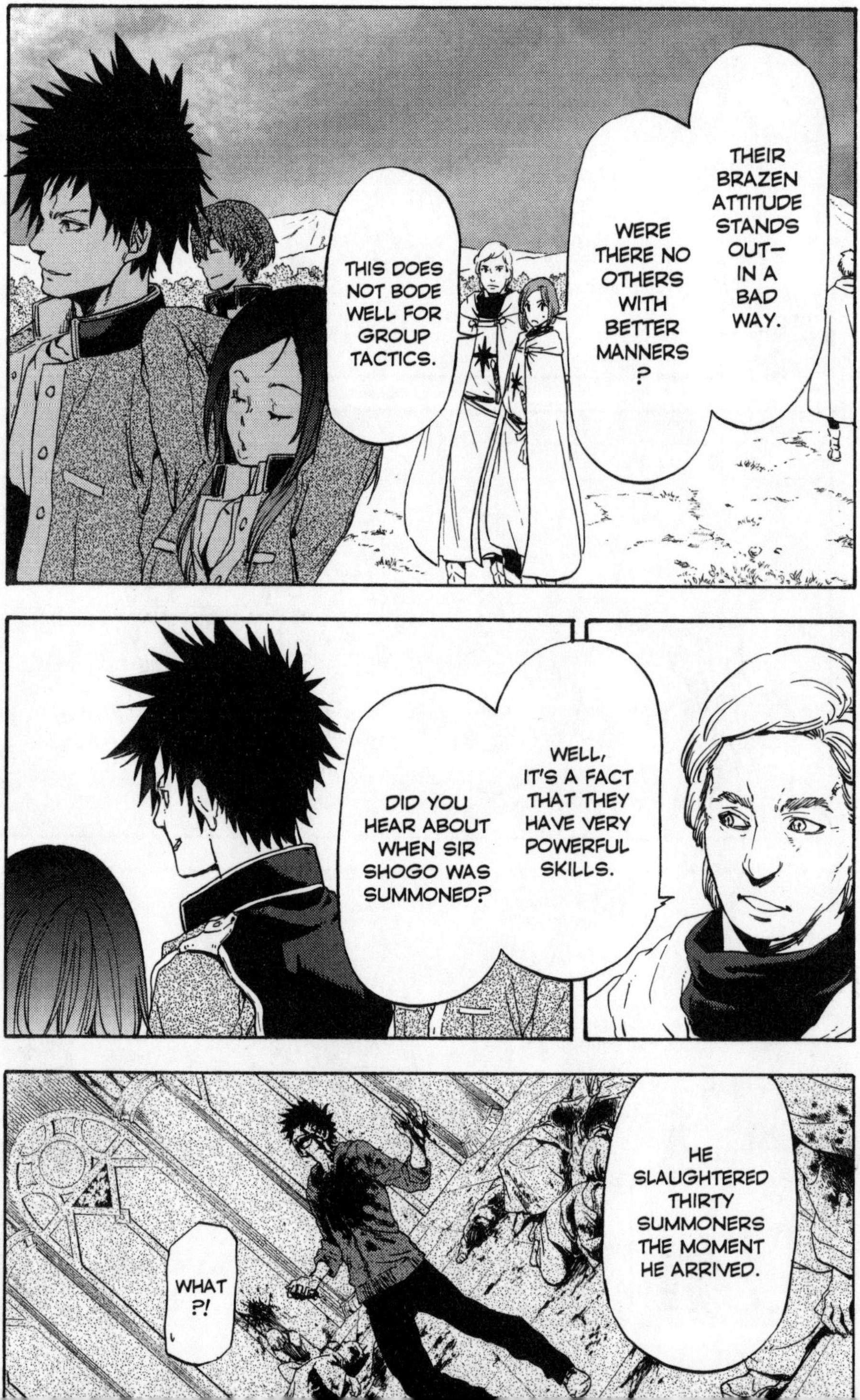
THEIR BRAZEN ATTITUDE STANDS OUT— IN A BAD WAY.
WERE THERE NO OTHERS WITH BETTER MANNERS?
THIS DOES NOT BODE WELL FOR GROUP TACTICS.
WELL, IT'S A FACT THAT THEY HAVE VERY POWERFUL SKILLS.
DID YOU HEAR ABOUT WHEN SIR SHOGO WAS SUMMONED?
HE SLAUGHTERED THIRTY SUMMONERS THE MOMENT HE ARRIVED.
WHAT?!

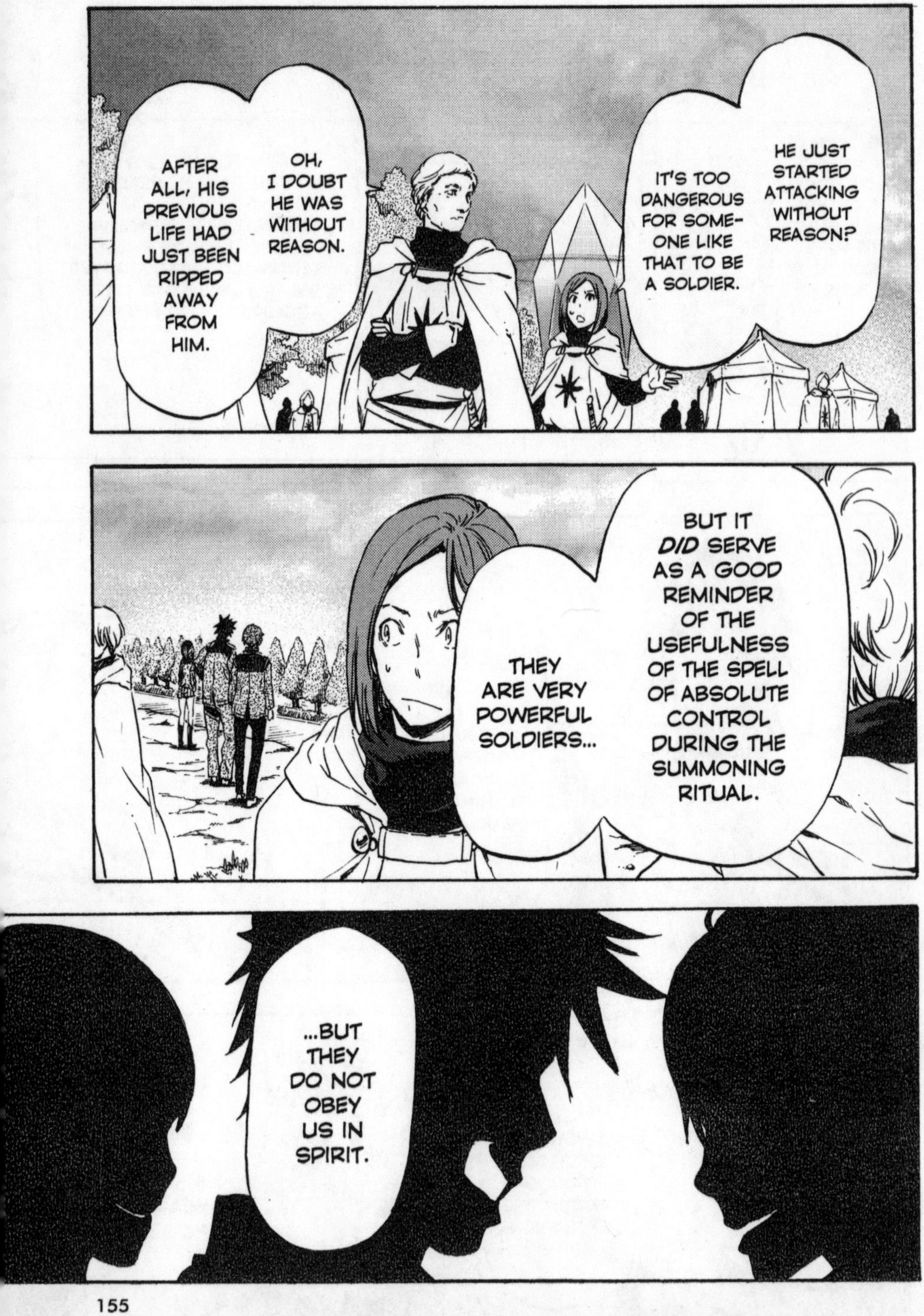
HE JUST STARTED ATTACKING WITHOUT REASON?
IT'S TOO DANGEROUS FOR SOME-ONE LIKE THAT TO BE A SOLDIER.
OH, I DOUBT HE WAS WITHOUT REASON.
AFTER ALL, HIS PREVIOUS LIFE HAD JUST BEEN RIPPED AWAY FROM HIM.
BUT IT *DID* SERVE AS A GOOD REMINDER OF THE USEFULNESS OF THE SPELL OF ABSOLUTE CONTROL DURING THE SUMMONING RITUAL.
THEY ARE VERY POWERFUL SOLDIERS...
...BUT THEY DO NOT OBEY US IN SPIRIT.

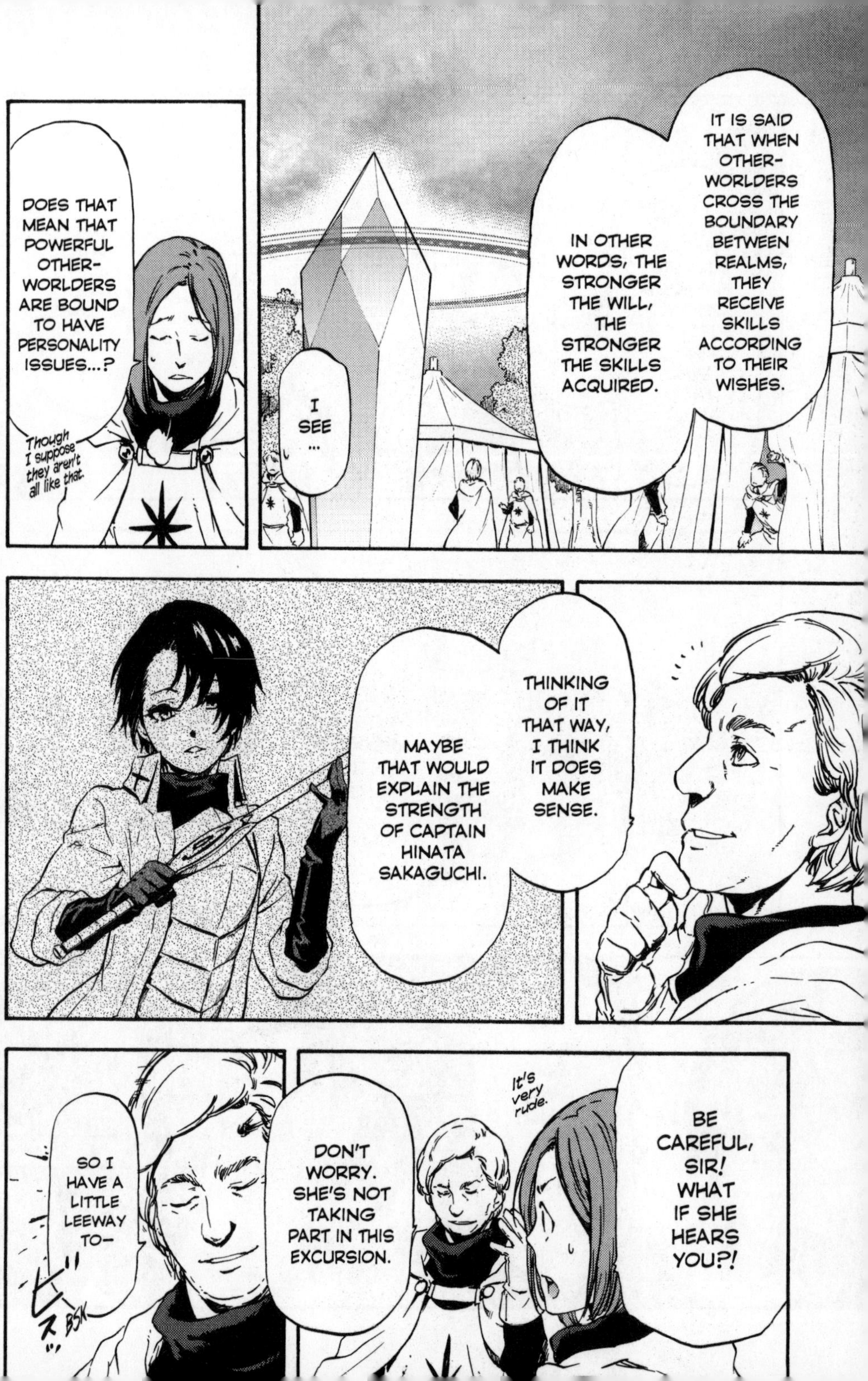
IT IS SAID THAT WHEN OTHER-WORLDERS CROSS THE BOUNDARY BETWEEN REALMS, THEY RECEIVE SKILLS ACCORDING TO THEIR WISHES.
IN OTHER WORDS, THE STRONGER THE WILL, THE STRONGER THE SKILLS ACQUIRED.
I SEE ...
DOES THAT MEAN THAT POWERFUL OTHER-WORLDERS ARE BOUND TO HAVE PERSONALITY ISSUES...?
Though I suppose they aren't all like that.
THINKING OF IT THAT WAY, I THINK IT DOES MAKE SENSE.
MAYBE THAT WOULD EXPLAIN THE STRENGTH OF CAPTAIN HINATA SAKAGUCHI.
BE CAREFUL, SIR! WHAT IF SHE HEARS YOU?!
It's very rude.
DON'T WORRY. SHE'S NOT TAKING PART IN THIS EXCURSION.
SO I HAVE A LITTLE LEEWAY TO—
BSK

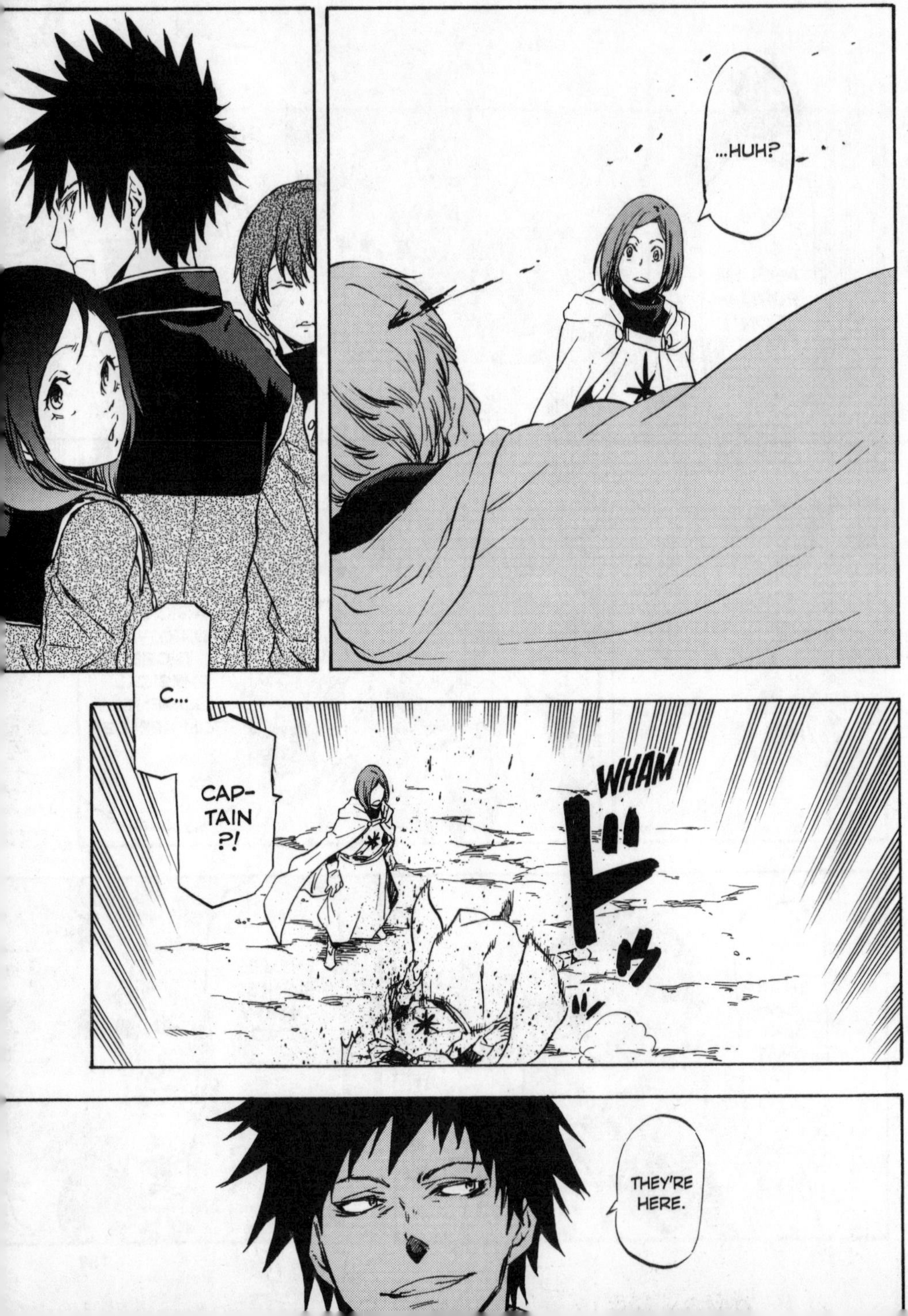
...HUH?
C... CAP-TAIN?!
WHAM
ドッ
THEY'RE HERE.

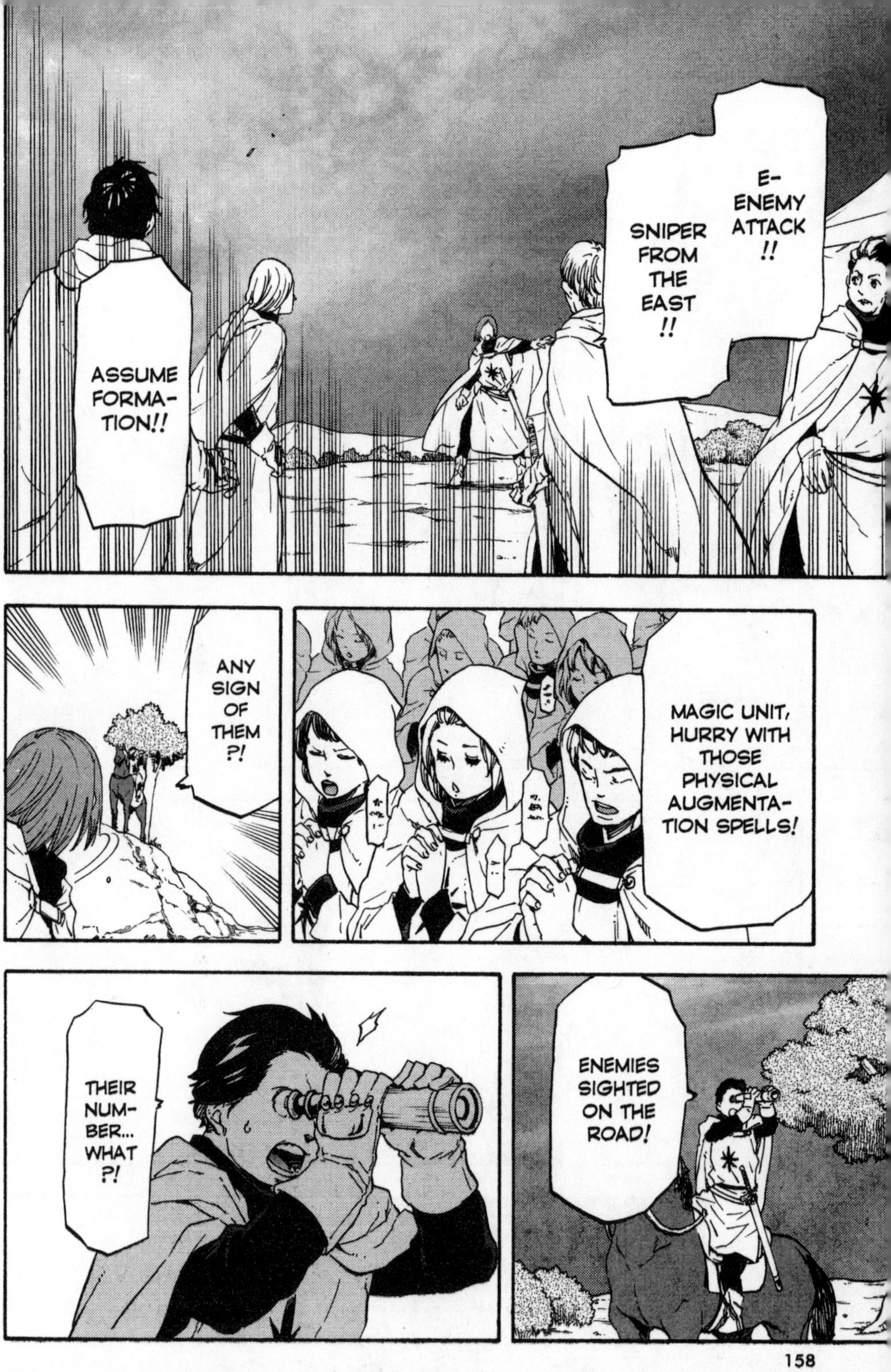
E-ENEMY ATTACK!!
SNIPER FROM THE EAST!!
ASSUME FORMATION!!
MAGIC UNIT, HURRY WITH THOSE PHYSICAL AUGMENTATION SPELLS!
ANY SIGN OF THEM?!
ENEMIES SIGHTED ON THE ROAD!
THEIR NUMBER... WHAT?!

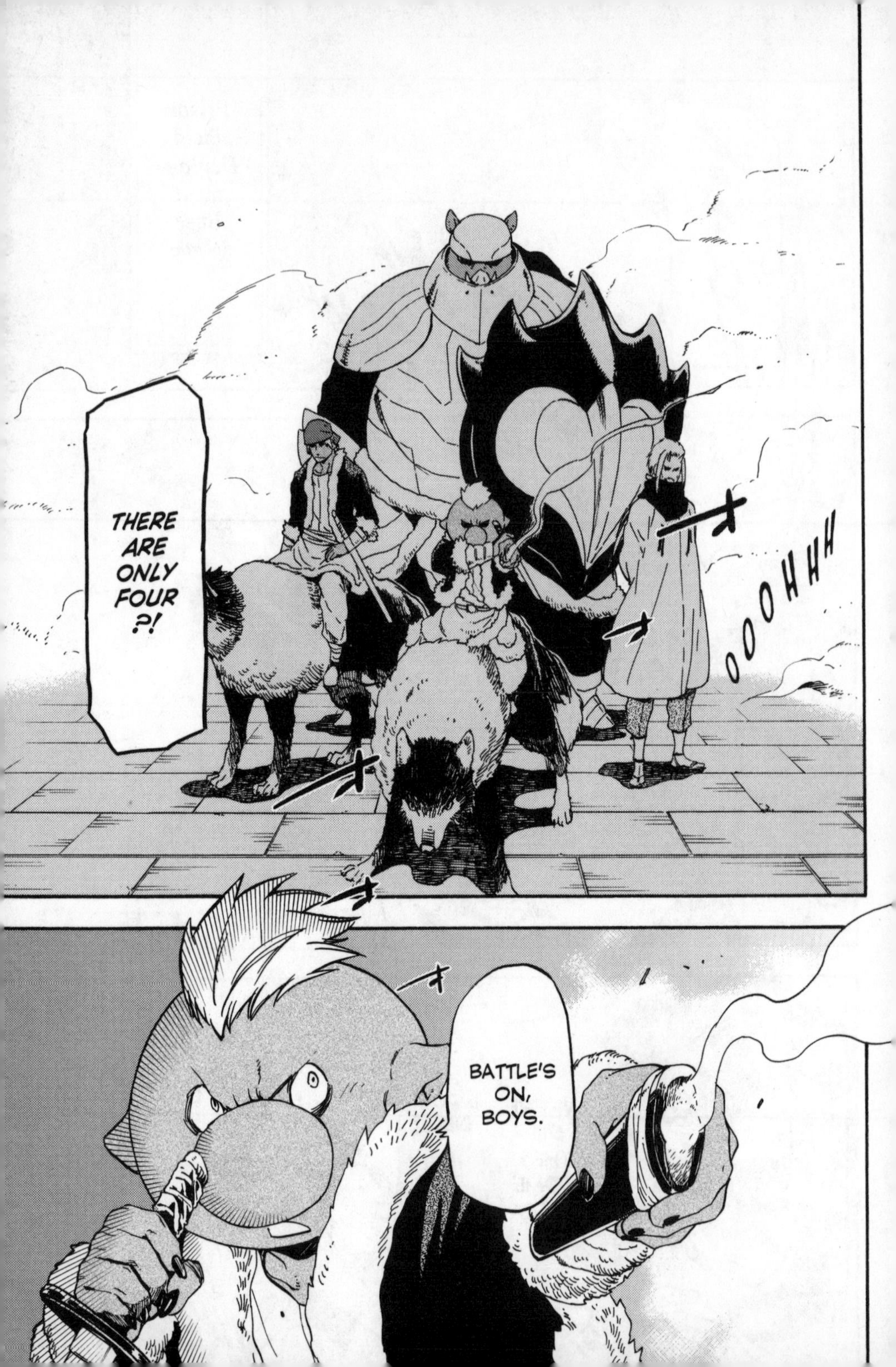
OOOHHH
THERE ARE ONLY FOUR ?!
BATTLE'S ON, BOYS.

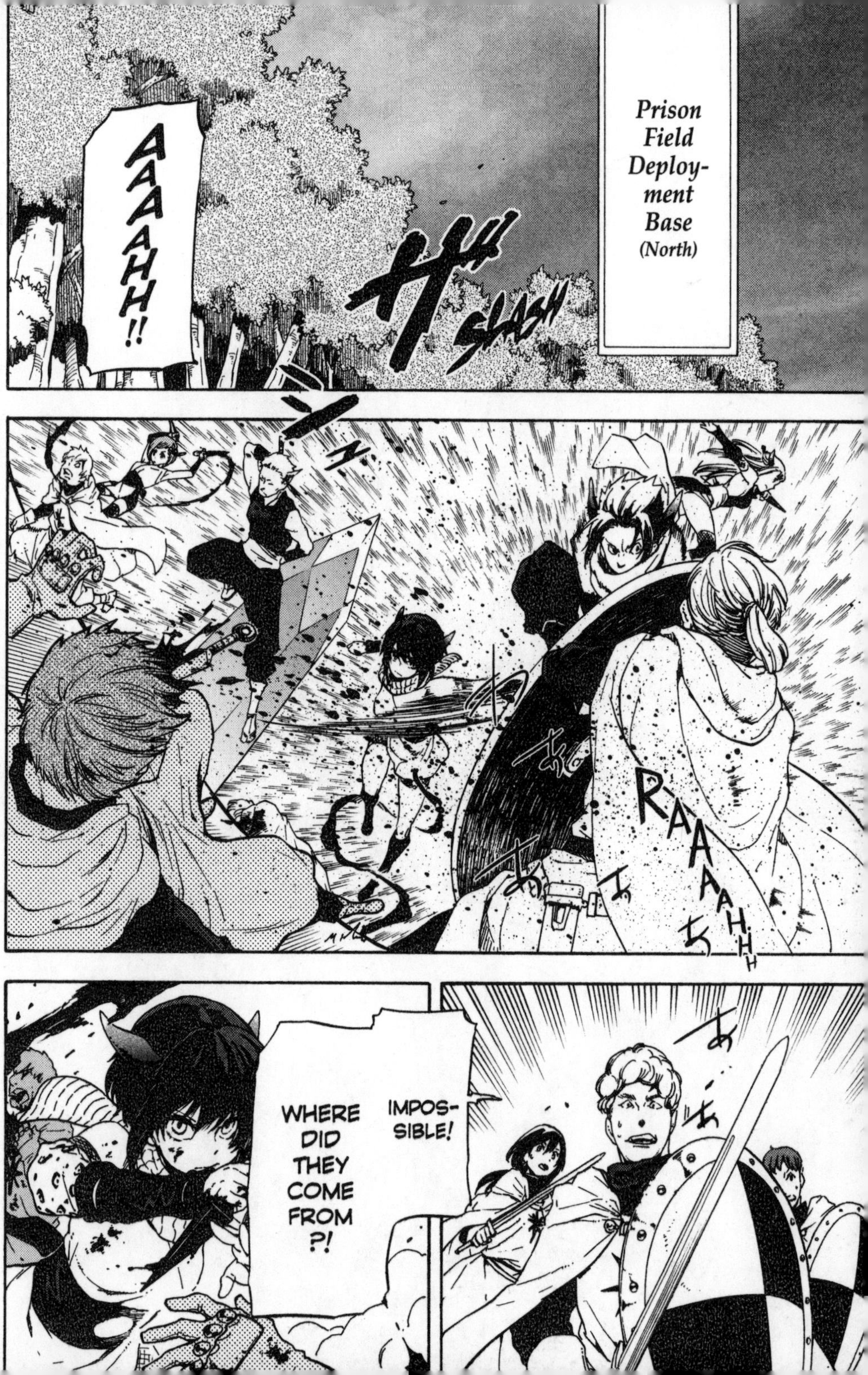
Prison Field Deployment Base (North)
SLASH
AAAAAHH!!
RAAAAAHHH
IMPOSSIBLE!
WHERE DID THEY COME FROM?!

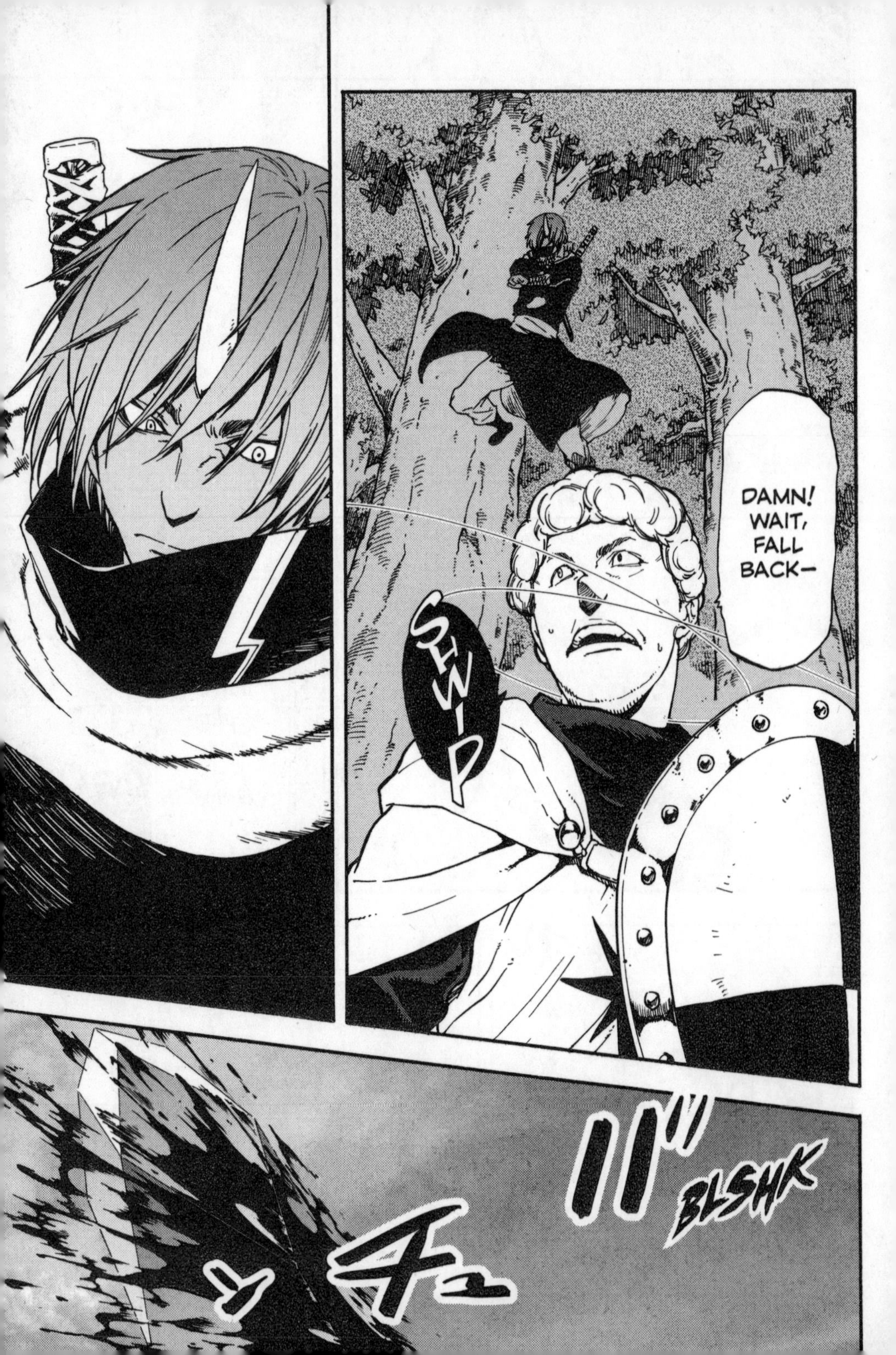
DAMN! WAIT, FALL BACK—
SHWIP
BLSHK

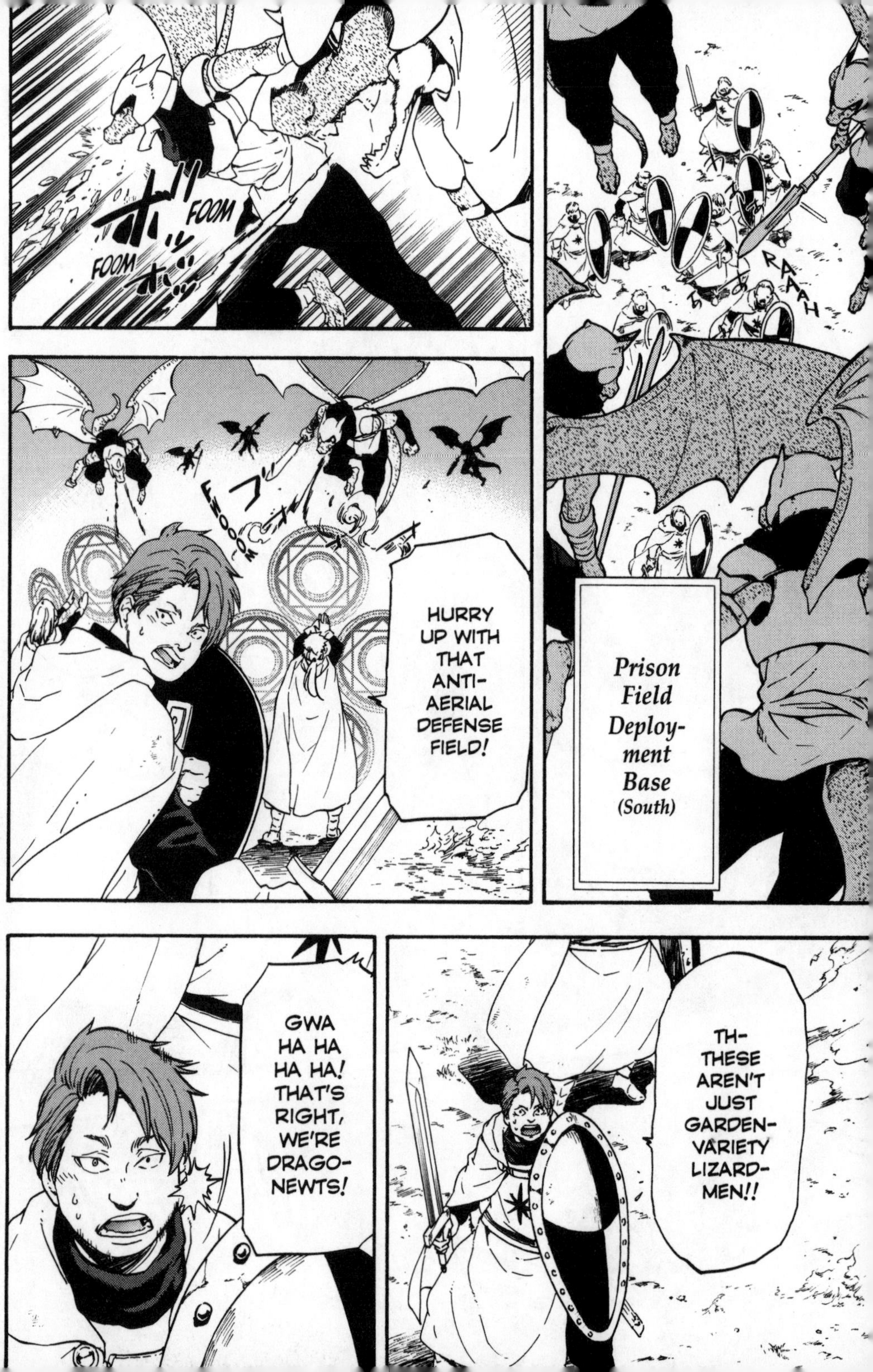
RAAAAH
FOOM
FOOM
Prison Field Deployment Base (South)
FWOOOM
HURRY UP WITH THAT ANTI-AERIAL DEFENSE FIELD!
TH-THESE AREN'T JUST GARDEN-VARIETY LIZARD-MEN!!
GWA HA HA HA HA! THAT'S RIGHT, WE'RE DRAGO-NEWTS!

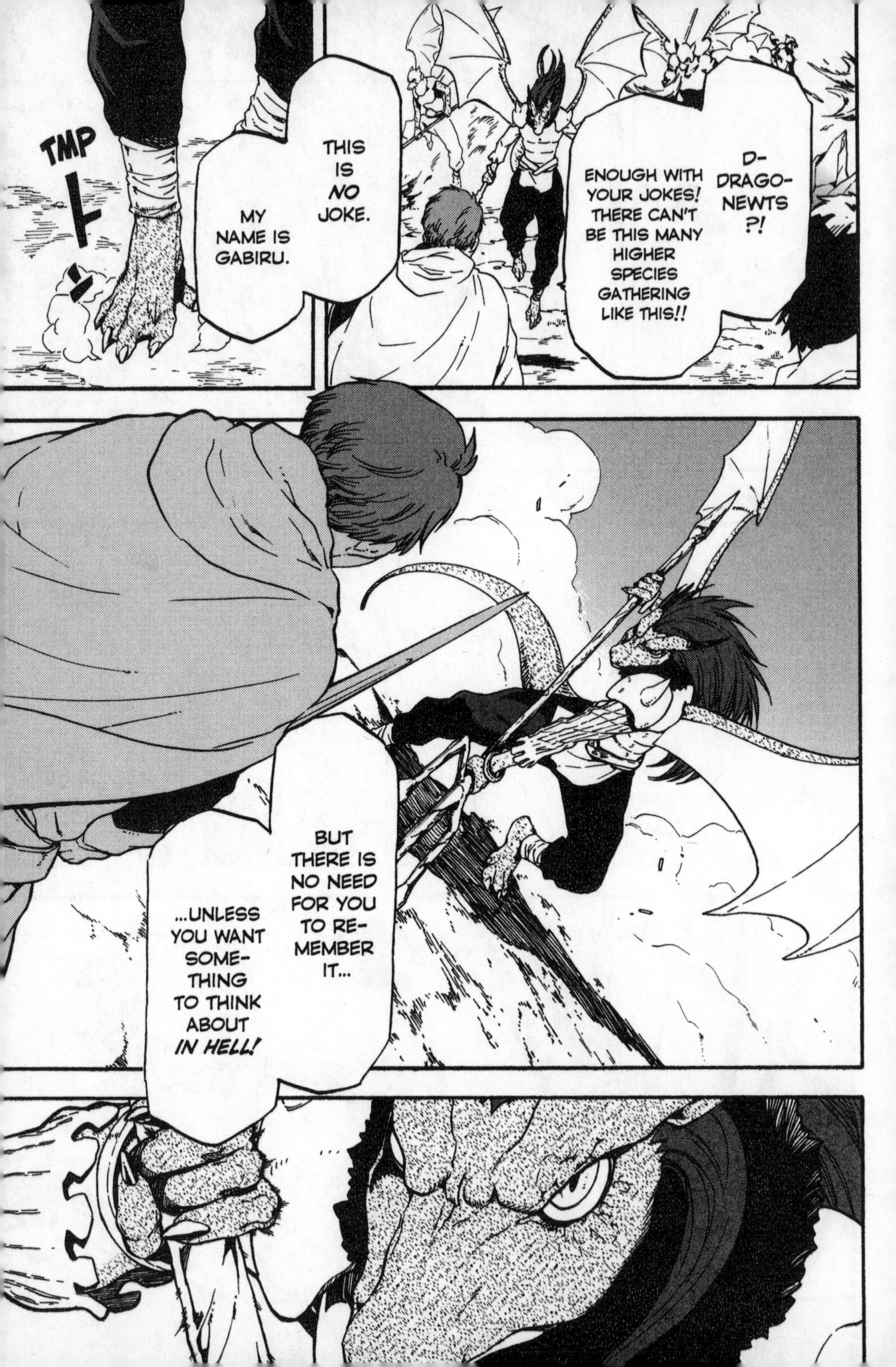
D-DRAGO-NEWTS?!
ENOUGH WITH YOUR JOKES! THERE CAN'T BE THIS MANY HIGHER SPECIES GATHERING LIKE THIS!!
THIS IS *NO* JOKE.
MY NAME IS GABIRU.
TMP
BUT THERE IS NO NEED FOR YOU TO RE-MEMBER IT...
...UNLESS YOU WANT SOME-THING TO THINK ABOUT *IN HELL!*

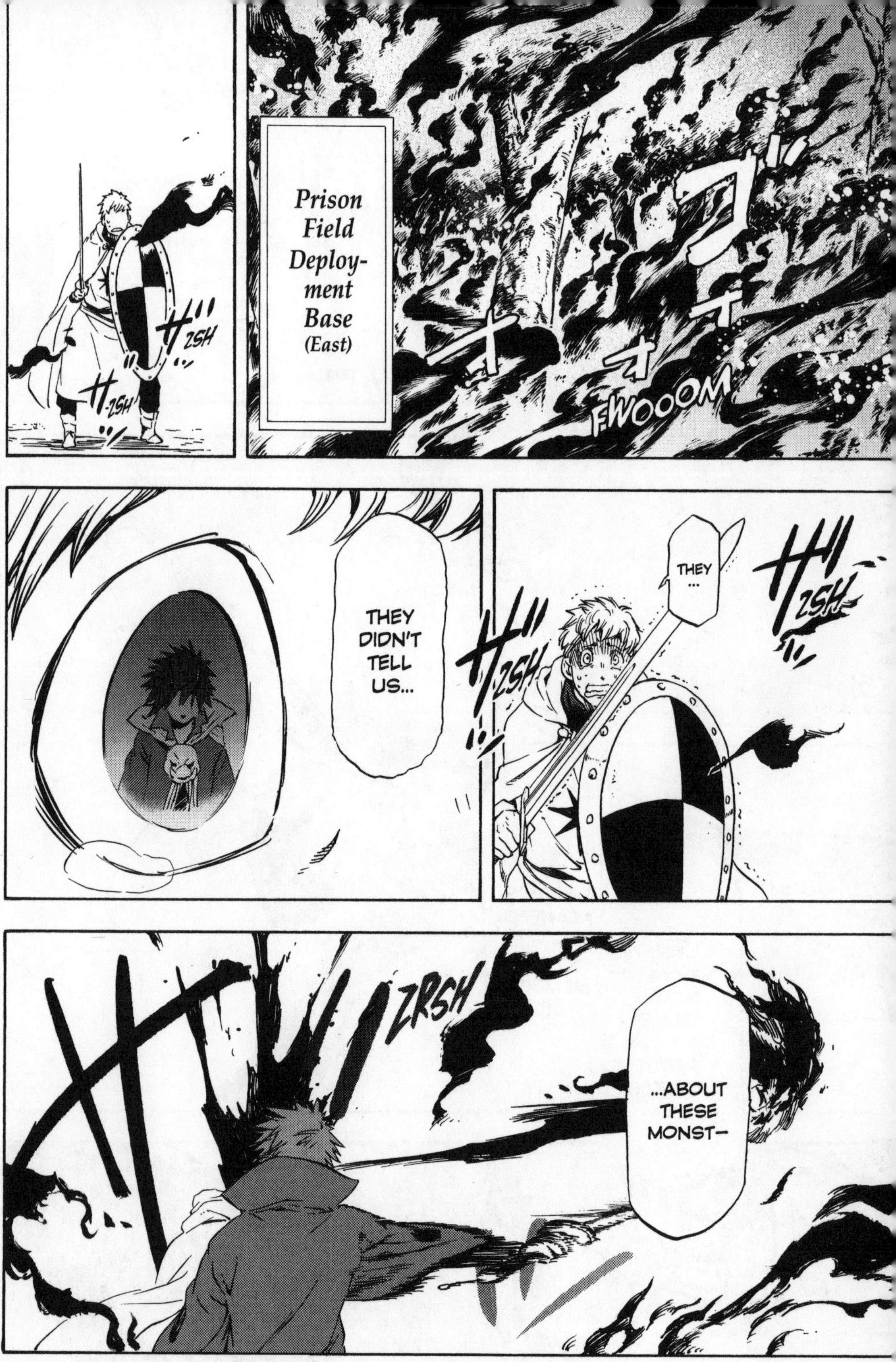
FWOOOM
Prison Field Deployment Base (East)
ZSH
ZSH
ZSH
THEY ...
ZSH
THEY DIDN'T TELL US...
ZRSH
...ABOUT THESE MONST—

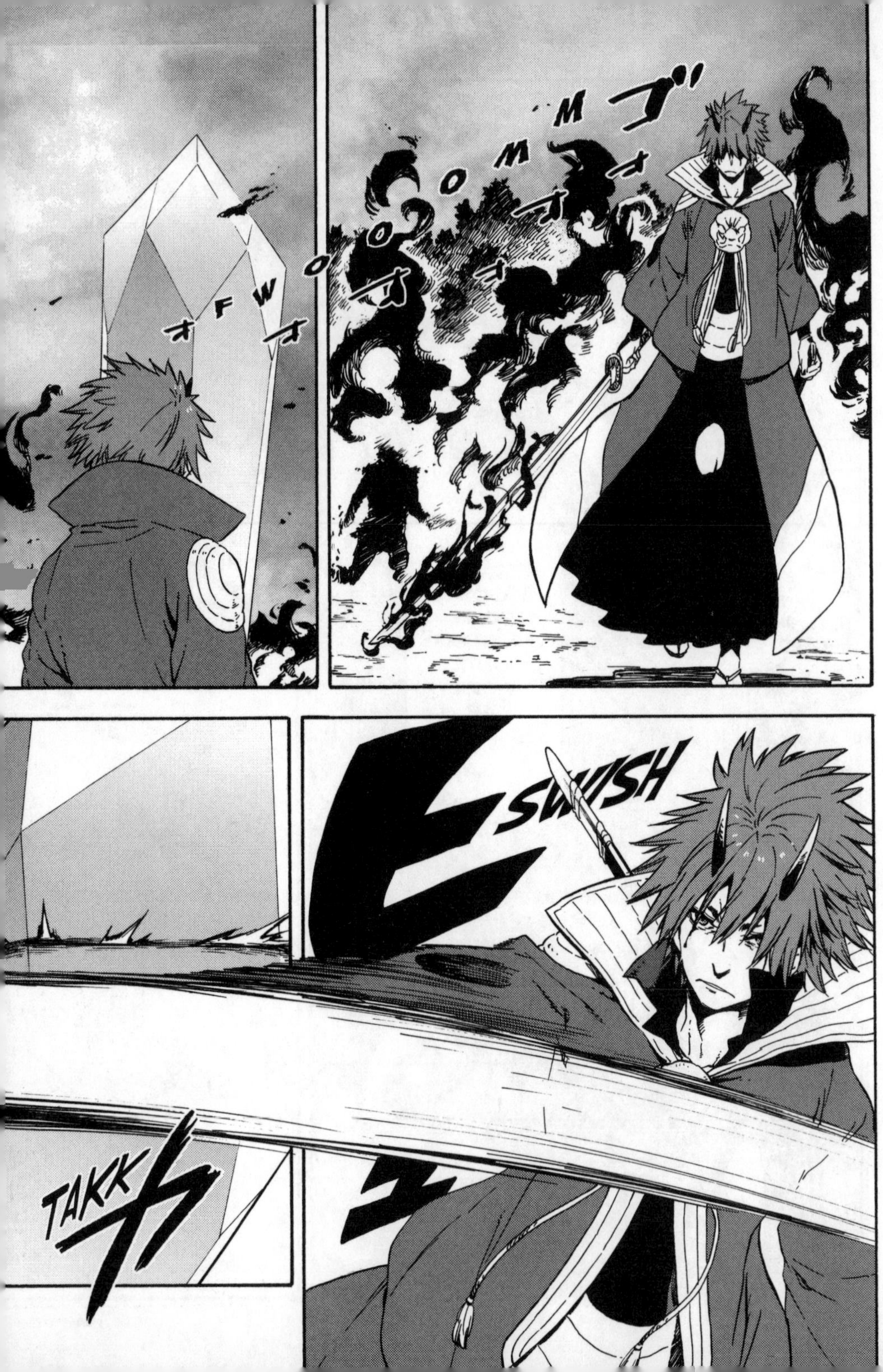
FWOOOMM
SWISH
TAKK

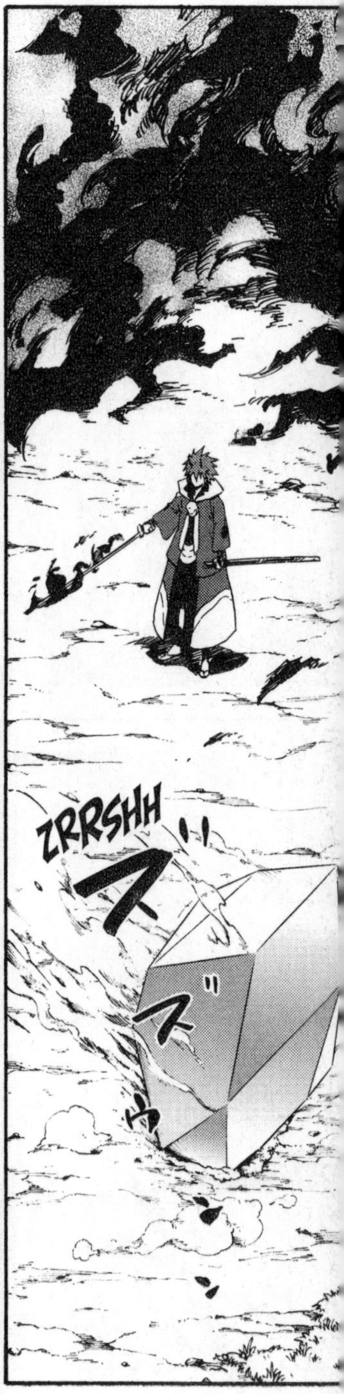
ZRRSHH

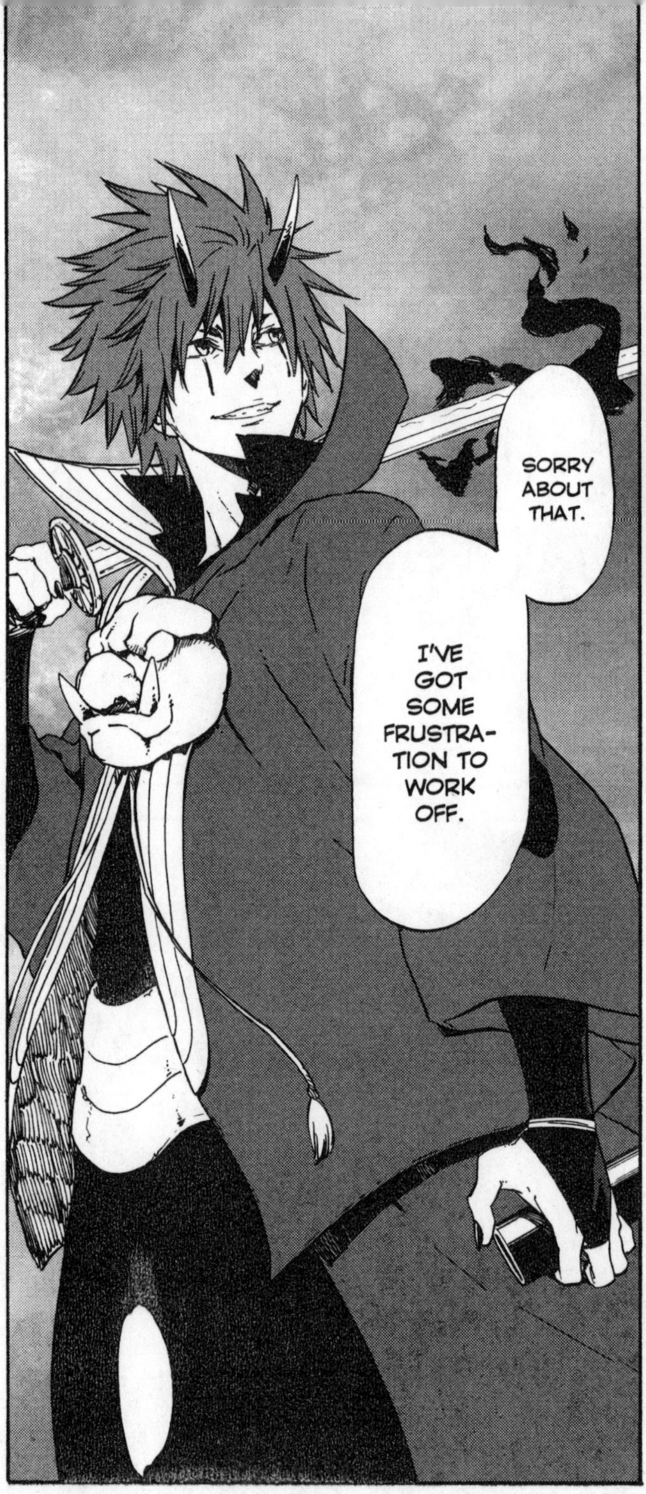
SORRY ABOUT THAT.
I'VE GOT SOME FRUSTRA- TION TO WORK OFF.

Reincarnate
in Volume 14?

→YES

NO

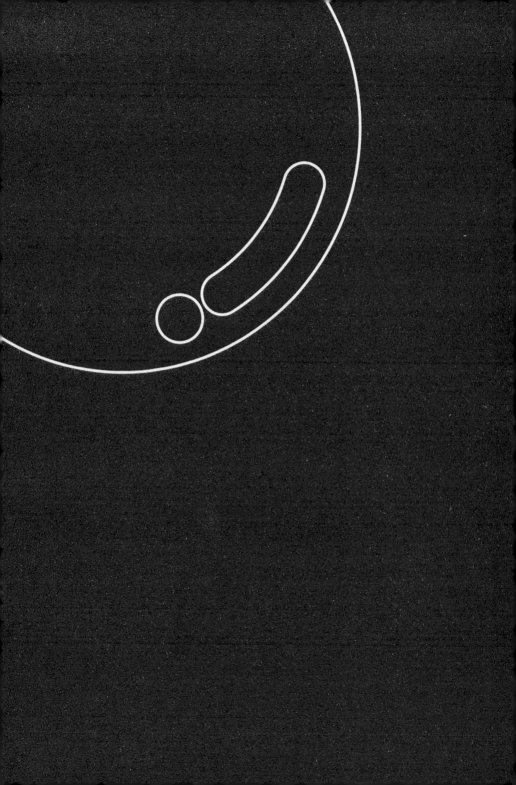

Bonus Short Story

Veldora's Slime Observation Journal

~HOPE~

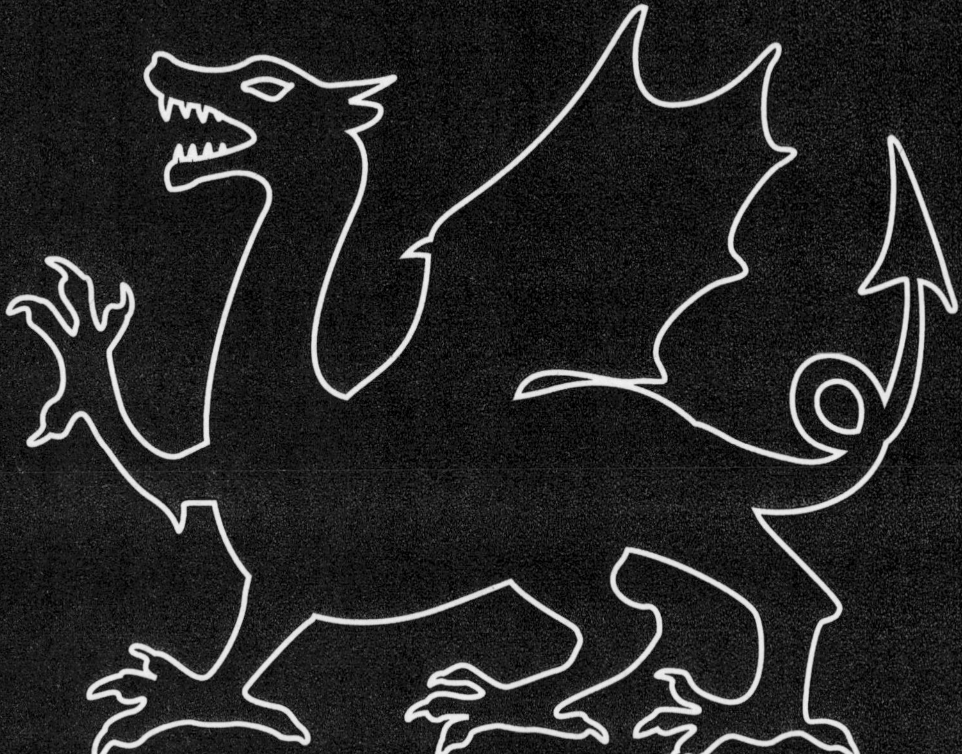

Veldora's Slime Observation Journal
~HOPE~

◆DESPAIR AND HOPE◆

When Rimuru returned, he found Gabiru and Vesta. There is a grim mood here. The ominous premonition has come to pass, it would seem.

Hearing the situation has proven this true. Tempest has been covered by a barrier enacted by unknown agents.

And that was not the only bad news.

Milim issued a declaration of war against Demon Lord Carrion, and refugees from the Animal Kingdom of Eurazania are bearing down as well. Apparently, their arrival will not happen for a while, but there's something more important to deal with now.

"This is a difficult situation, isn't it, Master...?"

"When it rains, it pours, as they say. It seems likely that this is no mere coincidence, but a part of someone's plan."

"I agree, Master. Especially about Milim. She is too cautious to take such rash actions for no reason. We should presume that whoever is pulling the strings behind this possesses tremendous power."

Yes. I suppose so.
It is difficult to make a judgment about Milim. She is so capricious, and it is impossible to predict what she will think about any one thing. But because I am certain she would never do another's bidding, I assume that there is a reason behind her actions.

At any rate, if it were to come to hostilities with Milim, Rimuru's chances of winning are zero. We need to keep a close eye so that it does not come to that. Now, let us focus on the next step.

After ordering Soei to investigate the situation, Rimuru entered the city.

"I have a bad feeling about this."

"Yes, me, too."

It was different from usual. In fact, it was almost a different place entirely. The usual liveliness was gone, and a deathly hush hung over the city.

The reason became clear at once. Surprisingly, Rimuru's hand-appointed regent, Benimaru, was in the middle of a fight. His opponent was Grucius the lycanthrope. Whatever his reason for fighting, Benimaru was merciless and nearly out of control.

What could have happened to put the monsters in such an extreme mental state...?

"Stop, Benimaru!!"

With Rimuru's arrival, it seemed that the situation would at last be brought under control. But that hope was soon proven to be naive. Benimaru guided him to a sight that was utterly grisly.

A great pile of fallen monsters. Adults and children, all indiscriminately slaughtered.

I was stunned.

For some reason, there was a feeling in my breast, something hot and surging. I wanted to shout, to rage, to fight...

"What a strange feeling. What is this emotion I feel?"

"Master Veldora..."

"I admire Rimuru. Even in this situation, he is calm, working to get things under control. If it were me..."

Would I seek vengeance? Me...?

From ancient times to the present, I have never spared a thought for anyone but myself. Would I truly act for the sake of others? Even without anyone wishing that I would do so?

What a strange thing. Even I cannot help but wonder what has gotten into me. Would Rimuru have the answer to that question?

And what is Rimuru thinking now, for that matter? I would very much like to know.

Rigurd explained the situation. A country by the name of Falmuth was responsible for the attack, and their reason was to compete for trading profits. They are trying to seize this place that Rimuru and his companions built from nothing, all for their own greed—is what this all amounts to.

"What a pain these humans are."

"Indeed, Master. Monsters are much simpler. If we see something we want, we take it by force. We live by the survival of the fittest, but unlike them, we do not need special ideals to justify our actions."

"But Rimuru seeks coexistence with these humans."

"…"

"So is he following the humans' rules, and unable to act upon his emotions…?"

If he doesn't like it, he should strike them back. That is what I would do, but Rimuru seems to be very calm about it.

His surface consciousness is placid at the moment, and he is hiding what lies beneath it. But it would seem to me that whatever is beneath the surface, it threatens to burst out into the open. I can only hope that he holds strong. Please let his heart not suffer any more than it already has.

However—the world is very cruel and uncaring.

"Where is she?" Rimuru asked.

Yes, I do not see the secretary, Shion. She is always hanging around Rimuru.

My sense of foreboding increased. There was still misfortune ahead.

There was Shion, lying on the ground, as though asleep.

But she was dead.

To think that beloved Shion—the type who could get away with anything—could have been killed so easily seems like a lie...

"I cannot believe it."

"No."

I only interacted with her through Rimuru's eyes, but even still, I felt a fondness for Shion. I even respected her in a way—she is someone with lessons to teach others.

And now Shion is dead, just like that...

Zwoosh!

At that moment, the shackles around Rimuru's heart seemed to break loose. I'd thought he was standing there emotion-less, listening to the explanation. But I was wrong.

Of course I was wrong.

Even *I* am upset by this development. So it stands to rea-son that Rimuru, who actually interacted with her directly, would feel more strongly about it.

Rimuru asked to be left alone, and so all the rest quickly left the scene. He sat down right there on the ground. What is he thinking now?

It is time for me to think as well—about something I have never had cause to consider very deeply before: death.

"What is death anyway, Ifrit?"

Ifrit said nothing. Despite his increase in wisdom as of late, he had no answer for the question.

What *is* death?

If one's body is moving, one is alive; that much is clear. Even if the flesh is not destroyed, if the individual loses their particular nature, one might say they are no longer alive.

If the "soul" is lost—what you might call the true quality of life—that is equivalent to death. Under this interpretation, Shion and all the other monsters lying around her are undoubtedly dead.

But I do not think that is sad. I have seen death countless times.

"I cannot stand to see Rimuru saddened...but I do not feel sad for the death of monsters. Their souls will simply be returned to the cycle of rebirth, where they may refine themselves and strive again for greater heights. That is the natural way of things, is it not?"

"Yes, Master. I believe you are right..."

"Then why can he not simply compartmentalize the matter that way?"

Why doesn't Rimuru cease his mourning...?
Dragons are immortal beings. We do not die. If our bodies are destroyed, we always come back to life. It does not work that way for Shion and her kind, but eventually, their souls will be reconstructed to gain new life.

Of course, they will not come back as the same beings, and their memories or even wills may not exist in the same form...but that, too, is the natural way of things.

"Aren't you sad, Master Veldora? Knowing that Shion, that bright and carefree individual with so much to teach, will never be heard from again?"

"Yes, that is true, but…"

Ifrit's observation took me aback.

"The depth of sadness felt corresponds to the depth of the connection, let us say. That is a fact of life that I believe I finally understand," Ifrit said gravely.

I believe that I understand what Ifrit is saying, too. I can tell from Rimuru's reaction. Though it may not be polite to say, it seems as though losing Shion is causing him more grief than the rest of the great crowd of dead monsters. As Ifrit says, the depth of the connection between individuals makes a difference in the sense of loss.

And I am no different. I was trying to explain Shion's death through the laws of nature and the universe, because doing so helped to distract me from the sadness.

"I once killed a girl named Pirino who was Shizue Izawa's friend. I only had the tiniest sliver of self-awareness then, and I acted only in reaction to hostility, but even still, it was a sin that I committed. And that very event was the reason that Shizu and I could not truly commune our hearts…"

"Ifrit…"

"Ha ha ha, it is too late to bring this up now. And because I thought of death as only part of the natural way of things, and nothing more, I failed to be aware of Shizu's sadness. Shizu thought my sin was her own, and her attempts to atone anguished her, but I didn't know… If I hadn't been observing Lord Rimuru with you, Master, I might not have understood this, even if centuries went by."

"Ah…"

Ifrit's words were heavy. They seemed to be telling me that death was not something to be considered lightly. Not at all.

Not that I needed to be told…

"I suppose. By watching what Rimuru does, I have come to understand just how much he treasures the connections he has to others. Even the way that he interacted with me seems very much in character with the person I know. I was going to come back to life anyway, but Rimuru swore to save me. He must have considered that my sense of self vanishing was equivalent to death. My memories will be preserved up to a point, and even my soul will remain virtually the same. Most would consider me to be the very same individual, but to Rimuru, I would not be. And given that this is Rimuru's nature…"

"Then he cannot give up on Shion and the other victims of the attack…"

Soon it was midday, and then night. Morning came again, and the sun spun about.

Three days passed. Shion did not wake.

Rimuru seems to be on the verge of giving up. I know of no magic with the effect of perfect resurrection of the dead. The ritual to reincarnate souls must be performed ahead of time. God's miracle of resurrection must happen before a soul can disperse. Because the chances of success decrease over time, it will fail if not performed within a few minutes of death.

In other words, there is nothing to be done. Like Rimuru, I tasted the bitter flavor of futility.

Then it happened, right as Rimuru was about to erase the dead bodies forever.

"Rimuru!" cried a voice.

It was Eren. She came in a terrible rush, and her usual smile was nowhere to be seen.

"…Um, Rimuru, I know the chances are low," she continued. "In fact, they might as well be nonexistent…but there is a way."

And that was enough to cause Rimuru to pause.

I listened intently as well, because she said there was "a fairy tale about bringing back the dead."

It was an impossible task *not* to have hope.

"Master Veldora!!"

"Yes. If there is a way, then I would certainly like to hear it," I said, placing my hopes in this possibility…fairy tale or not.

◆THE CONDITIONS FOR HOPE◆

What Eren described was a story I already knew.

"Master Veldora, is that dragon princess…"

"It is Milim. Though I do not know the details, I am aware that she destroyed an entire country."

I hadn't known the reason for it. Apparently, her friend was taken from her by force. This is not entirely meaningless to me. What if I were to lose Rimuru…? Just the thought of it is frightening.

But that is not what I should be pondering now. It is the resurrection of a follower when its master evolves. As Eren says, the real issue to be wary of is the presence or absence of the soul.

If the soul is still intact, then resurrection might be a possibility. Without it, all of this is mere fantasy…

"This city is surrounded by a barrier right now, isn't it?"

Oh…!!
Yes, of course!!

"Searching information within barrier limits… Failed. Lacking precision required to detect the presence of infons, the building blocks of the soul…"

You just leave that to me.

"I will use the full strength of my skill, Inquirer, to aid your search."

"Understood. Searching information within barrier limits again... Search successful. Presence of infons confirmed. Probability of reformation upon evolving..."

3.14%, it says. That is enough.

Rimuru has reached the same conclusion. His face lights up, brimming with intent to fight!

He's made up his mind now. He is ready to do what it takes: to sacrifice the lives of over ten thousand humans, and become a true demon lord.

"Lord Rimuru is a very kind leader. Couldn't he spare himself the bloodshed and order his followers to do it...?"

"You have it wrong, Ifrit. In fact, you just said it yourself: Shizu bore your sin. Even if there is no sin within an act of taking life, there is guilt. That negative act will become negative karma. Rimuru knows that he should not involve others in his act."

"I see. So that is the weight of his decision..."

Rimuru decided that he would resurrect them all, even at the cost of so much wrongdoing. I would likely make the same choice.

So be at ease, Rimuru. You are not alone.

I shall bear that karma with you, I swore to myself.

◆THE WITCH'S PUNISHMENT◆

With his mind now made up, Rimuru jumped into action with a sense of purpose so bold it seemed to be designed to make up for the three days he lost.

An army of twenty thousand bears down upon the city of monsters, they say. Now they are preparing to fight back.

The first step is to reinforce the barrier. Rimuru placed a firm and very careful seal, so as not to allow the souls of the dead to vanish into thin air.

This thoroughness is admirable, and in this case, it had unexpected benefits. As a side product of the barrier, Rimuru discovered the presence of Clayman's trump card.

Apparently, he was sending and receiving coded information in the form of electronic signals. Rimuru tracked the source to a majin named Mjurran.

Without revealing his knowledge, Rimuru began to question Mjurran. In fact, he seems to have other ideas in mind as well...but I do not have the slightest ability to focus on such things now.

"Are you all right, Master Veldora?"

"I am not. I believe I shall cry. *Gwababababaaa!*"

I was in terrible pain. It was a simple backlash from using my skills at full power.

I opened up the use of my Inquirer skill to assist Rimuru, but the demands upon me were extreme. Though it was only for a short time, the calorie burn was intense enough to completely exhaust me.

I was put to my very limit performing analytical identification, with my consciousness split to maximize processing load. Rimuru sifted through the information I gleaned, but I was so busy that I had no ability to pay attention to it.

"I want to eat something sweet..."

Yes, like the greatest of all foods: sweet, delicious flan...

"Understood. Here is an expression of gratitude."

I said it because I had nothing to lose, and what do you know: a collection of ten flans!

I was very pleased, indeed.

Apparently Mjurran's life has been saved as well, from what I can see now. Things are looking up.

The dead coming back to life is a common story, eh? That seems like just the sort of thing Rimuru would say.

◆WHETHER MONSTER OR HUMAN◆

Rimuru deceived Clayman, who had been cunningly pulling strings from the shadows, and won the trust of Youm and his followers. With that momentum behind him, he now heads toward the big meeting.

As for me, I am being tended to by Ifrit, and eating flan.
This…is not so bad.
In fact, this is the life for me, I think.

"Don't you agree?"

"W-well…I don't think this is the best time, perhaps…"

"Kwa ha ha ha! Don't worry. I will set some aside for you, too!"

I am not the selfish sort, to hog all the treasures to myself. I have ten of them, so I could certainly give three or so to Ifrit.

What do you mean, "not half?" Don't be preposterous! For one thing, I am bigger, and more importantly, I'm in my growth spurt. I must eat a lot to grow at a healthy rate.

And for that reason, I requested a nice massage.

"Yes, yes, as you wish, Master."

I thought Ifrit's response a tad uncharitable, but the finger pressure is undeniable. A spiritual being should not have any

experience with stiff shoulders or back pain, but for some reason, this is very soothing to me.

I watched the meeting in a state of bliss.

After Rimuru announced that he would become a demon lord, there was a quick flurry of traded opinions.

"Their reactions are surprisingly varied, aren't they?"

"Hmm?"

"I mean, lower monsters like goblins are absolutely subservient to more powerful monsters. The words of their superiors are everything, and they will never express their own will. And yet..."

"You find it amusing that there is such change in them?"

"Yes, Master."

Hmm. Ifrit does have a point, I admit.

Evolving does not mean changing one's inherent disposition. That was the common knowledge, at least, but the people of this city are anything but common. They each have their own firm will, which they express without fear or hesitation.

And who would expect shortsighted creatures like goblins to be so prudent and wise? It has not even been years since their evolution. How much could they have possibly learned in this time?

I suppose it is an environment that raises a person. That must be the ideal for which Rimuru is striving.

In order to judge a matter from many different angles, one must not be taken in by a single opinion, but value the thoughts of many different minds. By hearing out many ideas, one can search for a better direction.

Rimuru is not meant to be a tyrant.

But judging from the forces of the other Demon Lords, I suppose this is not an impossible idea. And even I am not exactly pleased when others defy my statements.

"In your case, Master Veldora, I'd describe that more as selfishness..."

"Hmm? Did you say something, Ifrit?"

"No, nothing at all."

"I did not think so. Very good! Now move down to my legs."

"Very well..."

I returned my attention to the flow of the meeting, allowing Ifrit's fingertips to do their work.

◆MOMENT OF COUNTERATTACK◆

Rimuru's followers have come to understand how much they have relied upon him. And they realize that it was not his strength that they admire, but his character. They are so very unlike monsters, and yet they are oddly likeable for that. I happen to agree with them on this point, anyway.

Rimuru tells the group of his ideals. Some, like Kaijin, say he is too soft and naive, but the entire group is in favor of his plan. The direction is set.

Next the topic of discussion turned to the crushing of the invading armies. At this point, Rimuru proclaimed, "I want you to leave that alliance to me."

Some were afraid this might be too dangerous, but Rimuru has already accepted the risk. He shows no doubt, nor does his resolve waver, so none of his subordinates dared speak out against him. Benimaru appeared to want to say something...but he recognized the will of his master.

There were no objections to his plan. Everyone has faith in Rimuru.

Now the stage is set for Rimuru to become a Demon Lord. The first counterattack will be the signal to fight, and the curtain rises on battle…

To be reincarnated in Volume 14!

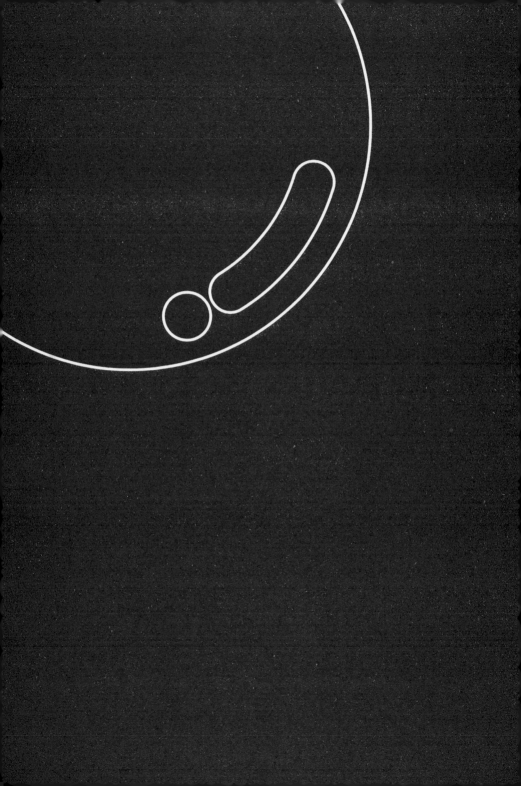

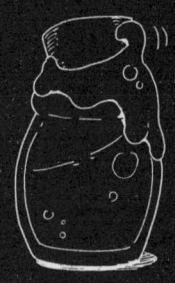

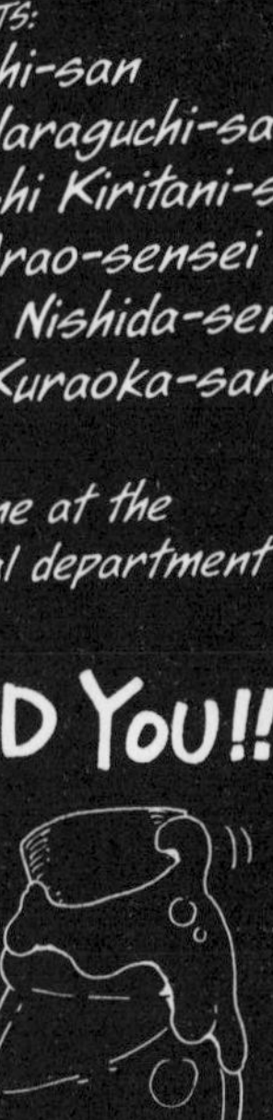

FATHERLY SENTIMENT AMONG LIZARDMEN

Abiru, Chieftain of Lizardmen
I WONDER HOW MY CHILDREN FARE THESE DAYS.
SOKA WILL BE FINE.
SHE'S HAD THINGS TOGETHER EVEN AS AN EGG.
I HEAR THAT SHE'S BEEN TRAINING WITH SOEI.
AS AN EGG
AND GABIRU ...
The chieftain's heir!
ONCE HE GETS ROLLING, HE JUST DOESN'T STOP...
WORRY...
HE COULD JUST GO AND SEE THEM...

LIST OF ACKNOWLEDGMENTS

AUTHOR:
Fuse-sensei

CHARACTER DESIGN:
Mitz Vah-sensei

THE WAYS OF THE MONSTER NATION:
Sho Okagiri-sensei

THE SLIME DIARIES:
Shiba-sensei

REINCARNATED AS A WAGE SLAVE:
Shizuku Akechi-sensei

TRINITY IN TEMPEST:
Tae Tono-sensei

TENCHURA!:
Chacha-sensei

ASSISTANTS:
Muraichi-san
Daiki Haraguchi-san
Masashi Kiritani-sensei
Taku Arao-sensei
Takuya Nishida-sensei
Daiki Kuraoka-san

Everyone at the editorial department

AND YOU!!

Bottled Slime

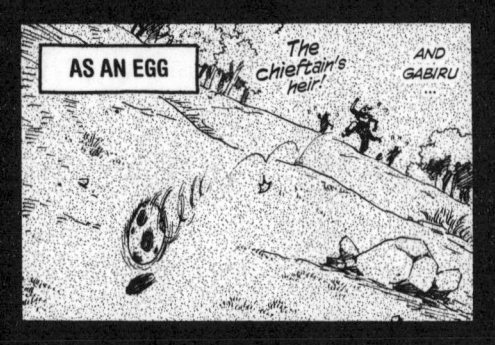

From character designer
Mitz Vah-sensei

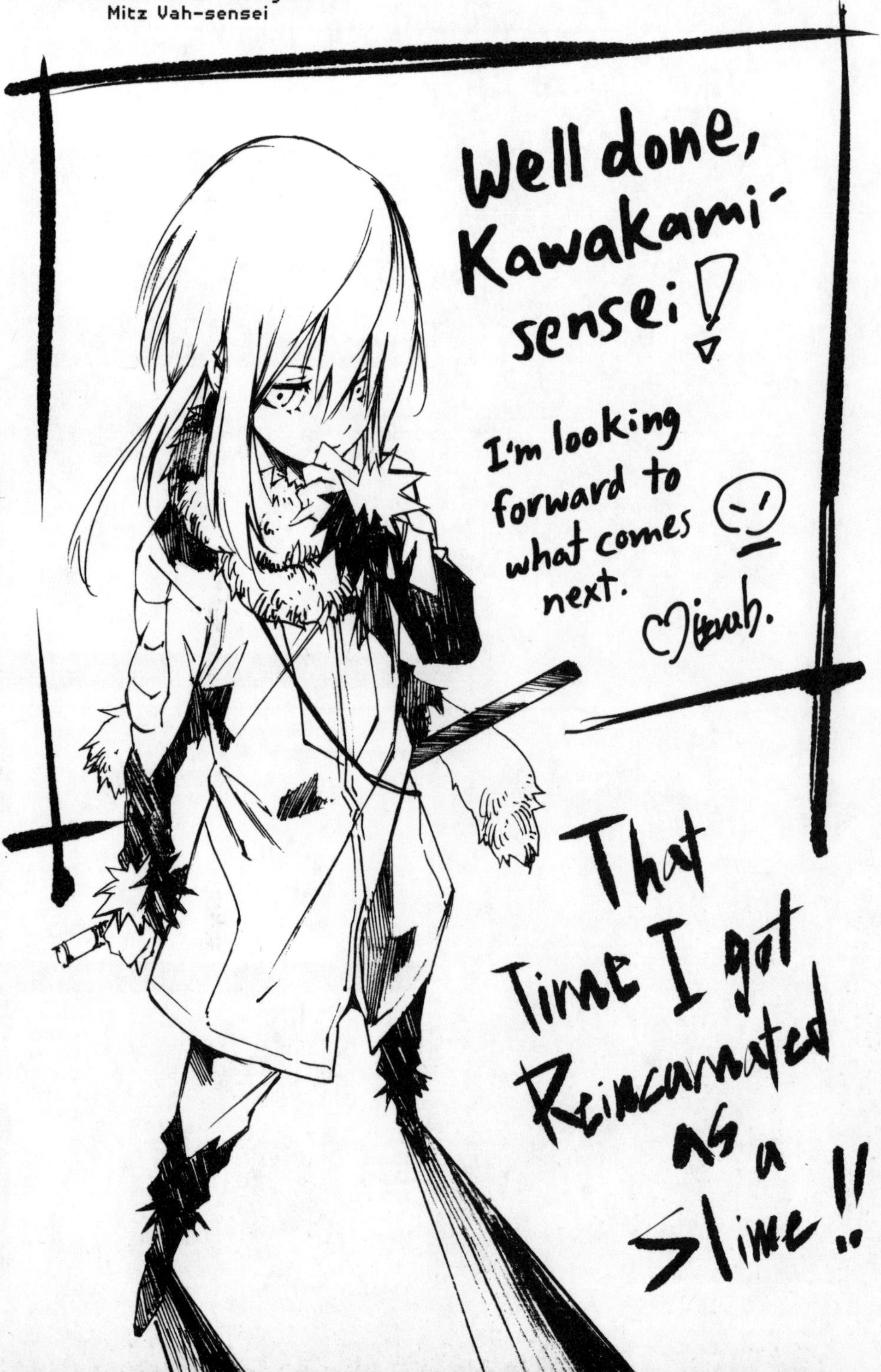
Well done, Kawakami-sensei!
I'm looking forward to what comes next.
That Time I got Reincarnated as a Slime!!

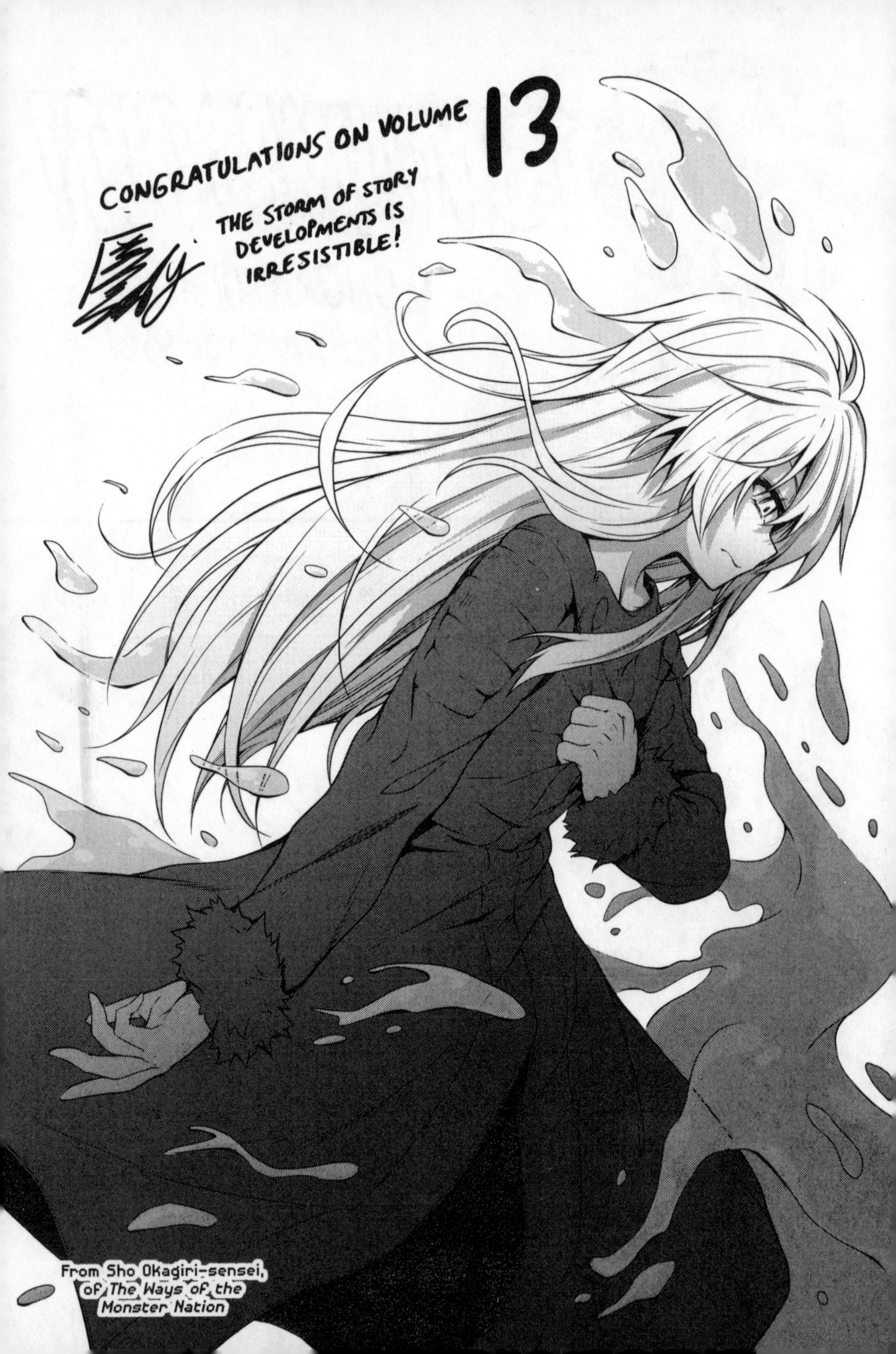
CONGRATULATIONS ON VOLUME 13
THE STORM OF STORY DEVELOPMENTS IS IRRESISTIBLE!
From Sho Okagiri-sensei, of The Ways of the Monster Nation

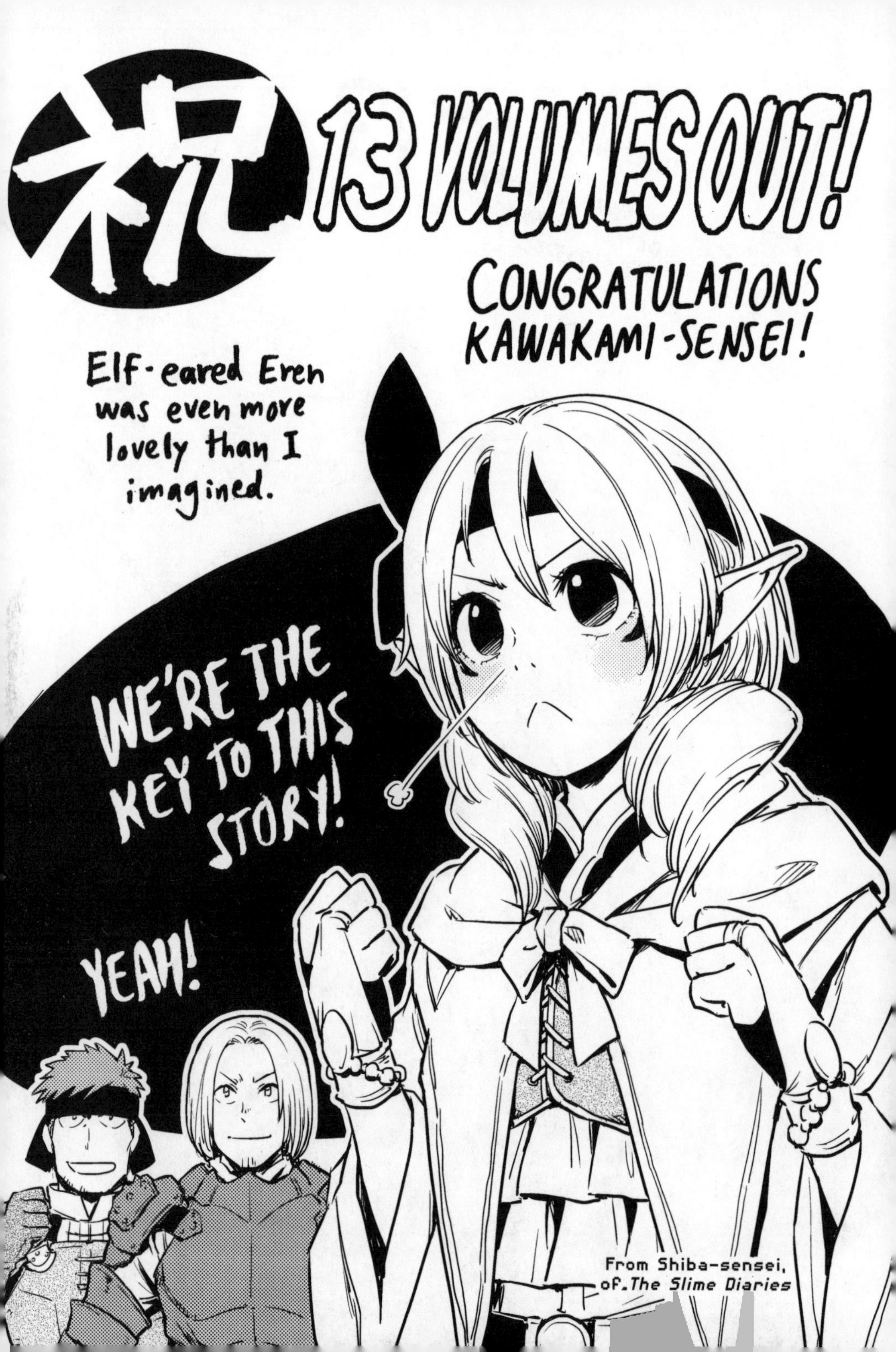
祝
13 VOLUMES OUT!
CONGRATULATIONS KAWAKAMI-SENSEI!
Elf-eared Eren was even more lovely than I imagined.
WE'RE THE KEY TO THIS STORY!
YEAH!
From Shiba-sensei, of *The Slime Diaries*

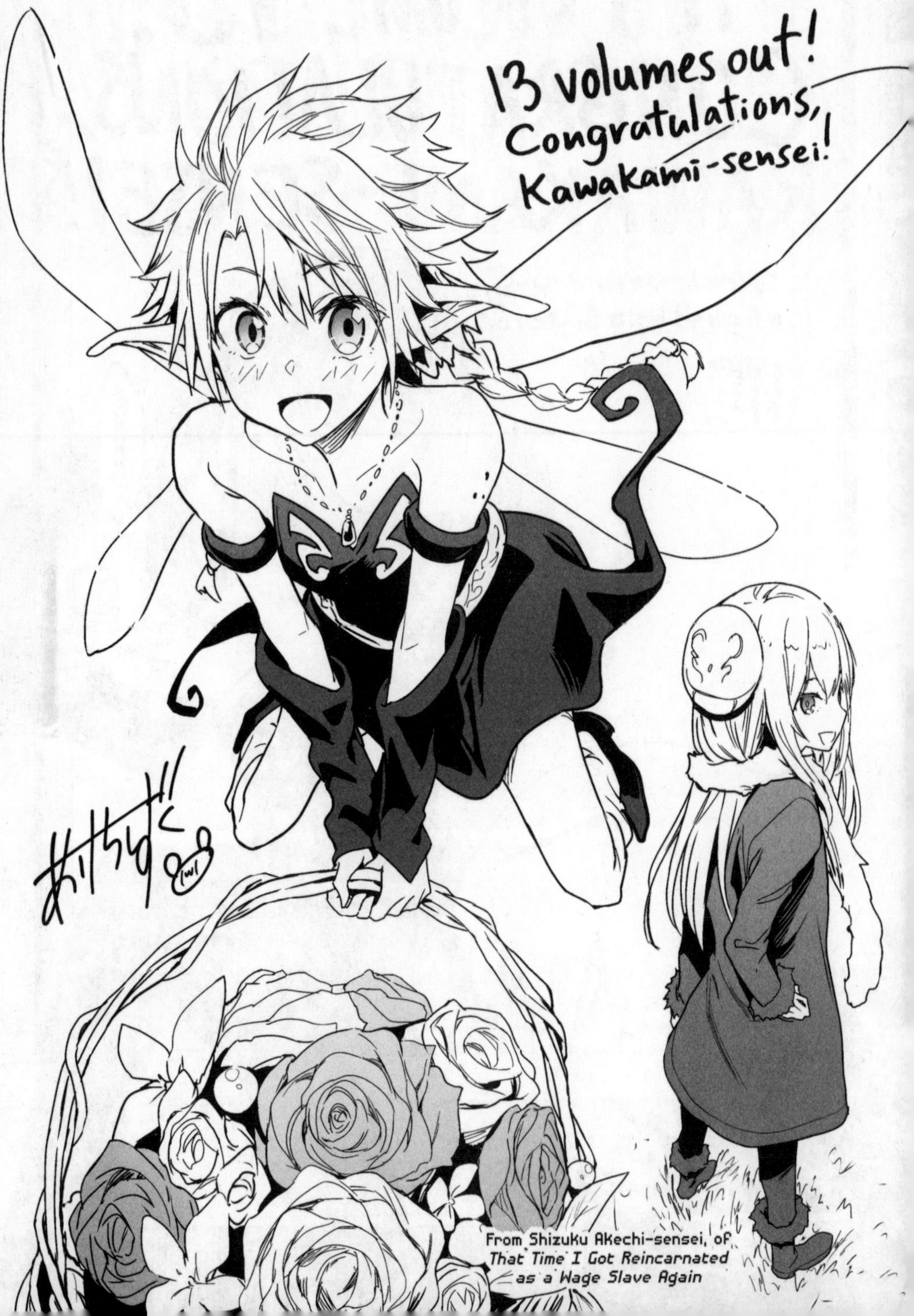
13 volumes out! Congratulations, Kawakami-sensei!
あけちしずく

From Shizuku Akechi-sensei, of *That Time I Got Reincarnated as a Wage Slave Again*

IT'S VOLUME 13! CONGRATULATIONS, KAWAKAMI-SENSEI!
So we've hit this part of the story... It'll only get better from here on!!
OHHH!
From Tae Tono-sensei, of Another Story: Trinity in Tempest

From Chacha-sensei, of *Tenchura! That Time I Got Reincarnated as a Slime*

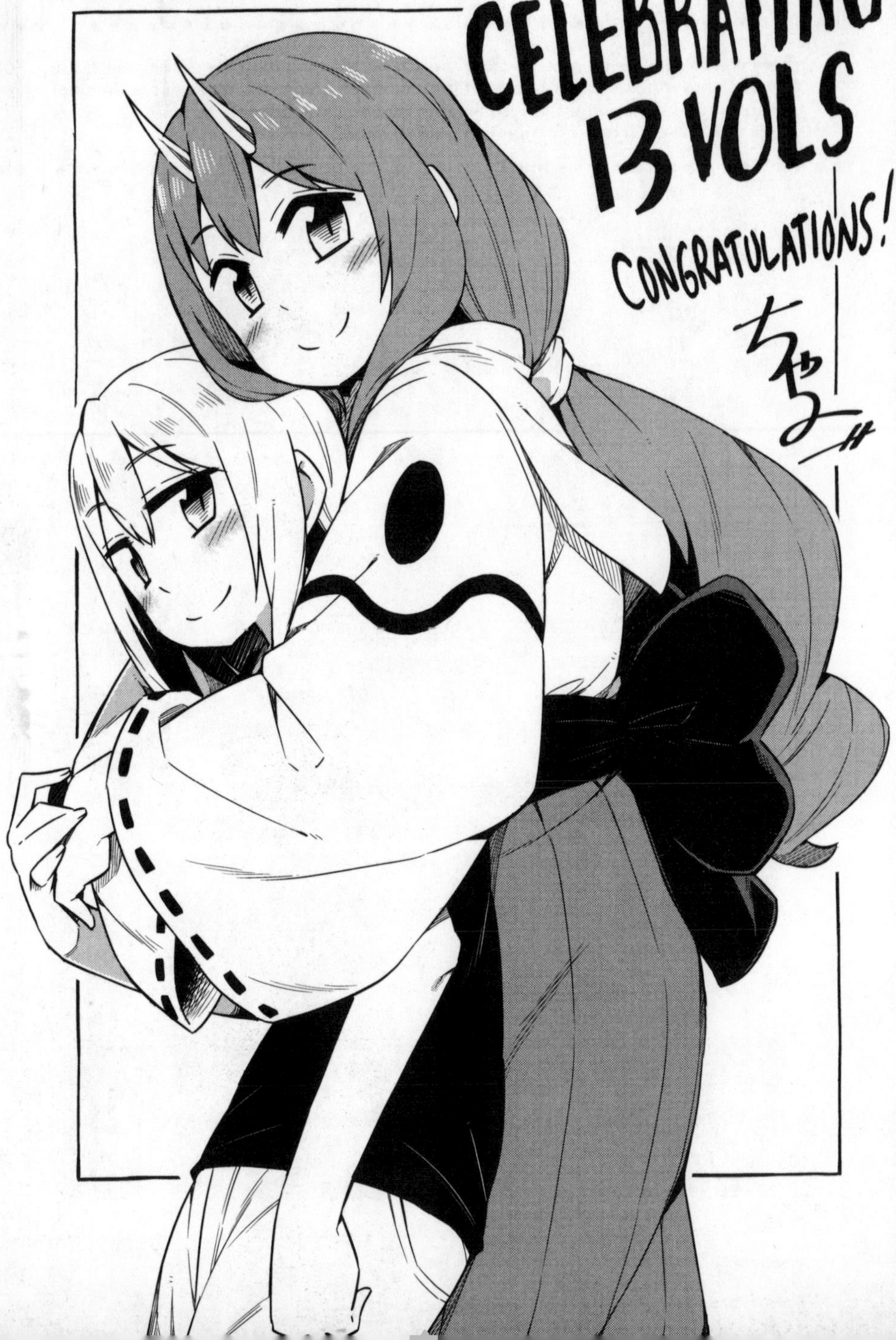
CELEBRATING 13 VOLS
CONGRATULATIONS!
ちゃちゃ

To commemorate the airing of each episode of the *Reincarnated as a Slime* anime, the *Shonen Sirius* official Twitter account (@shonen_sirius) made a series of promotional tweets. Here are the various congratulatory illustrations from other artists in the Sirius magazine, uploaded between March 4th, and 11th, 2019!

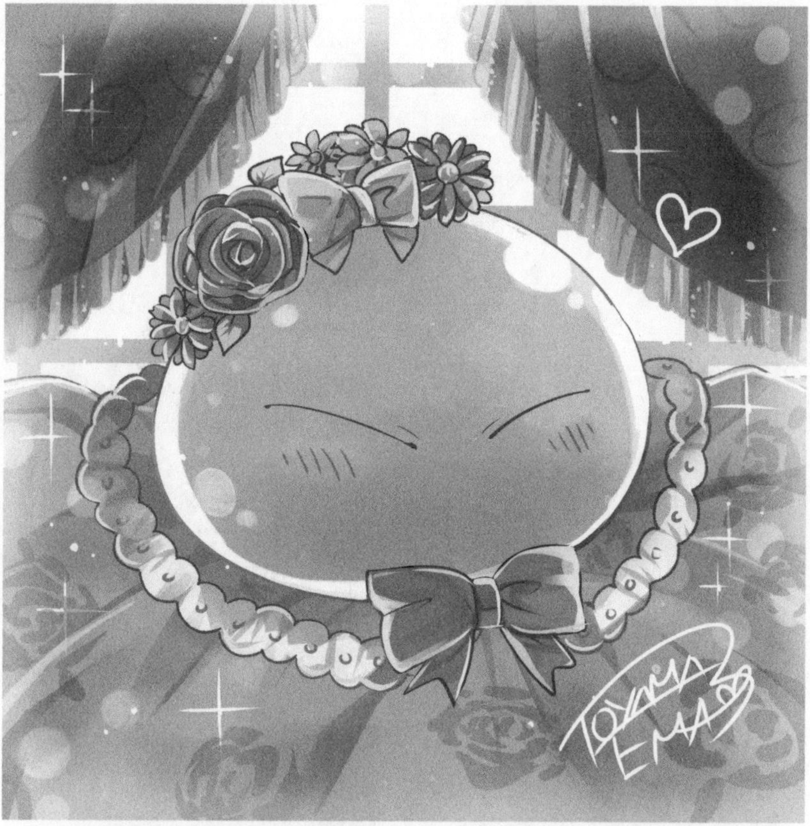
TOOYAMA EMA

Ema Tooyama-sensei (@tooyamatsuri)

Artist of I Became the Mom of the Strongest Demon Lord's 10 Children in Another World in Monthly Shonen Sirius

ZZZ
Deh heh heh...

Hoshino Taguchi-sensei (@taguchihoshino)

Artist of *Me, the Mistress* in *Magazine Pocket*

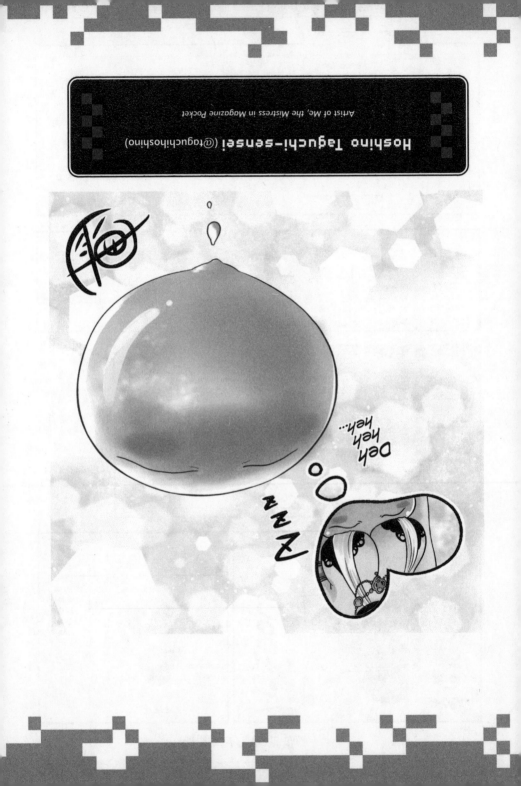

『The Almighty Vesta Theory』

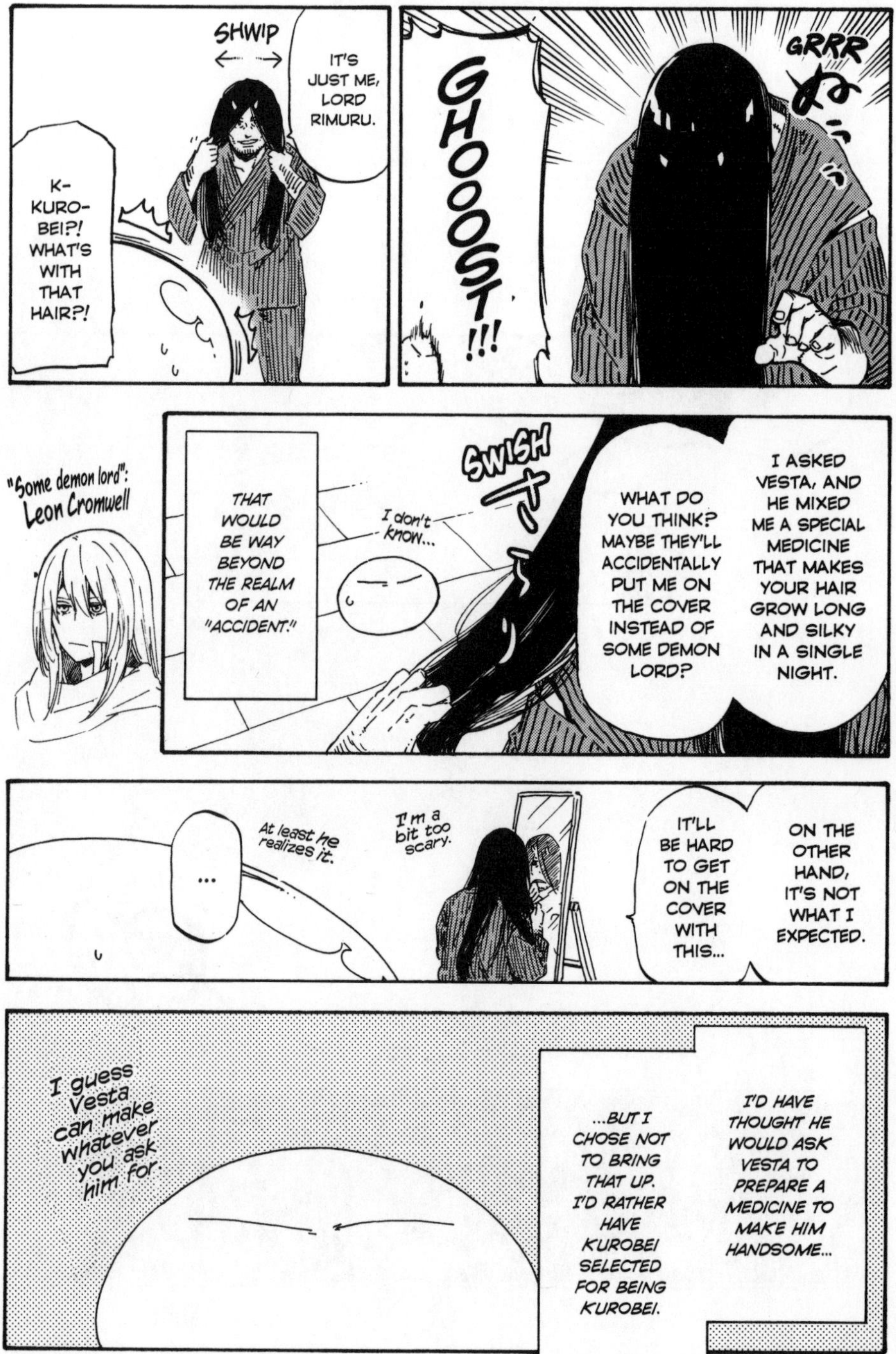
GRRR
GHOOOST!!!
SHWIP
IT'S JUST ME, LORD RIMURU.
K-KUROBEI?! WHAT'S WITH THAT HAIR?!
I ASKED VESTA, AND HE MIXED ME A SPECIAL MEDICINE THAT MAKES YOUR HAIR GROW LONG AND SILKY IN A SINGLE NIGHT.
WHAT DO YOU THINK? MAYBE THEY'LL ACCIDENTALLY PUT ME ON THE COVER INSTEAD OF SOME DEMON LORD?
SWISH
I don't know...
THAT WOULD BE WAY BEYOND THE REALM OF AN "ACCIDENT."
"Some demon lord": Leon Cromwell
ON THE OTHER HAND, IT'S NOT WHAT I EXPECTED.
IT'LL BE HARD TO GET ON THE COVER WITH THIS...
I'm a bit too scary.
At least he realizes it.
...
I'D HAVE THOUGHT HE WOULD ASK VESTA TO PREPARE A MEDICINE TO MAKE HIM HANDSOME...
...BUT I CHOSE NOT TO BRING THAT UP. I'D RATHER HAVE KUROBEI SELECTED FOR BEING KUROBEI.
I guess Vesta can make whatever you ask him for.

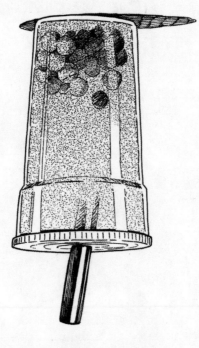

Bubble Slime Tea

At Granbell Kingdom, an abandoned amusement park, Shiki has lived his entire life among machines. But one day, Rebecca and her cat companion Happy appear at the park's front gates. Little do these newcomers know that this is the first human contact Granbell has had in a hundred years! As Shiki stumbles his way into making new friends, his former neighbors stir at an opportunity for a robo-rebellion.... And when his old homeland becomes too dangerous, Shiki must join Rebecca and Happy on their spaceship and escape into the boundless cosmos.

A high-flying space adventure! All the steadfast friendship and wild fighting you've been waiting for...IN SPACE!

HIRO MASHIMA IS BACK! JOIN THE CREATOR OF *FAIRY TAIL* AS HE TAKES TO THE STARS FOR ANOTHER THRILLING SAGA!

EDENS ZERO

EDENS ZERO © Hiro Mashima/Kodansha, Ltd.

The adorable new odd-couple cat comedy manga from the creator of the beloved *Chi's Sweet Home*, in full color!

Praise for Chi's Sweet Home

"Nearly impossible to turn away... a true all-ages title that anyone, young or old, cat lover or not, will enjoy. The stories will bring a smile to your face and warm your heart."

—School Library Journal

Sue & Tai-chan
Konami Kanata

Sue is an aging housecat who's looking forward to living out her life in peace... but her plans change when the mischievous black tomcat Tai-chan enters the picture! Hey! Sue never signed up to be a catsitter! *Sue & Tai-chan* is the latest from the reigning meow-narch of cute kitty comics, Konami Kanata.

THE SWEET SCENT OF LOVE IS IN THE AIR! FOR FANS OF OFFBEAT ROMANCES LIKE *WOTAKOI*

VOL. 1

SWEAT AND SOAP

KINTETSU YAMADA

Sweat and Soap © Kintetsu Yamada / Kodansha Ltd.

In an office romance, there's a fine line between sexy and awkward... and that line is where Asako — a woman who sweats copiously — meets Koutarou — a perfume developer who can't get enough of Asako's, er, scent. Don't miss a romcom manga like no other!

KC KODANSHA COMICS

A SMART, NEW ROMANTIC COMEDY FOR FANS OF *SHORTCAKE CAKE* AND *TERRACE HOUSE!*

LIVING ROOM

Keiko Iwashita

MATSUNAGA-SAN

KC KODANSHA COMICS

A romance manga starring high school girl Meeko, who learns to live on her own in a boarding house whose living room is home to the odd (but handsome) Matsunaga-san. She begins to adjust to her new life away from her parents, but Meeko soon learns that no matter how far away from home she is, she's still a young girl at heart — especially when she finds herself falling for Matsunaga-san.

Something's Wrong With Us

NATSUMI ANDO

The dark, psychological, sexy shojo series readers have been waiting for!

A spine-chilling and steamy romance between a Japanese sweets maker and the man who framed her mother for murder!

Following in her mother's footsteps, Nao became a traditional Japanese sweets maker, and with unparalleled artistry and a bright attitude, she gets an offer to work at a world-class confectionary company. But when she meets the young, handsome owner, she recognizes his cold stare...

KC/ KODANSHA COMICS

![Knight of the Ice — Yayoi Ogawa](Knight of the Ice book cover)

SKATING THRILLS AND ICY CHILLS WITH THIS NEW TINGLY ROMANCE SERIES!

A rom-com on ice, perfect for fans of *Princess Jellyfish* and *Wotakoi*. Kokoro is the talk of the figure-skating world, winning trophies and hearts. But little do they know... he's actually a huge nerd! From the beloved creator of *You're My Pet* (*Tramps Like Us*).

Chitose is a serious young woman, working for the health magazine *SASSO*. Or at least, she would be, if she wasn't constantly getting distracted by her childhood friend, international figure skating star Kokoro Kijinami! In the public eye and on the ice, Kokoro is a gallant, flawless knight, but behind his glittery costumes and breathtaking spins lies a secret: He's actually a hopelessly romantic otaku, who can only land his quad jumps when Chitose is on hand to recite a spell from his favorite magical girl anime!

KC KODANSHA COMICS

1 PERFECT WORLD

Rie Aruga

A TOUCHING NEW SERIES ABOUT LOVE AND COPING WITH DISABILITY

An office party reunites Tsugumi with her high school crush Itsuki. He's realized his dream of becoming an architect, but along the way, he experienced a spinal injury that put him in a wheelchair. Now Tsugumi's rekindled feelings will butt up against prejudices she never considered — and Itsuki will have to decide if he's ready to let someone into his heart...

"Depicts with great delicacy and courage the difficulties some with disabilities experience getting involved in romantic relationships... Rie Aruga refuses to romanticize, pushing her heroine to face the reality of disability. She invites her readers to the same tasks of empathy, knowledge and recognition."
—Slate.fr

"An important entry [in manga romance]... The emotional core of both plot and characters indicates thoughtfulness... [Aruga's] research is readily apparent in the text and artwork, making this feel like a real story."
—Anime News Network

The boys are back, in 400-page hardcovers that are as pretty and badass as they are!

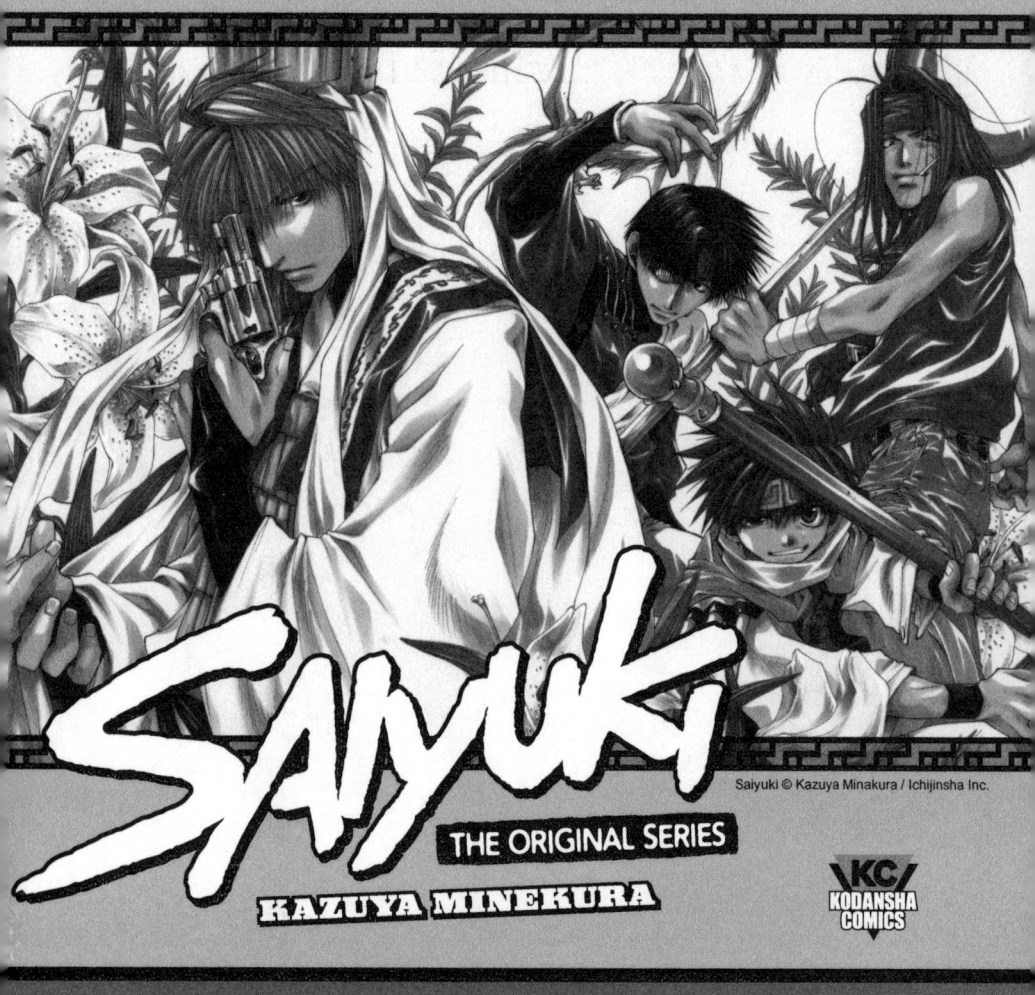

Saiyuki © Kazuya Minekura / Ichijinsha Inc.

Genjo Sanzo is a Buddhist priest in the city of Togenkyo, which is being ravaged by yokai spirits that have fallen out of balance with the natural order. His superiors send him on a journey far to the west to discover why this is happening and how to stop it. His companions are three yokai with human souls. But this is no day trip — the four will encounter many discoveries and horrors on the way.

FEATURES NEW TRANSLATION, COLOR PAGES, AND BEAUTIFUL WRAPAROUND COVER ART!

Young characters and steampunk setting, like *Howl's Moving Castle* and *Battle Angel Alita*

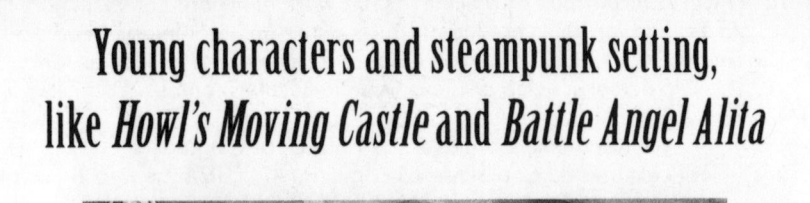

Beyond the Clouds © 2018 Nicke / Ki-oon

A boy with a talent for machines and a mysterious girl whose wings he's fixed will take you beyond the clouds! In the tradition of the high-flying, resonant adventure stories of Studio Ghibli comes a gorgeous tale about the longing of young hearts for adventure and friendship!

A Kodansha Comics Trade Paperback Original
That Time I Got Reincarnated as a Slime 13 copyright © 2019 Fuse / Taiki Kawakami
English translation copyright © 2020 Fuse / Taiki Kawakami

Published in the United States by Kodansha Comics, an imprint of
Kodansha USA Publishing, LLC, New York.

Publication rights for this English edition arranged through
Kodansha Ltd., Tokyo.

First published in Japan in 2019 by Kodansha Ltd., Tokyo
as *Tensei Shitara Suraimu Datta Ken*, volume 13.

ISBN 978-1-64651-007-8

Original cover design by Saya Takagi and Ayaka Hasegawa (RedRooster)

Printed in the United States of America.

www.kodanshacomics.com

9 8 7 6 5 4 3 2
Translation: Stephen Paul
Lettering: Evan Hayden
Editing: Vanessa Tenazas
Kodansha Comics edition cover design by Phil Balsman

D0557299

Publisher: Kiichiro Sugawara
Vice president of marketing & publicity: Naho Yamada

Director of publishing services: Ben Applegate
Associate director of operations: Stephen Pakula
Publishing services managing editor: Noelle Webster
Assistant production manager: Emi Lotto, Angela Zurlo